Taking the Floor

Models, Morals, and Management in a Wall Street Trading Room

Daniel Beunza

PRINCETON UNIVERSITY PRESS
PRINCETON AND OXFORD

Published by Princeton University Press
41 William Street, Princeton, New Jersey 08540
6 Oxford Street, Woodstock, Oxfordshire OX20 1TR

press.princeton.edu

Library of Congress Cataloging-in-Publication Data
Names: Beunza, Daniel, author.
Title: Taking the floor : models, morals, and management in a Wall Street trading room / Daniel
    Beunza.
Description: Princeton : Princeton University Press, [2019] | Includes bibliographical references
    and index.
Identifiers: LCCN 2019019273 | ISBN 9780691162812 (hardcover)
Subjects: LCSH: Investment banking--Moral and ethical aspects--United States--Case studies. |
    Investment bankers--United States--Case studies. | Corporate culture--United States--
    Case studies. | Organizational behavior--United States--Case studies.
Classification: LCC HG4930.5 .B48 2019 | DDC 332.640973--dc23 LC record available at https://
    lccn.loc.gov/2019019273
ISBN (e-book) 978-0-691-18599-6

British Library Cataloging-in-Publication Data is available

Editorial: Meagan Levinson and Jacqueline Delaney
Production Editorial: Leslie Grundfest
Jacket/Cover Design: Layla Mac Rory
Production: Erin Suydam
Publicity: Nathalie Levine (U.S.) and Kathryn Stevens (U.K.)
Copyeditor: Karen Verde

Jacket Image: Photo by Stéphane Brügger

This book has been composed in Adobe Text Pro and Gotham

Printed on acid-free paper ∞

Printed in the United States of America

10 9 8 7 6 5 4 3 2 1

To my parents, Joaquín and Maria Dolores

CONTENTS

ACKNOWLEDGMENTS

Over the almost two decades that elapsed from the beginning of my fieldwork until the submission of this final book manuscript, I have built up a long list of mentors, colleagues, relatives, and friends to whom I am indebted.

I owe a great debt of gratitude to David Stark, who over the years played a succession of roles, as supportive teacher, generous coauthor, helpful mentor, and close friend. Back in 1999, David's enthusiasm for my term paper in his doctoral seminar, Economic Sociology—Sociology 8200, marked the beginning of an exceptionally fruitful collaboration. Together, we wrote five articles based on the initial fieldwork that informs this book project, and our regular meetings in his grand professorial office in Fayerwhether Hall at Columbia's Department of Sociology make for some of my best memories of the doctoral years. Beyond our collaboration, David also must be credited with organizing, together with Monique Girard, the inspiring and thought-provoking dinner seminars (the CODES series) at their New York residence.

Donald MacKenzie has been a major source of intellectual support. In many ways, this book is a conversation with the prodigious body of work that Donald has produced between the years 2000 and 2017 on topics ranging from the performativity of Black-Scholes to the political economy of high-frequency trading. Donald was kind enough to read through the entire book manuscript, and his insightful comments have elevated the rigor of my study.

I owe a special mention to Karin Knorr Cetina, who expressed genuine interest in my book project at a meeting we had in Madrid 2011 following the SASE academic conference.

Eric Schwartz, now at Columbia University Press, deserves to be credited for putting the first contract on the table, back when he was sociology and cognitive science editor at Princeton University Press. From our very first meeting at a café in Grand Central Station, Eric provided valuable advice about the craft of academic book writing. Since 2014, Meagan Levinson took over the editorship of the book with very effective results. I am very grateful to both, as well as to the rest of the team at Princeton University Press.

This book has benefited greatly from proofreading by Megan Peppel and Hannah Weisman, whose command of English prose, constructive criticisms, and enthusiastic reactions were a source of improvement and encouragement.

I would like to thank the traders at International Securities, including Todd, Max, and numerous others, for granting me access to their workplace, and in some cases their private homes. I am grateful to Quinn for his generosity in introducing me to Bob, back in 1999. I owe a heartfelt thank you to Bob, the undoubted protagonist of this book. Only a very special kind of Wall Street manager would welcome an ethnographer to his trading floor. Had it not been for Bob's extraordinary intellectual curiosity, this book would not exist.

A number of friends and colleagues have commented, read through, or provided crucial ideas for different parts of the book. These are, in alphabetical order, the following: David Barberá, Charles Baden-Fuller, Katherine Chen, Vicente Cunat, Will Davies, Joe Deville, Gary Dushnitsky, Fabrizio Ferraro, Roger Friedland, Santi Furnari, Raghu Garud, Joel Gehman, Matthew Gill, Martin Giradeau, Paul Ingram, Bruce Kogut, Monika Krause, Vincent Lépinay, Jan Lepoutre, Michael Lounsbury, Anette Mikes, Yuval Millo, Mary Morgan, Gina Neff, Woody Powell, Michael Power, Joel Shapiro, and Balazs Vedres. The conversations I had with them turned this book project into a source of friendship and intellectual stimulation.

Closer to home, I would like to thank my sister Helena, whose complicity and appreciation for my research always reminded me of the value of my work beyond academic circles. Having both a cousin, Enrique, and a brother-in-law, Jose, with successful careers in the City of London proved of invaluable help in steering clear of stereotypes of finance professionals. I was also lucky to have yet another cousin, Carmen, whose research in theology contributed to my book thanks to memorable conversations on religion and society in New York, Madrid, and London.

This book was part of my very first conversations with my wife, Itziar Castelló, as we began our acquaintance in the summer of 2011 in Jávea, Spain. Itziar's reactions, suggestions, and even objections, proved a crucial stimulus for my project. Years later, and once we were engaged, Itziar provided valuable comments on the entire draft, and her love and affection kept me going through multiple drafts of the manuscript. In particular, I will not forget our early-morning breakfast outings in Valencia ahead of long days of writing during Christmas 2016—early enough that it was difficult to find an open bar that would serve us.

Finally, this book is dedicated to my parents, Joaquín and Maria Dolores. Their regular visits to New York City were a vital source of emotional support as I completed the various stages of my doctoral studies. We shared the joy of my early discoveries in endless after-dinner conversations in the lounge of their hotels in Midtown Manhattan. Their love, support, and ability to overcome the geographical distance that separates New York from their home in Valencia made my doctoral studies—and, by extension, this book project—possible.

TAKING THE FLOOR

1

Introduction

Whether in the form of toxic derivatives or fake Libor submissions, the growing list of financial misdeeds that emerged from Wall Street since the beginning of the global financial crisis has fueled a decade-long debate about financial reform. Consider, for instance, the Dodd-Frank Wall Street Reform and Consumer Protection Act of 2010, often described as the most significant change to financial regulation in the United States since the 1930s. Opponents of Dodd-Frank object to its excessive rigidity, arguing that it will starve US companies of the necessary capital. Proponents of stricter regulation, on the other hand, fault Dodd-Frank for its limited effectiveness, pointing to the continued problem of the too-big-to-fail banks. While resolution of this debate remains elusive, one intriguing outcome of the discussions has been the recognition that the moral standards on Wall Street, and not simply the standards set by the law, are critical to a healthy financial system. For instance, the National Commission on the Causes of the Financial and Economic Crisis concluded in 2011 that "there was a systematic breakdown in accountability and ethics," adding that this erosion of standards of responsibility and ethics "exacerbated the financial crisis."[1]

Concern about ethics underlies a visible shift in financial regulation within the United States and United Kingdom. In the United States, the initial regulatory response to the crisis took the form of structural reform, based on laws, rules, and prohibitions. This was exemplified by the Volcker Rule and its stipulated ban on proprietary trading in commercial banks. Subsequent efforts by American regulators, however, shifted to the norms and values in Wall Street banks. For instance, in October 2014, the president of the New York Federal Reserve, William Dudley, organized the Workshop on Reforming Culture and Behavior in the Financial Services Industry, including among its attendees the chief executives of major Wall Street banks. In his opening speech, Dudley announced that "improving culture in the financial services industry is an imperative."[2] Using the word "culture" as many as forty-five times, Dudley emphasized its inescapable presence and importance: "culture," he remarked, "exists within every firm, whether it is recognized or ignored, whether it is nurtured or neglected, and whether it is embraced or disavowed."

A similar shift has taken place in the UK. Shortly after the financial crisis, the Independent Commission on Banking Report of 2011 took a structural approach to reform, issuing recommendations to "ring-fence," or legally separate, the retail and investment arms of British banks. In subsequent years, however, the emphasis turned to culture. The Salz Review of Barclays Bank, published in 2013 after the Libor scandal, concluded that "bankers were engulfed in a culture of 'edginess' and a 'winning at all costs' attitude," adding that these traits contributed to the bank's malpractices.[3] The Kay Review, commissioned by the British government to address short-termism in the City, found that "a culture of trust relationships, which is actually central to making financial services work, has been displaced by essentially a culture of transactions and trading."[4] The bank culture agenda culminated in the creation of the UK Banking Standards Board in 2015, an organization that aims to "raise standards of behavior and competence across the [financial] industry."

What emerges from these developments is a novel approach to financial reform, ostensibly aimed at bank culture but substantively centered on morality in the financial industry. Indeed, when a journalist pressed Dudley to specify what he meant by reforming culture, his response was that "culture is too broad a way to describe this. I think, reflecting on it, it's really about ethics and conduct."[5] The bank culture agenda thus stands in contrast with the traditional regulatory emphasis on outlawing misconduct and aligning incentives. Moral norms, unlike laws or incentives, do not speak to interests, but to underlying assumptions, prevailing customs, and the institutionalized definitions of right and wrong. By underscoring the moral dimension of markets, the new approach equates to an implicit admission that no amount of tinkering with bonuses or legal rules can, in the absence of ethical change, address the shortcomings of the financial industry.

Predictably, the culture agenda has been met with skepticism among Wall Street executives. Some have objected that culture is too vague a concept to prove effective, while others have added that culture lacks practical and actionable implications. The bankers' resistance was poignantly captured by the words of the US Comptroller of the Currency, Thomas J. Curry, who was tasked with the unenviable job of listening to the bankers' complaints. "I've had some bank executives and directors say, 'I'm not a damn sociologist,'" Curry explained to a reporter from the *Wall Street Journal*.[6]

Disparagement aside, the bankers' response is remarkable for its accurate reflection on disciplinary expertise. Ever since Max Weber's study of the

Protestant work ethic, sociologists have claimed for their own discipline the problem of how culture shapes the economy. In Weber's case, the celebrated German sociologist first hypothesized a connection between moral beliefs and economic development. "Calvinist believers were psychologically isolated," Weber famously wrote, adding that "their distance from God could only be precariously bridged, and their inner tensions only partially relieved, by unstinting, purposeful labor." Once material success came to be seen as a sign of God's favor, people were free to engage in trade and accumulation of wealth, and capitalism grew and expanded in Northern Europe. Weber's approach was central to sociology for much of the twentieth century, bolstered by the view—subsequently developed by the midcentury sociologist Talcott Parsons—that society is held together by shared values and "moral consensus."[7] In Parsons's formulation, moral norms and values are the central guide of action. Situations provide the means and conditions of action, values motivate the pursuit of certain ends rather than others, and norms limit the choice of the means to achieve those ends.

Over the past decades, however, Parsons's formulation has come under attack from contemporary sociologists, culminating in an alternative perspective of culture centered on practice. The alternative is chiefly associated with the work of Ann Swidler, who disputed the Parsonian contention that values are the key link between culture and action. A values-based account, Swidler argued, overlooks the fact that people may share common aspirations while remaining widely different in their behavior. For instance, explaining the absence of economic achievement by the urban poor in terms of a "culture of poverty" presupposes that the poor do not share the values and aspirations of the middle class, but working-class youth surveys repeatedly report that they value middle-class aspirations such as education, secure friendships, stable marriages, and steady jobs.

Instead of shaping action through internalized norms and values, Swidler added, culture influences action by creating a set of cultural competences that allow people to achieve some ends and not others. After all, one can hardly pursue success in a world where the accepted skills, style, and informal know-how are unfamiliar. Returning to the culture of poverty debate, Swidler wrote that "if one asked a slum youth why he did not take steps to pursue a middle-class path to success, the answer might well be not 'I don't want that life' but instead, 'Who, me?'" Lack of familiarity with an environment, in other words, is a roadblock to success. Swidler adds that culture influences action not by providing the ultimate values toward which action is oriented, but by "shaping a repertoire or toolkit of habits, skills, and styles from which people construct strategies of action." Swidler's emphasis on practice, often referred to as the "toolkit" perspective, stands in clear contrast to Parsons's view of culture as values. "Action is not determined by one's values," Swidler concludes. "Rather, action *and* values are organized to take advantage of cultural competences."[8]

Taken together, the positions adopted by the bankers, regulators, and sociologists discussed so far suggests a peculiar landscape of intellectual alliances. Although sociologists have steered clear of Parsons's emphasis on shared norms and values, the latter has resurfaced in economic reports and reviews of the crisis, a phenomenon that is apparent in characterizations of banks in terms of a "culture of edginess," or a "culture of transactions and trading." A similar take on culture is found among academic economists. Thus, a well-known economic study by Luigi Guiso, Paola Sapienza, and Luigi Zingales equated culture with values, drawing from survey data on "how values are perceived by employees."[9] Similarly, Andrew Lo has proposed the existence of a "Gordon Gekko" effect in financial organizations (making reference to the infamous Hollywood villain) whereby "an epidemic of shared values" can lead to excessive risk-taking.[10] Culture is presented by Lo as an all-encompassing determinant of behavior. As with a nasty virus, once an organization catches the wrong sort of culture, there is little that their members can do. At the risk of oversimplifying, one is tempted to conclude that the global financial crisis has posthumously granted Parsons his much-desired wish for intellectual influence over economists.

Paradoxical as the above might sound, the alternative is no less surprising. Skepticism toward the cultural reform program on Wall Street, certainly in its values-based version, includes sociological followers of Swidler as well as bank executives who resist the supervisory expansion of the Federal Reserve. This is admittedly not a real coalition, for the said sociologists are chiefly opposed to Parsons, while the bankers are simply against additional rules. Indeed, this would not even be a happy coalition, for as we learned from Thomas Curry, bankers are keen not to be taken for sociologists. Nevertheless, it is not too much of a stretch to argue that opposition to the vagueness and ineffectiveness of a values-based cultural reform places academic supporters of Swidler and profit-minded Wall Street executives in the same intellectual camp.

The post-crisis debate, in sum, seems to have bred some unusual travel companions. The odd pairings are revealing of the depth with which financial devastation in 2008 has shaken up the intellectual foundations that traditionally sustained the financial industry. The idea, central to financial economics, that morality can be analytically extricated from the study of finance, has been thoroughly called into question by the official reports and reviews of the crisis. The study of finance, these reports emphasize, should be broadened beyond approaches that omit references to ethical dilemmas. They should incorporate, as Maureen O'Hara has written, "more focus on ethical issues in finance."[11] The same conclusion applies to the practice of bank supervision: whereas regulators traditionally entrusted the elimination of misconduct on Wall Street to the care of the legal system, they now favor an approach that targets the bankers' ethics directly.

There is, in sum, an emerging consensus that if financial reform is to make progress, morality needs to be brought back into finance, both in practice and the study of finance. Yet, given the sociological arguments noted above, moving beyond well-intended but often ineffective interventions on bank values calls for answers to two pending questions. The first concerns the moral diagnosis of the crisis: if not through overly materialistic values such as greed or impatience, how exactly did morality contribute to the banks' troubles? Put differently, once one abandons the enticing but ultimately unsatisfactory idea that bankers have fundamentally different morality than the rest of people in society, the moral drivers of the crisis suddenly become obscured. The challenge then, as with the analyses of underachievement among the urban poor, is to formulate an understanding of what went morally wrong on Wall Street that does not caricature bankers as Hollywood villains. A second pending question concerns the prognosis for financial reform: if presenting bank employees with a brand-new set of values—much in the way that they might be given a new corporate uniform—is unlikely to alter their actions, what type of reform might avoid a repetition of the problems that led to the crisis? That is, if moral interventions solely centered on values are unlikely to do the trick, what form of cultural change will?

A partial answer to these two questions can arguably be found in the literature on morals and markets associated with Viviana Zelizer. The work of this influential sociologist has systematically explored the ways in which morality enables and legitimizes the development of otherwise controversial market transactions. For instance, her seminal study of life insurance in the early nineteenth century showed that insurers had to grapple with the moral resistance of their potential customers, American wives, who objected to profiting from a husband's hypothetical death.[12] Their qualms were only overcome when insurers reframed their product as compensation for economic rather than affective loss, presented insurance as a form of preserving the welfare of orphan children, or claimed that insurance was a way of avoiding the indignity of a pauper's burial. Zelizer's analysis thus suggests that morally ambiguous markets can be made viable if the necessary frames and practices are put in place. In a similar vein, Michel Anteby has documented how adherence to certain practices makes commerce in human cadavers for medical research morally acceptable.[13] He found that buying and selling of such specimens for research purposes is nowadays deemed satisfactory if it is not for profit, if it has the doctor's consent (not only that of the family), and if the cadavers are kept whole rather than cut into pieces. In sum, and as Marion Fourcade and Kieran Healy have observed, markets can be seen as "moral projects," that is, enabled and made possible by arrangements that create moral boundaries and draw moral distinctions between the sacred and the profane.[14]

While insightful, the morals and markets literature has not yet offered specific prescriptions for financial reform, nor engaged financial markets. In this regard, one promising point of departure is the sociological literature on finance. One of the early contributors to this literature, Mitchel Abolafia, paid special attention to the institutional mechanisms that create restraint. Building on a comparison across three financial settings (bond traders in a bank, pit traders in a commodities exchange, and specialists at the New York Stock Exchange), Abolafia challenged the argument that a trading culture inevitably leads financiers down the path of opportunism, as a Parsonian analysis would contend. He argued instead that restraint can be instilled through the "norms, rules and procedures to which members of the trading community are habituated."[15] For instance, he argued that the Treasury bill auction scandal of 1991 that brought down Salomon Brothers was the result of an environment, constructed by the investment banks in the 1980s, "with minimal interdependence, extraordinary incentives for self-interest, and minimal constraints on behavior." It was the lack of restraint created by such structures, Abolafia argues, rather than opportunistic moral values, that led bankers to withhold information from clients, post false bids in trading platforms, or front-run customers.[16]

There is one sense, however, in which Abolafia's account is of limited relevance to the debate about financial reform. Over the past four decades, Wall Street has been reshaped by the adoption of economic models, electronic trading, and derivative instruments, to the point of undergoing what some have described as a "quantitative revolution." Yet, partly because of the time in which Abolafia's fieldwork was conducted (the early 1980s), his analysis does not engage with quantitative finance. The resulting gap is problematic, because quantitative tools have not only made it possible for traders to measure and calculate formerly incalculable magnitudes like option value or expected loss. Tools like the Black-Scholes equation, Value at Risk, or those that determine variable compensation, have introduced a distinctively instrumental dimension to decision-making. Thanks to them, a trader can precisely calculate the personal gains to be had from various courses of action. For that reason, reforming Wall Street along the lines of Swidler and Zelizer would not only entail drawing moral boundaries between the acceptable and unacceptable, but also would grapple with the fact that traders have been explicitly equipped by models and formulas to be calculative in their actions and address the moral implications of such orientation.

The Social Studies of Finance

How, then, do economic models mediate morality on Wall Street? Over the past fifteen years, an emerging literature known as the "social studies of finance" has laid out the theoretical groundwork to address this question. Scholars in this discipline have built on a seminal essay by Michel Callon that called for a new focus on the tools and devices used by market participants.[17] Examples of such tools include an auction house for strawberries, or the algorithm that set the closing price for stocks at the Bourse de Paris. Artefacts such as these, Callon noted, are of key significance to markets. They frame choice, reduce uncertainty, and have the potential to make calculation possible. Before such technologies were available, Callon explained, markets could reasonably be expected to depart from an economist's ideal of rational choice, and plausibly be subsumed within the sociology of networks or institutional theory. However, once markets are conceived as "collective calculative devices," as the title of an article by Callon and Fabian Muniesa reads, the mediating role of market devices becomes crucial to explain economic outcomes.[18]

Of particular interest is Callon's contention that market tools such as economic models may have an active, rather than passive, role in valuation. As economic theories and models are incorporated into practical tools, they can influence the outcome of economic decisions, and in some cases corroborate the theory that inspired the tool in the first place. Callon refers to this mechanism as *performativity*, a concept originally used by philosopher John Austin to argue that speech not only describes but also consummates— that is, performs—action. For example, the utterance "I apologize" allows an actor to simultaneously ask to be forgiven as well as describe a statement. In a similar vein, Callon wrote, the incorporation of material tools in markets implies that "economics [. . .] shapes and formats the economy, rather than observing how it functions."[19] In other words, that economics is performative.

Over the past fifteen years, a vibrant literature in the social studies of finance has developed these ideas, shedding light on the mediating effect of economic models on markets. In a landmark study on the topic, Donald MacKenzie and Yuval Millo examined the effects of the Black-Scholes equation on the prices of stock options, documenting the performative effect originally hypothesized by Callon. These authors showed that although the predictions of the Black-Scholes formula were inaccurate when first developed in 1973, once the formula was adopted by financial exchanges and Wall Street banks, option prices changed in line with the model's predictions.[20] As the authors wrote, "option pricing theory [. . .] succeeded empirically not because it discovered preexisting price patterns but because markets changed in ways that made its assumptions more accurate."[21] In a related vein, Karin Knorr Cetina and Urs Bruegger examined the mediating effect of trading terminals on the social relations among traders and their subjective experience of the market. They found that as market participants abandoned one-to-one telephone conversations and began interacting through text in trading terminals, the importance of social relations within trading floors diminished, and social order was reconstituted as interaction on-screen.[22]

As these analyses illustrate, the social studies of finance have provided scholars with key building blocks to understand the effect of economic models on markets. While other economic sociologists remained focused on the effects of networks and institutions on markets, scholars in the social studies of finance placed the mechanistic world of theories, artifacts, and formulas at the core of their research program. This approach afforded a unique opportunity to engage with the content, and not just the social context, of markets, moving from questions such as "who talks to whom?" to questions around valuation. In doing so, the social studies of finance became a source of enthusiasm and inspiration for young scholars.

I can attest to such excitement, because I was a direct witness to it. Although I missed the first gatherings of the sociologists of finance in Germany and France during the late 1990s, I understood full well the theoretical significance of the ideas that were being woven together. In the year 2001, my coauthor David Stark and I organized an international workshop of the Social Studies of Finance in New York City and debated the findings of our fieldwork on Wall Street with Callon, Knorr Cetina, and other pioneers.[23] Over the past two decades, this literature has grown to encompass a long list of topics such as the history of the stock market ticker, the social consequences of credit scoring, or the political economy of high-frequency trading.

Models and Morals

Nevertheless, the financial crisis has also laid bare the limitations of the social studies of finance. The material view of markets and society that underlies most of this literature has barely considered morality, much less the effect of economic models on moral norms. Furthermore, this gap was not the product of casual oversight, but happened for a reason. Callon's theory of performativity, which underlies much of the social studies of finance, is based on a broader sociological perspective—Actor Network Theory—that he developed with Bruno Latour and others, and that presents material objects as the glue that makes society durable. As such, research on performativity is generally skeptical of explanations based on invisible social forces.[24]

Perhaps the clearest illustration of such skepticism is Latour's discussion of the effect of speed bumps on car drivers. City planners often build speed bumps in the roads next to schools in order to ensure that drivers moderate their speed. The driver's goal, Latour notes, will be altered by the speed bump, from slowing down to avoid risk to the students to slowing down to protect the car's suspension. "The driver's first version appeals to morality, enlightened disinterest, and reflection," Latour writes, "whereas the second appeals to pure selfishness and reflex action." "In my experience," Latour concludes, "there are many more people who would respond to the second than to the first," implying that norms are less dependable than self-interest.[25] Objects, in other words, beat morals as means of social control.

As much as the example of the speed bumps demonstrates the need to add objects to social theory, Latour's illustration also points to the limits of such an approach. It is not difficult to find counterparts of a speed bump in a Wall Street bank. One example is the legal mandate for US banks to invest in securities that have a minimum credit rating of BBB or equivalent—a provision originally aimed at ensuring that banks did not make overly risky investments. Another speedbump-like requirement is the imposition of capital requirements aimed at limiting the extent to which banks can take risks with borrowed capital. The performance of these two financial speed bumps during the crisis, however, has been decidedly disappointing. The ratings of subprime mortgage turned out to be inaccurate, to the extent that even the highly rated "super senior" tranches of mortgage derivatives lost almost their entire value. Furthermore, the presence of capital requirements made things worse, as they pushed banks into investing in mortgage securities. Speed bumps, and more generally the use of material devices in markets, are thus not always sufficient to instill restraint. The Wall Street version of a car driver that confronts a speed bump cannot be assumed to be willing to slow down near the school but might well find a way to avoid the constraint: buy better tires, adjust the suspension, or perhaps even drive on the sidewalk and endanger other pedestrians.

As the above example suggests, scholars in the social studies of finance may have gone too far in their attempts to redress the sociological neglect of material devices in markets. When it comes to restraint, there are limits to the effectiveness of material artifacts that have no concern for broader norms. Stripped of their normative associations, devices like ratings or ratios become a practical obstacle to sidestep, rather than an effective instrument for control. This much was implicitly recognized by Callon himself in his more recent concept of "*homo economicus 2.0*" and his call for a model of individual action that combines materiality with sociological traits such as sociability, identity, or affect.[26] The goal, then, is not to replace decades of social theory with hard material objects, but to arrive at an understanding of markets that combines both. The role of morality has not yet been considered in this new approach.

One notable exception to the above is Caitlin Zaloom's research. Traders, she argues, attribute moral significance to being alert, to a reflexive engagement with the market, and to being disciplined—to the point that many see trading profits as "market-based virtue" (p. 177). But whereas Zaloom's research has persuasively challenged an amoral view of traders, it has not considered how economic models can give rise to moral complications such as those that surfaced in the 2008 crisis. (See Zaloom 2012.)

The limits of the social studies of finance bring me back to the central question that Abolafia left unresolved: what are the effects of economic models on morality in financial organizations? When taking stock of the existing literature, one cannot but conclude that there is a gap. Cultural sociologists like Swidler have developed a toolkit perspective that emphasizes concrete practices over abstract values, but this literature has not yet considered financial markets, nor economic models. The same can be said of Zelizer's literature on morals and markets. On the other hand, the social studies of finance has grappled substantially with the effect of economic models on markets, but has not considered the effects on morality. The interplay between models and morals, in other words, remains unexamined, leaving a number of questions unanswered. For instance, are moral norms simply abandoned when traders use equations like Black-Scholes and resort to calculative decision-making? Alternatively, are models used differently when traders adhere to certain ethical norms? If so, how? In sum, a full decade after September 2008, understanding how morals and models come together remains a crucial but pending task in our diagnosis of the crisis, as well as in addressing the problems that led to it.

Why This Book?

The above brings me to my own motivation for writing this book. The global financial crisis that started in 2008 might have seemed like a golden "opportunity" for an academic like myself. Although trained in management, the subject of my research is Wall Street, and my studies draw on organizational and sociological theory. Starting in 1999, I spent three years conducting fieldwork at the equity derivatives trading room of an international bank located in Lower Manhattan, which I will designate with a pseudonymous name, *International Securities*. Between 2003 and 2007, I published several articles based on this research, coauthored with David Stark, and won two research awards for them.[27] Starting in 2006, I joined the faculty of Columbia Business School and gained intellectual as well as geographical proximity to the banks on Wall Street. From the window of my office at Columbia, I could almost see the towers that housed these banks in Midtown Manhattan. To the extent that the cause of the global financial crisis of 2008 was located somewhere on Wall Street, I may have seemed ideally equipped to unearth it.

This was not, however, how the crisis felt at the time. The billion-dollar losses and controversial practices that came to light at Lehman Brothers and other banks in September 2008 put me in a state of perplexity. I could not grasp the connection between the misbehaviors at the failed banks and the practices of the traders that I had witnessed years earlier at International Securities, for the executives I had followed seemed hard-working and ambitious, but also honest and prudent. I could only imagine two possible explanations for this inconsistency: either my traders had managed to dupe me for the three years of my fieldwork, or their trading room that I had observed operated on a different planet than that of Lehman Brothers. Both alternatives, however, seemed equally implausible, so I spent the fall of 2008 suffering from an academic version of cognitive dissonance, unable to reconcile what I believed to be true with the daily events reported in the news.

The solution to the puzzle came to me as I recalled an event that took place one year earlier. Back in the fall of 2007, that is, four months *before* the failure of Bear Stearns in March 2008, I invited the manager of the trading room of International Securities to give a presentation to my MBA class at Columbia. I will refer to this executive as "Bob," again a pseudonym. At the time, I was teaching a core management course that was distinctively unpopular with some of my Wall Street-bound students. Inviting Bob was not just a form of intellectual recognition but also a self-interested attempt to improve my deficient teaching ratings, as I thought that my students would enjoy listening to a successful Wall Street executive.

What happened during that session changed how I think about Wall Street. In his presentation to my students, Bob shared an aspect of his career that had not previously surfaced in my fieldwork. Before managing the trading floor that I studied at International Securities, Bob had occupied a high-ranking position in the derivatives division of another bank, which I will refer to as Premier Financial. This bank experienced a number of scandals and eventually disappeared. Bob had left the bank untainted by scandal in the 1990s and took early retirement at an age when most people are still hoping for their first career break. Retirement gave him plenty of time to think about what had gone wrong. Two years later, when he decided to go back to work and run the equities division of International Securities, he put the lessons from Premier Financial into practice, and designed a trading room that was unlike the rest of Wall Street.

Fast forward now to my MBA classroom at Columbia in November 2007. In his lecture to my students, Bob focused on his experience at Premier Financial in the 1990s. In front of eighty MBA students, many of whom were eager to join Wall Street after graduation, Bob spoke candidly about the problems he confronted during his time at Premier, and about the challenges that persisted on Wall Street. He was critical. The large banks, he said, were too big, and too complex. They were badly managed. "Mark my words," he told my class, "when the next crisis comes, which it will, *not one but two* of the large banks will disappear."

At the time, the failure of two Wall Street banks did not seem even remotely plausible to me. Indeed, none of my students picked up on Bob's prophecy in their questions at the end of the lecture. However, barely four months later, Bear Stearns was being acquired by JP Morgan at the fire-sale price of $10 per share. Six months after that, Lehman Brothers was filing for bankruptcy. Had I not taken the trouble to tape Bob's talk and write the date on the audio file, I would have scarcely believed that Bob was so prescient in his prediction.

Bob's lecture cast in new light the research I had conducted at International Securities in the early 2000s. I now understood that the trading room that he had assembled was his own attempt to address the problems he had confronted at Premier Financial, including the excessive size and complexity of Wall Street banks. Furthermore, Bob's timely prediction of an impending bank failure suggested that his diagnosis of Wall Street's dysfunctions was not too far off the mark. When I put these two observations together, I understood that the trading room I had observed for three years was not *representative* of the average investment bank on Wall Street, but *illustrative* of what a possible solution to the challenges that plagued the financial industry might be. In other words, the trading room was less useful than I had hoped as a *description* of other banks on Wall Street, but a potentially valuable guide as a *prescription* for them.

Hence this book. In the chapters that follow, I unpack and clarify the insights from my original fieldwork at Bob's trading floor, placing them in the broader context of the financial crisis. The research design that I adopted is primarily ethnographic, combined with revisits and oral history interviews. Like other studies of trading floors, such as Karen Ho's *Liquidated* or Vincent Lépinay's *Codes of Finance*, my study relies on participant observation, and specifically on the practices that I observed on the equities trading floor of International Securities from 1999 to 2003. Yet this book differs from the first generation of Wall Street ethnographies in that it combines my original fieldwork with subsequent revisits to the bank's trading floor and its protagonists. My research design thus conforms in part to Michael Burawoy's concept of "punctuated revisit," that is, an ethnographic project where the researcher returns to the original site over a time period spanning at least ten years.[28]

Why such revisiting? The simple answer is a combination of curiosity and necessity. Before 2008, returning to the bank satisfied my genuine interest, supported my teaching, and helped me complete the academic articles that I was writing. After Lehman's bankruptcy, the revisits served a different goal: they were my way to try to reconcile my original findings with the media representations of reckless trading on Wall Street. Once I grasped that International Securities held relevant lessons for the policy debate on financial reform, my revisits became a means to articulate such lessons.[29]

My Core Argument

In the chapters that follow, I make two core claims. The first one concerns the key question that motivates the book: what are the effects of economic models on morality in financial organizations? I argue that the introduction of models threatens to exert a reconstitutive effect at various levels of the bank, altering the degree to which ethical norms are enforced, self-enforced, and interpreted. Specifically, I contend that the use of models for the purpose of corporate strategy and risk management can lead to a shift away from business relations between companies and the banks that lend them money, and toward transaction-based banking where banks treat each lending transaction as a single deal and focus on its risk. In addition, I posit that the introduction of models in top management may contribute to a managerial discourse based on rationality and self-interest that sacrifices the customers' interests. Furthermore, in the relationship between managers and traders, the use of models for risk management can erode managerial authority as well as generate perceptions of injustice when these models fail. Such perception may then invite retaliation and reckless decisions on the part of the traders. Finally, in the relationships between traders and the bank's customers, the informational asymmetry created by models helps traders capture most of the value they generate, incentivizing them to develop needlessly complex models. Taken together, models thus pose a risk of transforming a bank's strategy, discourse, control, and commercial relations, giving rise to perceptions of injustice and to what social psychologists call moral disengagement.[30] Moral disengagement disables the mechanisms of self-condemnation that are typically associated with immoral conduct, opening the bank to the unrestrained pursuit of self-interest. I refer to this phenomenon as *model-based moral disengagement.*

Models, however, need not create disengagement. Such outcomes can be avoided through organizational strategies and practices that I also identify. At the level of strategy, banks can avoid asset classes that create information asymmetries between them and their corporate customers, as such asymmetries invite abuse. One example is the use of "over-the-counter" derivatives such as interest rate swaps, where banks structure a made-to-measure contract with the customer that may be difficult for them to understand, making them vulnerable to abuse. At the level of discourse, managers can put forth a rhetoric that underscores the importance of organizational norms over financial returns. These norms may include collaboration, compliance with the law, or respect for back-office employees. They can be mobilized and enforced in offsite meetings, internal labor markets, or through an organizational layer of middle managers, but the primary enforcement vehicle is one-on-one interactions between employee and line manager. This enforcement of norms, however, also requires limiting the use of models for the purpose of control, as models constitute a rival and often incompatible source of authority. I refer to the deployment of organizational measures to prevent model-based moral disengagement as *proximate control.*

Proximate control builds on contemporary sociological understandings of culture, in that it provides a toolkit of strategic directions, framings, and practices, thereby approaching what Swidler termed a strategy of action. By relating a toolkit approach to the use of economic models, proximate control combines a cultural and a material sociological approach to financial reform. Proximate control also builds on the morals and markets literature developed by Zelizer, bringing economic models into the debate over how to improve moral standards in finance. Specifically, it invites parallels between the post-crisis debate on financial reform and the reforms initiated by insurance companies in the nineteenth century that made a morally dubious market morally acceptable. In this regard, proximate control is different from the values-based "bank culture" regulatory agenda, providing instead a practice-based approach to reform that is not driven by speeches, workshops, or attempts at inculcating values. Given its rejection of a consensus view of morality, proximate control is not aimed primarily at corporate responsibility units, compliance departments, risk management, or human resource teams that aim to influence an organization as a whole. Proximate control aims instead at the concrete and all-important relationship between a trader and his direct line manager, as it is in that close vicinity where the nuances of right and wrong can be established and practices can be modified.

Performative Spirals

The second key argument in this book concerns the organization of modeling on Wall Street. The topic became central to sociological debate over the financial crisis following MacKenzie's claim that the billions lost by Wall Street banks were due to silos in their modeling process.[31] The organization of modeling is especially important when the models are performative rather than simply descriptive, because in a performative context those models can actively change market value. I thus ask, how should banks organize the use of economic models to take into account their performative effects?

I consider one of the key applications of economic models on Wall Street—modern arbitrage. My observations of this trading strategy on the equities floor of International Securities suggest that as much as models help make calculation possible by reducing informational uncertainties, they also leave numerous uncertainties unresolved. As a result, modern arbitrage is neither mechanistic nor purely calculative, but requires instead the use of judgment, social cues, and inputs from various traders, both within and outside the trading room. In other words, modeling is not simply technical, but social. The arbitrageurs' need for social cues calls for organizational integration across desks, but such integration is problematic given the differences in assumptions, methods, and standards that characterize the various trading strategies. Integration, however, can to some extent be accomplished through the managerial promotion of informal relations across desks on the floor.

I further argue that modern arbitrage is performative in several ways. I document how arbitrageurs conceptualize stocks in terms of narrow *financial properties* such as mean reversion or merger probability, and these properties are dependent on the models and tools required to evaluate them. The relationship between models and stock prices is performative, in that the models are not external to the valuation process but an integral part of it. Such performativity is in some cases weak, in the sense that the models only provide the infrastructure needed to isolate and measure financial properties without impacting prices. In other cases, the performativity is strong, in that the model impacts prices and brings them closer to the model's predictions.[32] For instance, the use of implied probabilities in merger arbitrage relies on models that assume an absence of arbitrage opportunities. Over the years, the growing adoption of this strategy has contributed to reducing arbitrage opportunities, thereby bringing the market closer to the model's assumption.

Finally, I contend that the performative relationship between models and financial properties is not stable over time, but marked by a spiraling dynamic. Once an economic model becomes widely adopted, the arbitrage strategy that it sustains becomes less profitable. As a new model is subsequently developed, new financial properties will come into view and overlap with the existing ones. There is thus a reciprocal relationship between economic models and financial properties, which I denote as a *performative spiral*. The presence of such a spiral has implications for how a trading room should be structured: as a trading room incorporates new models and tools, novel forms of organizational integration will become necessary. This changing need for integration explains the shifting layout of the desks in the bank I studied, and I refer to this organizational pattern as a *performative trace*.

In conclusion, my two core claims in this book are centered on the moral and knowledge-related effects of economic models on financial markets. Models have a moral dimension and a knowledge dimension; their joint effect has implications for the sociological debate on the global financial crisis, as accounts of the crisis have advanced an organizational or moral perspective but have barely integrated the two. While MacKenzie and other scholars have centered their account on the problems created by organizational silos in the credit rating agencies and Wall Street banks,[33] others such as Neil Fligstein and Alexander Roehrkasse have attributed the crisis to unethical activity on Wall Street.[34] I contend that both problems were in part an outcome of the reorganization that took place on Wall Street at an organizational, technological, and regulatory level, starting in the 1980s. This included the disappearance of the investment banking partnerships (in which partners were jointly liable, and forced to monitor each other), the adoption of economic models, and the repeal of the Glass-Steagall Act. These changes had problematic moral consequences such as model-based disengagement. Furthermore, the introduction of new models, including those involved in the growth of credit derivatives, gave rise to new evaluation practices without the organizational changes that were necessary to integrate such practices.

Chapter Outline

In the chapters that follow, I divide my arguments in two sections. The first section, which encompasses chapters 2 to 7, introduces my original fieldwork from 1999 to 2003 and my account of how modeling was organized on the trading floor of International Securities. Chapter 2 situates my study within the original sociology of finance and introduces the core ethnographic breakdown that motivated my project: while existing studies described trading floors as loud, stressful, and chaotic, the trading room that I encountered at International Securities in 1999 was quiet and orderly. The reason for such disparity was the introduction of information technology during the 1990s, which had replaced loud oral communication as the key information exchange mechanism. This change in turn led Bob, the manager of the floor, to rethink the trading room as a space for interpreting and debating economic news and events.

Beyond the addition of the Bloomberg terminal, the key difference between the trading strategies I witnessed at International Securities and those reported by sociologists of finance in the 1980s was the widespread use of economic models. What challenges did those models pose? Chapter 3 considers this question by introducing a statistical arbitrage trader named Todd and his use of financial algorithms. Todd's strategy also illustrates the novelty entailed in modern arbitrage, that is, the exploitation of mispricings across markets for securities whose value is ambiguously related. There was a tension, I also noticed, running through Todd's work: whereas he sought to avoid psychological biases by relying on rigid decision rules, the uncertainty introduced by his algorithms often forced him to abandon his rules and rely on his judgment, as well as on social cues from the floor. Such tension is illustrative of a broader challenge posed by uncertainty in quantitative finance, which demands that traders develop precise numerical estimates and subsequently call them into question.

If, as the case of Todd suggests, social cues were a valuable complement to the use of models, how to ensure that those cues are present on the trading floor? Chapter 4 considers Bob's answer to this question by introducing the sales desk at International Securities, along with its convivial work atmosphere. Sales traders such as Scott, Joe, and Jim did not buy or sell stocks for the bank's proprietary account but executed trades for their customers instead. Their skills and resources, including humor, excitement, charisma, or business contacts at the stock exchanges, were different from and complementary to those of other traders on the floor. In the course of my observations, I also noted that the sales traders appeared to be engaged in a number of seemingly controversial practices such as earning soft-dollar commissions, crossing the Chinese Wall, or pulling pranks on accidental callers to the bank's phone line. By examining the ways in which these sales traders adopted, modified, and conceived of these practices, I was able to learn about their practiced, as opposed to stated, morality.

What are the distinctive advantages of using economic formulas on a trading floor? In chapter 5 I consider this question by introducing Max, a senior trader at the merger arbitrage desk and a mathematically gifted trader. Max bet on whether announced mergers would actually be completed. More important, he was able to combine stock prices with economic models, plot them on a Bloomberg terminal, and estimate his rivals' expectations about a pending merger. He then used these inferred expectations to refine his own estimates of merger probability. This allowed him to test his own hypothesis against the rest of the market, question his assumptions, or ponder what he might be missing. Such possibilities reduced the risk of mistakes in Max's bets, allowing him to take larger positions and realize higher returns. The case of Max revealed to me what was truly new, different, and to some extent magical, about the use of models in trading.

While the cases of Todd and Max pointed to social cues as a key aspect of quantitative finance, there was another, less salient but equally important social dimension: management. Chapter 6 shifts the book's focus from the traders to the managers who supervised them. I consider three different managers: the head of Risk Management at International Securities, a senior trader who was in charge of Todd's desk, and a manager whom Bob had tasked with promoting collaboration across desks. The challenges and difficulties these three individuals encountered revealed the organized and to some extent hierarchical nature of professional trading and the need for an organizational lens. My observations of these managers also point to a difficult tension between technical and managerial expertise.

As much as economic models give traders a unique ability to observe aspects of a stock that the naked eye cannot see, my study revealed another, even more intriguing aspect: performativity. In chapter 7 I consider the performative effect of economic models and their influence on the financial properties of securities such as stocks. New representations of value, typically in the form of new economic models, devices, and tools, reveal new properties of the securities, which can themselves be represented and profitably exploited. I capture this dynamic with the concept of performative spiral, defined above. Bob exploited the successive waves of innovation in modeling by aligning the layout of the trading room with the emerging interdependencies between the properties of the stocks. I refer to this dynamic as performative trace, also defined above.

The first half of the book, in sum, concerns the use of knowledge on the trading floor, focusing on models, traders, and the connection between them. The second half turns to morality on Wall Street, and the moral consequences of economic models. Chapter 8 is motivated by an observation that changed how I thought about the bank: the integration of knowledge across desks that I had originally observed was not simply the result of material processes such as the rotation of the desks or a low-monitor policy, but of organizational norms of collaboration that Bob enforced on the trading floor. Norms were enforced by Bob and a dedicated team of middle managers who fired or shamed deviant employees, constructed shared experiences in offsite meetings, and introduced a system of internal careers that rewarded following those norms with career promotion. Organizational norms, and not simply spatial features or material objects, were behind the remarkable degree of collaboration across desks that I observed.

While my emphasis on social relations might evoke an idyllic narrative where social factors dominate technical imperatives, the two were in fact interrelated. Exploiting social relations on the floor, as Bob did, gave rise to new challenges and pitfalls. In chapter 9, I examine Bob's handling of risk in light of his own reluctance to rely on the figures produced by the bank's Risk Management department. If not by means of numerical risk estimates such as Value at Risk, how did Bob promote restraint among his traders? As I found out, he limited the potential scope for losses by exercising judgment: he and his team considered potential scenarios, comparing alternative courses of action in the future. However, such judgment could also prove problematic. In 2001, Bob's judgment compounded the losses experienced by Max at the merger desk; upon further analysis I understood that the losses were an instance of model-based loss amplification, which David Stark and I called *resonance*. By resonance, I mean the spurious confirmation of a trader's estimate arising from the use of economic models. The solution that Bob subsequently adopted entailed a greater reliance and appreciation for his traders' ability to intuitively sense danger.

None of the accidents, errors, or disasters that I witnessed on the trading room prepared me for the scale of losses that beset Wall Street in September 2008. Chapter 10 presents my observations of the global financial crisis from Bob's vantage point. By September 2008, Bob had joined a different bank, Global Trust (pseudonym), and had become chief executive of one of its US subsidiaries. My regular meetings with him from August 2008 until the summer of 2009 thus provided me an insider's perspective into the crisis and exposed to a domain that had barely surfaced in my study: morality. I observed the moral outrage at the crisis experienced by Bob and other Wall Street insiders, as well as Bob's contention that moral judgments can help managers evaluate their subordinates' use of models in situations of uncertainty. Bob attributed the global financial crisis to the organizational changes that had taken place on Wall Street since the 1980s, along with their moral side effects. Wall Street, he told me a few days after Lehman's bankruptcy, did not die in September 2008, but had already been dead for years.

What did Bob mean by "dead"? In chapter 11, I unpack Bob's comment by turning to the modern history of Wall Street, as seen through Bob's professional trajectory in the securities industry since the early 1980s. This trajectory included the growth of the derivatives industry, the disappearance of the partnership form, and deregulation. I focus on the derivatives scandals of the mid-1990s, leveraging Bob's experience at another major bank, Premier Financial. Although largely overlooked, the 2008 crisis arguably had its predecessor in the derivatives scandals of 1994 and 1995. At the time, Wall Street banks signed over the counter derivatives agreements with corporations that resulted in sizeable losses for the latter. Also at that time, pioneering banks like Premier Financial began using risk management models as a tool for control and restraint rather than as a way to ascertain overall exposure. The mid-1990s crisis reveals the moral complexities posed by new and unfamiliar financial instruments, especially when the standards for prudent behavior are set by a mathematical formula such as Value at Risk. My analysis theorizes this dynamic with the concept of *model-based moral disengagement*, defined earlier in this chapter.

While an abundant literature on the global financial crisis has documented its devastating economic consequences for American workers, few ethnographies have documented its impact on Wall Street employees, or what it meant for them. In chapter 12, I consider this point, revisiting the protagonists of my fieldwork at International Securities in 2015, Todd, Max, and Bob, seven years after the crisis. By that time, Todd had left Wall Street, Max was closing a hedge fund he had recently founded, and Bob was running a conservative public-interest law firm. My meeting with Todd underscored the scarcity of committed and competent top management on Wall Street. My conversations with Max revealed his nostalgia for the investment banking partnerships of the early 1980s, as well as the advantages of Bob's management approach, which sought to replicate elements of the partnerships. Finally, my meetings with Bob spoke to the current debate on financial reform, alerting me to the presence of a feedback loop that connects bank size, economic models, and moral disengagement. In light of this loop, Bob advocated the breakup of Wall Street banks.

I conclude in chapter 13 by bringing together the emerging themes of the book into an overarching framework. I consider integration, organizational norms, judgment, moral disengagement, and the breakup of Wall Street banks. I propose the concept of *proximate control*, a hands-on approach to management that stands in contrast to what governmentality scholars such as Peter Miller and Nikolas Rose have called government at a distance. Proximate control calls for better supervision of quantitative traders by resisting the temptation to evaluate those employees using models. It entails a combination of the social and the technological, such as preserving face-to-face interaction on the trading floor, the use of personal evaluation of quantitative results, or the qualitative judgment of financial calculations.

2

First Impressions

Precisely how I ended up conducting an ethnographic study of a Wall Street trading floor was as much a matter of intellectual curiosity as of luck and happenstance. I landed in New York City in 1998. I was twenty-seven years old. I had completed a master's degree in business economics in Barcelona, and I had been admitted to a PhD program in Management at the Stern School of Business in New York University (NYU). Because living near NYU in Greenwich Village on a doctoral stipend was out of the question, I moved into an inexpensive graduate student residence in Harlem and commuted daily to the university. Every day, I took the number 1 subway train downtown, got off in Greenwich Village, and walked along West 4 Street toward NYU, where I had my own desk in a windowless room (the "bullpen") with six other doctoral students. Every day, as part of this commute, I caught sight of the Twin Towers. They were actually far from NYU, at least twenty blocks away, but because of their extraordinary size, they were clearly visible to me. They looked impressive, a perfectly identical pair of rectangular plinths, standing tall against the irregular skyline of Lower Manhattan.

I would regularly catch a second daily glimpse of the Towers on my way back home. In the dark, they were even more striking than in broad daylight, for some of the offices were lit up while others had gone dark. As in the black and white photographs of Manhattan taken by Berenice Abbott in the 1930s, the dotted pattern of lights hinted at the presence of life inside the buildings. Some of the executives in them had gone home for the day, while others were still working. But what, I wondered, were they doing? The image kept me company as I walked by the busy cafés and student bars of Greenwich Village on my way back to the graduate residence, burdened by the weight of choosing a dissertation topic.

Back in my residence in Harlem, I took to discussing the Towers with fellow graduate students. I mentioned the Towers to an MBA student who lived on the same floor as I did, and he remarked that they also made him think whenever he walked by. "Every lit office I see," he explained, "is a networking opportunity." To me, by contrast, the Towers meant Wall Street. They evoked the information processing function of markets, which I had come to appreciate in my late-night readings of Friedrich Hayek during my previous studies. As I imagined them, the Towers broadcast the prices of stocks and bonds to the rest of the country, optimally guiding the movement of capital from one company to another in reaction to, as Hayek wrote, "knowledge of the circumstances."[1] If one thought of the American economy as a body, Wall Street would be the brain, and the Towers, I concluded, were as close as one could get to the actual embodiment of that financial brain.

It was difficult to live in New York City in 1998 and not think about Wall Street. In September 1998, barely a month after I arrived in the city, a hedge fund called Long-Term Capital Management collapsed in the wake of the Russian debt default, losing $4.6 billion and forcing the Federal Reserve to assemble a consortium of investors to rescue it. Before failing, the fund had achieved prominence for its extraordinary returns, which were reputedly realized through the use of mathematical models to trade stocks and bonds. Two of the fund's partners were academics economists and recipients of the Nobel Prize in Economics. The failure of Long-Term Capital Management prompted multiple warnings in the business press against the dangers of quantitative finance. Wall Street also permeated the life of a doctoral student in Management like me in other ways. As the Nasdaq rose to historic highs, for instance, the business school at NYU where I studied installed a large, flat-screen television next to the elevators, tuned to the financial news channel CNBC.

Two months into my doctoral studies, I was struck by a realization, almost an epiphany. I was living in New York City, the financial capital of the world (Londoners would of course disagree). If I was going to spend my next four years writing a doctoral dissertation, it made little sense to write about the laser industry, chemical plants, or car companies. It *had* to be about financial markets. My interest, however, did not lie in financial models. I had already learned how to derive the Capital Asset Pricing Model in my previous studies. I had also read the original papers on market efficiency written in the 1960s by Eugene Fama, and I had marveled at the intellectual ambition exhibited by Harry Markowitz in laying the foundations for financial economics. However, those models could not satisfy my curiosity about the actual people on Wall Street: the bankers, traders, dealers, brokers, and analysts. In fact, the little I knew about actual Wall Street executives came from watching Hollywood films and reading fiction. I had watched Oliver Stone's *Wall Street* and was moved by the drama of corporate takeovers. I had read Tom Wolfe's *The Bonfire of the*

Vanities and imagined the trading rooms of Wall Street to be overcrowded and dominated by emotion and, as Wolfe wrote, full of "young men [. . .] sweating early in the morning and shouting" (p. 58). None of these markedly human traits, however, appeared to be captured by the financial models I had studied.

My goal, instead, was to understand what went on inside a Wall Street bank. What were the practices, motivations, and strategies of the bankers and traders inside them? Could I figuratively pry open the concrete-and-glass walls of the Towers and take a peek inside? My curiosity, in many ways, was no different from that of a tourist walking around Greenwich Village, gazing up toward the skyline of Lower Manhattan and wondering, *what's inside*? My hope, too, was that by studying Wall Street in this manner I might be able to tap into the social milieu that surrounded me: New York City and its hurried inhabitants. I was supposed to be living in "the greatest city in the world," but beyond sitting next to fellow subway travelers and sharing the sights on the street, I had yet to gain access to the wonders and magic of the metropolis and its people. I wanted, in other words, to connect, and I hoped that by studying Wall Street I would be able to understand New York City.

My goal, finally, was not just voyeuristic. As I saw it, there was a remarkable gap in the academic understanding of finance, and that gap concerned the managerial and organizational aspect of Wall Street. I concluded this from my own efforts to locate such perspective within the confines of the Stern School. As someone who had just left the intellectual rigidities of an academic discipline (in my case, Economics) I was keen to explore other fields and paradigms during my time at NYU. I began by attending seminars in the Finance Department, located one floor above Management. But as I ventured there, I noted something unusual: only two academic perspectives were represented in the study of financial markets. By contrast, my own Management Department had faculty from three different disciplines. It had economists who studied business strategy; sociologically informed organization theorists who studied networks, structures, and institutions; and psychologists who studied individual well-being, justice, or identity. All three groups shared the fourth floor of the Kaufman building and battled each other in the weekly Management research seminars. When I walked up one floor to the Finance Department, however, only two academic perspectives were in evidence. There were orthodox economists, who studied capital markets from the standpoint of rational choice; and there were psychologically informed behavioral economists, who explored the ways in which decision-making biases impacted financial markets.

In sum, there seemed to be one perspective missing from the study of finance within the confines of the Stern School, namely, an *organizational* approach. For instance, what effect did the presence of social networks on Wall Street banks have on the prices of stocks? How did organizational structures in investment banks influence trading? How did the culture and institutions of the trading floors shape the transactions that took place inside? Indeed, the business school offered a course on this very topic, but in the form of evening classes for part-time MBA students, titled "Managing Financial Businesses." I enrolled in this course as soon as I heard of its existence but was primarily taught by clinical faculty and finance practitioners, with an exclusive emphasis on practice and lacking a body of theory.

I resolved to fill that gap. The opportunity seemed both exhilarating and daunting, a research gap wide enough to make a meaningful contribution, though also wide enough to sink my future academic career. Successful doctoral dissertations, an older student had told me, typically asked a question that was *moderately* difficult. Seen from that perspective my plan seemed like an act of irresponsibility. Agitated, I arrived at my desk in the business school and immediately wrote an email to a classmate from my undergraduate days in Barcelona, who was completing a PhD in Economics in Boston. "Does this make sense?" I asked after a long description of my plans. "Go right ahead," he replied. "This could be huge."

Several months passed, and after a number of failed attempts, I eventually gained research access to the trading floor of International Securities. The way in which this happened was again unexpected. Aware of the need to better grasp the sociological dimension of markets, I decided to enroll in a doctoral course on Economic Sociology. I found one at Columbia University, and in September 1999 I took the subway uptown from NYU to Morningside Heights, walked across the campus of Columbia University to Room 801 in the brutalist-style building that housed Columbia's School of International and Public Affairs, and joined what proved to be the most influential course of my doctoral studies, a PhD seminar taught by David Stark: Economic Sociology— Sociology 8200. The highly charged intellectual atmosphere and tight community that emerged from that seminar equipped me not only with the ideas that would guide my dissertation, but also with the key contact for my project.

I came across this contact by happenstance. While discussing my dissertation plans before the start of a seminar, a fellow student offered to introduce me to an ex-colleague who worked on Wall Street. The student, whom I will refer to as Quinn, had been a banker in the 1980s, retired, and enrolled in Columbia's PhD program in Sociology. He explained that one of his former colleagues had also retired but then returned to work on Wall Street to run a derivatives trading floor, and might be willing to speak to me. His name was Robert, or Bob (again, pseudonymous). Thrilled by the opportunity, I took Quinn up on the offer and contacted the ex-colleague, requesting a meeting. Bob replied to my message right away, and I made an appointment for a visit to the bank where he worked.

In preparing for that first visit, I took stock of what I knew about organizations on Wall Street. A year had elapsed since I had first decided to study an investment bank. I had been turned down by two already, and I had also learned about the existence of a small but important sociological literature on finance. Two sociologists were of special relevance to my project. The first was Mitchel Abolafia. His research on bond traders seemed particularly applicable to my project, in that the traders he studied worked in a trading room like the one I was about to visit. Abolafia's portrait of those traders presented them as uniquely self-interested and opportunistic: "traders are dying to make money," one of them said to Abolafia. "That's all they care about."[2] Such reductionism only added to my curiosity, for it implied that traders might have lost basic human qualities such as sociability, compassion, or morality, their personalities somehow altered by their bonuses. If the words of Abolafia's trader were accurate, visiting Bob's trading room might reveal a strange alien tribe in a skyscraper.

Research by a second sociologist of finance, Wayne Baker, provided me with the preliminary hypotheses that guided my visit. Baker had analyzed how social networks shaped prices on the floor of a securities exchange. A trading pit, Baker found, was so noisy, uncertain, and open to such abuse that pit traders limited themselves to buying and selling from known and trusted traders. As a result, transactions were structured in small networks. When a given crowd in the pit reached a certain size, trading broke down into two separate networks, increasing price volatility. This was a remarkable finding, because both common sense and economic theory suggested that the greater the number of traders in a pit, the greater the liquidity, and the smoother the price changes, that is, the lower the volatility. However, Baker showed that, beyond a certain size, additional traders did not reduce price volatility but actually increased it. As he wrote, "trading among actors exhibited distinct social structural patterns that dramatically affected the direction and magnitude of [. . .] price volatility."[3]

Baker's study focused my attention on the patterns of oral information exchange in trading rooms. In other words, *shouting*. When do traders shout? Why? I prepared to examine these questions in my visit to Bob's trading floor by developing a 20-point questionnaire to explore the relationship between oral communication in the trading room and the evolution of prices and traded volume. For instance, I wondered: when the *traded volume* (that is, the total number of shares bought and sold) increased, did the *spoken volume* (that is, the sound intensity uttered by the traders) rise accordingly?

International Securities

On the date of my visit to International Securities, and armed with the aforementioned questionnaire, I searched for some semblance of formal wear in my sparse closet with the goal of looking inconspicuous on the floor. I put on a jacket and a tie, and took the subway to Wall Street.

The visit, however, did not go as planned. The offices of International Securities were located in an imposing corporate skyscraper in Lower Manhattan. I entered the lobby, gave my name to a security guard, and continued to an elevator. Once the elevator stopped on the relevant floor, the doors opened up to a sign that read "Equities" and a corridor leading down to a glass door. I walked past the door and announced to the receptionist that I was coming to see "Robert." An executive assistant appeared and walked me down another corridor to the trading room.

As soon as we turned the corner, I had to pause for a second. In front of me were row upon row of traders, each of them sitting in front of a multitude of screens. The image was a powerful one, a visual display of smart people, hard at work in front of scrolling text and up-to-the-second numbers. Yet nothing in that trading room seemed to fit my preconceived notion of what the space would be like. For one, the trading floor was not the overcrowded box that Tom Wolfe had described; instead, the space featured tall ceilings, wide corridors, and a panoramic view of Manhattan. Of greater concern to me, the traders were not shouting as Baker had described, but speaking to each other at a normal volume, creating a quiet buzz. Furthermore, no one seemed overly stressed; some traders were in fact reclined in their Aeron chairs, pointing and clicking on their Bloomberg terminals, while others talked to one another in the corridor, holding cups of Starbucks coffee and looking relaxed. Indeed, and in contrast to the sartorial standards featured in Hollywood films, nobody was wearing a tie. It was Friday, and the bank had recently adopted a "casual Friday" dress code.

I then met the manager. Bob's executive assistant took me to a desk in the middle of the room where a man was sitting. "That's Bob," she said. The man, once again, looked the opposite of what I imagined a Wall Street executive to be: he was short, young-looking, and dressed in a casual shirt and cotton chinos. Bob stood up to greet me: "I'm honored that you dressed up for the visit," he said with a visible hint of irony, highlighting the conspicuousness of the jacket and tie that I had put on for the purpose of looking discreet. He suggested I call him Bob.

As we sat down to talk, it quickly became clear that the questionnaire I had prepared was going to be of little help. I had intended to study the patterns of shouting among the traders, but I could not hear a single shout. My only option was to come clean: "my objective was to study information sharing," I explained to Bob, "and I had put together a set of questions for you. But nobody is shouting, the trading room is not crowded, and no one seems stressed. So, my actual question is, *why don't your traders act like in the movies?*"

Bob smiled. The trading rooms I had in mind, he explained, did exist, but they were typical of the 1980s. Things had changed with the arrival of information technology such as the Bloomberg terminal. "Thanks to technology," he said, "you don't need to hear from your neighbor on price action." In the old times, before all the quotes were on screens, a trading room was a quick and efficient way to find out the price of securities. "If you were on the phone with a client and he wanted to know the price of IBM, you stood up, shouted the question at the IBM dealer and he shouted the price back. Nowadays, if a trader started shouting about the price of a stock, the others would ask him what's the fuss and tell him to calm down."

Why, then, did banks continue to use trading rooms? Bob agreed that the question was worth asking. In fact, he added, trading rooms were expensive. "Not because of the real estate," he added, "but because of the changes that have to be made to the building to accommodate the equipment." The ceiling and floor had to be adjusted to make space for the wiring, and the air-conditioning had to be reinforced to cool the heat generated by the computers. Furthermore, the traders could trade from home. "For $1400 a month," Bob said, "you can have the machine at home," referring to the Bloomberg terminal, which could be installed at a private home with a high-speed connection. "You can have the best information, access to all data at your disposal, at home." Bob still found that incredible. Yet, despite having this technology at their disposal, banks were not sending traders to work from home. "The tendency is precisely the reverse," Bob said, "banks are building bigger and bigger trading rooms."

What, then, was the point of *his* trading room? "Understanding each other," Bob replied. "When I have something complicated to explain to someone else, I hate to do it on the telephone, because I need to know if the other guy is getting what I say." Bob gave me the example of his own location on the floor. As the manager of the entire unit, he had a glass-walled private office overlooking the floor a few meters from where we were talking. But he preferred to sit in the middle of the room. "The other role that the trading room plays is, it's a social place. You can overhear other people's conversation. The market sometimes doesn't move. You get bored. You like to have contact with the other guys." Almost on cue, a trader came by and interrupted our conversation. He did not come to tell Bob about an urgent problem, but rather to share a story that he thought Bob "would really enjoy." From the sound of it, his story seemed to me more like gossip than work.

"For example, look at this," Bob continued once the trader left, pointing to the price of Apple Computer on the screen of his Bloomberg terminal. "The price of Apple has just dropped. Is this interesting? No. Because anybody has access to it. On the other hand," he continued, "look at that," displaying on the screen the price chart of a small company with a sharp price decrease in the middle of the day. "See this company? Its price fell because of a lawsuit. Now, this is interesting because it is a very small company and one would not normally pay attention to it. If I know about it, I can tell this to the people who are doing program trading, whose computer does not take this into consideration."

Beyond managing the traders' attention, having all traders in the same room facilitated collaboration across teams, or so-called desks. Bob gave the following example: on July 9, 1999, the chemical company DuPont announced its intention to "split off" one of its oil units, Conoco Inc. A company "split-off" is a corporate sale, but a sale to its shareholders rather than to another company. The legal terms of Conoco's split created some uncertainty regarding the shareholders' reaction to it. DuPont shareholders were given the option to exchange their shares for those in Conoco. However, the offer only applied to US investors; for international shareholders, DuPont extended a cash offer up to a maximum of eight million shares. Thus, while there was some usual uncertainty associated with the deal (would it be completed, or called off?), most of the uncertainty investors faced resulted from not knowing whether shareholders would take DuPont stock or not. Some of these shareholders were domestic, and some international; some were retail investors, and some institutional. Any trader who understood how these dynamics would play out ahead of time could make lucrative returns.

Bob's traders were active in this trade and engaged in an unprecedented degree of communication across desks. However, Bob added, talking proved challenging. "Sharing and collaborating does not come naturally for these guys," he explained. "A trader is like an engineer type. Difficult when they think they're right. Abrasive. And not very social. Not socially adept." In fact, Bob added, "I can easily find you ten traders in the room who would be miserable at a cocktail party. Until you catch something that's in their field, and then they will express their opinion without concern for the others."

Interestingly, the lack of communication across desks was partly rooted in a cultural norm on Wall Street. Bob explained that back in the 1980s, and while working at Premier Financial, "there were areas of the trading floor I would never venture into. People I never, absolutely never, talked to. There was no reason why I should go there, since we traded completely different things." This lack of interaction posed a real problem when collaboration was actually needed. "Even if I just happened to want to go there, it felt strange. There were these cold looks. Somebody would ask, 'what do you want?' in a defensive tone. People did not like you to watch them trade." In the absence of actively promoted interactions across desks, Bob concluded, even the possibility of knowledge-sharing disappeared. The outcome was the proverbial "silos" that management theorists allude to when accounting for mistakes by corporate bureaucracies. "My point is, territoriality is a big issue," Bob concluded. "These people are all very qualified, very competitive. They will accept working in a desk with the people surrounding them. But they don't like strangers."

The Conoco trade was a success for Bob and the floor. To accomplish it, Bob explained, "we had to pull together information from all the different desks. Some were doing research on what the institutional investors were going to do. Others were contacting their clients. We had to meet and discuss all this to make sense and get a coherent picture. And we had to do it quickly." However, the trading room was not physically designed for extensive cross-desk collaboration, and the traders kept literally running into each other. Frustrated, Bob ordered an architectural alteration. In a corner where there used to be a traditional meeting room, four walls, a table, and chairs, Bob ordered the removal of two of the walls, the desk, and the chairs, creating a corner-shaped open space for quick meetings. "We put whiteboard all across the walls. Now, people just walk in, scribble on the wall, and move on." I was intrigued by this space. "What exactly do people discuss?" I asked. "They walk others through their trades," Bob replied. The space was so new that the three wooden stools that Bob had ordered had not yet arrived. But meetings were already taking place, as many as three or four times a day.

My conversation with Bob then evolved into a discussion of his own role within the trading room. "The job of the manager is to keep an eye on what is going on in the room," he said. "I have that office over there—you just saw it," pointing to the glass-walled office. "But I like this place better. Here I can get a feel for how the market is doing. I have to know this, because the atmosphere definitely influences the way traders trade. They know it does, but they don't know how. See there, for example?" He stood up and pointed to the group of four men drinking coffee in the corridor that I had spotted earlier as I walked in. "These guys are having a business meeting. How do I know? They are all from the same team, they are with their boss, and they are talking to that other guy who is from Equity Research. See those other ones? I can tell you, right off, that is a social meeting."

The idea of the atmosphere in the room influencing people's trades was intriguing, as well as the fact that Bob had built that influence into his job. How did *he* find out how the markets were doing? "I listen," he explained. "I like to hear a smooth sound, not very loud. I look for people having disagreements on the phone. That is conflict, which is a bad sign." Bob also paid attention to body language. "It's not deliberate, so it's a good source for what's happening. But I don't try to get too conscious of how I'm reading body language and facial expressions. I just let it work its way to where it's useful." In addition to listening, Bob saw himself as having a balancing effect on traders. "My role is as a cooling rod. I walk the floor. I talk to people about non-substantial issues. I try and find out who is stressed. We pile up all this," Bob said, gesturing to the entire room, "to get a reaction. And sometimes we need to manage that reaction."

"Another role of the manager," Bob added, lowering his voice and adopting a more serious tone, "is to overrule the traders' decisions, and order them to close a position if they're losing too much. This is a very sensitive issue. If a position is losing money, it can always pick up, given enough time. The trader will always want to hold to his position for longer than the manager wants him to, in the hope that it will pick up. But that can lead to huge losses." Mounting losses typically forced the bank to force traders to liquidate their positions. "Other traders don't like to see this, because liquidating abruptly leads to losses, and they think, 'this could happen to me.'"

These situations created a complex relationship between Bob and the traders he managed. As Bob explained, in situations of continued losses, managers and traders appeared to have opposing incentives. If losses are moderately large, they will matter greatly to the trader, as they cut into his bonus, but not to the bank in any significant way. If, by contrast, losses become very large, the manager may lose his job over poor risk management, yet the impact would be limited for the trader. Once the trader's losses have wiped out the bonus, additional losses might not matter as much. Traders and managers thus faced a potential conflict, and Bob was mindful of that tension.

Grappling with the Quantitative Revolution

The hour that Bob had agreed to devote to our meeting soon elapsed, and my time was up. I gathered my notes and thanked him for his time. The visit had left me both exhausted and perplexed. I had walked into the trading room hoping to see shouting, stress, and emotional intensity; instead, I had seen hushed conversations, traders who behaved like engineers, and a thoughtful manager who was keen on his traders getting along. Compared with Abolafia's traders, the peace and quiet in Bob's trading room felt disappointing. *Is this*, I asked myself as I was leaving, *the real Wall Street*? As I entered the elevator, I made a mental note to look for another trading room, a more old-fashioned and authentic one, or at least more similar to the ones Abolafia described. As the elevator made its way down to the lobby, however, I realized that what I had witnessed offered a real research opportunity. As the case of Long-Term Capital Management had made clear, quantitative technology and economic models were the new development shaping financial markets. The equity derivatives floor at International Securities could, if I managed to gain continued access, provide me with a unique window into that exclusive world.

The subway commute back to NYU barely took fifteen minutes. As I returned to the PhD bullpen, I began to transcribe the fieldnotes that I had hurriedly jotted while Bob spoke. My fellow students, however, expressed great curiosity about the visit. I shared with them what I had seen and heard, taking care to preserve the anonymity of the bank. At some point in my recounting, I realized that the entire bullpen had dropped what they were doing and were standing around me, listening in silence. My fellow students were just as fascinated as I was. International Securities, I concluded, would make for a good dissertation topic.

Later that day, as I finished transcribing my notes, I took stock of the surprises and unexpected observations from my visit. These certainly included the lack of shouting, which stood in sharp contrast to the frantic pits described by Baker that largely preceded the rise of quantitative finance. Indeed, such was the level of peace and quiet in Bob's trading floor that my perplexity was now turned on its head: did people *really* shout in the trading floors of the 1980s?

There was, I discovered, an existing study of the traditional trading rooms before technology changed them. A team of London-based researchers, Christian Heath, Marina Jirotka, Paul Luff, and Jon Hindmarsh, had conducted observations in a City dealing room during the early 1990s, and found that the clustering of people and shouting of prices facilitated coordination.[4] Consider, for instance, the tight seating arrangement of trading desks. The researchers had found that trading required timely collaboration with other traders at the desk, but that a trader could not always simply interrupt a fellow trader if he was doing something else. However, sitting close together allowed each trader to send and receive visual cues that invited or discouraged interruption. A dealer that they observed, for instance, was once able to "time, with precision, an utterance which engenders collaboration, so that it coincides with a colleague . . . swallowing a mouthful of lunch."[5]

Shouting was equally useful. Heath and his colleagues were at first struck by the traders' practice of yelling names and numbers while on the phone, apparently without expecting an answer. This, the London researchers argued, was the solution to a problem of knowledge-sharing: traders not only needed to know about their own stocks, but also about some of the stocks that their colleagues were trading. Precisely who needed to know about which stock could never be easily anticipated. "Shouting aloud," Heath and colleagues wrote, "delivers the information in a way that does not necessarily demand that anyone responds." While this approach might seem relatively obtrusive, "it is perhaps less obtrusive than actually informing specific recipients."[6] A traditional trading room, in other words, was a material setup, comprised of desks, phones, monitors, and other artifacts, and designed to engender local and peripheral collaboration, that is, collaboration within each desk and across desks. In this regard, trading rooms were no different from other "control rooms" used by air traffic controllers or at the London underground.

The above, however, described the state of trading rooms in the late 1980s when Heath and his colleagues did their fieldwork, but by the late 1990s the shouting had disappeared from International Securities. A sociologist of science and technology, Karin Knorr Cetina, and her collaborator, Urs Bruegger, had recently studied the process by which information technology replaced the "peripheral collaboration" theorized by Heath and colleagues. In an ethnographic study of foreign exchange trading in Zurich, they found that the introduction of trading terminals had sharply reduced the frequency of face-to-face interaction among foreign exchange ("forex") trades. These traders preferred to interact with counterparts in other banks via text-based electronic conversations made possible by their trading terminals. The forex market, these sociologists concluded, was thus best described as a "collective disembodied system generated entirely in a symbolic space."[7] Based on their observations, Knorr Cetina and Bruegger concluded that electronic markets, that is, those where prices and orders traveled through computer terminals rather than the phone, had reduced the importance of physical proximity. The market was not physically located in a place, but constituted by numbers, letters, and currency symbols floating somewhere in cyberspace.[8]

The above was directly relevant to my own observations. The adoption of trading terminals seemed to explain the relative quiet in Bob's trading room, but a puzzle still remained, for the terminals could not account for the collaboration across desks in the DuPont-Conoco trade. In making sense of Bob's emphasis on collaboration, my mind turned to the writings of Frank Knight, an influential economist during the decades before World War II who was subsequently rediscovered by sociologists such as Harrison White.[9] Knight's original interest was to explain the extraordinary profits earned by entrepreneurs, and he accounted for these by distinguishing between risk and uncertainty. In situations of *risk*, all possible contingencies and their probabilities are known in advance, and market actors can safely make calculated bets. The classic example is the toss of a coin, in which there are only two possible contingencies, heads or tails, and their probability is known (50 percent) unless the coin has been manipulated. By contrast, in situations of *uncertainty*, the possible contingencies and probabilities are not known in advance, and calculation is therefore not possible.

Because of competitive pressure, Knight hypothesized, profitable economic activity shifts from activities marked by risk to those marked by uncertainty. That is why, Knight added, entrepreneurs are so richly rewarded: they confront uncertainty, so their decisions are less easily replicated by competitors. The same, I reasoned, could be said about the traders at International Securities. Because profitable trading strategies are imitated and their returns competed away, clearly defined trades (that is, situations of risk) do not remain profitable for long. By contrast, high returns will accumulate among ill-defined trades, that is, trades that are marked by uncertainty and are difficult to replicate. I thought this pattern explained why Bob looked for complex and interdependent trades, like the DuPont-Conoco trade.

In sum, my observations in the trading room of International Securities were partly consistent with the research by Heath and associates, as well as that by Knorr Cetina and Bruegger. There was a need for collaboration, as Heath and others had identified. However, this collaboration no longer took the form of shouting due to information technology such as the Bloomberg terminal, as Knorr Cetina argued. At the same time, there was still one important way in which International Securities differed from the existing literature: unlike Knorr Cetina and Bruegger's traders, who appeared to be so engrossed in the black-and-white, text-only, world of their trading terminals so as to be absent from the physical space of the trading room, Bob had described a picture of presence and collaboration within his trading room, and my observations of people speaking corroborated this. While the forex traders that Knorr Cetina and Bruegger described appeared to be traveling through some form of financial cyberspace, Bob's trading room tried to recreate a sort of cocktail party, with impromptu meetings and social congregation, made possible by the shared physical space. Similarly, Knorr Cetina and Bruegger made little mention of the role of managers, while Bob assumed a central role in his own floor, at least according to his own account.

The importance of space for collaboration was aptly captured by the whiteboard area in a corner of the floor. Bob's emphasis on collaboration had led him to create a customized space for it. In the whiteboard area, the lack of the traditional office furniture such as chairs, a table, or for that matter, walls, altered how meeting participants interacted with each other. Instead of engaging in the elaborate corporate ritual that people identify as "a meeting," the traders appeared to simply show up to the whiteboard and discuss without wasting time or engaging in formalities. In this sense, the whiteboard illustrated how material objects could mediate social action: to reduce the time wasted on symbol and ritual, Bob had simply removed the tangible accessories that complemented the time waste. That the whiteboard might have an effect on the traders' behavior was not difficult to believe, because I had already seen that Bob was willing to forgo status symbols—both a private office and formal business attire.

Second Visit

I contacted Bob again in January 2000 and asked for another appointment. I wanted to verify my first impressions, and specifically understand whether informal relations were the key to his traders' profits. To keep Bob interested in my research, I sent him a sanitized version of my fieldnotes, free from my own speculations and references to obscure theories. The notes just summarized what Bob himself had said and gave me an excuse to come for another visit.

That second visit also did not go quite as planned. I showed up on the agreed day and hour, but Bob's assistant explained that he was in a meeting and could not see me. I left the building in disappointment. The following day, however, I received an email from Bob, who apologized and suggested we reschedule. "Join me for lunch," he wrote. One week later I thus returned to the bank, this time at lunchtime, and not quite sure of what to expect. Bob met me at his desk, and from there we took an elevator, going up two floors above the trading room. We then walked further up through what seemed to be the staircase of a duplex apartment, tastefully decorated in glass, steel, and dark green granite. We arrived at a luminous space, outfitted in the style of a luxury boat with echoes of Art Deco style. This was the bank's executive dining room. The place had very few tables, a panoramic view of Manhattan, curved leather sofas, and Egyptian sphinxes carved into the furniture. A maître d' welcomed us and ushered us to a reserved table. Sensing my bewilderment, Bob explained: "my reward to you for keeping you waiting last week. I was retired for two years, working from home, and these small luxuries are definitely something you miss."

"I have thought a lot about your notes," Bob continued once we sat down. "When I read them, I realized it is not easy to see yourself in the mirror." But the theme of promoting collaboration had somehow struck a chord with him. "I am doing more construction work," Bob continued. "Did you see the area just in front of the entrance?" I had indeed noticed that part of the trading room was enclosed in translucent plastic. I vaguely recalled that there used to be a lounge area in there. "I am demolishing that. This would mean nothing if I were to use the space to put more people in it, but I am actually *reducing* the number of people in the trading room."

Bob's objective, he explained, was to free up space to move the Technology desk and Operations group closer together. One key function of Operations, Bob said, was to keep a record of which corporations the bank's clients had invested in. For instance, if a client defaulted on an interest payment, Operations officials were expected to communicate this to the traders. But such communication, Bob added, was fraught with social hazards: someone from Operations would not typically have a graduate degree, much less an MBA, as did some of the traders. Traders got upset when Operations officers missed corporate actions, or when they relayed news that the traders disliked. This often led to yelling, so traders and Operations officers tended not to get along. Placing them physically closer, Bob thought, would improve the flow of information. He even made the space in Operations look more similar to that of the traders. The windows in the Operations area were initially blocked by stacked computer manuals, empty boxes, and unused hardware. Bob had them uncluttered. "This integration," he said to me, visibly pleased, "you will not find in the rest of Wall Street." In bigger banks, the Operations department was located on a different floor, even a different building. For the purpose of communication, Bob said, once a team is on a different floor, "they might as well be on a different planet."[10]

The conversation turned to the corner meeting room that I had seen during my previous visit, the "whiteboard." Bob explained that he had been unsure about how often the whiteboard would be used, as he had not seen it in other banks. Initially, he had felt he had to encourage his traders to use it, but since my previous visit its use had increased. The dark wood stools had arrived, but "now people complain to me because they cannot recline back, so what they do is they drag their chairs over and use the stools as tables."

Both the whiteboard and Bob's decision to have additional construction done appeared to confirm my initial impression: he placed a great emphasis on collaboration. My attention had also been drawn to the idea of limiting the number of traders on the floor, as this resembled Baker's argument that beyond a certain number, adding traders to a pit did not reduce volatility but increased it instead. The implication was that a relational perspective, as used by Baker, was key to understanding Bob's trading room.

I began to explore this idea in the conversation with Bob, but my knowledge of network theory had not prepared me for the exchange that followed. "Have you read *The Tipping Point*?" he asked. Bob was referring to a book by Malcolm Gladwell on critical mass phenomena, lucidly written for the general public.[11] I knew of the book but had not yet read it. I told Bob as much. "You should," he replied, in the tone one would use to recommend that someone sign up for the gym. Bob went on to explain his interest in the book. In it, Gladwell discussed the optimal size of an informal group, citing anthropological research that put this size at 150 people. Above that number, trust supposedly breaks down.

Where did Bob's interest in the topic come from? "Before joining International Securities," he said, "I invested in a dot-com company that was based on the idea of networks," he added. But whereas Gladwell was the inspiration that Bob relied on for his decision to limit the size of his trading room, Bob had also found a similar message from a very different source: the Mennonite communities that his ancestors belonged to. Mennonites, Bob explained, were similar to the Amish, but unlike the Amish they did not reject technology. Doing research on his ancestry, Bob found that the maximum size of a Mennonite community was about 150 people. "Once the group grew above that size, they would split into two," as above a certain number the communal connection that drove members to work for the common group started to weaken.[12]

Bob had even tested the idea of an optimal unit size in his trading room. "We gave everybody a list of the people in the trading room and asked them to mark who they spoke to at least once a day. We concluded that the maximum size was more or less the same as the Mennonites, 150." There was another reason for having a limited size. For communication to work, Bob argued, people have to be extremely comfortable with each other. "The key is to avoid social awkwardness," he explained. "Two traders are talking to each other. A third needs a piece of information. He has to interrupt. 'Can I interrupt? Can I interrupt?' The key there is the social cost of the interruption. There currently are 170 people in the trading room, and I intend to reduce that a little."

Was the trading room, I asked, deriving additional returns from this unique organization? Bob admitted that the question was relevant, but that it was difficult to discuss rates of return without discussing the level of risk, as one can always raise returns by increasing risk. One should compare the trading room with hedge funds that incurred the same level of risk. Bob estimated that hedge funds had a "market neutral" profitability between 15 percent and 25 percent. By market neutral he meant a level of risk commensurate with the overall stock market. He felt "very comfortable" giving me a figure for International Securities in the low end of this bracket. "But," he added, "this has management fees already discounted." Hedge funds typically took a 2 percent fee from the total volume of the assets they managed and a 30 percent fee from the profits. The implication was that Bob's trading room was doing better than comparable hedge funds.

I expressed surprise, since the efficient markets hypothesis argued that above-normal rates of return were not sustainable in the long term. "That is ridiculous," Bob replied, and recounted the well-known story of the two economists walking down the street who see, but do not pick up, a $50 bill on the ground, arguing that it could not possibly be there, because if it were someone else would have already picked it up. "Finance is the same," Bob added. "Over the long term, prices reach an equilibrium, but it takes someone making money through buying and selling for equilibrium prices to hold." Bob was also skeptical about mathematical models for risk management. "We do have the models, and we do run the numbers. And many people ask us for them, and we produce them. But I don't go by them." The reason is that these models never incorporate future possible risk scenarios. "I trust my subconscious to give me the risk."[13]

Social Relations on the Trading Floor

Back in my cubicle at NYU, as I transcribed my notes from this second visit, I reflected on what I had seen. The meeting had confirmed my first impressions about the whiteboard area, and in fact Bob had escalated in his efforts to use space to shape behavior, removing the lounge area that separated Operations from the rest of the trading room. Bob's approach seemed to be characterized by an emphasis on informal interaction across organizational structures such as desks, as well as by a commitment to egalitarianism that de-emphasized the standard markers of corporate hierarchy. In this, Bob's approach appeared to fit within the renowned concept of "organic structure" developed in 1961 by British researchers Tom Burns and Lawrence Stalker. These two noted that companies in new and emerging industries faced rapidly changing market conditions where a rigid division of labor, which the authors labeled "mechanistic" structure, limited the organization's ability to adapt to the environment.

Instead, they added, innovative companies followed an "organic" approach, with "fluid definitions of function and interactions that are equally lateral as they are vertical."[14] Organic structures, in other words, were non-hierarchical and non-bureaucratic. The distinction between mechanistic and organic established by Burns and Stalker proved influential and was the basis for more recent organizational concepts such as the network organization, the boundaryless organization, the flat organization, or the heterarchy.

That Bob's traders were organized to encourage collaboration and reduce status differences was surprising, in that it seemed to challenge Abolafia's study of bond traders in the 1980s. The traders that Abolafia interviewed openly declared that making money was "all they care about," and they engaged in morally dubious, even illegal practices like submitting false bids to the auctions of the US government's Treasury bills. But despite the superficial disparity, Bob's practices were consistent with Abolafia's ultimate argument, namely, that the materialist focus he had observed in the traders was not the outcome of a natural and inevitable psychological drive, but a cultural construction that was influenced in their case by the absence of structural features promoting restraint. Morally dubious practices, Abolafia argued, were one possible option within a culturally defined menu. Bond traders were consciously embracing opportunism because it advanced their objectives, but they might have chosen a different course of action had it been in their strategic interest to do so. Traders were not, in other words, immersed in their own culture to the point of being blinded to it. Their professional affiliation or social sphere was not the sole determinant of opportunism. Bob's trading floor seemed to be an example of precisely the alternative scenario that Abolafia hinted at: when faced with the need to collaborate to make money, and surrounded by a material setup that facilitated collaboration, Bob's traders seemed able to overcome their individualism.

A second surprise from my visit was the degree to which Bob relied on academic research for his design of the trading room, and especially on social anthropology and network theory. As soon as I left the trading floor, I purchased Gladwell's book and discovered that the idea that trust needs groups of 150 people at a maximum was first proposed in the 1990s by British anthropologist Robin Dunbar. He found a correlation between primate brain size and average social group size, and the figure of 150 people is now known as "Dunbar's number." By using the average human brain size and extrapolating from the results of primates, Dunbar proposed that humans can comfortably maintain around 150 stable relationships.[15] As important as the number itself was the source that Bob had relied on, a book that popularized social science research, much of it network theory.

Taken together, my two visits to the equities floor at International Securities left me with a sense of excitement and opportunity. I had realized my original goal: gaining access and catching a glimpse of the world that hid behind the façade of the glass and steel skyscrapers in Lower Manhattan. An opportunity now lay ahead of me, for grasping Bob's trading floor might allow me to contribute to an organizational understanding of financial markets, an emerging literature with leading contributions from the likes of Baker, Abolafia, Heath, or Knorr Cetina. As I examined the extant research on this topic, I had concluded that my observations did not quite fit academic accounts of shouting and stress, or of rampant materialism. The securities industry was in the midst of an extraordinary transformation, the quantitative revolution, and the arrival of trading terminals and economic models had altered the organization of trading floors. Even then, the peculiarities of Bob's trading room could not be entirely attributed to technology, because while other trading floors had made their trading terminals the new focus of attention, Bob was emphasizing collaboration on the floor, and altering its architecture to achieve it. The emerging story was not one of technology trumping social relations, but one where technology was redefining the nature and function of those relations. The task ahead for me would be to establish how.

3

Trading Robots and Social Cues

My first two visits to the equities floor of International Securities had satisfied my initial curiosity about Wall Street. Once inside, however, what I saw defied my expectations: the manager promoted collaboration across desks, and the traders no longer shouted prices at each other. The introduction of trading terminals and economics models, I learned, was altering the function of social relations on trading floors, but the precise way in which it did was far from clear. Indeed, I had understood from my two previous visits that the traders were engaged in *arbitrage*, that is, exploiting mispricings across markets, but the connection between arbitrage and economic models was also unclear to me. Understanding this point was critical, for it concerned the relationship between quantitative technology and social dynamics on the floor.

In search of an answer, I asked Bob for permission to observe one of his quantitative traders at work, ideally one that used models for his trading strategy. Bob suggested that I speak to Todd, a "statistical arbitrage" trader who specialized in the use of probabilistic models. His was the most technology-based strategy on the floor, Bob noted, and watching him would allow me to understand how traders combined computers and knowledge from other desks to establish equivalencies among securities. He then introduced me to Todd via email.

Todd

"I have a coin that comes up heads 55 percent of the time," said Todd in our first meeting. "The point is to flip it a lot." Todd agreed to let me watch him trade. I pulled up a chair next to him and took quick notes while he explained what he was doing. A thin and understated man, Todd was my introduction to the world of *quants*, or quantitative analysts, a specialized type of trader that applied mathematical and statistical methods to trading. Todd's career illustrated the confluence of science and finance that defined quants: he graduated in the late 1970s from an Ivy League university with an undergraduate degree in Operations Research, and then studied for a master's degree in Finance. His first job was at a large Wall Street bank, where he traded bonds using economic models in a pioneering and secretive group located at the bank's information technology division. This team was culturally as well as physically separated from the main trading floor. Todd's manager was an astrophysicist. The rates of return were legendary. After a few years, Todd moved to another bank, where he used models to price bonds before there was readily available commercial software to do it. The bank experienced legal troubles in the late 1980s, and Todd moved to International Securities.

I asked Todd about the nature of his trades. His strategy, Todd said, was arbitrage. "You start with a view of a misprice. This is often a relative misprice, of some assets with respect to others, and it involves some assumption that two securities are similar in some way. In order to get at that similarity, you use replication arguments." Arbitrage, in other words, was about relative rather than absolute prices: Todd did not make any claim about the future price of a stock, but about its relationship with some other security. Arbitrage was thus a more qualified form of claim than a directional bet. The arbitrage trader typically buys one security and sells another one, so that the trader is not exposed to changes in the absolute value. In addition, Todd's bets were based on a "replication" argument: he related one security to another by finding ways to recreate the cash flow provided by the first one with a modified version of the second one, and that replication entailed the use of economic models. Replication, in other words, was not about intuition but logic, and it was open to empirical testing.

Todd explained that he specialized in statistical arbitrage. This strategy was based on the premise that stock prices behaved according to statistical regularities. To exploit these regularities, Todd executed 8,000 trades per day with computer programs. Specifically, he used three "robots"—two developed by him and one by "outside advisors."[1] Among those he developed, one was based on the notion of statistical "mean-reversion" in prices. "The principle of the model," he explained, was that "if something goes down enough, it will go back up." On that morning, for example, Todd's book began the day with a short position on Lexmark Inc., the printer company. The stock opened at a very low price, however, so the mean-reversion robot "decided" that it was under-priced and put in an order for 2,000 shares, that is, bet that the price would increase. Then, as the price began to increase, the robot put in an order to short 5,000 shares, that is, bet that its price would decrease. Todd thus made money on the way up and on the way down. Furthermore, when the robot bought Lexmark, it simultaneously sold HP, not because it was unattractive, but because HP also sold printers and it provided a way to hedge the exposure to Lexmark. The second robot developed by Todd was "earnings-driven." Instead of predicting the convergence of stock prices to their historical average, it assumed that prices would react to changes in company earnings. That morning, Todd's robot was shorting shares in a gas company whose stock price was already very low, something the first robot would never do, because the company's earnings were even lower.

One striking aspect of Todd's approach to trading was his aversion to judgment. To avoid making judgment calls, he relied on a number of rules he had developed over the years. These related, for instance, to the type of information source he could use. "Rumors on CNBC, should I listen to them?" he asked rhetorically about this financial television channel. "I often need to find out when a stock is going to go through exceptional circumstances, like a takeover or a restructuring. In principle, it would be useful to anticipate what is going to happen. But there are ten rumors for every takeover. So, I just turn off the volume." And as he said this, he manually turned off the volume in the individual speaker on his desk. "There is an additional problem with rumors. You never know how they're going to be interpreted. Take Motorola, the big news today. They've done worse than expected. But the stock went up. Why? Because all tech stocks went up, apparently because some trader at Salomon decided that tech's so low that we should buy anyway." As Todd saw it, the market was unpredictable and it was better to not try to anticipate it by pursuing rumors.

Todd had also developed a rule for deciding what information to take into account. "What I do is, I read the second column on the cover of the *Wall Street Journal*." This column provided readers with a brief summary of daily business news, and Todd believed one could safely assume that anybody in business knew what was written in it. The larger point, Todd added, was the value of consistency. "The more that I can articulate simple rules for myself, the more I can be consistent in my own interpretation of events. If I start to interpret events freely, I'm using a 50 percent coin to go against a 55 percent one." Indeed, Todd was not only committed to the elimination of bias, but positively proud of his automated system. At regular intervals, he would look away from the conversation, point to the computer and say, "here! Another 'look ma, no hands!' trade," in reference to an automated trade his computer had executed.

As we spoke, Todd's telephone suddenly rang. Someone from Risk Management was calling to ask Todd about his results for the day. "I'm up $300,000," he said, after writing something on the workstation and punching a few keys on his HP financial calculator. In a corner of the screen, a number refreshed instantaneously, giving the results for the month. As of April 11, Todd had made $1,024,000 for the bank. However, the figure (expressed in thousands) went up and down every second: $1,030, then $1,015, then $1,020 . . . and so on. "In a month of losses, it is very difficult to deal with this figure and watch it grow more and more negative." He added: "this was a good year. I have made 6 cents per share traded. But in a bad year I will make 4 or 3 cents. Last year I had positive results for 11 months."

Todd devoted most of his time to monitoring the algorithm that bought and sold securities. "The key is to manage the flow," he explained. His trading setup reflected this emphasis on flow. He had three screens in front of him; two corresponded to two different Unix workstations and the third was a Bloomberg terminal. The first workstation provided real-time information about his trades. Across the top there was a slash sign that rotated and moved from side to side: a "pulse meter" to gauge the speed at which information on prices is arriving to him; the slash stopped moving when prices stopped arriving. "It is very important to realize when this happens," Todd said, "because the robot was not programmed to take this into account, and would take stale prices for fresh ones, leading to losses." Todd's reference to the robot was to his trading algorithm.

There were several more indicators on Todd's screen. The right corner of the second Unix workstation showed five colored squares; each of them was a version of a traffic light, signaling how quickly orders were getting through to the servers of the New York Stock Exchange or its electronic competitors. If the squares were green, everything was fine. If they were yellow, the network was congested, and the trades would get through slowly. If they were red, the servers were clogged. Todd also had a large display of an analog clock on his computer, synchronized every day to the Atomic Clock, and two "CPU-meters" that measured how busy the database was that dealt with the order flow at International Securities. When it was busy for long periods of time, orders took longer to execute. Other windows that Todd kept open throughout the day included a screen with a limit order book in Nasdaq stocks, an email screen, and a Unix-programming screen.

"Electronic execution has changed the appearance of the trading room," said Todd, confirming what Bob had told me. "As you can see, the place is fairly quiet." The flip side to automation, he added, was that when there were problems with the system, losses were much larger. Situations became more difficult, "and you scream at the programmers." The move to quantitative tools had also created execution challenges. One of these related to the price feed coming from electronic exchanges like Island and Archipelago: although these exchanges were already prevalent by the time of my meeting with Todd, they were nevertheless a recent development. "We use them to supplement the traditional Nasdaq market makers, but they do funny things. Sometimes they reject orders that we send them, and they don't send us a message back. So,

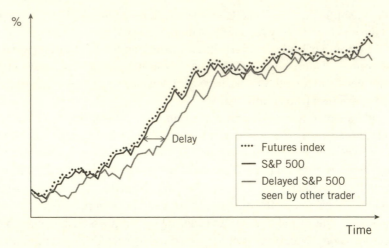

FIGURE 3.1. Effect of delay on a trading strategy.

we think the order went through, but it has not." This could create large losses amidst falling prices.

More generally, Todd's strategy created a great need for timeliness. "When you're buying some stock, the only reason you're doing it is that, at the same time, something else has another price." In other words, because arbitrage entailed connecting two markets, it required transactions to be synchronized. "What happens," I asked, "if there is a mismatch in the order flows?" This could be very problematic. "Three years ago, on a day of high volatility and a rising index, a rival bank got delayed information because of problems in the Reuters server." In a rallying market, traders at the rival bank consistently saw the index below its real level, so what seemed to them cheap was in fact expensive (see figure 3.1). "We, on the other hand, were getting timely data. While they were buying, we were selling. Traders here were writing tickets [i.e., trading] until their fingers started bleeding." Todd made $2 million in an hour until the competitors realized what was happening.

To avoid problems such as these, Todd combined the information coming from his system with social cues from other desks. His desk was located between the merger arbitrage and the technology desk. The latter was in charge of the IT systems, so Todd could overhear what its officials told other traders through their microphones. This gave him a sense of how well the computer systems were running. "When you hear screams of agony around you, it indicates that perhaps it is not a good time to trade." As if to illustrate the possibilities for multitasking, Todd's screen suddenly required his attention. I paused to let him deal with the developments, but he told me I could continue talking. "Here, you learn to do more than one thing at a time. In principle," he continued, "I would focus exclusively on execution. Speed of order flow, etc. But I can't ignore the general situation in the market. Execution problems coincide with a high volume of trading." The programmer's screams were not the only social cue. Todd obtained a sense of the market environment through the Bloomberg terminal, but he also listened to the futures desk. "If all our systems worked perfectly, I would not need to talk to any programmer." However, it was the nature of the system that it was never at an optimal stage.

Todd's account thus pointed to a paradox. He was keen on avoiding bias, but communication with other desks was critical, even to a quant like himself. Could he, I asked, possibly trade from outside the room? "I would need a squawk box to communicate to the programmers"—that is, an intercom system. "A phone would definitely not do, since sometimes they would be busy and I would not be able to get their attention. Physically, I can go there and grab the guy." Did he use the whiteboard on the corner? He traded alone, he said, so he did not. "I can have a meeting with myself in the men's room." I paused for a second, trying to process the unusual joke. "Occasionally, I have to walk to the back office when things are not well. Like, in my last day of last year—when they count your results—they made a clerical mistake in counting one of my trades, and it had to be resolved. It was on the one day that counted."

Another reason for communicating with other desks was the need to properly handle losing trades. "The secret in arbitrage," Todd explained, "is to make money from a narrow spread [i.e., margin] for a long time. The problem comes with large losses, which can wipe out your gains." Risk Management was located one floor below and was tasked with ensuring that traders kept to their strategies and cut their losses. For instance, he added, "I am not supposed to trade in crude oil futures," Todd explained. "If one of the guys in Risk Management found out I did, he'd probably call and ask, 'what, you woke up today, you were bored, and decided to speculate?'" However, the meaning of losses was not as clear-cut as it might seem, because an early loss could be the first stage of a lucrative trade. "Often, I find myself in the middle of a four standard-deviation event, like obtaining ten tails in a row with my 55%-heads coin. This can happen," Todd said. A four standard-deviation event was Todd's way to describe a statistical anomaly. If Todd's model was correct, any such event would only happen once every forty-three years. But unlike a coin toss, where the probabilities remain constant with every toss, the odds that Todd confronted could vary if the underlying situation had changed. "You don't know whether things have changed fundamentally or not, and you have to decide what to do. Shall I keep the position, increase it, or reduce it? If the stock's properties have not changed, I'll make extraordinary profits and make up for the losses, but if I'm wrong then losses pile up."

I asked for an example. "Summer of 1998," he answered. At the time, lack of liquidity caused by losses in the bond markets forced hedge funds such as Long-Term Capital Management to close other perfectly reasonable positions, leading to bizarre and inexplicable price patterns. "In these cases, I will have an informal conversation with Bob, and he will persuade me to reduce the position. Well, I could also persuade him of my view, but it is not like a 'one man, one vote' situation," he conceded with a smile. Extreme events such as these also called for informal conversations with the rest of the trading room. For instance, "sometimes I become an accidental merger arbitrageur," he said, in reference to the merger arbitrage desk near him, which bet on companies undergoing acquisitions. "I will have a position in a stock, and the company is taken over." This created a complication, because stocks undergoing mergers were unsuitable to his strategy, as merger likelihood dominated every other movement reason for price movement. "Then the question is, shall I liquidate my position right away, or hold it for a while? It no longer is my trade, and it is useful to have casual conversation with the merger arbitrage team. It is no big deal to walk over and ask them for help."

Exceptional situations like the ones just described happened with surprising frequency for Todd. They also happened when there was an important change in the "microstructure" of the market, that is, in the details of how trades occurred in stock exchanges. At the time of our conversation, the Nasdaq had recently adopted "decimalization," that is, trading in decimal price increments rather than fractions of one-sixteenth of a dollar. Decimalization had reduced the minimum spread between the bid and ask prices but also the level of liquidity at each price level. This had put great pressure on Todd's returns. An even more unusual situation took place during the peak of the dotcom bubble, which had only recently begun to burst then. "I have utterly no sympathy for day traders, because they caused me grief. For three months, I made no profits," Todd explained. "It paid to buy the most over-valued stocks. Then, for the rest of the year while these guys were getting killed, I went back into profits."

Todd's antipathy for day traders was not exclusively caused by losses. "I think day traders are very exposed to their own emotions." The type of emotional interferences that they suffered were the key weakness of the gambler. "A gambler will either re-interpret the same information differently as the game evolves, or will alter his degree of risk-taking." Todd's trading algorithm, by contrast, creates the discipline to stick to strategies. "Also, day traders fall prey to superstition. My favorite article in behaviorist psychology is by Skinner, titled 'Superstition in the Pigeon.'" Skinner shows how hungry pigeons can be made "superstitious," that is, made to believe in false cause-effect relationships, by giving them food or electric shocks. One of Skinner's pigeons took to turning around in the cage two or three times between being fed, not just in any direction, but counterclockwise, because it associated that behavior with getting food. Like pigeons, Todd thought, day traders attempted to see regularities in the random patterns of stock price movements and ended up developing spurious beliefs.

My last question centered on arbitrage. Aside from profits, what were the *societal* benefits of his work? Arbitrageurs like him, Todd explained, act "like shepherd dogs" toward stock prices. That is, if an index security should truly be worth the same as the basket of the underlying stocks, then a disparity in price between the two was an incorrect signal that would lead to capital being misallocated. "By enforcing the relationships between assets, we keep prices in line." Nevertheless, he admitted, arbitrage also had the potential to be destabilizing. Since competition pushed down profitability, arbitrage had gradually deviated from its less risky forms.

Arbitrage, Technology, and Social Interaction

Following my meeting with Todd, and as I typed my fieldnotes, I reflected on what I had seen and heard. I was relieved to have finally understood the role of economic models in arbitrage, at least in the contemporary version that I had just witnessed. The finance literature on arbitrage drew a clear distinction between classic and modern arbitrage. Classic arbitrage was a riskless activity that entailed exploiting mispricings in markets for the same security. To use the textbook example, if the price of a gold bar is 95 cents in New York, and one dollar in London, an arbitrageur could profit by simultaneously buying gold in the United States and selling it in the United Kingdom (assuming no transportation costs). Of course, opportunities like this do not last, as arbitrage alters supply and demand, thereby eliminating the very price differences that make it profitable. In the gold example, as arbitrageurs exploit the five-cent price disparity by shipping gold from New York to London, gold prices in the two cities would converge, eliminating the margin.

Given the above, contemporary arbitrageurs like Todd engaged in modern, or risky, arbitrage. This entails the exploitation of mispricings across markets for *different* securities. Modern arbitrage had entered the public debate following the numerous analyses of Long-Term Capital Management two years earlier. "Using extensive statistical databases and theoretical reasoning," MacKenzie wrote in the *London Review of Books*, Long-Term Capital Management "identified pairs of financial assets the prices of which ought to have been closely related, which should over the long run converge, but which for contingent reasons had diverged [. . .] The fund would then buy the underpriced, less popular asset, and borrow and sell the overpriced, more popular one."[2] Modern arbitrage, in other words, was about locating pairs of securities that were different but closely related, understanding the precise, mathematical way in which they were connected, and betting that over the long term this relationship would hold, leading to a convergence in prices. The classic example was the 30-year US Treasury bond and the 30-and-a-half-year Treasury bond. In the short term, one was more liquid and therefore valuable than the other, but this difference disappeared with time, and traders could exploit that convergence.

Todd's approach to arbitrage, statistical arbitrage, differed from the Treasury bond example in that it was centered around the use of a computer program, or "robot," to trade shares. Todd was like a bird watcher, or a train spotter: he sat in front of his computer for most of the day and observed with anticipation as his algorithm executed individual trades, following its actions with paternal pride. My observation lent partial confirmation to Knorr Cetina and Bruegger's thesis on electronic markets, namely, that trading terminals held an irresistible allure for the traders' attention that displaced social interaction on the floor. Like the forex traders described by Knorr Cetina and Bruegger, Todd spent a substantial amount of his time relating to his screen rather than interacting with colleagues in the room or other traders on the phone.[3]

My observations, however, ultimately pointed to a different dynamic, namely, that networks and quantitative technology *complemented* each other. Information technology and economic theory had certainly brought to Wall Street new people, new practices, and new tools. However, these novelties had not eroded the value of sociability, but merely altered the way in which social relations and communication could prove valuable. Before quantitative finance, social interactions helped traders answer questions such as, "what is the price of IBM?" After the terminals arrived, the questions traders answered were about the state of the technical infrastructure (is the server clogged?), or about the statistical properties of the stocks (is this company being acquired?).

Such complementarity had not yet been adequately theorized. While existing accounts of modern arbitrage gave the impression that arbitrage was fundamentally about the use of mathematical techniques in selecting which securities to connect, Todd's case suggested that the creative work of connecting markets was not the primary focus, and that statistical arbitrage traders had responded instead to competition with a race for speed, using automation to be ahead of their rivals. Furthermore, this use of algorithms or "robots" posed its own problems, for Todd's systems could be down, receive slow price feeds, or be experiencing clogged servers or unresponsive stock exchanges. Even if the algorithms worked well, a stock could stop behaving as Todd's models expected it to because of a merger, a financial bubble, or an operational change at the NYSE, as occurrences such as these altered a stock's statistical properties. Addressing such essential questions (e.g., is this stock what I thought it was?) on a daily basis, rather than establishing whether two securities were mathematically related in the first place, was Todd's major challenge. In sum, while existing accounts of modern arbitrage presented the activity as a creative task of drawing connections across seemingly disparate securities through mathematical replication, Todd's work seemed to center on the different task of operational effectiveness, such as ensuring that his equipment did not let him down or that working assumptions remained valid.

This more prosaic understanding of statistical arbitrage had one important advantage. It explained the way in which Todd managed to combine his theoretical knowledge of economic models with the tacit knowledge of the market collectively held in the trading room. Equipment malfunction might, in the extreme, not be detected through the equipment, so Todd relied instead on social cues from the IT desk. A change in the statistical properties of a stock might be impossible to statistically identify precisely as it happened, for statistics need cumulative observations to establish inflection points. However, Todd could rely on the advice from the merger arbitrage desk. In these situations, Bob's encouragement of communication across desks proved helpful. My observation of Todd's work thus accounted for the question that motivated my visit to his desk in the first place: how did tools and social relations come together? Quantitative tools and social cues, I found, were complementary *because* of competition among arbitrageurs, which had led to a form of speed arms race that restored the very uncertainty that the models were originally supposed to eliminate.

Another remarkable observation emerged from my visit, and it concerned Todd himself and the nature of Wall Street's quants. Several accounts of Long-Term Capital Management had described quants as stereotypical geeks: mathematically gifted but socially detached and introverted. Todd certainly fit this description, but his self-awareness and reflexivity were nowhere to be seen in existing accounts. The quants I read about seemed to be warped by their own scientism and beset by a degree of social awkwardness that rendered them incapable of recognizing even the most obvious market departures from economic rationality. This was why, for instance, Nicholas Dunbar's and Roger Lowenstein's accounts of Long-Term Capital Management's demise blamed the fund's failure on its traders' blind faith in economic models.[4] By contrast, Todd was reflexive and self-critical. He was acutely aware of his own cognitive limits and mindful of the dangers of his own biases; hence his resistance to any decision that departed from his own rules. Indeed, Todd's reflexiveness went beyond self-awareness to the point of drawing on the academic literature on psychology and behavioral economics. Just as the anthropology of Robin Dunbar (not to be confused with journalist Nicholas Dunbar) had made its way to a socially skilled executive like Bob, Todd was well versed in academic theories that played to his own mathematical strengths.

There was, however, a paradox in Todd's interest in behavioral finance. Despite his awareness of how individual judgments often proved inconsistent, the persistence of uncertainty in Todd's computerized strategy meant he could not avoid intervening in his algorithm, for sometimes the computer could not be trusted, and stocks had to be removed from his trading book. Todd confronted this irreducible uncertainty through the use of rules, as in "when I hear cries from the IT desk, I halt the algorithm" or "I only consider news on the second column of the *Wall Street Journal*." Such rules were reminiscent of the "satisficing" rules of thumb that were posited by early behavioral economists such as Herbert Simon, and that were seen as a remedy against cognitive constraints. However, while Simon's rules were presented as an outcome of mental limits and a driver of suboptimal choices, Todd's rules were a product of his own concern about bias. In other words, whereas the use of rules of thumb has traditionally been regarded as a departure from rationality, Todd's reliance rules were an attempt to bring common sense into decision-making and doing so in a world that was changing and technologically mediated, and that for those reasons it escaped simple definitions of what "acting rationally" meant.

Motivation on Wall Street

Days after my conversation with Todd, I requested a meeting with Bob. I wanted to discuss with him my emerging impressions of the trading room and, more important, ask him for additional introductions. Bob agreed to meet, and once we did, we started talking about my meeting with Todd. As it turned out, Todd was one of four statistical arbitrage traders in the trading room. "Stat arb one" was Todd, who had developed an algorithm a long time ago, and had "rented" two more. (The fact that one could rent an algorithm was news to me, but I learned that it was possible with only some additional complexity: "you share the earnings with the company that built it.") Stat arb two was a Russian mathematician. "If you met him, you'd agree that the line between genius and insanity is unclear," Bob added. Stat arb three was a mathematician from Hong Kong. "He comes back to work at night to pore over the data because he enjoys it." Stat arb four was a Taiwanese mathematician, but his algorithm was "more corporate, in the sense that it was developed in-house."

I then sought confirmation of the general points Todd had made, taking care to avoid any allusion to anything personal or controversial that he might have told me. Did overhearing traders at the merger desk really help establish whether a stock was undergoing a merger? Bob agreed with my question and added another reason to the one that Todd gave: the price of a company being merged may not settle immediately after the announcement but experience ups and downs instead. In that situation, "the traders at the merger desk can tell you, 'you'll be able to sell back, no problem.'"

I then brought up technology. Given that speeding up trading can accelerate profits as well as losses, did the bank have any position limits or stop-loss arrangements for its algorithmic traders? "Not at International Securities," he answered. It was true, Bob added, that mistakes were sometimes made in statistical arbitrage; for example, a trader at Lehman Brothers had recently lost $6 million when he made a "fat finger" mistake, adding a zero to his buy order. However, Bob rejected the use of position limits, for they could potentially cut the trader off just at the wrong moment. They also signaled a lack of trust. "If you're watching, people know you're watching. 'I know you don't steal but I'm just going to take a look . . .' But the trader will say, '*bullshit*, you're lying to me.'"

We then returned to the problem of encouraging collaboration across desks. The traders on Bob's floor, even quants like Todd, benefited from communication across desks. However, collaboration created a tension when it came to compensation. The room was formally divided into desks, and traders were paid a fixed percentage of the profits generated by their desk; for instance, a trader might receive 5 percent of the profits of his desk. This was a number agreed upon in advance of the financial year. It was also standard practice at the hedge funds where Bob's traders could find alternative employment so, Bob said, he did not really have the choice of not adhering to it. However, while this compensation scheme facilitated communication *within* desks, it made cooperation *across* desks more difficult, because a trader's bonus did not increase when a trader in another desk made a profit because of his advice.

I replied with the inevitable question: "how about paying traders to talk across desks?" Many corporations, I knew, followed this approach. General Electric, for one, used a matrix with two separate dimensions to decide on pay, economic performance, and cultural fit. Bob dismissed the idea out of hand, for two reasons. First, the size of the bonuses he was paying posed problems for tying compensation to collaboration. "I pay $8 million, $15 million bonuses," he said. How do you motivate a guy that just received an $8 million bonus? Do you say, here's $40,000 for collaborating? If you're a nice guy, you say 'thank you.' But most people would just give it back and say, 'get out of my face.'" Furthermore, some of the traders Bob hired were already wealthy, especially as he hired numerous midcareer traders. In conclusion, Bob said, "I cannot pay them to be friendly. They were not hired to be friendly."

There was a larger problem with paying traders to collaborate. It required a subjective assessment of how collaborative they had been, which in turn, Bob added, posed concerns about how that assessment was determined. In other units of International Securities, and in most other Wall Street banks, individual bonuses were determined by a compensation committee, which relied on subjective measures. However, Bob argued that this led to conflict because it involved assessing the value of the contributions of others. "If the boss does not give a trader the same as others, he can say 'you did a good job, but weren't very cooperative. You get four hundred thousand.' And the trader will go, 'I heard Joe at a party, he got five hundred thousand. What, don't you like me?'"

The problem was not simply one of fairness. "Say you give the trader what he wants," Bob added. "What is he going to say? 'Thank you for seeing my value?' What a subordinate status! It gives the traders an opportunity to complain about other things they are frustrated with in life. *And that is the heart and soul of what Wall Street is all about.*" Bob, in other words, was not only sensitive to the problem of unfair outcomes but also unfair processes such as having one's collaboration with others appraised by one's supervisor. Bob's point, and in particular his generalization to Wall Street at large, was surprising to me, for while I had imagined Wall Street to be chiefly about money, Bob's policy suggested that perceptions of justice or injustice were key. To the outside world, Wall Street traders led a life of privilege and wealth; from the inside, many experienced their outsized bonuses as insufficient and unfair.

By contrast, the peculiar bonus arrangement at Bob's floor seemed to avoid those difficulties. "At the end of the year, you don't have to come to me," Bob said, "you go to the accountant and find out the profits at the desk," implying that because the bonus was an arithmetic percentage of the total profits, it could be objectively measured. Or, as he put it, "you don't have to kiss my feet." Furthermore, if a trader tried to renegotiate the agreed percentage at year-end, Bob would refuse to budge. "The social system we built is a zero complain environment." Once again, I was intrigued by Bob's insistence that fairness, and not only the total size of the material gain, was a driver of trader motivation. I insisted: was money *really* not the chief, if not sole, goal of your traders? "Here's a paradox," Bob replied, smiling. "Say someone lost money and is due no bonus, but you give them forty thousand. What happens? He's insulted. He quits. So, sometimes, if the guy wasn't rich and needed to pay the mortgage, I made up an excuse [to pay him a bonus]. Otherwise, it's 'leave me alone.' Money is not a good a good driver of cooperation."

Conversely, Bob believed proximity to be a much better driver of cooperation. For that reason, he had resorted to regularly changing the seating arrangement in the trading room. "I rotate people as much as I can," he explained. "They resist. My rule of thumb is, they only talk to people around them." For that reason, Bob rotated traders, sometimes as much as twice a year. "They can complain about me, and they get to know each other in doing so." The frictions and animosities created by these moves were moderated by the fact that any move was temporary. "The trick is to put people who don't know each other together just long enough for them to get to know each other but not so long that they're at each other's throats."

Bob's goal was to make traders share their judgments and analyses, not just facts and information. "The typical sharing of information is, 'Joe, what's the ratio of Time Warner to AOL?' It's like at the copier: 'Joe, how do I do it?'

'Hit the reset button.'" This was just normal teamwork; the key, however, was sharing opinions in complex and uncertain situations. Achieving that required habituation to each other: "there are now a lot of conversations about the elections," he added, "and I would never discourage them, because it helps traders know each other. Once two traders have been sitting together, even if they don't like each other, they'll cooperate. Like roommates. Everyone in the trading room got moved every six months on average. But not everyone at a time." Bob likened the policy to children's "sliding block" puzzles, which have one hole only so that only one block can be moved at a time. The changes in the seating arrangement were similarly gradual. "More than shifting, drifting," Bob noted.

In engineering social interactions, Bob added, architecture had proved helpful. In addition to the whiteboard and integrating the Operations Department, Bob enforced a "low monitor" policy. "We try to keep the PCs at a low level so that they can see the rest of the room. But people are insecure on the floor and build themselves a nest." At the same time, Bob was aware of the limitations of using space to shape interaction. "We have this guy; he has a degree in mathematics from Princeton. If you see him in the subway, you would think he's a postal inspector. But he makes millions. Personally." The trading room, Bob continued, had another desk, the agency sales desk, where the traders typically shouted as they worked, and this bothered the Princeton trader. "They will get the order from their clients and shout 'AOL Time Warner's *up*!' The guy hates this, because it influences him. He likes to arrive at his conclusions through careful deduction and logic. He wants to be sequestered." Bob had gone as far as offering him to sit in a glass-enclosed room, so that no noise would bother him, and the trader considered it for a moment, but in the end decided to stay with the rest.

Similarly, Bob admitted, there were complexities associated with the whiteboard. It was located at the center of the trading room, so it was very visible. Others could read what was written on it. Bob had recently decided to stop walking over to it, because "when people want to please, they don't listen." Indeed, he also explained that new trading ideas were not originated on the whiteboard. "Breakout thinking leads to a victory lap. First you talk to others. You tell someone else, 'I've got this great idea,' and if he tells you, 'I read it yesterday in *Barron's*,' you say, 'Oh, I did too.'" The whiteboard was the final stage of that lap, but not the beginning. "People go there when there is a high degree of complexity. They'll say, 'let's clarify this.' But the whiteboard is not a launching site."

Beyond the use of space, Bob had developed a more directive policy to promote collaboration. This entailed an executive that Bob had tasked with engineering conversations across desks. Bob referred to him as the "minister without portfolio," in reference to an innovation famously introduced by the

French king Louis XVI. This monarch first introduced the figure of a government minister with cabinet status but no department of state under his authority. At Bob's trading room, this "minister" was a trader who was not located in any desk, but whose job was to find desks doing related trades that could benefit from communicating with each other and were not yet doing so. This executive had proved to be controversial on the floor. "He is not liked," Bob admitted.

Another limit to Bob's policy of encouraging collaboration, he confessed, was that it did not benefit all parts of the trading room equally. For instance, a sizeable part of the floor was dedicated to producing research on listed companies aimed at institutional investors. "This is a mature business, and very specialized," added Bob. "It is more like a factory than anything else. The layout is not at all that critical. Sure, these guys want to sit together, but I don't know how much they speak to each other. The number of people they need to talk to is very small, around five or six. It's the I-bring-you-coffee-you-bring-me-coffee thing. They want to sit together because they want to be in a team."

My last question for Bob probed the extent to which the aforementioned practices were typical of other trading floors. Was Bob's approach common on Wall Street? He did not claim to be the only one doing it, but could not point to other firms following a similar policy. "Not many people, including myself ten years ago, have given a lot of thought to trading rooms. Managers, they'll tell you, 'communication, communication,' but you wonder. For example, you should visit [the Swiss bank] UBS and its trading room in Connecticut, it is the size of three aircraft carriers. And the reason for it is that it is a source of pride to the manager. It is difficult to see how traders can communicate shouting at each other across two aircraft carriers. At UBS, what you'll find is chaos that looks grand."

Informal Networks and Quantitative Finance

Bonuses. Architecture. A "minister" without portfolio. Back at NYU, as I reflected on my third conversation with Bob, I realized that I now had a deeper understanding of how he conceived his trading floor. While our conversation had broadened our previous discussions on communication and architecture, this time Bob had added his own views about motivation and compensation. His arguments challenged, or to be precise, qualified, the view that the only motivation on Wall Street was material, as some of Abolafia's traders reported. Bob certainly paid large bonuses, and his "percentage payout" scheme made profitability the only measure of value in a trader's work. However, the lack of subjective assessments that Bob had instituted also made clear his view that what motivated people on Wall Street was not exclusively money. Fairness, as in not making less than someone else who had contributed equally, was just as important. Dignity, as in not depending on someone else's whim, mattered too. The seemingly simplistic nature of the percentage payout, which did not take into account nonfinancial contributions to the trading room, concealed a complex reasoning: subjectively attaching a monetary value to collaboration created difficult problems of fairness, dignity, and autonomy.

Bob's practices spoke to existing research in the field of organizational behavior on the problem of *organizational justice*, a concept introduced by Jerald Greenberg to describe the reactions of organizational members to the decisions made by the organization.[5] Greenberg established that perceptions of injustice can impact job attitudes and behaviors at work, and Bob appeared to have an intuitive understanding of this dynamic. Far from considering fairness a peripheral aspect of an industry otherwise shaped by greed, Bob put fairness, or the lack of it, at the *center* of his subjective experience of Wall Street. As Bob said, perceptions of injustice were "the heart and soul" of Wall Street. The comment proved intriguing, in that it revealed Bob's ambivalence toward his own industry, hinting at some unhappy experience that might have led him to think this way. I found that surprising, for I somehow assumed that Wall Street executives, especially the well-paid and high-status ones, would be proud of working in finance. To my surprise, it seemed that traders' attitudes were less straightforward, at least for Bob.

Bob's appreciation for the complexity of human motivation was also clear from his approach to promoting collaboration across desks. Bob's bonus scheme system did not automatically promote collaboration, but his solution was to use proximity and the architectural layout of the trading room: the whiteboard, rotating the desks in the room, and the low-monitor policy. Far from working flawlessly, one of Bob's experiments, the minister without portfolio, had already backfired. Another one, the rotating of desks, had strong detractors. Finally, the whiteboard space turned out to be ineffective for brainstorming during the early stages of idea generation. The common thread running through these limitations, I concluded, was the reactive and social nature of the trading room: people resisted being acted upon, whether it was being exposed to the screams of others, seen by others to make a flawed argument, or being told to whom they should talk.

A final surprise, prompted by my conversations with Todd and Bob, was the remarkable degree to which they drew on academic concepts to justify their practices. Todd had a sophisticated sensitivity to the biases created by judgment and could cite classic articles in psychology articulating this concern. He could even account for his trading strategies in terms of these ideas, arguing that he was seeking to exploit the presence of biases in *other* investors. In the case of Bob, I already knew of his sensitivity to the effect of trading room size on trust and communication, was well as his use of Dunbar's Number via Malcolm Gladwell. After the conversation described above, however, I now understood that not only Bob was sensitive to social relations, but he also grasped the problem of organizational justice and put it well ahead of materialism as an explanation of behavior on Wall Street.

What accounted for the academic bent of Bob and Todd? I realized that I had bumped up against the problem of what ethnographers call "studying up." In 1964, the renowned anthropologist Laura Nader observed that ethnographic studies had until then for the most part studied remote tribes or inhabitants of depressed urban areas with lower social and economic status than that of the researchers. It was easy, in that context, for ethnographers to disregard the theories espoused by the natives as alienated, superstitious, or unscientific, and to cast themselves as the proper theorists and true discoverers of empirical regularities and broad patterns. Instead of studying the underprivileged, Nader called on ethnographers to turn to the privileged and powerful; as she put it, "the colonizers rather than the colonized, the culture of power rather than the culture of the powerless, the culture of affluence rather than the culture of poverty."[6] I hoped my project was contributing to advance Nader's vision, but I had to grapple with the unexpected theoretical sophistication of my subjects and the difficult question it posed: how did my theories speak to their theories?

4

Animating the Market

My conversations with Todd and Bob had proved revelatory: the trading room, I now understood, was a social system that equipped traders to better confront the uncertainty inherent in the use of financial models. One way in which it did so, I had learned, was through the provision of social cues across desks, such as those that helped Todd understand when to stop using his trading algorithms. The trading room fostered these social cues by facilitating informal interaction across desks. Such appreciation for the social aspect of trading, however, did not seem to extend to other banks on Wall Street. One consequence of the recent shift toward financial models and electronic markets, Bob had explained, was the reduced importance of the so-called sales desk, where traders executed orders for clients. "In the old times," Bob said, "sales traders enjoyed close relations to floor brokers and clients." These traders had extraordinary physical presence and relational skills. "The people that ended up gravitating toward these jobs," Bob added, "were like pilots: self-confident, charismatic." Unfortunately for these traders, the move toward electronic markets had diminished the advantages conferred by these interpersonal traits.

In other words, more technology, fewer interactions. This change not only raised critical questions for those traders who had specialized in professional relations (what challenges were they facing? How were they adapting their work practices?), but also had important implications for conceptualizing the effect of technology on the stock market. It lent support to Knorr Cetina and Preda's thesis that electronic markets had re-centered financial markets around the trading terminal, that is, transformed markets from *pipes* (or social networks) to *scopes* (or trading terminals). I expressed to Bob an interest in meeting sales traders. "It would be ideal," I said, "to compare them to the quantitatively oriented arbitrageurs in the trading room, like Todd." As it turns out, Bob replied, such comparison was feasible, for he had kept a small sales desk within International Securities. That desk was actually located directly behind him. Bob agreed to introduce me to them, and suggested I email them to ask for permission to conduct observations of their work. The traders said yes and agreed to being observed for two days.

The chapter that follows thus presents the findings from my observations and conversations at the sales trading desk. This subunit at International Securities, also known as the "agency sales" desk, was composed of four traders, one analyst, one intern, and one administrative assistant. Among these, two senior traders, Joe and Jim, sat next to each other and conducted their own research to find trading opportunities for their clients. Two junior traders, Scott and George, sat behind them, executed trades, and followed the prices of specific stocks. Kelly, the administrative assistant, sat nearby, next to the intern and the analyst. Most remarkable among these was Joe, a tall, fit, and elegantly dressed senior trader who looked like the charismatic bond traders originally described by Abolafia, and whose powerful voice resonated well beyond the desk to the rest of the trading room. Joe's desktop featured automatic weapons with the barrel pointing out aggressively. Immediately next to him sat Jim, the other senior trader, who was thinner and more cerebral, and more understated in his dress style. In splitting their jobs, Joe styled himself as "the marketer" and explained to me that Jim was "the strategist."

As I describe below, the customer sales desk was the closest I ever got in my study to a traditional Wall Street trading desk, that is, one characterized by hectic activity, bold decisions, and tight camaraderie. The desk comprised an intricate social entity that helped the traders divide their attention with precision, cultivate tight relationships with customers, give meaning to the numbers displayed on their screens, and develop useful emotional attachments. At the same time, not everything that I saw there was uncontroversial. During my days of observation, I witnessed sensitive information traveling across the bank's Chinese Wall, and a prank to a Haitian caller that, at the time of writing this book (almost twenty years after the fact), still seemed to me insensitive and inappropriate.

First Day

My first day of observations at the sales trading desk was centered on one of its junior traders, Scott. I arrived at the desk at 8:00 am for my first morning of observation, but Scott and George had not yet arrived. I was received by Kelly, the administrative assistant, who was already at her seat and who suggested I take a chair in between those of the two junior traders. Just before 8:30 am, Scott walked in. "Hi Kelly, how're you doing? How's the baby?" said Scott, making friendly conversation with the administrative assistant, who was mother to a toddler. "I've got the photos from the honeymoon on Shutterfly," he added in reference to a photo-sharing website, "I'll email you the link." Scott had recently been married and displayed a proud wedding photograph of his wife on the wallpaper of one of his workstation screens. "Four hun for the wedding album," he added. "I can't believe I paid that much." Physically thin and mild mannered, Scott had some resemblance to a high school teacher. Like others in the trading room, he defied the stereotype of the physically imposing Wall Street trader.

Soon after, George walked in. Young and agreeable, though somewhat less earnest than Scott, Greg had snowboarding photographs on his wallpaper, and he wore a sports watch and somewhat sporty, casual clothes. Both Scott and George were in charge of executing arbitrage trades for clients, that is, of doing the actual buying and selling of shares. Customers such as hedge funds turned to Scott and George because if these customers executed their own orders, others might learn of their intentions and have an adverse impact on prices.

Sitting next to me, Scott began to customize the various windows on his screens, arranging them in specific ways. The stock market would not open until 9:30 am, which gave him a few minutes to prepare. Scott followed market movements by relying on price and volume data that he could monitor. There were three high-contrast flat panel screens in front of him, populated by several windows containing price information about stocks. Each screen was divided into several areas: on the left screen, a series of windows provided general information on the market, including news from Bloomberg and price charts for stocks in the Dow Jones Industry Average. The middle screen showed what Scott called a "magnifying glass," that is, a selection of sixty stocks that he considered representative of key sectors such as electronics, oil, or broadband Internet firms. The numbers on these windows grew in size when an order was received, giving it a pulsating quality. On the right screen, Scott had opened several windows and placed them in the appropriate corner, creating a "trading basket" (the set of securities he intended to buy and sell) in advance of the market opening. He did this by executing and canceling a trade, which could save up to 15 seconds in the actual trade. "What matters," he said, "is being fast, efficient and organized."

Scott then began to work on "setting up" an arbitrage trade for a large customer. Doing this arbitrage trade entailed "buying the spread" between two merging companies, AmeriSource Corporation and Bergen Brunswig, whenever the difference in their stock prices exceeded 80 basis points (that is, 0.80 percent). The challenge was to buy and sell as closely in time as possible, for doing a single leg of an arbitrage trade (i.e., longing the target company without or shorting the acquirer, or vice versa) would expose the customer to directional price movements, defeating the very purpose of arbitrage. Scott referred to this scenario as "getting hooked." To avoid getting hooked, he needed to anticipate immediate price movements and execute a sell order right after a buying order.

By 9:30 am, the two senior traders, Jim and Joe, arrived at the desk. They sat directly behind Scott, creating a setup of extreme proximity that resembled the cockpit of an armored vehicle. The proximity allowed the traders to communicate verbally about what they saw without taking their eyes off their own screens, much like watching sports on television in the same room as someone else. Sometimes Scott's utterances even resembled sports talk. For instance,

SCOTT [in a cheerful tone]: "Jim, Bergen at $35!"
JIM: "Snap 'em up!"

Indeed, according to Scott, trading was "like a sport." That was one reason he liked his job. "When the pressure goes up," Scott asked, "are you gonna yield or not?" This pressure, however, sometimes spilled onto the trading equipment. "We break these a lot," he added, pointing to the phone handset. "Jim breaks one a month." Scott himself had cracked one of his flat screens only the month before, "because I was mad, and threw the pencil at it." The bank ordered a new one immediately.

In turn, the use and misuse of the equipment created fodder for jokes at the desk. For instance, a few minutes later Jim made a joke about the intern, who was working two seats to his left. "Oh, I know why you need a headset! *Because you cannot hold the phone!* I saw you holding it yesterday, so close to your ear, it hurt." The banter was received with comments and chuckles from everyone, including the intern. "There's going to be telephone-holding classes here every day at four," Joe added.

Stan's exchanges with Jim were not only about stock prices. "These guys," said Scott, referring to Jim and Joe, "often ask, 'what do you think of the market?'" When Scott was new at the bank, he was reluctant to give his view. "I thought, 'what if I'm wrong?'" However, he eventually understood that his fellow traders were not looking for a forecast, but an opinion. "It's your view. You have to take a stand. When you tell where you stand, you're not jeopardizing your career."

While Scott explicitly addressed one of the senior traders in his comments, the senior traders were engaged in a different form of dialogue, seemingly aimed at no one. "These guys are constantly yelling out shit," Scott explained, in reference to Jim and Joe. "Some of it matters, some of it doesn't." The point was economy of language. "Joe will give an order out of the blue, and he'll assume I heard it. He'll yell something, and I know it's at me. I just know. It's one thing you learn when you first come to work in a trading room—no one wants to say things twice." To facilitate this form of interaction, Scott used a small rearview mirror beneath his monitor that allowed him to look behind him without taking his eyes off the screens in front of him. The bank's logo was on the mirror, and George also had one, which suggested to me that it was an institutionalized tool at International Securities.

Giving Looks

At 10:50 am, I noted that Scott's phone call with a broker had suddenly become intense. "A long seller," Scott said to the broker, "came in and knocked the shit out of AAS. What's going on?" Scott was referring to an accumulation of selling orders that had arrived for AmeriSource. For the past hour, Scott had been looking for opportunities to buy the stock, but the spread was not wide enough—it was "tight." At around 10:30 am, however, Scott began to see an accumulation of selling orders, and at 10:44 am, the price dropped. What made these moves extraordinary was that the price of Bergen, which was supposed to move in lockstep with AmeriSource as merger stocks tend to do, had not changed at all. What accounted for the divergence? Would there be additional sell orders of AmeriSource? And, more to the point, was Scott likely to get hooked if he went ahead and bought stock in the company?

The broker that Scott contacted, however, replied he did not know the reason for those sell orders in AmeriSource. Lacking a satisfactory answer, Scott checked the news on the Bloomberg, but again this provided no conclusive answer. Scott then asked the analyst at the desk for additional research on the two companies. "You know anything?" He didn't. He posed the same question to Jim and Joe, who did not know much either.

Minutes later, Scott found the answer he searched for from somewhere else, a floor broker at NYSE that he contacted on the phone. "Morgan Stanley," the broker had told him, "came up with this long seller." By "long seller," Scott meant an investor who was merely selling to reduce his exposure to the stock, rather than for the purpose of the arbitrage deal Scott's client was interested in, and that had executed his trade through Morgan Stanley. This was good news for Scott, for had the seller been an arbitrageur, the profit opportunity that Scott's client was pursuing might have vanished. As it was, the price movement was not a red flag. "I know it was not a deal-related issue," Scott explained to me, which meant that he could proceed with executing the customer trade, safe in the knowledge that he would not be hooked.

This episode illustrates the peculiar nature of information flow on Wall Street. Information is not bought and sold explicitly but indirectly exchanged legally for trading commissions. As Scott put it, "the floor brokers we use at the NYSE will lead us if something is going on, say someone is buying many IBMs. He'll give us a look. And maybe when I do a trade, I'll give it to this guy." Giving looks, I learned, typically entailed conveying something about the identity of a buyer or a seller that allows others to infer that individual's strategy from it. But, according to Scott, "it's deeper than that. Floor brokers [at the stock exchange] will tell you when things are going to happen—so much news takes place in between the closing of the market and the following morning." For example, "at what price is a certain stock going to open?"

Scott not only received looks, but also passed them on to his customers. At some point during the morning, for instance, Jim called Scott's attention to the situation of another company, Galileo Inc. Jim then called one of his clients: "I'd just like to give you a look on Galileo. [The spread] is a little tight. I know that you're active on it, and I thought you'd be interested." Scott went as far as asking for looks from his own customers. "We are in the heart of the deal," he explained to me. "When we talk to our customer it's like, hey, do you see anything? What's happening? They're customers but, hey." On the other hand, there was no communication with others in the room. I asked Scott, are you in contact with the merger arbitrage traders? "No," he answered. "There's a Chinese Wall. Those guys sit over there, they don't know what we're doing." As he said this, Scott pointed to a distant desk past the whiteboard room where two traders worked, clearly out of earshot.

In the delicate task of combining the information they had with that of their clients, the traders at his desk relied on a special technology. Instead of a traditional telephone, Scott used a "telephone turret," a digital switchboard with a microphone, a handset, and direct lines with various brokers, customers, the New York Stock Exchange, CNN, and CNBC. I was particularly interested in a special mute button on the phone's handset. This allowed Scott to prevent his customers from hearing him talk to a colleague at the desk, even as the customer might be talking. "I can go, 'Jim what do you think about this?' without the customer hearing it," Scott explained. The system was quicker and smoother than putting the customer on hold. "All traders on Wall Street have this," Scott added. The phone turret also had a speaker that connected Scott to the sound of the financial news television network CNBC, which he had "always on."

The morning went by quickly, and as lunchtime approached, the activity at the desk began to slow down. At some point, Joe stood up and began to ask each of the traders on the desk what they wanted for their meal. There was a well-appointed cafeteria inside the trading room, but on that day the sales traders wanted to order out. "Bacon cheeseburger," said one trader. "Chicken sandwich," went another. Joe then turned to me and asked what I wanted. Surprised, I decided to join in and asked for the same sandwich as Scott. After Joe had taken all the orders, he asked, "OK, who's the least senior trader here?" He then gave the order list to the intern, and Joe paid for everyone.

Once the food arrived, the conversation turned to nonwork matters. Jim and Joe debated the following issue: which was the best SUV on the market? Joe argued vigorously for the Mercedes. While they talked, I asked Scott additional questions about his experience of working at the desk. Scott was grateful, he explained, for the work environment at the bank. "When I decided to come here," Scott said, "I was very nervous. I had a rival offer. I didn't know what to do, so I walked the streets, wondering. I was going to take that other offer, but then someone told me, 'come in, you just have to come in and meet Bob.'" He then met Bob and accepted the job at International Securities. "And you know what?" he added, "this is home." Once Scott joined the bank, the rival bank raised the offer, but Scott chose to stay, and he had "not regretted it one moment."

He added in a lower voice, "these guys [Jim and Joe] are very generous to us, and especially to me. Here, it's very relaxed. At other places such as [another bank] they're very stiff. Bob is very laissez-faire. When I made my first mistake and lost $100,000, you know what these guys did? They took me out for dinner. They buy me lunch every time. Also, I play ice hockey. When I came, I told Bob I wanted to create a hockey team here. He said he'd sponsor it, right away. He pays $20,000 a year for the hockey team."

"So, this is lunch at the desk," Scott noted as we finished our sandwiches. "Today we ate at normal speed because it is a slow day. If it's busy, then it's either no lunch, or wolf it down as fast as you can. And I like it that way. You get it over, and that's it."

Distributed Cognition

I left the trading floor after lunch and spent the afternoon back at my cubicle at NYU, taking stock of what I had witnessed that morning. My observations at the sales trading desk offered two core insights about the role of social interaction in trade execution. The first pertained to the problem of rapid coordination and information processing, and specifically the need to avoid "getting hooked" while executing an arbitrage trade. To this end, Scott relied on a careful disposition of technological tools that allocated his own attention to whatever was happening at the time: the elaborate screens, phone turrets, and rearview mirror. In addition to these tools, sitting close to the senior traders allowed Scott to overhear them and access their sense of events on the market at any given moment.

In this regard, the desk resembled the airplane cockpits described by psychologist Edwin Hutchins. In *Cognition in the Wild*, Hutchins documented the numerous ways in which information "travels" in an airplane cockpit. Information, Hutchins argued, not only moves from the several dials to the pilots, or from one pilot to the other, via conversation; in addition, each pilot's action provides information to the other pilot, even if those actions are not explicitly meant to serve as communication. For instance, when, a pilot pulls the yoke toward him, the co-pilot instantly learns that the plane is being pitched nose-up. Hutchins refers to these as *unintended information trajectories*. In fact, before the advent of electronic controls, the pilot's and co-pilot's yokes of large planes were connected and moved together, thus providing each pilot with an instant indication of what the other pilot was doing and thinking. This form of information sharing had the advantage of being cognitively inexpensive, in that it did not require talking and allowed the pilots to develop a shared sense of the situation.

As with Hutchins's pilots, the close proximity among sales traders meant that initiation and interruption of individual tasks could be done in tight coordination with each other. Similarly, the loud remarks to events on screen created a shared common ground that helped the traders interpret subsequent utterances, as well as to know that theirs would be equally understood. In doing so, the traders at the sales desk behaved in line with the findings reported by Heath and colleagues in their research on dealing rooms during the mid-1980s. As they wrote, the physical disposition of traders in desks made it possible for them to establish "mutually focused collaboration."[1]

A second key aspect of Scott's work was his reliance on "looks" from a floor broker at the NYSE. Such looks were a legal and legitimate activity. The specialists at the NYSE shared selective elements of their order books to floor brokers to account for the reasons behind larger orders or quick price movements. By doing so, specialists allayed the traders' suspicions that there might be hidden reasons *not* to buy a stock, while at the same time protecting the identity of the other buyers and sellers. The requests for and provision of looks comprised a key relational part of the activity of the sales traders like Scott, and one that the shift toward electronic markets noted by Knorr Cetina and Preda had not eliminated. Indeed, the look at AmeriSource provided that morning by a NYSE floor broker gave Scott information that was *not* displayed on any screen, and therefore sat outside any of Knorr Cetina and Preda's scopes. This information had come from the book of a NYSE specialist, who had verbally shared it with a floor broker at the post, who in turn had mentioned it to Scott via the telephone. In other words, events at the desk suggested that the introduction of electronic markets had not placed *all* information on public display. For that reason, it had made those relationships that could provide off-screen information all the more valuable.

Finally, what to make of the broken headsets and flat screens? I was surprised to hear that Scott and others frequently abused their equipment. What accounted for this seemingly irresponsible treatment of the bank's technology? I eventually understood that the broken headsets might be part of an overall performance at the sales desk, where affective and emotional behaviors were not only accepted but in fact promoted by the senior traders. The actions and utterances of the junior traders formed a decisive part of the social cues that were used in the rest of the room ("everyone listens to us," explained Scott). As a result, the cost of broken IT might be deemed acceptable. After all, junior traders like Scott had quickly learned from their senior colleagues to develop opinions about future stock prices on the basis of how they felt about it. While traders like Max's at the merger arbitrage desk flatly rejected this approach to trading, I concluded that relying on instinct might be appropriate in the context of the sales desk and trade execution, where the horizon was short and prices were more influenced by the flow of other investors' orders than by the intrinsic properties of the listed companies. Adopting a speculative orientation to trading execution could be an adaptive way to be attuned to "market sentiment."

Second Day

On my second day at the desk, I was to sit next to Joe and Jim and watch them work. I arrived at the desk after lunch and found Jim looking relaxed, staring at an Excel spreadsheet. The spreadsheet had a table with the largest companies in the Nasdaq and NYSE, along with their sales. "I've got a lot of theories about why these companies have such high sales. Look at that," he said pointing to the sales of GM. "GM sold 180 billion. Can you believe that? And then there's JC Penney, which is going up like crazy for no special reason." He mentioned the debate over how analysts had been valuing Internet firms. Jim saw his work as very much influenced by cycles. "I like to anticipate broad trends and get ahead of the next trend."

"Liberty Media has no plans to buy ATT cable," he quoted aloud minutes later, reading from the Bloomberg screen. "That means he wants it, right there!" he added, in reference to Joe Malone, the owner of Liberty Media, and added: "why would they say that otherwise?" This type of remark was one of several ways in which Jim located opportunities for customers: reframing public news. Jim read out Bloomberg newswires that he found interesting, providing his own interpretation. "I don't want to read spreadsheet to clients," he said in reference to prices on the screen, "I give market color."

"I fucking hate Yahoo," Jim shouted shortly after, having read a press release about the company's earnings on the Bloomberg terminal. He then explained to me that he rejected sources that provided a ready-made interpretation. "I never read the *Wall Street Journal*. It just poisons me. Once I see those nice charts, I would get here and say just what everybody else is saying. I read press releases instead. I phone the companies and listen for the tone of the voice." Jim was also in communication with the traders at the stock loan desk a few meters away. "Scott will tell me, 'the stock is going higher,' and someone from stock loan will say 'it is getting harder to borrow,' " suggesting that the stock was the target of arbitrageurs.

As the conversation continued, Jim corrected my initial sense about the division of labor at the sales desk. I thought he only did research, but he did also execute some of the bigger trades. "I take more risks than Scott, because I have less patience, but that is also a product of my seniority. If I screw up, it comes out of my own pocket. If Scott screws up, it also comes out of my own pocket. Scott takes fewer risks, even if we [him and Joe] would sometimes prefer that he did [take greater risks]." This was surprising to me, for it reversed the traditional account of conflicts of interest in the economics literature, which was often attributed to agents that work for others on a commission (e.g., salespeople).

As we talked, Bob came over the desk. He approached us smiling and joking like a welcome guest at a party, ready to share some gossip: there had been an announcement in a trade magazine that an ex-employee who had left the bank had now been promoted at his new bank. "You never forget about anybody in this business," Jim remarked as Bob left. "I may end up working for him. Or he may end up working for me." The statement seemed to confirm the value of social networks despite the prevalence of electronic markets. He added: "International Securities is very different from other places. Bob has a vision of where he wants to be, and that allows people to stay and wait out the bottom of the cycle." In turn, this confirmed Bob's self-described interest in creating greater stability and cohesiveness at International Securities than at other banks.

A few minutes later, Joe arrived at the trading room. The sales traders' attention automatically shifted to him. He was coming from the floor of the NYSE, where he had gone to visit "a friend who is a floor broker, who's been there for 35 years, and is about to retire." He went on to list in detail the people he had talked to, whom others in the desk also knew. "You guys have to go. I saw everyone!" He described the case of a trader that "Lehman fired because they couldn't understand his strategy, and risk management got freaked out at the volume he was dealing with." He gave career updates on everyone and a brief report on the level of activity in the market.

Once Joe settled in his seat, Jim and I returned to our conversation. Another way in which Jim generated ideas was by considering what customers were doing and thinking about it with the proprietary traders who sat across from him. "Josh [the proprietary trader sitting in front] will say, 'everybody is doing this,' then I'll work backwards, and maybe there's something, maybe there's not. For example, if someone pays a lot for a stock, it could be interpreted as, 'why would someone want to pay that much for that stock?' But it could also be seen as 'what does he know that I don't?' " In sum, Jim concluded, "this is real brainstorming, not like the bullshit brainstorming you have in corporations, where a bunch of people go into a room and one forces his views on the rest. Here, we really don't know what we're going to think at the end. I could've told 'buy' to those guys [the proprietary traders] and conclude five minutes later that it was 'sell.' "

I asked Jim for an example of the type of brainstorming with proprietary traders he had described. Earlier that year, Jim explained, Tyson Corporation (the multinational food company) had announced its intention to acquire meat-maker IBP, Inc. Three months later, Tyson tried to cancel the deal, arguing that IBP had provided misleading information about the company's own value. After two months of vacillation, however, Tyson Foods finally agreed to complete the $2.7 billion deal. The transfer of ownership would take place as a "cash conversion," that is, the shareholders in IBP would be able to sell some of their stock for $30 per share, and the rest would be converted into Tyson Class A common stock, at a preestablished ratio. As with simpler mergers, the conversion gave shareholders a choice to take cash or IBP stock, and that choice could be used by Jim and others for the purpose of arbitrage.

Jim developed an idea for an arbitrage trade that arose from a conversation with a client. Jim received an order: "I looked at it and said, 'why does he do that?' I then talked to Josh [a proprietary trader sitting in front of him] and it didn't make any sense. 'That guy's crazy,' we thought. That was the tip-off. We structured what we thought was a better trade. So, I phoned back the client. 'This is the trade you should be doing. And this is why.'" In doing so, Jim said, he was able to tap into Josh's expertise and the productive friction created between the customer's order and Jim's own plan. The ultimate beneficiary was the customer. Granted, Jim added, these calls did not always result in the client following Jim's suggestion. "He might say," Jim continued, "'You're an idiot, and that's never going to happen.' So, I'll say, 'Great. Do you want to take the other side?' You know, it takes two sides for a trade."

I was somewhat troubled by Jim's reliance on a customer for the Tyson-IBP trade. Was this a form of insider trading? Alternatively, was it an illegal case of front-running of the customer? And more generally, should there not be a proverbial Chinese Wall between customer activities such as Jim's and proprietary traders like Josh? As I looked into the matter more carefully, however, I realized that the Tyson-IBP trade was *not* insider trading, for although Jim had used information about the customer's trade that only he knew, Jim had also shared the opportunity he saw with that same customer. Similarly, the practice was *not* front-running (i.e., trading ahead of a customer's order) for even though Jim was using information about the client's order as the basis for his strategy, he was not trading that same order for his own account before executing the customer's order.

Nevertheless, the practice was fraught with complexity. The communication between Jim and Josh was indeed crossing the legal partition (or Chinese Wall) between proprietary and customer trading. Indeed, the two desks were physically located in front of each other for the explicit purpose of sharing information. Yet far from taking advantage of his customers, Jim felt this approach was beneficial for them, for according to him, what made sales traders like himself valuable for hedge funds and mutual funds was that Jim and his colleagues were part of the broader trading room, and as a result they understood complex events in the market. "We are all in this together," said Jim. "Our thing is a loyal customer base," he added, explaining that he elicited such loyalty by constantly telling customers about opportunities. "Our customers have a vested interest in our success," and as a result they gave them business.

I was initially unsure about what Jim meant by "gave them business," but I soon found out. Minutes after our exchange, and while I was going through my notes, Jim received a phone call. As he answered the caller, Jim lowered his voice, alerting me to the sensitive nature of the call. He turned his eyes in my direction to check whether I was listening, but I saw him turn his face before he could see me, and pretended to be staring at my notes. The call was about a so-called soft-dollar arrangement, or indirect payment for research and advice through trading commissions. These arrangements were legal and performed on a daily basis: clients compensated Jim and Joe for their advice about opportunities by trading with them. However, on this specific occasion the client on the phone did not want to trade through the United States for tax reasons. "No," Jim told the client after a while, "even if you want to trade from Bermuda [where the bank had an office], you have to direct the trades through New York."

As I subsequently learned, soft-dollar arrangements were the core business model at the sales trading desk. The senior sales traders offered their customers ideas free of charge and were paid by the commissions that the desk charged for executing orders. The arrangement called for having *both* trading ideas and execution within the same desk. Quick and inexpensive order execution by the two young traders, Scott and George, would not attract as much business as they currently did, for clients were also drawn to the ideas provided by Joe and Jim. At the same time, without trading commissions the customer had no established way to pay for Joe's and Jim's ideas, so the desk needed to have execution services to be compensated for them. (There was another and more visible source of complementarity, which was the way in which Scott monitored the ups and downs of the market and relayed them back to Jim or Joe.)

Jim went on to describe the role of the customer trading desk within Bob's trading room. The desk, I now understood, sought to create strong client loyalty by providing them with opportunities that originated from conversations with the proprietary trading desks. Such loyalty created a steady stream of revenue that reduced the fluctuations in volume stemming from the economic cycle. "We are a niche player," Jim noted, in reference to the small size of the floor. That, he argued, was clearly the result of Bob's vision. However, Bob's decision to keep the overall activity of the client sales desk relatively small had broad organizational effects: "if you're not a niche player you can only stay competitive by being large . . . but being large forces you to lay off people when the cycle turns against you." In International, as noted above, their aim was to stay small and avoid layoffs.

More broadly, Jim added, Bob's management approach sought to limit too much attention to the short term. "Your value comes from the results. Every day, you get this email," and as he said so he clicked in his email program and showed me a spreadsheet displaying the returns that his desk had made on that day. "It's very easy to concentrate only on this number. But you shouldn't. This is a cycle. You build up goodwill with clients." If people concentrate too much on results, Jim said, they will end up doing something excessively risky, "and we don't want that."

As we spoke, Jim and I were suddenly interrupted by unexpected agitation at the other end of the trading room. An external caller had confused the bank's phone number for the number of New York's Department of Motor Vehicles, and had called to find out whether he had passed the driving test. A trader at another desk used his phone turret to pull an elaborate prank, which involved pretending to be the administrator of the driving license official, and then transferring the call to Joe at the sales desk, who pretended to be the senior official. The dialogue went as follows:

CALLER: I'm calling about my license.
TRADER A: [who had first received the call]: Yes. May I have your name, last name, date and place of birth, and social security number? [Then, muting his phone and shouting at others in the trading room] Hey! Here comes another for the driver's license!
JOE: I'll take it! It's mine!
TRADER A: Ok, Joe, line two.

At this point the caller gave all this information, spelling it out in detail. He was from Haiti, he explained. As he did, Joe was listening on his phone and writing down that information. Other traders had stopped working, and many were waiting to see what happened next.

TRADER A: Very good, I'll put you through to the person in charge.

The Haitian caller had now been transferred to Joe, and the conversation was being broadcast on the trading room's speaker system. Everyone in the room could hear it.

JOE [in a commandeering tone, as if he was reading the caller's file from a computer screen]: Good morning. Are you [name] born [date] in [place] with social security number [XXXX]?
CALLER [in a humble tone]: Yes, yes, that's me, sir.
JOE: Well, I'm afraid I don't have good news for you. My file here shows that there were some traces of drugs found in your urine.

CALLER [even more humble, nervous, shocked]: Drugs?

JOE: Yes, I show here cocaine and heroin. Do you take drugs?

CALLER: No sir! No drugs! Never in my life. Never, I swear!

JOE: Well, we'll have to re-do the urine tests then. And one more thing. Your file here says you come from Haiti. Now, I happen to know there is a lot of voodoo going on there. Black magic. Are you engaged in any of this?

CALLER: No, sir, no magic, no sir.

JOE [with magnanimity]: We'll have to take your word for it. [Then, more seriously] But the urine tests definitely have to be re-done. Present a sample of your urine tomorrow at ten at the fifth floor of number 12, 34th Street. Did you take that well?

DRIVER: Yes, thank you, sir, thank you very much. I'll be there.

As Joe hung up, the traders broke out in laughter, congratulating Joe for the originality of the prank with cheers, expletives, and high-fives. "How did you come up with the voodoo thing?" Jim asked. "I know that in Haiti people either do voodoo or are completely against it," Joe answered.

I had laughed with everyone else. But as soon as the collective laughter died down, I felt troubled by the prank. Scott, sensing my bewilderment, offered a justification. "They do these pranks often," he explained, "because the bank's phone number is very similar to several other numbers." Further-more, he said, Joe's pranks were also directed at the fellow traders. "You can't get away with anything here," Scott explained, "lots of joking, lots of messing around." For example, "if these pants were a little bit too yellow, you'd hear about it in two minutes. But then you snap right back into work, that's how it goes."

Jim had a more elaborate theory on how their trading strategy matched their use of humor to the job at hand. " 'You're crazy!' We want everybody to tell us that," Jim said. "In order to make the point that you should take a stand, we find stuff we shouldn't have an opinion on, like a women's basketball league, and bet on it." Indeed, a few minutes later, Joe began playing with a voice synthesizer he had loaded in his computer. While a nearby trader called Matt had left his seat for a few minutes, Joe typed something about him. "Listen to this," he exclaimed, "this is gonna be an all-time winner." A loud metallic voice then announced from Joe's computer: "Matt Corigliano, please report to the pizza parlor for your paycheck." The utterance was a humorous reference to Matt's tendency to leave the floor to buy food in the middle of the day. Joe then played it four times, ahead of Matt's return. When, minutes later, Matt returned to the desk, everyone was waiting to see his face when Joe played the voice synthesizer one more time. He did, to the shock of Corigliano and the delight of fellow traders.

At 4:00 pm, markets closed. Some of the sales traders left their desk minutes later, once they had closed their systems. Scott said he would stay for an hour, registering the transactions he had done for the day and reading and preparing some documents for the senior traders on the following day. I left too, in order to transcribe my notes at my cubicle in NYU. As I made my way out, a trader from another desk remarked, "Joe and Jim . . . they have their own gig going on."

Affect

Soft dollars. Breaching the Chinese Wall. Pranks. My observations during the second day at the sales desk underscored the social aspect of the trading room, shedding fresh light on the question of how electronic markets were reconfiguring, rather than simply phasing out, networks and social relations on Wall Street.

The first observation that surprised me on my second day was Jim's insistence on reading and reframing Bloomberg's news. I initially wondered whether Jim might not be too fond of hearing his own voice. However, the literature on computer-supported collaborative work provides an alternative explanation for these actions. In *Technology in Action,* Christian Heath and Paul Luff examined similar undirected utterances in media newsrooms and argue that these play the crucial role of "animating" the dry information coming from the screen. These allow for journalistic articles to be developed collaboratively through physical co-location. Specifically, Heath and Luff note that the banter solves a problem of *search*: different journalists have access to different information; some of this information will be interesting to other journalists, but it is not clear who that might be. How, then, to share the relevant part without swamping everyone else with data? This, they argue, is facilitated through tongue-in-cheek remarks that do not require a response and hence they do not interrupt anyone's workflow.

Jim's loud readings from his screen thus reinforced the parallel I had already seen between the sales trading desk and Hutchins's plane cockpits. Unintended communication trajectories, both in the forms of banter and of serious talk at the desk, helped traders focus on the relevant news and price movements without the associated interruption cost. This might provide a crucial speed advantage that would then translate into profits.

In turn, this observation led me to reflect on the problem of *attention*, one of the pillars of the literature in behavioral economics. A tenet of this literature was the observation, originally made by Herbert Simon, that humans have a limited cognitive capacity to process decision alternatives, a form of limited attention span. Simon's observation had important implications, because decision-makers with limited attention span will typically opt for a suboptimal course of action, or as Simon put it, one that is "satisficing," namely, good enough, but not the best. The implication is that markets will settle for sub-optimal decisions.

My observations at the sales desk added a twist to this argument. Unlike the abstract decision-makers that featured in behavioral studies, the real-world traders that I observed used a cockpit-like setup to manage their attention. This included both social mechanisms and material tools, from the elaborate setup of windows and screens that Scott arranged every day, to the overheard utterances that shaped the traders' attention and helped them distinguish the important from the accessory. Thanks to this organization of the desk, traders might be able to go beyond their normal cognitive limits in attention span.

However, managing attention was only one form, perhaps the least important, of finding profit opportunities. Beyond attention, the sales desk also managed *affection*. The traders' comments, attitudes, and reactions animated the otherwise lifeless flow of numbers and news presented on the Bloomberg screen. One senior trader "hated" Yahoo. Another one pulled pranks. The junior traders were encouraged to develop views about stock prices despite having limited information and experience, in order to feed into brainstorming. This flow of attachments was then broadcast to the rest of the room by way of loud remarks, banged headsets, broken monitors, and outrageous bets. Affect, Bob had previously remarked, was particularly important in a trading room during moments of slow trading, both in a seasonal sense—the summer period—and on a daily basis, the midday lull. The sales trading desk brought this type of noise and affect to the room.

Another surprise from my second day of fieldwork was the fact that Jim used his clients' trades as the starting point of brainstorming conversations with Josh, the outcome of which was then shared with clients in the form of ideas for trades. This was consistent with Bob's rationale for placing a customer trading desk in a proprietary information floor: customer trading was, in a sense, the opposite of proprietary trading. However, Bob explained, there was an inevitable overlap between customer and proprietary business, and he would rather err on the side of including all relevant information for proprietary trading by engaging in a modicum of customer business.

Practiced Morality

Finally, I now return to the original question that prompted my visit to the sales desk. What did the sales trading desk suggest about the effects that the introduction of electronic trading had on Wall Street? Taken together, my observations from the two days could be summed up in two metaphors about the changing role of the sales trading desk: the sales desk as a cockpit (distributed attention), and the desk as a stage (projecting affection). However, a narrow focus on the activity at the desk ran the danger of overlooking a third and perhaps even more important source of profit opportunities—social relations beyond the four walls of the trading room. Information circulated on Wall Street through the exchange of soft-dollar commissions, whereby the ideas were free but trades were generously paid for via trading commissions. Such information also obeyed the logic of reciprocity, flowing along informal networks of former colleagues and service providers. Interestingly, the information conveyed in the "looks" given by NYSE floor brokers was not self-explanatory, in the way that an accounting number or a macroeconomic figure would be. The data that pointed to a profit opportunity was typically not unequivocal, but ambiguous and partial. Indeed, a broker's look only revealed the identity and strategy of the buyer or seller behind some puzzling price movement. However, such information was invaluable in the context of the calculative and deliberative process taking place at the desk.

As much as my description so far presents a picture of a well-run, effectively organized desk, I remained troubled about the prank to the Haitian caller. Had there been any trader on the desk of the same ethnicity or geographical origin as the unfortunate caller, a prank like this might not have been possible (but then again, it seemed that the traders pulled pranks on callers from multiple origins). The prank thus reflected a clear insensitivity to cultural diversity.

More broadly, the prank also illustrated the risks that Bob was taking by having the sales trading desk in the midst of his proprietary trading floor. They were salespeople. By including them in the trading room, Bob had introduced an element of the old, relationship-based, irreverent Wall Street sales culture into an otherwise serious group of engineer-traders. The sales traders seemed willing to jump to conclusions for the sake of conversation. Their insistence on taking a view reflected a time when intuition and personal charisma, including humor, made up for missing argumentation and analysis. The danger that the sales traders posed to the trading floor was real, because information was after all crossing the Chinese Wall. Information was flowing in the legal direction, that is, from proprietary trading to customer trading, rather than the other way around; however, it created a chain of reciprocity that meant it could potentially flow in the reverse direction. Furthermore, the use of soft commissions invited discussions of the type I had overheard of opaque offshore payments. Paradoxically, however, my conversation with Jim revealed that Bob's insistence in having this desk was legitimate: the desk not only produced affective cues for the rest of the room, but also provided a steady source of returns that were uncorrelated with those of other desks. These returns allowed Bob to avoid layoffs and avoid short-termism among his traders.

My initial motivation for the visits to the customer trading desk was to better understand the traditional role of social relations in trading. My initial premise was that electronic markets had displaced phone calls and loud utterances as the core vehicles for information exchange on the floor; and that financial models had displaced structural network positions as a source of trading advantage. However, and despite these trends, the customer trading desk still relied primarily on social relations and social interaction, making it a unique setting in which to examine how those dynamics had been reshaped by the new quantitative technology. I concluded from my visit that social relations had coalesced around the surviving sources of advantage, such as looks from floor brokers at the NYSE. The trading room could be seen as an instrument for what Hutchins had called "distributed cognition," yet this cognition was not only distributed across instruments, but also across social networks that crossed sensitive organizational, economic, and legal boundaries. The question that this posed for Bob was how to adequately manage this process. That is, how could he foster animation without exuberance?

5

Models and Reflexivity

In contrast to the highly relational work that I had seen at the customer sales desk, my earlier observations of Todd's work had opened a window into a strangely hybrid world, both technical and social, made up of data feeds as well as social relations, of algorithms and personal ties. In grasping the diverse activity I witnessed on the trading floor, however, one element still proved elusive: economic models. As much as trading terminals had displaced the market's location onto the screen, the adoption of economic models seemed to exert a different and altogether more transformative effect. The demise of Long-Term Capital Management in 1998 was illustrative of both the opulent gains and dangerous perils entailed in using models for investment purposes. Economic models, that is, simplified mathematical representations of economic processes, gave its user access to a wealth of possibilities: algebraic manipulation, statistical measurement, or econometric calibration. These techniques had the potential to alter or even reverse the meaning of a given number, thereby yielding unique and valuable new insights. However, models also created the danger of oversize errors and losses if their assumptions proved inaccurate.

How, I wondered, did the trading floor at International Securities facilitate the use of models? My observations at Todd's desk had made clear that statistical arbitrage was not a purely solitary endeavor, as he combined algorithms with social cues and conversations with other desks. These allowed him to exclude some stocks from the book that his algorithm traded, or stop his algorithm altogether. Now that I had a good grasp of the integration of algorithms and social cues, I needed to understand the analogous process with economic models. How did traders incorporate social cues in their models?

Answering this question called for observing the work of a trader who relied heavily on economic models. I recalled that Bob had mentioned one such trader, the "Princeton mathematician," with particular admiration. (I will refer to him with a pseudonymous name, Max.) I asked Bob about him. "Everything Max knows," Bob said, "he knows down to the smallest details." Indeed, Bob attributed to Max the rare ability to use quantitative tools without falling prey to them. "The guys in his desk," said Bob, "talk in probabilities, as in, 'this has a 60 percent probability of happening.' It's not real, but it's real to them. Max calculates the most sophisticated Bayesian formulas to get at a probability number, and then he'll say, 'it's all guessing.' " In other words, while Max's colleagues seemed to be essentializing the formulae, he was the exception.

Max's ability to simultaneously attach and detach himself from his models seemed to me a logical implication of Frank Knight's distinction between risk and uncertainty. Traders needed to navigate uncertainty with quantitative tools that presumed a simple world of risk that did not quite correspond to the actual complexity of the stock market. Instead of abandoning the models altogether, the traders needed to find ways to remain mindful of their limitations and incorporate them into their practices: as anthropologist Hirokazu Miyazaki wrote, successful arbitrage lay in a combination of "belief and doubt."[1] Such a balancing act, however, prompted numerous additional questions: how could a trader commit to a model and simultaneously remain skeptical of it? For instance, what affective state would this imply? Similarly, how would a trader divide his attention between numbers and social cues that disconfirm such numbers? I imagined Max operating in a schizophrenic world of attachment and detachment, distance and proximity, belief and disbelief.

With this in mind, and once Bob had introduced me to Max, I emailed him to request a meeting, and he agreed to see me at his desk. On the day of my visit, I found Max sitting in front of his Bloomberg screen, dressed in an elegant form of business casual and sporting a calculator watch that gave away his quantitative orientation. The first question he asked me was about the correct pronunciation of my last name. He then introduced me to the junior traders at his desk with an impeccable pronunciation of my last name. Max had read a summary of my project, which I had prepared ahead of our meeting, and went on to offer stylistic corrections, suggesting, for instance, the use of "among" rather than "amongst."

Max's refined taste, I found out, was easily offended. He winced when, as part of our conversation, I used the expression "buy a stock." "We don't say that," he cautioned. "The most obvious thing that differentiates the professional from the amateur is that you talk about how you are positioned toward the stock. You are short or long. But you don't 'own it,' with the commitment that it implies. It is much more dispassionate, professional, even-handed. In fact, while many amateurs consider selling at a loss to be the result of some fault of character, taking losses early and in small amounts is a sign of professionalism.

There are horror stories about traders who roll losses." Modern arbitrage, Max implied, called for dispassion and cool-headedness. The point was to limit one's attachment to one's trades, thus preserving one's rigor and accuracy when they were challenged by colleagues or a client. Max's correction of my sentence was thus highly informative, although it made me feel somewhat inadequate. I would have to be mindful of what I said in front of him.

Like Todd, Max engaged in arbitrage, but the specific arbitrage strategy he specialized in was *merger* arbitrage. As any basic finance textbook explains, this strategy leverages the announcements of mergers between companies to find mispricings. For instance, suppose company A announces today a merger with company B, to be completed in nine months. Company A will typically add how it plans to pay shareholders in company B. Suppose it plans on paying one share in A for each of their shares in B. Nine months after the announcement, if the merger is successfully completed, any investors will be able to hand over one share in company B to the management company A, and receive in exchange a share in company A. This can provide an arbitrage opportunity. If, nine months after the announcement, the merger between companies A and B is successfully completed, the price of stock in company B will be exactly equal to the stock price of company A, as the two will be the same company. Furthermore, this will be true regardless of contextual vagaries such as movements in the Dow Jones index performance, the state of the US economy, or the competitive fortunes of the two companies in their product markets.

A merger, in other words, creates a radical simplification of the problem of valuation. Simplifying is key to merger arbitrage, because certainty over the value equivalence between A and B on merger day can then be brought forward to the present. If the price of B today is significantly lower than the price of A, an arbitrage opportunity thus exists: a trader could buy shares in B, which amounts to betting that its stock price will rise; and sell short shares in A, that is, bet that its price will fall. If the merger is successfully completed, the trader will then exchange the shares he bought in company B for shares in company A and use those shares to pay off the shares in company A he borrowed to short it, and pocket the difference. This "relative value" trade has the additional advantage of insulating the trader from the overall movements in the market, because if stock prices fall, the profits from shorting company A would offset the losses from longing company B.

In practice, there was a further twist to this trading strategy due to the uncertainty associated with merger completions. There is never full certainty that a merger, once announced, will actually be completed, and on average 5 percent of mergers are not completed. Accordingly, the stock prices of companies A and B will reflect this less-than-certain equivalence. In the extreme, and assuming many other arbitrageurs are active and have had time to respond to a merger when it is announced, a trader could use the difference in price between companies A and B (also known as the spread) to quantify the probability that other arbitrageurs attribute to a successful merger completion. For instance, if the stock price of company B is half of company A's, that can be taken to mean that arbitrageurs attribute a 50 percent probability to the completion of the merger. Thus, although betting on merger arbitrage entails buying and selling shares in companies A and B, it effectively means betting on the probability that the merger, once announced, will be completed.

As much as merger arbitrage (or at least the textbook explanation noted above) seems straightforward, Max's account was anything but: "the on-off character of merger completion," Max explained, "means that the probability distribution of returns is not lognormal but bimodal." Merger arbitrage, Max was implying, was chiefly about operational details. Because arbitrageurs like him only entered a trade once it had been announced, the merger spread (or difference in prices) between the merging companies was never very wide. Other traders, betting on the merger before it had been announced, had already narrowed the spread for arbitrageurs like Max. This meant that the potential margin available to Max was not wide. On the other hand, if the merger was canceled at the last minute, the prices of the merging companies could move substantially, leading to sizeable losses for arbitrageurs. As a result, the two possible outcomes that Max effectively faced were either a small profit if the merger was completed, or a very large loss if it was not. This is what he meant by "bimodal." Max's goal, then, was not to make outsize returns on any individual trade, but rather to accumulate a steady stream of reasonable returns while avoiding any single disastrous bet. As Max explained, "in Vegas, people bet on small odds with big payoffs. We do the opposite. High odds, small payoffs."

Beyond the above, Max proved elusive. He resisted revealing to me the operational details that allowed him to bet for high odds and small payoffs, as well as the ways in which working from the trading floor facilitated such activity. "There is really no mystery to what we do," he said. This, to me, was a sign that there was *a lot* to learn. I asked, "could I spend a morning observing how you trade?" Max was not keen: "I am unclear," he replied, "as to what you are going to learn." And then, pointing to the summary I had sent him, he added, "I am a little wary about going into so much detail about the integration we have achieved of the different desks in the trading room. We have done very well, and other banks have not managed it, so I don't know how much we should share." I could not help but be pleased by this comment. Never before had I seen such direct corroboration of a hypothesis of mine during fieldwork. Max's comment left me with even greater interest in watching him trade, though of course that was precisely what he wanted to avoid.

Merger Arbitrage

Back at NYU, as I transcribed my notes, I realized that my visit to Max's desk had left me both intrigued and frustrated. Max's arbitrage strategy was a revealing example of so-called modern arbitrage, that is, arbitrage that did not simply relate markets for the same securities but connected seemingly unrelated markets. In other words, Max was not exploiting mispricings across the same market, as in the classic example of gold in New York and London that Todd had described (see figure 5.1). Instead, Max was exploiting differences in prices between two different securities, such as the stock prices of company A and company B. These securities were in principle unrelated, but the announcement of a merger suddenly brought them together (see figure 5.2).

My conversation had not made clear the precise ways in which he used models to make bets on merger probability. The extraordinary returns associated with such a model-based strategy had been well documented, and a growing literature on the economics of arbitrage had emerged during the late 1990s. This literature had quantified the returns from merger arbitrage, identifying returns that exceeded the normal rate of return by 100 percent[2] (this figure was subsequently challenged).[3] Despite its remarkable profitability, it was also clear that merger arbitrage carried substantial risk, suggesting that part of those excess returns was a compensation for its risk.

In sum, my first conversation with Max had allowed me to understand the basics of merger arbitrage, but it had also led to a number of additional questions about the use of economic models in trading. How did Max use models to bet on merger probabilities? Why was the use of models so lucrative? Finally, how were those models integrated with the knowledge produced by the rest of the trading room?

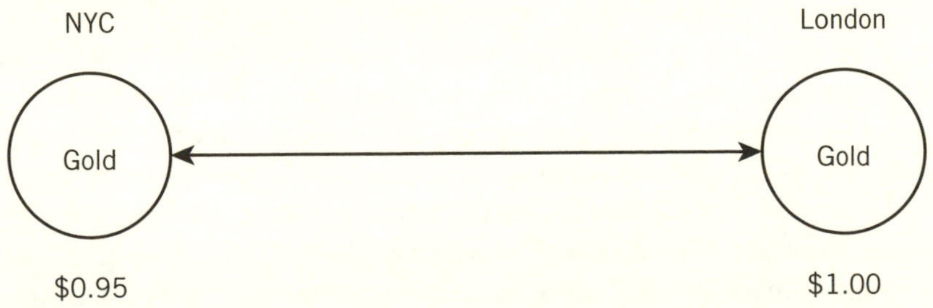

NYC   London

Gold   Gold

$0.95 $1.00

FIGURE 5.1. Classic arbitrage. In this example, the presence of a mispricing between two geographically separate markets for gold creates, assuming zero transportation costs, an arbitrage opportunity.

Company A   Company B

Merger announcement

$0.95 $1.00

FIGURE 5.2. Merger arbitrage. The announcement of a merger between companies A and B creates an arbitrage opportunity if the difference in prices between the two exceeds the expected difference between the value of the acquirer and the merger value of the acquisition target.

One Morning at the Merger Arbitrage Desk

Several months after our first conversation, Max finally agreed to let me watch him trade. On the day of our appointment, I arrived at the merger desk after 9:30 am, just after the market had opened. As I arrived, however, the traders barely acknowledged my presence. They looked busy. Max and a trader sitting next to him, Andy, were entering data in their respective computers, checking with each other every row they typed. Next to them a young analyst named Oscar was listening intently to a webcast PowerPoint presentation, sealed off from the desk by large headphones. "There's been a merger announcement this morning," Max explained, offering me a seat between him and Oscar. The news had landed on the traders' Bloomberg terminals at 5:58 pm the previous day, with the market already closed. This merger would combine two barely known *for-profit* educational institutions, Whitman Education Group and Career Education Group. Mergers such as this one were the raw material of merger arbitrage, so the announcement was big news for Max's desk. The three traders had been at the desk since 7:30 am, preparing for the opening of the market at 9:30 am. I was late to the party.

What had I missed? As I looked around, I noted that Max and Andy were both glancing at a sheet of paper that sat on top of a low bookcase separating them. The paper was the second page of a memo that summarized the details of the merger. Oscar had prepared the memo earlier that morning, based on the PowerPoint presentation that Whitman's management had webcast. Oscar had passed this memo on to Max and Andy "for modeling." At the bottom of the memo I saw a diagram that represented the "collar structure" of the deal. This referred to a set of legal provisions that altered the "conversion ratio" between Whitman and Career shares, that is, the number of shares that Career was offering to buy Whitman. The typical collar reduced, or "choked," the rate at which the acquiring company exchanged its shares for those of the target, hence the name. This choking took the form of a legal clause, and it typically applied if the target's stock price dropped severely as in, for example, the case of a financial scandal. The collar thus protected the acquirer but also created difficulties for arbitrageurs as it altered the value equivalence between the two merging companies, adding an extra piece of uncertainty to the puzzle.

Having represented the merger memo as a collar diagram, Max and Andy were incorporating this information into a spreadsheet. "When we go down from here, we're gonna have negative gamma," Andy said. He was looking again at the collar structure. "Do you wanna revisit the volatility assumptions?" Max answered. "50 days, 44 . . ." The dialogue was illustrative of the manner in which traders interacted with one another. They smiled, but not too often, and always in a subdued manner. They spoke in a whisper, so low, in fact, that I sometimes could not hear them even though I was sitting between Andy and Max.

Max then turned to me: "the deal is so complex, you cannot just eyeball it and say 'oh, volatility is good for us.' It is good on some tranches of the collar, and negative on others." Why, I asked, pursue such complex trades? "We go for collared deals," Max replied. "Fifteen years ago, I had the models and no one else did, and what looked to others as a two-dollar spread looked to me really as a dollar-and-a-half spread." However, he added, the quantitative tools he had were now diffused. "Here at International Securities we have a PhD in fluid mechanics in Risk Management. A lot of it has been the result of the influx of Russian and Chinese expatriates."

In sum, my first minutes at the merger desk revealed a different way to trade than what I anticipated. The traders were not just reacting to the ups and downs of the market, but spent their time creating models that revealed profit opportunities too complex for the eye to see. On the day of my visit, this entailed two hours of work for three people before the opening of the market, and a combination of tools that included a webcast presentation, a written memo, a model, and a spreadsheet. The final outcome of this work was another spreadsheet, a summary document, showing red brackets around the cell corresponding to Whitman when the price of the stock created a buy opportunity. In this regard, Max was truly representative of the shift toward models and formulas on Wall Street. In my subsequent observations, I sought to understand whether economic theory had shaped the tools used by the arbitrageurs, and if so, how.

Taking a Position

"Amex hasn't really opened on WIX," said Andy with bewilderment at 10:00 am. Andy was referring to the stock ticker symbol of Whitman Education, WIX, which was listed on the American Stock Exchange ("Amex"). By 10:00 am Max and the others had the trade already "set up" (native expression) and all they needed to know to start trading was the price of Whitman. Although trading at the Amex normally opened at 9:30 am, by 10:00 am the stock had not yet started trading. Some delay was typically expected when there was a merger announcement, but at thirty minutes the delay was taking longer than usual, suggesting that something problematic might be taking place.

As they waited, the traders turned to other mergers they had been working on. On that day, they were active in thirty-one deals in total, at different stages of completion. On Max's screen, a window called Trading Summary listed these trades as rows. In the rightmost column of each row Max had included keywords like "Judge," "Chinese," "Justice approves," or "watch," to remind himself of the key aspect he needed to follow for each deal. For instance, one of these mergers involved General Electric (GE), which was in a second-stage merger discussion with the European Commission's antitrust unit. Max was also active on the merger between DHL and Deutsche Post; this one needed approval from the US Transportation Department, as it would entail a government (the German one) owning an American airline. "Both mergers involve a European and an American firm, and they are both pending a political decision," Max explained. The background story, he added, was a gradual souring of international trade beginning with the US decision not to sign the Kyoto agreement and then enacting steel tariffs.

A few minutes later, Whitman finally began trading. The spread, or difference in price between Whitman and Career, was as wide as ten cents. "Things were so simple, this looked like an okay deal," Max remarked, "but it may turn out to be better." Sensing an opportunity, the traders began to scrutinize the merging companies. "Do they have regulatory approval?" Max asked Oscar. Max was asking for potential risks to merger completion. "Do they have accreditation?" he added. Oscar explained that they did. "What schools are these anyways?" Max insisted, his eyes squinting at the computer screen as he sought to grasp the big picture. "Technical, for adults," responded the analyst. "They teach you things like how to be a dental assistant." Max's probing continued: "Is it true that there's a summer drop for this business?" Oscar replied that the drop Max was wondering about was in fact the summer recess.

I asked Max about the reason for these questions. "This guy Edison," Max explained to me as he looked at the screen, "a few years ago wanted to manage the primary school system, but then went down in flames." The entrepreneur that Max was alluding to was in fact named Christopher Whittle, but he was the founder of Edison Schools. Edison began operations in 1995 with the promise to bring "private-sector discipline" to the education industry, which according to him was heavily "bureaucratized," but Edison's company soon saw its stock price plummet in 2002 amidst accusations of corruption. A scandal of the type that Edison experienced would immediately ruin the merger between Whitman and Career, so the probability of a scandal had to be factored in. Max was thus analyzing the Whitman merger based on a rough industry categorization. Once he established that the proposed merger belonged to the "for-profit education" sector, he had drawn an analogy between two *secondary* education companies such as Whitman and Career, and a scandalous *primary* education company like Edison Schools.

Turning to his Bloomberg terminal, Max saw that Whitman's owner held a large proportion of the stock, which suggested he had a stake in the future of the company. This led Max to conclude that corruption was not the reason for the wide spread he was seeing. "The reason why the spread is not zero is that other traders have their own proprietary models for it. And they can all be right. At this point, it's all about the future, and we don't know the future. So, their assumptions on volatility, for example, could be different than ours. Or their assumptions about timing. If it were just a cash deal, it would have a much lower spread."

"Let's bid $13.60 for 10,000," said Max to Andy. Max had decided to "have a presence" in the deal and buy ten thousand shares at $13.60. Why? "There may be many issues with this company," he explained, "but I can invest right away by knowing that they're a five million and a two million company. This means it's not one company acquiring another one of the same size, which right away means that there are not financing issues involved. If there were, it would be a whole different game." Following the instruction to buy, Andy lifted the headset to call traders at other banks to buy shares in Whitman. To do so, Andy had specialized tools to track the market: a telephone turret, screens filled with stock prices, etc. "We want to have a presence in the deal, but we don't want to be the ones setting the price," Max explained.

Max's decision-making process came as a surprise to me, in that he did not rely on quantitative tools to arrive at a numerical point estimate of the value of Whitman before deciding to buy. Unlike what I anticipated, his equations and databases were not producing a single number. I asked him why he did not use the models to calculate merger probabilities. "We do not have a formula for that. This is an art. It is not like statistical arbitrage," he replied, in veiled criticism of Todd's trading strategy. Categories and analogies, I concluded, were instead what helped arbitrageurs anticipate possible merger obstacles. They allowed the traders to glean the future from the past. "We look for patterns," Max explained, "precedent, similar deals, either hostile or friendly, degree of product overlap, and earnings variability."

Talking to Other Desks

While Andy was buying stock in Whitman, Max turned to one of his daily routines, updating the prices of the stocks in all the mergers that were active in their book. "What's your price for XYZ? I've got bad data on it," Max said in a low voice, without taking his eyes off the screen. Sometimes, he explained, these prices do not automatically update correctly.

The traders' attention soon turned to another deal. "Let's see what the NYSE says about Household International," said Max, logging on to the website of the New York Stock Exchange. Five months earlier, the Hong Kong and Shanghai Bank (HSBC) had announced its intention to acquire Household International, an American bank that specialized in subprime mortgages. Max and his traders were actively betting that this merger would be completed. Max entered his password on the NYSE site to check whether the original date, March 28, still held for the closing on the deal. "If they had some doubts that they're merging on the 28th," Max said, "they would use different wording." And if the merger were delayed, "it could be a big problem, because the index guys are shit-load long on HSBC." Max knew about the position taken by index arbitrageurs from his frequent contact with the index arbitrage desk barely a few meters away. Unless these traders correctly anticipated the precise day of the merger, they stood to lose from the derivatives that they were using to take a position. As it turned out, the wording was as expected. But then this prompted Andy to check another source. "Bloomberg is using 31st," he noted, renewing their doubts.

At 11:30 am, Max got a call about the timing of the HSBC-Household International deal; he spoke on the phone for a few minutes and then walked two desks over to the index arbitrage team. He had left to speak to them about the timing of the deal. He came back excited: "it turns out there are really many possibilities, many moving parts: they could take it on Friday, on Monday . . ." he said in reference to HSBC-Household International. "If the deal does go through," he learned from the conversation, "Symantec will be replacing Household in the S&P 500." Immediately, Max checked Symantec's price: "Let's see, perhaps we should expect a jump in the price . . . it's a midcap stock, the indexers are going to have to buy 4 percent of it."

In calculating the impact of the merger on the price of Symantec, Max was thinking strategically about how passive funds would affect the stock price. Passive mutual funds were committed to mimic the S&P 500 index in their portfolio, so when a stock was included in the index, they had to buy large blocks of it. Knowing this, index arbitrageurs could anticipate the moves of passive mutual funds by buying the company that was expected to enter the index, thereby pushing up its price ahead of time, creating a signal that Max would read. Max's rule of thumb was that if the newly entering stock was a large firm, its price would increase by 8 percent. Symantec was a medium-sized firm, so Max only expected its price to rise by 4 percent. The price of Symantec already reflected that upward pressure, which meant that other index arbitrageurs believed that the Household International-HSBC deal was going to come through. This lent support to Max's hunch.

In sum, talking to the index arbitrageurs and tracing back their strategy (which, in turn, traced back the strategy of passive mutual funds) had allowed Max to read the price of Symantec as a relevant signal of the likelihood of a merger between Household International and HSBC. To do so, Max was anticipating what other actors would do by thinking ahead and mentally rolling back their actions to the present. This was the type of rational discounting of the future that financial economists attribute to market actors, but I was struck by one difference: Max understood that there were many different types of investors, with as many different strategies. Understanding the motivations of each type allowed Max to make sense of stock prices and to arrive at a better estimate of merger probability and merger date. To do so, Max relied on conversations with other desks in the trading room that were similar to the investors he needed to understand.

Visualizing Merger Likelihood

Max's attention soon returned to the Whitman-Career deal. He called up a black-and-white window on his screen that displayed old fashioned, 1980s-style Microsoft DOS characters. Pressing a combination of command keys, Max obtained some information on Edison Schools. He was looking for similarities with the Whitman-Career deal. The screen he had displayed corresponded to a proprietary database that Max had meticulously assembled over the years with information about all past mergers in which the desk had been involved, and that classified the deals along several dimensions. This gave him "thumbnail" information about each company that merged. "You think you would remember," Max says about it, "but you don't. Memory is very deceiving."

The database often proved helpful. Max recalled a merger between two junkyards that had incompatible computer systems. In the low-tech world of junkyards, one might not anticipate that information technology would be a key factor in derailing a merger. But, Max added, "if the point of a junkyard is to find a door for that 1996 Volvo, you can imagine how important computer systems are." The arbitrageurs had previously encountered another deal in a different industry that also entailed incompatible systems, and that merger reminded them of the junkyard deal. They correctly predicted the failure of the latter, closing their positions early enough to avert outsize losses. "Drawing parallels and linkages, saying 'this reminds me of that,' is at the heart of what we do," said Max.

FIGURE 5.3. Plotting implied merger probability. Screen shot of a Bloomberg terminal showing the spreadplot of Household International and HSBC Bank, November 2002–May 2004. *Source*: International Securities.

As he finished this sentence, Max typed a command in his Bloomberg terminal, producing a large graph in black and blue colors. The chart, reproduced in figure 5.3, displayed the evolution of the *spread* between HSBC and Household. As noted, the spread is the difference in the prices of the merging companies, adjusted for the terms of the merger. In this case, the spread was the difference in the prices of HSBC and Household, weighted by the stock conversion ratio agreed to by the merging partners of 0.535 shares in HSBC for each share in Household International. The graph, known as the "spreadplot," played a key role in Max's work. Max interpreted movements in the spread as signs of changes in the likelihood of merger completion. The completion of a merger would turn the two merging firms into a single entity, and the difference in their stock prices (the spread) would then be zero. Conversely, a widening spread was evidence that the merger was likely to be canceled. If a merger was canceled, the value equivalence between the two firms would disappear, and the spread would revert to its wide level before the merger announcement. For that reason, a narrowing of the spread was an indication that the market expected a greater likelihood of merger completion, while a widening of the spread indicated lower likelihood.

The spreadplot gave Max access to information that would otherwise be impossible to obtain: what arbitrageurs on a rival desk on Wall Street were thinking. Using the spreadplot was akin to predicting the weather by looking at whether pedestrians on the street are carrying umbrellas: if one assumes that other pedestrians are rational, well informed, and keen to stay dry, their decision to carry an umbrella will reveal their assessments of the weather. And although the street might be filled with wild optimists and pessimists, on average the extremes will cancel out, offering insight on what weather people expected on average. Similarly, by relating the changes in the spreadplot to ongoing news and events, Max was able to infer how his rivals thought about the merger.

Max's use of the spreadplot, however, went further. He was able to numerically calculate the estimates of merger probability that rival traders were making. Max referred to this as the "implied probability" of merger completion. To quantify this magnitude, Max assumed that the prices of both companies were already the result of his rivals' trades. If that was the case, the size of the spread would reflect their perceptions of merger likelihood. With this and other assumptions, Max was able to mathematically infer, or "back out," the numerical probability associated with a given merger.

The spreadplot offered even more information. By using the implied probability repeatedly over several months and not just on a one-off basis, the traders were able to access not only the average assessment of merger likelihood, but also the reasons for such assessments. The HSBC-Household merger illustrates this approach. The spreadplot for HSBC-Household (see figure 5.3) shows two spikes along a descending line. These correspond to the two instances in which market participants lost confidence in the merger. The first, on November 22, 2002, was motivated by funding concerns, as investors wondered whether HSBC was financially sound or buying Household to get funding. The second instance took place on March 20, 2003, following news that Household International was shredding documents. This reminded arbitrageurs of similar shredding activity at Enron. The two spikes thus illustrate how plotting the spread brought into relief potential merger obstacles. By plotting the spread over time, Max's traders were thus able to identify the magnitude of these risks, and the types of risks that other traders saw in the deal (funding concerns at the acquirer, and governance problems at the target). These variables then structured their attention.

Are We Missing Something?

By 11:30 am, the spread between Whitman and Career had not narrowed. "I'm concerned," Max said. One hour earlier, Max had interpreted a wide spread as a good thing, but now the profit opportunity seemed too good to be true. "Are we missing something?" Max wondered, "or can it be that the deal has gone under the radar screen of other traders?" Perhaps, Max reasoned, someone's worried by an earnings surprise that we're not worried about. To check, Max turned to a proprietary database called Relegence FirstTrack. "It gives you all the information published about some company in very different sources." According to the database's brochure, Relegence offered capabilities for aggregating, filtering, and managing information from "tens of thousands of external sources." Max typed WIX into the database. He obtained several results, but all of them were familiar to him. He was looking for news from some unexpected regional newspaper. "We ran Household International in it," he explained, "and it turned up shredding practice in its Washington office." This could have potentially derailed the merger with HSBC, "but then Relegence uncovered this story from AFX, a European News Agency, with a quotation on HSBC saying that the firm was aware of these things when it announced the merger."

Following an inconclusive database search on WIX, Andy picked up the phone and called a floor broker who handled orders for Whitman at the stock exchange. "John says buy this WIX, no one's really hedging it," he said to Max. No other arbitrageur, the floor broker had implied, was active in the Whitman trade. From this, Max concluded that the merger had effectively gone under the radar of other arbitrageurs. He reacted by increasing the desks' exposure to the merger. "Let's work another ten [thousand], but pick your spots," he said to Andy, asking the junior trader to purchase additional shares in Whitman, but to do so carefully so as to avoid inflating the stock price.

Why had Andy called up the floor broker? Until 11:30 am, the traders had interpreted the spread as the implied probability of the merger. The persistent discrepancy between the wide spread and the traders' confidence in it, which would imply a narrow spread, had led them to question their own interpretation of events. Having re-checked the Relegence database, they decided to inquire about the identities of the shareholders, partially lifting the veil of anonymity that protects securities trading. By doing so, the arbitrageurs were able to clarify whether backing out the implied probability from the spread made sense: was the spread effectively reflecting the information in the hands of rival arbitrageurs? The traders concluded it was not, because they were not active in the deal.

This last step was important to understanding merger arbitrage. Backing out, I now grasped, can only be done under certain conditions. In translating prices into implied merger probabilities, arbitrageurs typically make two key assumptions. First, that movements in the spread are dominated by merger considerations; if on the contrary the spread moved for reasons unrelated to the merger, interpreting the move as a change in merger likelihood would be erroneous. The second assumption the traders made was that markets equilibrated rapidly, which amounts to assuming that rival traders had seen and paid attention to the spread, compared it to their own information, and acted upon it. Max was mindful of these two assumptions and had come back to them once the spread began exhibiting a puzzling behavior.

The spreadplot allowed Max to see what his rivals were doing. Was Max thus attempting to mimic them? I would argue this was not the case, and that Max was instead attempting to read his rivals' actions to improve *his own* understanding. On learning that no other arbitrageur was hedging the stock, he concluded that the spread could not be interpreted as a measure of implied probability, and decided to do the opposite. In other words, Max's was not a case of blind imitation aimed at short-cutting the need to analyze the deal. Indeed, as Max explained to me at a later date, the ultimate point of the implied probability is that it allows for confrontation rather than imitation. "It is a reality check, it's a number that's out there and it challenges you every day, when you come in, to have 85 percent confidence in this deal, whatever that is. You could have a little sign saying, 'Are you challenging yourself every day on every deal?' "

The significance of the spreadplot could thus not be overstated. Its use provided merger arbitrageurs with a measurement of the extent to which their estimates deviated from their rivals'. It also warned them against missing information, prompted additional search, pushed them to use their business contacts, and ultimately gave them the necessary confidence to expand their position. Indeed, this use of the spread was illustrative of the trading strategies generally described as "quantitative finance." Max emphasized this with an example. "Look at this jump," he said, in reference to the brusque price movement of Household International on the day its merger with HSBC was announced (see figure 5.4). "This is the value that [mutual] fund managers and the guys on the Street are after," referring to those that were seeking to anticipate the merger announcement. "Once the jump has taken place," that is, after the merger is officially announced, "it's a matter of pennies. The value investors don't have the fine-tuned tools to position themselves in this spread, to determine if it's too wide or too narrow for them. *We do*."

As the morning came to an end and the work pace began to slow down ahead of the lunch hour, I left the trading room and returned to NYU. Before I left, I noticed a small drawing taped to one of Max's screens. It showed Snoopy, the cartoon character, in full airplane pilot gear, piloting his doghouse: Goggles, helmet, scarf flapping in the wind, and arms stretched out holding an

```
.HI ↑  -.37 -.42   0s                              Index  GP
 At 12:33 Vol 4 Op .06   Hi .06  Lo -.42  Prev .06
                    Line Chart  .HI Index                     1/5
Range        3/27/02 - 3/27/03      Period  D Daily
Upper Chart: 1 Line Chart           Moving Averages  ▮ ▮
535 * HBC US Equity - HI US Equity                        1) News
```

Chart data box:
```
        Close
Last         -0.3658
High 11/12/02  7.9775
Average      -6.9151
Low 04/19/02 -30.7359
```

Chart axis labels (right side): 10, 5, 0, -5, -10, -15, -20, -25

X-axis: 01 08 15 22 | 01 08 15 22 | 03 10 17 24 | 01 08 15 22 | 01 08 15 22 | 03 10 17 24 | 01 08 15 22 | 01 08 15 22 | 02 09 16 23 | 02 09 16 23 | 03 10 18 | 03 10 17 24
2002 Apr | 2002 May | 2002 Jun | 2002 Jul | 2002 Aug | 2002 Sep | 2002 Oct | 2002 Nov | 2002 Dec | 2003 Jan | 2003 Feb | 2003 Mar

```
Australia 61 2 9777 8600      Brazil 5511 3048 4500      Europe 44 20 7330 7500      Germany 49 69 920410
Hong Kong 852 2977 6000 Japan 81 3 3201 8900 Singapore 65 6212 1000 U.S. 1 212 318 2000 Copyright 2003 Bloomberg L.P.
```

FIGURE 5.4. The jump in the spread on merger announcement date. Spreadplot of Household International and HSBC Bank, before and after the merger announcement. The jump in the spread on November 14, 2002, corresponds to the merger announcement. Contemporary arbitrageurs, however, focus their trading on the post-announcement period. *Source:* Bloomberg.

FIGURE 5.5. Cartoon taped to Max's monitor. PEANUTS © Peanuts Worldwide LLC. Dist. By ANDREWS MCMEEL SYNDICATION. Reprinted with permission. All rights reserved.

imaginary plane yoke (see figure 5.5). Intrigued, I made a note of it before leaving the floor.

The Use of Models in Arbitrage

Back at NYU, I felt a combination of fatigue and accomplishment. My observations at the merger arbitrage desk had produced twenty-three pages of nearly illegible notes, but proved exceptionally rich in findings. In the three hours that elapsed between 9:30 am and 12:30 pm, the desk comprised of Max, Andy, and Oscar had produced a memo, created a valuation spreadsheet, taken a position, and brainstormed with other traders inside and outside the trading room. They had made elaborate inferences from a graph that led them to increase one of their positions. The traders had also worked on three different mergers: Whitman-Career, HSBC-Household International, and Deutsche Post-DHL. In following those, the news of the day had taken them from business scandals in the obscure world of the for-profit education industry to the emergence of the subprime loan industry, as well as the political context of post-Kyoto international trade. Through all this, the traders had displayed a remarkable ability to multitask. "The best predictor of your skill at merger arbitrage," Max had remarked in passing, "is your potential as taxi dispatcher— the skill to do lots of things in parallel."

My original goal when approaching Max and his desk was to understand how financial models were used in merger arbitrage, and more specifically, how their output was combined with social cues from the rest of the trading room. In this regard, several surprises emerged from my morning of observation. The first related to the ways in which traders used the models. Based on the idea, as Todd originally explained, that traders used models to relate the value of different securities, I expected Max to use economic models to make numerical predictions. To my surprise, this was not how Max and his colleagues used models. Instead, Max quantified a new variable, implied merger probability, and monitored it through a graphical representation, the spreadplot.

Reflexivity

Two entities, the spreadplot and the implied probability, held the answer to my original question. Max did not simply combine quantitative tools with social cues, as Todd did to determine when to stop relying on the algorithm. Instead, Max used models to *infer* a form of social cue from market prices, and specifically, to infer the market's average implied estimate of merger probability. Max's approach is captured in figures 5.6 and 5.7. The spread, or difference between the prices of merging companies (see figure 5.6), is expected to converge as the date of merger completion approaches. Arbitrageurs thus plotted the spread over time on their Bloomberg screen and looked for an L-shaped pattern as in figure 5.7.

In a subsequent conversation, I checked with Bob about my interpretation of Max's technique. "Is it really the case," I asked, "that Max backs out prices to find out the opinion of his competitors?" He confirmed this point. "It's like being able to tap into the wisdom of the crowds, but only a few people can do it. This is very topical, this recognition that there is some kind of collective crowd knowledge. This is powerful stuff," he added. "The conventional idea is that 'oh we have a scientific valuation model and then we go out and trade.' But that is not what's happening. The scientific model is actually a reverse flow, more often than not. The scientific model is a way of deriving what the crowd is deciding."

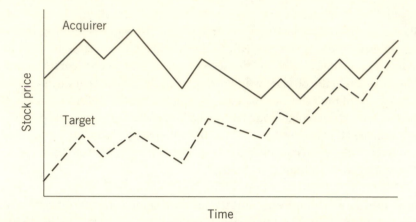

FIGURE 5.6. Mergers create price convergence. Two companies that merge success-fully typically start from disparate values, but as the likelihood of them becoming a single economic entity increases, their stock market values become the same.

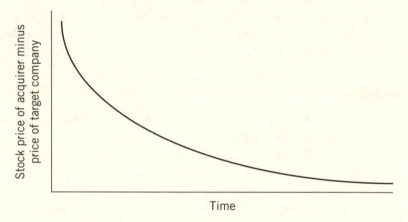

FIGURE 5.7. Spread and successful merger completion. The difference in prices or "spread" between two companies that merge successfully decreases over time in an L-shaped pattern of gradual decay. Arbitrageurs look for this pattern to identify whether market investors believe that the merger will be completed.

Max's use of models in reverse was at first genuinely shocking to me. How-ever, I soon discovered that the finding was consistent with those of other soci-ologists. MacKenzie and Millo's study of the use of the Black-Scholes formula reported a similar mechanism in options trading. As they wrote, "central [to the problem of pricing options] was the notion of 'implied volatility,' calcu-lated by running the Black-Scholes model 'backward': using observed option prices to infer, by iterative solution, the stock volatilities they implied."[4] The outcome of this exercise, MacKenzie and Millo argued, allowed the traders to capture something as abstract as volatility, which would not have been possible otherwise.

Studies like MacKenzie and Millo's, however, did not report on the intriguing way in which Max used the spreadplot. Instead of relying on the implied probability to replace his own estimates of merger likelihood, Max used it to question them. His was a reflexive and dispassionate orientation to trading, and key to it was Max's focus on what variables could go wrong, rather than on the outsize returns to any given trade. Equally important to Max was to ensure accurate data entry, and to question his own beliefs by reading correctly the ups and downs of the spreadplot.

I realized at that point that I had come full circle. I had begun my research inspired by cultural accounts of financial markets such as Abolafia's depiction of bond traders. What I had observed at Max's desk, however, was the opposite. Three decades before my visit, a mathematics graduate from an Ivy League university like Max would not have found a job on Wall Street. Thanks to the development of quantitative tools, and thanks to the public reaction against the insider trading excesses of Ivan Boesky and others in the 1980s, merger arbitrage had been reinvented as a quantitative activity. To the extent that the protagonist of Oliver Stone's film, Gordon Gekko, had been inspired by Boesky, what I had just witnessed at Max's desk was a form of anti-Gekko.

Materiality

A second surprise that emerged from my visit was the tangible and material way in which the traders used financial models. Max was not using models in his head, as economic accounts appeared to imply. Instead, the model was programmed into an Excel spreadsheet and turned into a graphical form—the spreadplot—on the Bloomberg terminal. The cognitive complexity of the collared trade, as Max had said, was otherwise too high. In this sense, the spreadplot fit with the category of what Muniesa, Millo, and Callon had called "market devices," or material artifacts that helped market actors make decisions.[5] Its use was also consistent with other findings reported by MacKenzie and Millo, who also found that Black-Scholes was introduced into the pits of the Chicago Board of Trade through a material device. As these sociologists note, Fisher Black printed tables with theoretical option values for each volatility level and maturity date, so that the traders could roll these papers and take them to the pit to trade.[6] Finally, research by Caitlin Zaloom has also identified a graphical representation that serves as a material tool for Treasury bond traders: the "yield curve," which represented yield rates paid on Treasury securities against various maturity dates.[7]

It took me some time to fully grasp the implications of the above. If the traders were reading prices and feeding these prices back into their estimates, acting and reacting to their screens, their actions amounted to an invisible form of collaboration across the various banks active on the trade. In other words, while I was sitting by Max's desk, another desk of merger arbitrageurs somewhere in another Manhattan skyscraper was working on the same mergers as Max. In doing so, the entire "arbitrage community" (a peculiar expression that Max and others used) was thinking more or less as a whole entity, thanks to the use of the spreadplot. The merger desk, I then realized, had given me a distinctly modern experience, a sense of connectedness with people I did not know or see, but whose presence made itself felt through the trading terminals, in the movement of the spread. This peculiar form of belonging spoke to research by Knorr Cetina and Bruegger that claimed that electronic markets had redefined the grounds for shared experience in finance, shifting those grounds from being in a common space to operating at a simultaneous time. As the authors wrote, "the screen gives a gestural face to the signals that are transmitted through this information technology; it instantiates the market as a life-form that inhabits the technology."[8]

Social Networks

My visit produced a third notable observation. Max was not only relying on quantitative technology, but also on social networks within and outside the floor. During my morning at his desk, Max had relied on other people to overcome the limitations of his setup. He leveraged fellow traders at his desk for spotting errors, conversations with other desks for insight on the mergers, and looks from a floor broker at the exchange to interpret the spread. Without question, the key moment of the morning took place at 11:30 am, when the same figure for the spread was interpreted differently from what it had been at 10:00 am. The conundrum the traders experienced ("are we missing something?") emphasized the ambiguity involved in interpreting the data produced by the combination of models and prices. As with the case of Todd, Max's quantitative sophistication was not enough to eliminate the irreducible uncertainty of his trades. Max's own response was the addition of social ties and informal conversations to his highly mathematical and technological setup.

In this, Max's thinking was based on the premise that his models were imperfect, that data entry was prone to errors, and that the spreadplot was not always an accurate representation of his rivals' views. Max turned to his network for checking errors and clarifying ambiguities. Had he used established models and tried-and-tested strategies, fewer of these interactions would have been necessary, but because Max pursued highly profitable and complex deals such as mergers with collars or with unclear completion dates, his models remained imperfect, and social relations were crucially important. In this regard, my morning of observation had also impressed on me the enduring applicability of Knight's framework for the use of financial models: whenever economic models involve the future, there is an irreducible uncertainty that makes simple calculation impossible.

The above, I felt, might explain the Snoopy cartoon that Max had taped to his monitor. At one level, the cartoon illustrated Max's self-deprecating humor: "if you think I am a powerful trader, steering the world's financial markets, think again. I am a plain dog in trader gear." At another level, the cartoon exemplified the strong interdependencies entailed in working at the merger desk with thirty open deals at a time: the multitasking demands of trading—like those of running a taxi dispatch, as Max himself had said—were similar to the multitasking demands of operating a warplane. Finally, Max's cartoon could be seen as a metaphor for the balance between skepticism and belief that was needed to succeed as a quantitative trader. As Bob pointed out, traders required the ability to move from careful discussions of Bayesian probability to recognizing that it was "just guessing."

Performativity

My observations also speak to the sociological debate on the performativity of economics. Callon's performativity thesis posits that economic theories have the potential to alter the economy and bring it closer to the theory. The theory has proved both intriguing and controversial; one frequent critique is that there are few clear empirical examples of performativity beyond Mac-Kenzie and Millo's study of the Black-Scholes formula. In this regard, the case of merger arbitrage offers another instance where the introduction of economic models altered, rather than merely described, stock prices, and did so in the direction predicted by model.

In recent years, the literature on merger arbitrage has documented that merger arbitrage funds have altered the stock prices of merging companies. As Jetley and Ji note, between 2002 and 2008 merger arbitrage spreads have declined by more than 400 basis points (see figure 5.8).[9] This decline, which these authors found "both economically and statistically significant," corresponds to a simultaneous decrease in the aggregate returns experienced by merger arbitrage hedge funds, as well as an increase in the capital inflows going into these funds, suggesting that the narrowing in spreads was due to the arrival of more and more investment capital to this strategy rather than to external factors such as regulation or the business cycle. The authors further argue that the reason for the diminishing spreads is the diffusion of highly quantitative and model-based "post-announcement" strategies (similar to that used by Max), as opposed to the traditional "pre-announcement" merger arbitrage

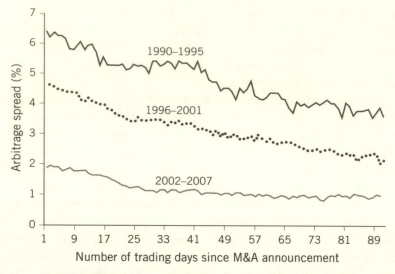

FIGURE 5.8. Arbitrage spread in percentage points of successful M&A deals, in the first 90 days of trading after the M&A announcement. *Source:* Jetley and Ji (2010).

strategies, which typically relied on market tips. As Jetley and Ji write, "part of the decline in the arbitrage spread may be explained by increased trading in the targets' stocks *following* the merger announcement."[10]

Such development can be seen as a form of performativity. If merger spreads have narrowed, and such narrowing has been due to the activity of model-based arbitrage, one may conclude that the narrowing of the spread was caused by the diffusion of arbitrage models and tools. Indeed, Max's own account of his work confirms that this narrowing took place. As he explained, the initial introduction of models and tools such as the spreadplot allowed Max and his colleagues to identify lucrative profit opportunities that were invisible to the naked eye. Once the existence of these opportunities became widely known, the arrival of competing traders with similar models reduced merger spreads. Seen in these terms, the narrower merger arbitrage spreads can be attributed to the diffusion of economic models and tools.

Furthermore, such narrowing of merger spreads brings stock prices in line with the predictions of the models. More specifically, the model used by Max and others in merger arbitrage is based on the Law of One Price, which dictates that the stock market value of an acquisition target should correspond to its merger value. Such value can be calculated as the price at which the acquiring company will buy the target, adjusted by the likelihood of such acquisition. Thus, unlike the earnings value of a stock, which amounts to the net present value of its cash flow, the merger value of a stock is only defined by the merger.

Given the above, the secular reduction of spreads in successful merger deals documented by Jetley and Ji suggests that the stock prices of merging companies are increasingly determined by their merger value. Put differently, the development and diffusion of no-arbitrage pricing models in merger arbitrage has made such models a more accurate description of stock prices. The case of merger arbitrage is thus not simply an instance of performativity, but specifically an instance of strong or "Barnesian" performativity, where the model alters stock prices in the direction predicted by the model. In this manner, the case of merger arbitrage contributes to the debate over performativity by providing an instance of Barnesian performativity that complements the case documented in MacKenzie and Millo's study of the Black-Scholes equation.

My observations also speak to the way in which the models gave rise to performativity. As noted above, the models derived from the Law of One Price did not provide a direct way to calculate stock value, because the probability of merger completion remained unknown. Instead, the model proved useful by providing calculative tools that supported Max's trading strategy. This strategy entailed comparing his own estimates with the market's estimate. The role of the model was thus enabling the traders' calculative practices or, as MacKenzie writes, to act as an engine.

Finally, merger arbitrage also speaks to the *consequences* of performativity. A subsequent industry research report on merger arbitrage explicitly agrees with the analysis by Jetley and Ji, and considers its implications.[11] The document, titled "No Free Lunch: Plain Vanilla Deals Offer Little Upside," notes the presence of "spread compression" in basic merger arbitrage strategies.[12] Crucially, it adds that the solution adopted by arbitrage funds has been to resort to more complex traders and economic models: "confronted with shrinking spreads, merger arbitrage players have had to climb up the scale of complexity to deliver higher returns" (p. 6). This included "topping bids, hostile deals and transactions taking place in multiple jurisdictions or exposed to antitrust risk." Such a dynamic suggests that performativity was followed by a turn to strategies with greater uncertainty, as first posited by Frank Knight in the context of entrepreneurship. It thus suggests that the performative adoption of an economic model may lead to additional, more elaborate and complex, models. One performative cycle therefore leads to the next.

Models, Technology, and Social Interaction

Taken together, the tight integration with which Max weaved models, technology, and social interaction spoke to the literature on the social studies of finance, and in particular to the work of Callon, MacKenzie, Knorr Cetina, and others. Consider first Callon's argument that market devices allow market actors to calculate gains and losses, and generally behave in ways that approximate the conception of rational actors put forth by orthodox economics.[13] A tool like the spreadplot illustrated this dynamic: the introduction of economic models had turned merger arbitrage into an arena where calculative decisions were now possible. This was visible in the historical shift in arbitrage strategy from trying to anticipate merger announcements before they happened (pre-announcement trades) to betting on mergers that were already announced (post-announcement trades). The former hinged on creating and maintaining social ties to industry insiders, while the latter called for superior modeling skills.

However, there is a twist to this seemingly simple illustration of the Callonian argument. The reduction in uncertainty that Max had achieved was not an outcome of the model itself but sprang from a distinct possibility afforded by such models, namely, the ability to contrast his own estimates against those of his rivals. Furthermore, while the use of models had increased the accuracy and sophistication of Max's trading, it had also given rise to a new type of uncertainty that centered on the modeling process itself: did the spreadplot truly capture his rival's estimates? This secondary uncertainty was addressed by turning to social mechanisms that Callon originally imagined would disappear with the arrival of market devices: networks, social cues, and cultural conventions.[14]

Arbitrage had thus not gone from social to mathematical, but from predominantly relational to a combined activity that relied heavily on both models and networks. Max's case thus illustrates a subsequent distinction that Callon drew between "homo economicus 1.0," or the textbook decision-makers of orthodox economics—calculative, asocial, devoid of feelings—and his subsequent conception of market actors as equipped with tools but also socially embedded, which he labeled "homo economicus 2.0." Callon referred to the combined effect of devices and networks as *habilitation*, and illustrated this process with reference to disabled wheelchair users: by itself, a wheelchair or another form of prosthesis does not fully integrate its user; it is the combination of wheelchairs, accessible ramps, legal rules, etc., that restores accessibility for the wheelchair users.[15] In a similar way, it was the combination of Max's models and networks, his spreadplot and business contacts, that accounted for his profits.

A similar message emerged when I compared my findings to Knorr Cetina and Bruegger, subsequently elaborated by Knorr Cetina and Alexandru Preda.[16] At first blush, the use of the spreadplot and implied probability resembled the shift from pipes to scopes (that is, from networks to trading terminals) that Knorr Cetina and Preda had theorized. Indeed, Max's engagement with the market had many of the characteristics of the scopic market that Knorr Cetina had originally posited: the traders' sense of shared experience was grounded in simultaneous exposure to economic events, attention was centered on the screen, and high returns hinged on better technological infrastructure—in Max's case, a better spreadplot.

However, much of what Max did departed from Knorr Cetina and Bruegger's conception of the financial market, which was primarily screen-based. Chief among these departures was the critical importance of Max's local networks, which Max engaged to resolve the ambiguity that sprang from his instrument, the spreadplot. As I had witnessed, the same number had different meanings at different times of the morning, so that what seemed like an opportunity at 10:00 am could be a potential danger two hours later. Indeed, every time Max interrupted his on-screen experience to take a phone call or talk to traders at other desks, he was brought back to the physical reality of his colleagues sitting next to him. Max's morning could thus be described as an exercise in toggling back and forth between the screen world and his social milieu. It was no wonder, then, that Max referred to a good arbitrageur as a taxi dispatcher.

My findings also spoke to MacKenzie and Millo's claim that models had become an integral part of the market, rather than an external representation of it. I observed two aspects of this dynamic at play in Max's case. While the use of models was central to modern arbitrage, my observations at Max's desk suggested that modeling was not the only activity traders engaged in. The traders spent almost two hours modeling the Whitman-Career merger, but once the arbitrage trade was thus "set up," the traders merely relied on the model to observe their competitors' estimates, test their own views, and increase or decrease their trading positions on the basis of their relative comfort. The resulting level of exposure, which for the coming nine months would rise and fall with Max's degree of confidence in his own views vis-à-vis those of his rivals, was not a result of the model but of his prior experience, his database, and his networks. From that standpoint, Max's models were an input into his trades, but his trades were a combination of models, technologies, and social relations.

The implication is that models have not reduced the role of social relations in markets, but have transformed it instead. Specifically, the combination of models and social relations provided Max with a level of rigor, empirical scrutiny, and reflexiveness that was suggestive of an academic department at a university. Models had not eliminated the social aspect of trading, but had altered trading, turning it into an activity that is given to deliberation. David Stark and I sought to capture this transformation with the expression "reflexive modeling."[17]

6

Managers

My conversations with the various traders piqued my curiosity about a functional area of the bank that I had not previously considered: risk management. Given the traders' concerns about risk management, and Bob's skepticism of the figures and estimates that this department produced, I had become intrigued by (if not downright suspicious of) risk management. A quick search in the academic literature revealed that the use of models in risk management was developed in the 1970s at a now-defunct Wall Street bank, Bankers Trust. Such models were developed further at JP Morgan during the 1990s and had been globally adopted after the Basel II Accord of the Committee on Banking Supervision in 1999, as well as Sarbanes-Oxley in 2003. But despite widespread diffusion of risk management, a growing literature in critical accounting had expressed skepticism about its effectiveness. Michael Power, for instance, saw risk management as an ineffective tool that took place "in a climate of organizational defensiveness and a logic of auditability," where the emphasis was placed on avoiding institutional sanctions rather than reducing actual dangers for companies.[1] Similarly, several accounts of the downfall of Long-Term Capital Management, including MacKenzie's, had identified risk management as a key factor that aggravated the precarious situation of the fund in 1998. Risk management forced the fund's rivals to reduce the size of their positions, increased the temporary mispricings, and drained liquidity from the embattled hedge fund. Intrigued, I asked Bob to put me in touch with the executive responsible for risk management at International Securities. He introduced me to Lewis Cabot, head of the bank's Risk Management Department.

The Risk Management Department

A few days later, I met with Lewis in his office at International Securities' Risk Management Department. The unit, located one floor below Bob's trading room, presented an odd mix of similarities and differences with the trading room I knew well: it had the exact size, height, and views as the floor above, yet the two felt very different. As I walked in, instead of an open-plan layout with rows upon rows of traders and flat-panel screens, I found traditional cubicles with mid-height partitions and employees working in solitude. Because of the partitions, the employees had no view beyond their computer screens, but someone walking behind them could see what they were doing. There was also a striking silence, which contrasted with the humming sound of multiple conversations in the trading room above.

Lewis and I met in his glass-walled office, which was not unlike Bob's office upstairs. Lewis was prematurely bald and wore small round metal glasses, giving him the appearance of a scientist. He spoke in the language of the mathematical economist, with multiple references to agency problems and the "risk-return equation." But far from hiding behind technical jargon, Lewis provided an account of his work and challenges that was insightful and revealing. To him, financial institutions lived in a world of imperfect certainty, where the future was truly unknown. This seemingly simple premise, when taken to its ultimate conclusions, led to paradoxical implications. "Suppose," Lewis said of a fictional investor, "that you think prices are going to fall. Should you sell your entire portfolio?" No, he answered, because you might be wrong, so it would be wiser to sell only a part of it. "Now suppose," he added, "that you expect your trading strategy to lose millions in the following year. Should you close it?" No, he answered again, because in the end it might not lead to those losses, and the profits from it might be necessary to make up for losses in other desks. Lack of certainty, in other words, changed how decisions should be made.

Risk management, Lewis explained, was an attempt to confront that uncertainty in an organized fashion. One of his department's functions was to understand how the different positions taken by the traders affected each other. He referred to this as *portfolio optimization*. Equities and options traders, for instance, could tell what their respective positions were, but they did not know where they stood relative to other traders in the bank; as Lewis put it, "they can't define their risk-return equation." This is where Risk Management came in: "we aggregate the risks taken by the different divisions of the bank," Lewis explained. The key tool that Lewis employed for this purpose was a model known as "Value at Risk." This produced "risk capital," or the capital needed to offset the potential losses from a given trading position. Risk capital, or "risk dollars," to simplify, was a theoretical magnitude that could be used to compare between competing investment possibilities. "Consider two investments of

$100," said Lewis, "one in shares of Coca-Cola, and another in US Treasury bonds." If both securities offered the same return, one would quickly conclude that bonds are preferable, because stocks are generally riskier. However, what if bonds yield 7 percent and stocks yield 10 percent? This apples-to-oranges comparison problem was pervasive in a bank, and risk capital allowed them to make these comparisons. "We treat risk as a cost," Lewis added, because the bank had to set aside a certain level of risk capital for every dollar that was put at risk. According to the risk capital calculations Lewis used, an investment of $100 in equities was equivalent to one of $1,000 in US Treasuries in terms of the capital the bank had to set aside to offset its risk. Using these equivalences and looking at different possible outcomes and correlations between securities, Lewis decided whether a business within the bank was performing or not. "If it is not, we have to consider whether to change something or close it down."

The process, Lewis admitted, was necessarily imperfect and engendered suspicion. "The main reason for the mistrust is that risk capital ends up being meaningless, because of the many assumptions that are involved." A large number of those assumptions were often not satisfied. "Fortunately, many cancel each other out, so you trust the overall number thanks to the Law of Large Numbers." Lewis was alluding to the probability theorem stating that the larger the number of trials, the closer the average result will be to the long-run theoretical value. The Law of Large Numbers, Lewis cautioned, only applied at the level of the entire bank and not to individual businesses such as Equities (in reference to Bob's division). "The lower the level, the less you can trust the assumptions." Hence, Lewis concluded, the need to place strict, hardwired limits on each individual business. Another implication was that a change in risk capital could not simply be taken at face value. As he put it, "you see that risk capital went up today. Did *risk* really go up? This is why we can't rely on computers to do the risk management."

There were additional functions that the Risk Management department performed. One was ensuring the bank had enough capital to confront a reasonable level of losses, as measured by risk capital. This function was known as *capital adequacy* and was a way to protect the health of the bank, "even if its shareholders would want us to take on more risk, because they can offset it in their portfolio." From Lewis's perspective, shareholders might well push for risky decisions that could bankrupt the bank, as this might be in their narrow self-interest, and Lewis saw his job as preventing that. Furthermore, shareholders were not the only group with perverse incentives. "Traders basically have call options," Lewis said: if they did well, their pay went up, but if they lost money, they did not have to pay the bank back. "There is a conflict of interests," he concluded. For that reason, an additional responsibility of Lewis's department was to place risk limits on the traders' positions.

I knew from my conversations with Bob that placing limits on the traders' positions was very problematic, so I asked Lewis to elaborate. Lewis's perspective came down to the ultimate nature of arbitrage. "Traders say they're arbitrageurs. They all say they hedge. But just because you hedge you may not have eliminated all the risks." A trader may be buying in New York and selling the exact same security in Los Angeles, but what if the telephone line goes down? "Risk Management comes back and says, '*there's no arbitrage.*' They are taking risks." Lewis, however, also recognized that he could not just ignore the point of quantitative finance, which was to use models to develop a distinct perspective about risk and return. "If you look at the traders' positions with disregard for their models, what they're doing seems crazy. You would restrict them," but this would do away with quantitative trading in the first place, so a complete disregard for economic models was not sensible either.

The solution to the dilemma was, again, establishing limits, or risk controls, at different levels of the organization: the individual trader, the business, etc. Lewis's department allocated risk capital in fixed proportions to the different businesses. "Suppose risk capital is allocated 50–50 between equities and treasuries." If there were losses of 65 in equities and 30 in treasuries, Lewis added, "you might think this would be acceptable, as it still adds up to less than 100 in total. But it would not be. You want each individual business to be within its own internal limits." Rigidity, in other words, was the answer to the uncertainty Risk Management faced about the degree to which the models used by the traders really worked.

Regulators, Lewis added, had been instrumental in promoting the development of risk management. The American government, concerned that bank insolvency might negatively impact the economy, had traditionally protected the bank deposits of Americans. However, deposit insurance created a problem of moral hazard, as it encouraged bank depositors to choose the riskiest, highest-interest-paying bank, safe in the knowledge that they would get their deposits back. Similarly, "until twenty years ago," Lewis explained, "the guiding principle for risk management was a set of rules: banks cannot own stocks, and so on." But these rules sometimes had negative unexpected consequences. For instance, the rule that forced banks to operate in a single state, originally imposed to reduce systemic risk, had created a new form of risk. Because the main asset of a bank often was the real estate holdings on its book, limiting a bank's presence to a single state forced on it a geographically undiversified exposure. As a result, when house prices in a state experienced a crunch, banks in that state tended to go bankrupt. Partly for that reason, policy makers had switched to encouraging banks to control their risks themselves.

Our conversation then moved to a recurring theme in my observations at Bob's trading room: physical proximity. Lewis argued that proximity also played a key role in risk management. It was difficult, he noted, to interpret model-generated figures such as risk capital. For that reason, Lewis was in constant communication with the fifty or so main decision-makers at International Securities. He visited the equities trading floor frequently and found the interactions with the traders "very valuable." Indeed, this form of presence and conversations was not available to Lewis's supervisor abroad, the global Head of Risk Management. "I wouldn't want his job," Lewis said, to my surprise. "Finding out about risk at a distance is extremely complicated."

Our conversation closed with a discussion of Long-Term Capital Management. Lewis had read Lowenstein's analysis of the fund's demise, *When Genius Failed.* To him, the case of Long-Term Capital Management illustrated a fundamental paradox in risk management, namely that risk controls were potentially counterproductive, but nevertheless necessary. If every investor simultaneously revised up his risk estimates in the face of a new risk, every investor would reduce his investments at the same time, thereby impacting stock prices and creating a new form of risk, a second-order risk.[2] This was one reason for the adverse price movements that caused the initial losses at Long-Term Capital Management: the Russian bond default prompted market participants to pull back.

At the same time, Lewis added, it was important to remain skeptical of financial models, and to close seemingly correct positions when losses accumulated beyond a certain level. "When the market says that a bond is worth $3.80 and the model says $4.00, you know the real value must lie between $3.80 and $4.20. But traders at Long-Term Capital Management always took what their model said to be true." I understood the dilemma but countered that this was precisely the point of quantitative finance: the models inform the trading. What alternative, I asked, did they have? "That's right," Lewis replied. "The difference is that at some point the banks said, 'stop it.' Long-Term Capital Management did not. *When I read that book, I started believing in my own job,*" Lewis added, implying that he did not fully believe in risk management before the Long-Term Capital crisis. Confronted with such a candid confession of self-doubt, I did not quite know what to reply. "Thank you," I mumbled, and gathered my things to leave.

Understanding Risk Management

Back at NYU, and while transcribing the day's notes, I considered the surprising ambivalence that Lewis had expressed about his own department, Risk Management. This was new to me, in that none of the other traders I had spoken to before had professed any doubt about the value of their job, or their importance to the company. The skepticism that Lewis had conveyed, however, was consistent with Bob's rejection of quantitative risk management,

as well as with research by Power and others. But if Risk Management departments on Wall Street did not actually manage risk, why did they continue
to exist? The more I empathized with the dilemmas Lewis faced, the more
confused I felt about risk management.

In my search for clarity, I decided to return to the academic literature on
risk management. This revealed an intriguing history. In its original form,
financial risk management was developed at a Wall Street bank called Bankers Trust in 1973 by an executive named Charles Sanford, who went on to
become its chief executive officer.[3] It was originally conceived as a way to
systematically compare investments with similar rates of return to avoid the
customary reliance on subjective judgment and routine. Sanford reasoned that
a trader who took a position was introducing a new risk into the bank, so the
cost of that risk should be considered when appraising the trader's returns.
He proposed to estimate such cost in terms of the capital needed to offset the
maximum potential loss inherent in the trader's position. He called this "risk
capital," as Lewis had explained to me. Risk capital was then used in deciding
which projects to undertake by adjusting the expected returns of the various
projects to reflect their risk.

Risk capital was not only successful within Sanford's unit, but went on
to be adopted in numerous other departments at his bank, reshaping them
in the process and elevating Sanford to the position of CEO. Other banks
soon started imitating Bankers Trust's approach. Risk management was then
combined with probability theory in the 1990s: instead of using the *maximum*
possible loss, risk managers used a probabilistic loss, that is, losses with a 95
percent or 99 percent probability, to capture the concept of a *reasonable* loss.
This approach was adopted and further refined at JP Morgan at the request of
its CEO, Dennis Weatherstone, who famously called for a "4:15 report" that
would combine all firmwide risks on one page and be made available within
15 minutes of market close. The resulting indicator was called Value at Risk.[4]
Unlike the original version developed at Bankers Trust, where the concept of
risk capital was employed to choose between competing investments, at JP
Morgan it became a tool for managing the bank's overall exposure. Value at
Risk underwent yet another transformation on its route to global adoption.
In 1999, the Bank for International Settlements introduced it in its capital
requirements framework, known as the Basel II Accord, integrating it in the
supervision of the global banking industry. Thus, in the span of less than two
decades, Value at Risk was globally diffused, and risk management departments were created and charged with ensuring compliance with international
capital adequacy regulations.

The above helped me make sense of Lewis's dilemmas. Although in its
early development risk management had been a strategic initiative at leading Wall Street banks, its adoption in the rest of the financial industry was a

combination of imitation and compliance. Less successful banks had yielded to regulatory pressure and copied the practices of JP Morgan. A bank like International Securities, in other words, had few options but to have a Risk Management department. This explained why Bob had decided not to rely on the output produced by Risk Management. His response was a deliberate case of what institutional sociologists call decoupling, that is, disconnecting actual practices from formal policies. As I understood this, I also grasped Lewis's reservations about his own effectiveness. He was in charge of the Risk Management department, but senior managers like Bob did not find his numerical output useful, or relevant.

My conversation with Lewis also revealed the sophisticated rationale behind the use of bureaucratic rules in risk management. The bank's traders used economic models to attain extraordinary returns, but Lewis was expected to question the assumptions behind those models without simply replicating the traders' thought processes, as that might simply reproduce the traders' mistakes. Given the delicate nature of his position, Lewis had to walk a fine line between too much leniency and excess rectitude. His solution was to rely on bureaucratic rules, that is, hardwiring the use of capital across the various divisions of the bank, and fixing position limits for the traders.[5] The unit essentially created and administered fixed rules and limits. This explained why the Risk Management department was on a different floor than equity derivatives, and also explained the outdated appearance of its layout. As the issuer of impersonal rules, the department shared many characteristics with a Weberian bureaucracy.

Unlike a classic bureaucracy, however, Risk Management was hampered in its application of impersonal rules by the ambiguous meaning of the risk capital figures. To understand what a change in the Value at Risk number meant, Lewis needed specialized knowledge and social cues he could obtain only by talking to Bob and others in the bank. Thus, even Risk Management, predicated as it was on the social separation between its officials and the traders, required context to make judgments, and resorted to interaction with the traders to obtain it. In this paradoxical need for both distance and proximity, Lewis reminded me of Max and his complaints about excess noise: both were attempting to manage their relations in order to gain both insight and independence.

Finally, the dilemmas entailed in risk management brought me back to Lewis's reading of Lowenstein's book on Long-Term Capital Management. One of Lowenstein's core theses is that the fund failed because its founders and senior partners professed excessive faith in financial models. This claim has subsequently been challenged by MacKenzie's re-analysis of the case, which instead blamed the existence of limits to arbitrage, arguing that the fund's models were correct but market mispricings persisted for too long, making its position untenable.[6] Paradoxically, however, Lowenstein's thesis helped Lewis justify his own work as risk manager, for, in the presence of imperfect arbitrage models, the case for position limits becomes compelling.

My conversation with Lewis not only impressed on me the importance and significance of risk management, but also its limited effectiveness and the inner self-doubt that it created. Arbitrage was imperfect, I now understood, but so was risk management. My meeting with Lewis, in other words, had explained Bob's skepticism about risk management. It had also explained the reason for the widespread presence of this limited and imperfect practice: regulatory compliance. However, my meeting with Lewis had also given rise to more questions. At this point, I decided to email Bob to request another meeting with him. If risk management truly did not work, I planned to ask him, how did he instill restraint on the floor?

Heavy Losses

Bob and I met a few days later. On the day of my visit, I found him notably tense. "You seem to come in on days of heavy losses," Bob said, barely managing a smile as we shook hands. He was referring to an earlier visit of mine, which had taken place on a day of tumbling prices and trading losses during the dot-com crash of the year 2000. As we finished shaking hands, Bob led me to his private office, closed the door, and sat in front of an oversize Bloomberg screen in order to monitor ongoing market events while he spoke to me. As soon as he sat down, however, he quickly changed his mind and proposed that we move back to his desk. He wanted to remain in contact with the trading room, he said, and valued that more than having privacy for our conversation. "We lost a decent amount of money today," Bob said, "and the day before. I'm very bearish. Stanley is too." Stanley was the "minister without portfolio" that Bob had tasked with promoting communication across desks. He reported directly to Bob, and the two engaged in brainstorming whenever unusual market developments took place.

Bob's concern was not unjustified. In the two previous days, the Nasdaq composite index had experienced consecutive drops, leading to indiscriminate sales. "People were just chucking things out the window," according to the *Wall Street Journal*.[7] Yet the real cause of Bob's concern was not the declining prices but the fact that no one seemed to know the reason for it. Was it the fate of the US spy plane in China? Was it the latest round of corporate profit warnings? I brought up Knight's distinction between risk and uncertainty, and its implications for trading. This resonated with Bob: "uncertainty on the floor means you can't even identify what the problem is," he said, as was the case on that day. The effect of uncertainty on traders, Bob added, was paralysis: "the way traders normally operate is, they don't start with theories but with intuitive conclusions that they try to justify. If they can't fit them into a rational argument, they may give up."

In Bob's case, he dealt with uncertainty by turning to other people. "Yesterday I called Morgan Stanley. I usually try to find out what they're up to . . . and they're doing terrible. I spent some time at night yelling at the kids, what you usually do in these cases. I checked some screens, tried to find out what is going on in the market. Then today I tried to sell others my view of what's going on." In other words, like the traders that worked for him, Bob turned to others in response to uncertainty. Unlike them, however, uncertainty gave Bob a chance to influence his subordinates. Bob debated ongoing events with a few executives like Stanley, bracketed the relevant facts, and offered his own interpretation to the traders.

With a slight movement of the head, Bob shifted his gaze away from me and toward his Bloomberg terminal. I gestured to ask if he wanted me to leave, but he was happy to keep talking while he looked at the screen. Sitting in the middle of the room also gave him the ability to scan other traders and, more important, encouraged them to reach out to him if they needed to. Talking to me, I suspected, was helping him restore his emotional balance. He wanted me to keep talking about theories and take his mind off the market. Bob then received a phone call, and that gave me the opportunity to look around and take in the room in a special situation such as this.

I then saw something that startled me. A trader a few feet behind us had just stood up from his chair and was speaking on the phone with a volume and intensity I had not seen before. He was Joe, the head of the sales desk described in chapter 3. Unlike other desks in the trading room, this one did not do any proprietary trading. Bob had included this desk in the trading room because their conversations with customers gave the other desks a wealth of social cues, contacts, and an emotional tone that helped others understand the market, a form of soundtrack. Being salespeople, the traders in this desk also had a much more imposing presence and tone of voice. On the phone, Joe sounded like a general issuing commands: loud but controlled, urgent, authoritative. On any other day, the noise might just have been a nuisance. On a stressful and uncertain day such as that one, I panicked. Looking around, however, I saw that no one was reacting to the trader, so I decided to ignore it.

I turned to Bob, who had finished his call, and asked him about his managing of risk. How could he get away with not using the figures produced by Risk Management? "Typically," Bob said, "in firms like ours, Risk Management has little political power." The influence that such departments end up having, he implied, was independent of their technical merits and depended instead on their relative sway with the CEO. Bob was quite open regarding his skepticism about this department. But, I asked him, how did he do "his own" risk management? Partly through diversification, Bob replied. "I talk to the traders, try to find out if they are all doing the same thing, if the market is pushing them in the same direction." How was that diversity preserved? "First, we forbid people from imitating winning strategies. Traders cannot trade just what they want. An options trader has to trade options." Bob nevertheless admitted that some traders ended up replicating partial aspects of winning strategies, so he had put other measures in place. "We don't have formal meetings at the floor level among traders. But on the other hand, we don't forbid conversations at the water cooler." This was a surprise to me, as I thought that Bob favored all types of collaboration. Finally, Bob was mindful that imitation could take place at an unconscious level. "Sometimes," Bob said, "you don't know what's going on. You are ascribing some rationale to what you are doing after the fact." For example, "we are trying to have uncorrelated strategies. But all the strategies seem to be feeding off the same root. Even two trades as disparate as Morgan Stanley's fund portfolio rebalancing and the GE-Honeywell deal."

Our conversation then moved to the sensitive topic of position limits. How did Lewis decide that a trader's losses were high enough to justify closing his position? "We use comparable models," he replied. "Trade magazines provide indications on the performance of single-strategy funds." But again, this was of limited use, "because if you're not making a good comparison, you could be making a terrible decision. And if you are unique, looking at what others do does not help." Conversely, "sometimes it is traders who want to close their position, and it is the bank that is interested in keeping the position open."

Most important, Bob explained that he relied on his "management team" to handle risk. This was news to me, for I did not know there was such a thing as a management team on the floor. "I'll introduce you to Jerry, head of the stat arb units," he offered. "In order to manage traders, the cultural stuff is important. But it isn't enough. You need to have a real knowledge about what they're doing," Bob added. "You have to be a technician as well as a leader. And Jerry is, in essence, willing to be a technician." Jerry had worked with Bob for fifteen years at a previous bank, Premier Financial, and had done so in different locations. He was "emotional," Bob added, not very consistent, and became angry easily. "Jerry can get so angry," Bob said, "that I really should say that I am the one who works for him. He is an engineer, and you know how they are. I'll ask him, 'how's that model doing?' And he'll say, 'horrible, nothing's working.' And when I find out more, I realize the only problem is it has some slight inconsistencies that he dislikes. On the other hand, if then I go to him and refer to the model that does not work well, he'll deny it. 'Not well? Works perfectly!' " At the time, Jerry was working on improving the performance of Todd's robots. One of Todd's models was "discrete," in that it sought prices from the market once and then traded. Instead, Bob and Jerry wanted to turn it into a continuous one.

After almost an hour, it was time for me to go. Bob walked me to the exit, his frustration with the losses of the week becoming apparent. Out of the blue, he asked me about academic seminars in Manhattan. I told him about a few of them at NYU and Columbia, but my surprised tone prompted him to account for the question. "I don't get out of here enough," Bob added, by way of explanation. "I'd like to go somewhere where I can have complete anonymity."

Optimal Connectedness

Back at NYU, it took me a while to regain my own emotional balance. For the first time, I had experienced fear of the market. My own turmoil was only the result of emotional empathy, in that although I had no capital invested in Bob's bank and thus no money at risk, his troubled state of mind on that day had somehow transferred to me. Early in the visit, I now realized, the lack of a satisfactory emotional connection with Bob put me in a state of mild anxiety. This anxiety turned into fear when I became startled by the loud orders of one of the senior traders. Interestingly, the way in which my anxiety subsided was also social: based on the lack of reactions to the loud orders of the sales trader, I understood that there was nothing to worry about. Finally, the visit revealed something new to me: there was a vulnerable side to Bob. Like any parent, stress from the job ended up affecting him at home. In situations of stress, the carefully orchestrated sociability of the trading room was almost too much for him, and he wished he could disappear into an academic seminar.

Another novelty from my visit was the realization that Bob discouraged, rather than encouraged, the highest degree of integration among the desks. This contradicted my initial understanding, which was that integration was unambiguously desirable. Now I saw that there was an optimal degree of integration, beyond which additional connectedness was not desirable. The reason was the need to preserve diversity in the strategies pursued by the desk, and doing so was one important way to limit the overall risk the trading room faced. This, I now understood, was achieved through organizational procedures, encouraging informal interaction while prohibiting formal meetings across desks.

My final and more significant realization was that there was a layer of middle managers on the floor. This was consistent with Bob's view that the figures from risk management were of limited use; instead of using numbers, Bob had hired subordinates that he trusted—that is, former colleagues—to supervise the traders on the floor. I noted then that I knew very little about middle managers on Wall Street. They had been largely overlooked in the existing academic literature on finance, whether in the case of Baker, Knorr Cetina, or MacKenzie. What exactly did these managers do? What practices and tools did they draw on? How effective were they? I decided to pursue an answer to these questions by requesting meetings with Jerry and Stanley.

JERRY

Jerry and I met at a conference room on the trading floor. He was one of two middle managers with line responsibility over traders. He was in charge of several desks, including statistical arbitrage, to which Todd belonged. Jerry began our conversation by discussing his views of this trading strategy. "Stat arb," Jerry explained, "is the *opposite* of a traditional investment strategy. You look for patterns. You don't have to know the company you're buying or selling. The signals to buy and sell are coming from the computer." The strategy was relatively new to Jerry, he added, and he had taught himself stat arb in order to be able to supervise the four statistical arbitrage traders on the floor.

In doing so, Jerry had to overcome his traditional commitment to an orderly mathematical framework. "I was never a believer in statistics," he explained. "I was a foreign exchange trader, and studied bond math." Jerry's experience, in other words, had not prepared him to run a stat arb desk, where opportunities were not certain but happened with a certain probability. In his previous work as a bond trader, "you could lock in trades. You added it all up, it worked." The differences between locked trades and statistical arbitrage created initial friction in his relationship with Todd. "When I spoke with Todd, he said he traded based on some factors. I said, 'which factors?' And he said they were invisible. I hated him, and did not respect what he was doing." Eventually, however, Jerry found out about Todd's performance and his attitude softened. "He is not stellar. But he is consistent. He makes money every year, in a bull market as well as in a bear market. It is very difficult to do that, to make money every year, even if it is only a bit. I still hate him, but that's beside the point."

Jerry's interest in statistical arbitrage first developed after hearing about Renaissance Technologies and its exceptional performance. This New York-based hedge fund was founded in 1982 by a former academic mathematician, James Simons, and its flagship Medallion fund had had one of the best investment track records in financial history, averaging around 40 percent a year for nearly three decades. Renaissance was specialized in statistical arbitrage,[8] and its success had inspired Jerry. "So, I hired a couple of guys and set out to learn stat arb," Jerry explained. "My programming skills are not that good, but I tried to build a team. Along the way, we stumbled on a couple pathways, and now I understand Todd. I know what those invisible factors are." Jerry, however, still operated according to the premise that he needed to know why a trade made money, or, as he put it, he needed "to have principles." He added, "I realized that some rules really work. For example, my dad traded. Some old rules, like never sell on a down market, make sense. You put them in practice, and you realize that your returns are higher."

I asked Jerry about one of the challenges that Todd typically encountered, namely, situations where stocks lose their usual statistical properties: How do you know when to turn off the robot? To my surprise, Jerry had a ready

answer: "we back-test the models. We find out what is an acceptable deviation in returns and what is not, what is a three-standard-deviation event. We
have to distinguish a statistical mistake from a bug in the code. We put three
people side by side." Ultimately, Jerry thought, a model is a set of rules, so it
is possible to understand its rationale. "For example, the idea in the 'Dogs of
the Dow' is to buy the stocks with the highest dividend yield in the previous
year." Jerry was referring to the investment strategy popularized in 1991 by
Michael O'Higgins, who proposed that investors select the ten stocks in the
Dow Jones Industrial Average whose dividend is the highest fraction of their
price.[9] The difficulty, Jerry added, was that robots evolved. "If, for example,
you are following the Dogs of the Dow, the index may get reconstituted, and
you may find out that it works better on a quarterly basis, or that it works better
with the S&P 500 than with the Dow."

Ultimately, Jerry admitted, managing risk in statistical arbitrage entailed
a crucial difficulty: "it is not locked arbitrage; you can make the right decision and lose money." Statistical arbitrage thus called for a different way of
thinking about risk than in other forms of arbitrage: "you have to differentiate
between being blatantly wrong and making a bad bet." Also, it was essential to
understand the economic rationale behind an idea that worked. "The stat arb
trader has to be interested in markets, know statistics, and know computers;
if he just has quantitative skills, he might as well be doing biometrics." For
instance, Jerry added, "it is reassuring when you find out that the stocks the
model proposes as the main explanatory variable are the ones that everyone
is talking about. I need to have a rationale, that comfort level."

Jerry explained that his biggest challenge in managing the stat arb desk was
not conceptual, but interpersonal. "The mathematics are not that complicated.
It's linear algebra after all, factor models. You take a matrix of 3,000 stocks and
try to predict the movement of one with the rest. Much of the problem lies in
the execution." By execution, Jerry meant managing the stat arb traders. "We
have this Chinese mathematician, a genius. He has two PhDs. The problem
is, one of his positions will start to lose money, but he won't take it off." More
generally, "programmers are easily offended. If I say, 'Mike, this isn't working,'
he'll say, 'no, it works,' until I insist and show him that it does not, and then
he'll say 'oh, you're right.'" Similarly, Jerry could never praise someone's piece
of code in front of another programmer. "They'll say immediately, 'have you
tried *my* code?'" As a consequence, the stat arb traders sat separately from
each other. "Programmers are very antisocial. Paranoid. Schizophrenic. We
separate them. They don't talk to each other, but if you sit them side by side
with someone else, eventually they spill their view of the world."

Beyond that, Jerry's role was to flag problems: "I try to be noisy. If I see
something coming up, I'll shout." The programmer's reaction may not be

accommodating. "He'll say, 'you're fucking with my model.' I'll say, 'Look, I've saved your ass three times, and it's my money too, so you change that model.' That's how you build up your credibility. You impose something and then you turn out to be right." There were three actions that Jerry could ask a stat arb to do: pull a stock out, change an assumption, or switch the robot off. "The first one I have no problem with at all. Two I sometimes do. Three is tougher because you make the most money when the model is right and the rubber snaps back. But sometimes a model will not work, and I'll say, 'look, in two weeks we've made a very big hole.'" The rubber metaphor was used by traders to describe the quick reversion from losses to profits that takes place when the market comes around to a trader's perspective.

I was interested in one final aspect of Jerry's work. "What we do," Jerry said, "is data mining, and data is dirty." Data mining, that is, the search for correlations without drawing on prior causal hypotheses, was something I had been warned against repeatedly in my graduate courses on probability. I pointed this out to Jerry and asked him what potential concerns he had about data mining. "Well, I try out things that academics say do not work, and I find out they're working. Whenever I want to try something, I have this guy who is really good at finding what research has been done, so he pulls it out for me. I looked at a paper on stock option volatility, and the author found no correlation. But he mixed the options bought at the ask and at the bid. When I separated them, I found the pattern." Jerry thus appeared to draw from the academic literature on finance for his trading in the same vein as Bob, Todd, or Max. However, his relationship with it seemed more irreverent and instrumental.

Supervising Traders

Back at NYU, I realized that my conversation with Jerry had left me somewhat stressed, but also filled me with excitement and a sense of discovery. I had ventured into the unexplored realm of middle management on Wall Street. Sociological neglect of middle managers had privileged the work of traders and the buyer-seller transaction, whether in the form of tools, models, or networks, thereby overlooking the fact that those traders typically work in an organization, and that because this organization is structured as a form of hierarchy, they have a boss. Jerry's existence was a reminder that such structures and bosses could not be ignored.

One academic exception to this oversight was Abolafia's research, which presented supervisors as an effective source of structural restraint to Wall Street opportunism. In contrast to the bond traders Abolafia had once followed, his ethnography of the NYSE described two key layers of supervision, Exchange officials and "floor governors," that is, floor members who acted in a self-regulatory capacity, were distinguished from others by the red badges on their arms. The figure of the governor had been created to enforce the application of the formal "obligations" of specialist market-makers. According to Abolafia, the combination of officials and governors led to an "articulate, comprehensive and moralizing ideology consisting of the institutional rules of the trading floor."[10]

In light of the above, my own experience with Jerry was somewhat surprising. He certainly fit the role of norm enforcer documented by Abolafia, and indeed, the relationship between Jerry and Bob was symbiotic, for having a line manager like Jerry allowed Bob to focus on the big picture and liberated him from day-to-day interaction with all 150 traders. At the same time, Jerry did not quite fit my expectations of a supervisor that others would look up to. I was startled by his professing to "hate" a subordinate, his eschatological language, and especially by the verbal violence. Coming into contact with Jerry had left me somewhat frazzled. Meeting him after talking to Bob felt like moving from the center of a city to a different and more dangerous neighborhood.

In Jerry's defense, however, I also had to recognize that managing the statistical arbitrage traders seemed far more difficult than I had anticipated. Indeed, based on Jerry's description, it seemed that his work was not fundamentally about creative ideas, but about "execution." Once the math and the code came into contact with the stocks, complications cropped up. These included personal friction, caused by lack of work discipline and abrasive personalities, as well as social difficulties, including employees that disliked or imitated others. In short, managing stat arbs was rough, and this might justify some of the managing style that Jerry had displayed.

Beyond norm enforcement, another surprise from my visit was the extent to which Jerry found it difficult to accept the methods and techniques of statistical arbitrage, given his background in bond trading. The trading floor at International Securities seemed to possess something akin to what sociologists of science such as Karin Knorr Cetina had called epistemic cultures. These include the practices, arrangements, and mechanisms bound together by necessity, affinity, and historical coincidence that, in a given area of professional expertise, "make up how we know what we know." They are, in other words, differences between the various "machineries of knowing,"[11] and account for disparities across disciplines such as those that exist between high-energy physics and molecular biology. Like scientific disciplines, the different trading strategies on Bob's floor had different standards of proof and ways of establishing the value of securities.

In subsequent research, MacKenzie introduced a version of Knorr Cetina's concept into the study of finance with the idea of "evaluation practices," or locally bound beliefs about what is appropriate and inappropriate, shaped to a large degree by the calculative device. That knowledge-intensive disciplines such as science or finance fall into subgroups with common commitments to what is legitimate and appropriate, has important implications, because it highlights the problem of fragmentation. Differences across subcultures, in other words, constitute a barrier to communication. In the case of International Securities, my meeting with Jerry suggested that such differences could be addressed by his own willingness to retrain himself into the new practice he was supervising. My conversation with Jerry thus suggested he was engaged in two different forms of middle management: norm enforcement, and knowledge integration across desks.

The above were, however, preliminary findings based on a single manager. My next step, I concluded, should be to meet the other middle manager that Bob alluded to, Stanley. "Would that be possible?" I asked Bob. "Of course," he replied. "But there have also been changes to take into account," he added. Since my arrival at the trading room, Stanley's desk had moved from being close to the whiteboard to several meters away. Why? "Most people do not believe there is value in him," Bob explained. One reason was the difficulty in identifying his contribution. "If I take something from A and give it to B, do you think B thanks me when he goes home? No, he thinks, 'that was my trade.'" Knowing that Stanley could take their idea and share it with another desk, traders had taken to declaring they had nothing to give him. He would then argue with them to show them they were wrong and he was right. Given the animosity, Bob had decided to move him.

STANLEY

The first thing that struck me about Stanley was his youth. He was an overachiever who had made it to the managerial rank by age thirty-six, managing traders much older and more experienced than he. He also had the physical size and energy of a college athlete, and a degree of emotional intensity that came across as almost threatening. I started by asking him about his early career and learned that he started in finance in 1988 after obtaining an MBA from a prestigious business school known for its quantitative training. During the first year of his MBA he was fascinated by economic theory, but soon appreciated the practical side of life. After almost failing to secure a summer internship during his first year of business school, Stanley concluded he would have to be more pragmatic. "I learned," he said about his job interviews, "that it is very important to control everything that is happening in that [interview] room." In Stanley's final job search during his second year of the MBA, he received nineteen offers out of twenty job interviews.

Stanley met Bob at a bank where they both worked during the 1990s, Premier Financial. Unlike Bob, who never said much about Premier, Stanley felt inclined to talk about it. "Premier was a free, wild, crazy place. I learned a lot. Competitive, but not in a malicious way." The bank gave "an incredible amount of responsibility to young people, too much perhaps, which is maybe why some people abused it." He was making reference to a number of scandals in the mid-1990s that tarnished the bank's reputation. "It's funny, after that happened, there were a lot of references in the press about traders making derogatory remarks about customers. And it is true that they made them, because that was the culture of the place. But they were not serious. They were for play." After his time at Premier, Stanley decided to look for a smaller bank to leave his imprint on. Following a six-month sabbatical, he joined International Securities in 1998 "because of my relationship with Bob."

My conversation with Stanley provided me with the first temporal perspective on International Securities, and the changes that Bob had instituted there. When Stanley first arrived, he explained, "International Securities was a dysfunctional little firm full of fiefdoms. People didn't talk to each other. They were protective of their P&L [profit and loss accounts] and were compensated individually." There had been so much management turnover that traders were skeptical of any new management team. "They thought," Stanley noted, "that if they waited just a little bit, it would go just as the previous one had."

Bob, he recalls, set out to change that. He began to move people around. "Now, on the surface Bob looks very easygoing. Deep down, he can be ruthless. He does so by surrounding himself with very aggressive people. Like myself." Things were different now at the bank. "There is camaraderie and a sense that if people contribute to the general information flow and ideas, everyone can be better off. This is facilitated by the fact that there are no surprises in the compensation," he said in reference to Bob's percentage payout system. "There is also none of that false bravado of Premier. People come here because they want that freedom."

Once hired at International Securities, Stanley became part of the change process that Bob was introducing. Bob sought to promote communication by putting Stanley in charge of a common book of trades, a form of clearinghouse. "I looked at the strategies on the floor and realized that they were all very related. Trades would show up in different permutations in the different books." This placed Stanley in the difficult position of having to consolidate trades. "This ended up pinning me against them. I actually don't mind confrontation," Stanley said, "but I realized that for the traders this was not necessarily true." This, he thought, pointed to one interesting limit of transparency and open communication: "people resent being shown that they're wrong, that was one of the problems with the whiteboard."

After several months of perseverance, Stanley added, the duplication had been addressed. "The same trade appeared on several desks," but these desks used different strategies to profit from it. "Max may be betting on whether the deal will go through or not. The index arbitrage guys will be betting on index rebalancing. A lot of that cooperation used to happen at the whiteboard." How, I asked him, does being in the same trading room help? To benefit from the commonalties between strategies, he said, "you cannot do it unless you have a trading room," but that is only a necessary condition. "A culture of openness is even more important. The benefits of a trading room are sometimes exaggerated," Stanley said, "but I'll also tell you that, in the middle of all the noise, I am able to hear my [desk] phone ring. It has a particular tone."

Stanley thought about arbitrage as an essentially mental, rational, and logical activity. "I remember," he explained, "this TV show with three doors, and an option to choose between them. For thirty years, everyone was convinced that the order in which you chose was indifferent, but then a mathematician realized it was not the case. That, to me, is the definition of arbitrage. People know things when they have worked to find out." By contrast, he added, Bob operated in a very different way. "The way Bob manages is, he does not listen to what you say, but to the tone of your voice. If I say something to him and he finds me very committed, he'll tell me to go ahead with whatever it is that I propose. Then he'll ask how much I plan to commit, and since he knows I'm conservative, he'll suggest that I double it."

One of the reasons for the positive atmosphere in the trading room, Stanley added, was that "no one" was hoping to make a career in the upper ranks of International Securities, that is, to be promoted beyond the equity floor. "We are not looking to be bigger, or to take over fixed income. If anything, we would prefer to be smaller, which would make things easier to manage. International Securities lets us be part of them, and we share with them our profits." The bank's contribution to the trading room was the favorable credit rating, which allowed the traders to get capital at low rates. "In exchange, we are reasonable and don't take excessive risks during, for example, last year, which was bad. We could improve our results by playing Russian roulette, but then we might not be here again the following year."

Finally, the lack of rivalry within the management team was also important. "The way compensation is calculated for senior management means that there is no incentive for anyone to get more at the expense of someone else." The incentive for everyone was to help others make more money, and to be paid more in that way. "It is really what they call a true partnership. Have you ever come across the expression?" By "partnership," Stanley meant the traditional organizational structure of investment banks before the 1980s: small in size, and with joint liability. "Things are quite informal as a management team. We don't have very clear schedules, presentations, etc. At Deustche they say things like, 'I have gotten really good at setting someone up. It may take me some time, six months, nine months, but eventually I'll do it.'" At International Securities, Stanley implied, this did not happen.

From Risk Management to Line Management

I reflected on my conversation with Stanley while transcribing my field-notes. His "minister without portfolio" position was an intriguing one: he was expected to connect desks that were active on related trades, but which were not already collaborating. This emphasis on connecting was suggestive of the relational nature of trading, in line with Baker's research.[12] Baker's trading crowds, however, did not have a central figure that brought together and connected others like Stanley. Instead, the sociological concept of "brokerage" developed by Ronald Burt captured this active role. The broker in Burt's writings exploited and remedied the existence of "structural holes," or gaps between individuals who had non-redundant information. Such gaps typically exist because social life is arranged in clusters of strong connections that are weakly linked to each other. Thus, someone connected to more than one group will be able to transfer valuable information from one group to another.[13] In crafting the "minister" position and appointing Stanley to it, Bob seemed to have progressed down the path of a network-inspired trading floor that he initiated when drawing on the anthropology of Robin Dunbar. Bob was not only ensuring there was trust by limiting the size of the floor and creating spaces for open discussion, but also creating an intermediary role to guarantee that traders collaborated across desks.

Surprisingly, however, the "minister without portfolio" role was not quite working for Stanley. He had been moved away from the whiteboard. The reason for it, I could now see, was because Stanley's proximity discouraged traders from using the whiteboard, as they did not want him to take their ideas. I could hardly blame them, given my own unsettled feelings after meeting Stanley. He had been generous with his time, and his mental speed was impressive, but he seemed more skilled in conveying his own thinking, including the sense of anxiety that comes from intellectual discovery, than in having a calming influence on others. Like Jerry, Stanley seemed willing to win every technical discussion at the cost of his personal rapport with others. Indeed, his approach was consistent with his view of arbitrage as a game show with three doors: cognition and logic, rather than teamwork. Perhaps it was for that reason that Stanley was skeptical of the corporate aspect of Wall Street. The reason for the success of Bob's trading room, he had ventured, was that they were not trapped in the larger structure of the bank. Such an anti-hierarchical conception of the world—a form of libertarianism, applied to finance—was clearly informing Stanley's approach to his own job.

Norm Enforcement and Integration

Overall, my conversations with Lewis, Jerry, and Stanley opened up an unexpected window into an obscure but critical corner of Wall Street: its managers. While my original interest had centered on the traders, I had now come into contact with the less-known but equally important individuals that were responsible for them.

The limited attention to these managers in the existing literature suggests an implicit view of markets and organizations as separate realms, in which companies are purposively organized, while markets are self-organized. Such self-organization has been characterized as network structures or material configurations and spurred further theorizing about the effect of information technology and financial models on Wall Street. However, my interactions with Jerry and Stanley—and especially my direct experience of their intensity and stubbornness—was a theoretical wake-up call. Wall Street traders, I now saw with clarity, were themselves being managed. They had a boss. The organizations versus markets duality that economic sociologists had tacitly presumed needed to be revised, because those traders were not freely operating in a market, but were enabled and constrained by the organization they were part of.

Abolafia's research, by contrast, has resolutely emphasized the role of floor managers as promoters of restraint and enforcers of institutional norms. There is nothing inevitable, he contends, about opportunism on Wall Street, and financial organizations can be shaped through structural and cultural mechanisms so as to limit such opportunism. Middle managers are key to this process. The creation of a formal middle manager position such as "Floor Governor" at the NYSE had decisively contributed to the enforcement of trading rules and formal obligations and contributed to preventing floor brokers and specialists from taking advantage of investors.[14]

The two middle managers I spoke to, Jerry and Stanley, were also a reminder that there were limits to informality and space as the basis for organizing, suggesting that those elements were only a complement to an existing hierarchy. One way to visualize this hierarchy was by thinking of the trading room as a pyramid (see figure 6.1). At the top there was Bob, below him were his two subordinates, Jerry and Brian (I had not yet spoken to the latter), and below them were the various traders, grouped by desks. Separately, and interacting directly with the various desks, was Stanley. Finally, Lewis and the Risk Management department are left outside the figure because he reported directly to the head of the entire US subsidiary of International Securities.

What effect did such hierarchy have on Bob's trading floor? Norm enforcement was clearly at the heart of Jerry's work, which was expected to ensure that stat arb traders limited their losses so as to protect the bank. Another role

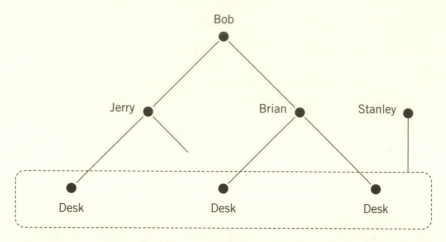

FIGURE 6.1. The organizational structure of the equities trading floor at International Securities.

undertaken by Bob's middle managers was integration. This was clearly evident in the case of Stanley and his efforts at ensuring collaboration across desks.

My conversations with both Jerry and Stanley also highlighted the challenges of creating a managerial structure on a trading floor. These middle managers were conduits for trust: they controlled, transmitted orders, developed expertise, and enforced the policies of their own manager, Bob. Both of them had worked with Bob in their previous bank, which illustrated the sheer difficulty of ensuring trust in a materialist environment such as Wall Street, with so many opportunities for malfeasance. Both managers also needed to possess an advanced technical understanding of the trading strategies, and indeed Jerry had to train himself in statistical arbitrage while Stanley seemed to be knowledgeable about quantitative finance in general. Finally, both managers needed skills for handling the interpersonal challenges of exerting authority, including addressing the emotional reactions of subordinates. My observations suggested this was not something they had yet completely mastered, nor developed an appreciation for.

My observations of Bob's management team thus spoke to a tradeoff between technical and managerial talent. The more technical finance became, the greater the technical requirements for managing such traders, and the narrower the pool of available talent that might also have the necessary interpersonal skills. Insensitive or offensive Wall Street managers limited the effectiveness of the exercise of power through formal mechanisms. This was particularly clear in Stanley's limited success at integration, to the point that the traders had cut down on their conversations at the whiteboard for fear of his intervention.

The above shed new light on how my conversation with Lewis, the head of Risk Management, spoke to the nature of management on Wall Street. Risk management, and specifically the use of Value at Risk, had developed in the previous three decades as a quantitative complement to the work of managers. It informed the problem of project selection by middle managers, helped with the task of monitoring capital adequacy that chief financial officers needed to do, and was a tool used by regulators across countries to restrain risk-taking in banks. But as much as Value at Risk was meant to be a *management tool*, Bob had clearly warned that it was used as a *management substitute*. It was easier, he implied, for regulators to demand the use of Value at Risk than to monitor the quality of a bank's middle management, even if the risk capital figures produced by risk management departments seldom captured the actual perils that banks confronted. It was for that reason that Bob had decided not to exert control through model-based indicators like Value at Risk. Line management, rather than model-based management, was Bob's approach to ensure that risk-taking was handled with judgment.

7

Performative Spirals

By the summer of 2002, my research reached a milestone. I had been visiting Bob's trading room since November 1999, interviewing the traders and observing their work.[1] However, I still felt I lacked the habituation and familiarity that arises from closer involvement. Could I, I wondered, spend more time on the floor? I asked Bob for a pass and a desk, and he agreed to it. I would be provided with an official magnetic bank ID, a Dell workstation, an Aeron chair, and an elaborate phone turret like those used by the traders. This would allow me to observe, overhear, and enter into casual conversation with whoever would be willing to speak to me rather than those Bob suggested I speak to.

On the first day at my own desk, I took stock of the new possibilities ahead of me. I could now eavesdrop with greater freedom than before, but my neighbors were not particularly high-ranking in the organization. To my right there was Ali, Bob's driver, who appeared to be browsing the web whenever Bob did not need him. To my left there was an empty desk. Behind me there was a corridor, and behind that corridor sat several summer interns, two of whom were leaving on that day. Because of the corridor, however, I could not hear what the remaining interns were saying, either. There was, in other words, not much to gain from attempting to overhear others from my seat. But I was in. I could come in and out as I pleased.

Earlier that day, as I obtained my pass, I had the opportunity to see the Human Resources department. This was located one level below Risk Management and shared the floor with other service units such as External Relations. Like Risk Management, Human Resources was laid out in cubicles and closed offices, but while the former was mostly staffed by men sitting in similar-sized partitions, Human Resources featured multiple departures from corporate minimalism: the walls were decorated with figurative paintings in the style of

Norman Rockwell, and the employees' cubicles had children's drawings pinned to them. There was also greater demographic diversity, with a dominance of females, many from ethnic minorities. Officially, I was an intern, but the staff in Human Resources were unclear and somewhat suspicious as to why I was not on the payroll like other interns. The confusion was deliberate. The only administrative means that Bob found to provide me with a pass was to make me into a formal intern, even though obviously I would not be paid.

LEAH

My experience at the Human Resources Department impressed on me an important shortcoming of my study: I had barely spoken to anyone in the bank who was not a trader or a manager (I had also barely spoken to female employees; see the methodological note for the limitations of such an approach). My first opportunity to interview an administrator arose after meeting Leah, a part-time employee at the New Accounts Department. Leah was a lively woman in her mid-thirties who spoke with a thick Long Island accent. She lived in Long Island with her husband, who had his own business as an electrician, and her two young children. Her commute to the World Financial Center took one and a half hours each way; on the days she worked, she woke up at 5:30 am and got back home at 9:30 pm, after her children had already been tucked in by Leah's mother. For that reason, she worked part-time, coming to the office three days a week. They never offered her the option to work from home. "I guess they want me to be in the office while I am working," she concluded.

Leah had been working for International Securities for twelve years, but she had only been at New Accounts for two. I asked her, "do you work for the traders?" and her answer was: "no, I work with actual human beings." But she said that laughing, and with no bitterness. "The majority of traders are very good people, it's just two or three who are difficult," she added. The source of conflict was that in order to open a new account, there was some information that the traders had to provide, and sometimes they did not do so, which meant she could not let them use the account, and they reacted negatively. "I mean, it's not that I don't want to, it's the regulations, what am I gonna do?" Instead of talking to the traders directly, she dealt with their sales assistants, "a buffer that helps a lot."

Leah acknowledged that traders made "a lot of money," but she said she did not feel a sense of injustice. She argued that they also had to bear a great weight and responsibility, pointing to the large box of Tums anti-acid pills in the middle of the trading room, next to the candies. They also "drank Maalox all the time," another anti-acid remedy. Furthermore, Leah pointed out, the traders left early, but they also arrived very early, many of them as early as half past six. She would not want to be a trader. She was more acquainted with analysts because she used to work as an administrative assistant in the Research Division. They also worked too much, she concluded. Lisa had always worked at International Securities. She knew a lot of the people there, as well as others who had left and with whom she still kept in touch. When asked, "how do you like it?" she said that her acquaintances who had left had found that International Securities was a good place. "They care for the business, but also for the personal."

THE OTHER WALL STREET

My quick visit to the Human Resources department, and especially my conversation with Leah, revealed a part of the bank that until then I had barely come in contact with. My experience with them reminded me of the campaign run by Fernando Ferrer, a candidate in the Democratic primary runoff for the municipal elections in New York City in 2001. His (unsuccessful) election campaign highlighted concerns of "the other New York," the part of the city excluded from the affluence of the stock market boom during the late 1990s. As with New York City at large, not everyone on Wall Street, or even in the same company, benefited from the riches generated by the stock market.

Leah, an administrative support employee, was arguably among those who had barely benefited. My conversation with her revealed her perspective on the traders, as well as the bank in general. Leah's world was one of sacrifice: long commutes, long hours on the days she worked, and difficult conversations with some of the traders. However, it was also one of job stability, family life, and a reasonable degree of stress from work. My conversation with Leah confirmed something that Bob had already alluded to, namely, the danger for social friction in the conversations between traders in the front and back office, given their status differences. Some of the traders, Lisa implied, were not "human beings." At the same time, the conversation with Lisa also revealed something about the traders: their level of stress, which was high enough to merit an institutionalized arrangement of free anti-acid pills.

TODD

A few days later, I did something that I had not attempted before: I casually walked over to Todd's desk for an informal chat, with no prior appointment. As usual, Todd was watching his algorithm trade, but he did not seem to mind my presence. He had a cynical theory about why I had been given a desk: there were too many empty places in the trading room. His performance during the year before had been unsatisfactory, and the trading room as a whole had had negative revenue and very high costs. Eighty-five people had been laid off firmwide, and there had been additional departures through attrition. Bob had been forced to lay off twenty employees from the trading room, mostly in operations and mainly in order to cut costs, so the total head count in the trading room had shrunk to 142 people. I had been offered a desk, Todd ventured, to give a sense that the room was less empty than it really was.

Todd's situation was not easy either. His trading strategy was "non-directional," that is, supposedly insulated from overall market movements. However, stock prices had moved so adversely during the preceding months that they had impacted the returns of even non-directional strategies like Todd's. The reason for such impact was that widespread losses had produced a new pattern in prices that, although not irrational, was inconsistent with the assumptions of Todd's models. "Large losses lead to forced liquidations among fund managers," Todd explained, adding that this had changed their strategies. "Redemptions of this sort turn fund managers into clerks. They just have to sell in order to raise cash." Indeed, stocks had become cheap, but investors kept selling them. As a result, stock prices did not "mean-revert," nor did they behave independently from corporate earnings, as Todd's model assumed. The corporate scandal atmosphere that started with Enron (the company had filed for bankruptcy in December 2001) had further altered market dynamics, creating additional difficulties for Todd. For instance, there often were 20 percent selloffs of single stocks "without any radically bad news," Todd said, "something unheard of." The outcome of such sharp falls in prices was that traders were constantly on the lookout for any sudden governance scandal in the companies in their portfolios.

To make things worse, internal turmoil at the bank had aggravated the losses experienced by the bank's traders. One month before I got my desk, Todd and others on the floor had been forced to cut their positions by a directive from corporate headquarters abroad. This was problematic, because a smaller position now meant that Todd would be unable to recover even if the market turned in his favor. To add insult to injury, and because of these unfair losses, Todd now received an email every day from Risk Management, copied to his boss, Jerry, about his daily performance. Todd felt scrutinized.

A Change in the Layout of the Room

A conversation I had with Bob a few days later spoke to this new environment. In response to the new and more difficult market dynamics, Bob had decided to change the layout of the room: "I am redoing the seating chart," Bob explained. But now it was proving more difficult than before. "After a couple years, everyone on the floor is thinking about what they're getting from their neighbors. People are asking, 'who are you sitting me with?'" This level of interest, paradoxically, created complexities for Bob. "It's funny," he added,

"I gave merger arbitrage the corner seats. People like them, they can look out the window, and so on. I thought they'd like them, but Max came to me and complained. In the past, he did not want to be near the sales force but now he does not mind." Max was now keen on avoiding being isolated. In sum, Bob felt vindicated in his attention to physical proximity, but his job had become more arduous because of it.

The changes that Bob was introducing in the seating chart, he added, sought to reflect the new market context. He had moved the "stock loan" desk to the periphery of the trading room because of the low-interest-rate environment. Stock loan was a desk that clearly interested Bob: "most people ignore stock loan," he said, "but their role is critical." They were necessary for merger arbitrage, he explained, because the latter involved shorting stocks (i.e., betting that their prices would fall), and shorting stocks required borrowing them through stock loan. "Most people put the stock loan desk on the operations floor, but we love to have it on the trading floor." Why? Bob pointed to the numerous quantitative cues that could gleaned from them: although using privileged information to trade ahead of a merger was illegal, it all too often took place among the less scrupulous banks, and this behavior ended up being reflected in the rates of lending and borrowing. "A stock is easy to borrow, suddenly gets tight, is tight all morning, and in the afternoon, a merger is announced," Bob explained. In other words, stock loan rates were predictive of merger announcements. As a result, stock loan traders could, without doing anything illegal, alert merger traders that something was about to happen simply by being attentive to the rates that were being quoted for borrowing stocks. (Unlike predicting merger announcements from tips from corporate insiders, which is illegal, using non-sensitive information such as borrowing rates, is not.) Bob continued: "then, as soon as the merger announcement has officially been made, the assistance can go the other way." Merger arbitrageurs could give stock loan traders a sense of merger likelihood and help them decide whether to borrow shares that could subsequently be lent back at a higher rate.

I asked if I could speak to the stock loan traders. Bob was happy for me to do so, but cautioned that this might not help me in my original goal of understanding quantitative finance. "In order to understand stock loan," he cautioned half-jokingly, "you would really have to change your mentality completely, or send a clone of yours. The desk is staffed a hundred percent by Italian Americans who live in Staten Island. The stock loan market functions with no screens. It is a guild. It's relationship-driven." Traders at stock loan, Bob added, socialized together on the weekends, drank together after work, and played soccer together. "They're more loyal to the guild than to the organization. If you tell one of them to name all the family relationships he has in stock loan, they'll come up with at least fifteen." This was yet another example of how different the practices, people, and types of knowledge prevailing in the various desks of International Securities could be. The importance of the stock loan desk on the trading floor, however, had recently decreased. In the previous bull market (between 1990 and 2000) and with the correspondingly high interest rates, borrowing stocks was difficult and stock loan was very important. Now, in an environment of lower interest rates and thus lower financing costs, the cost of borrowing was less important. Hence Bob's decision to send stock loan to the periphery.

The second change that Bob had introduced in the layout of the room was to place merger arbitrage next to the "long-short" desk. The latter specialized in betting on entire industries, such as healthcare, rather than individual stocks. Placing them next to merger arbitrage would allow Max and his traders to establish the potential antitrust risks to a proposed deal. Bob offered an example: "we had a merger between Ralston and Purina, the pet food companies. All of a sudden, the merger guys had to have a strong opinion about whether the Justice Department cares whether cat food and dog food should be consolidated into one company. True story. Well, if there's some guy doing consumer products in the long-short desk, he probably knows already, so rather than the merger arbs getting really heavy on Puppy Chow, there's some guy in the long-short desk who knows the sales cycle and how it works."

A third novelty introduced by Bob was to combine index arbitrage traders with the technology desk. This decision was due to technological changes in regulation that meant the practice of index arbitrage had changed completely. Index arbitrage traders exploited price differences between the S&P 500 index and the stocks that went into it. "Before, the way to make money was to have really large positions. Now, the key lies in fast turnover. For that reason, the index arbs are now mixed up with the technology guys. Of the sixteen tech people that we have, five are sitting with the index arbs." Yet another of Bob's changes was to move all the stat arb traders together, including Todd. This was part of a strategy, initiated by Jerry, to integrate their different algorithms. Finally, two of the customer sales analysts were moved to the periphery of the room for SEC compliance reasons (see figures 7.1 and 7.2).

To illustrate the gains from collaboration in the trading room, Bob had created a chart that captured his thinking (see figure 7.3). The chart showed the various potential sources of complementarity emerging from the merger arbitrage desk. Once a merger is announced, Bob explained, the merger desk is immediately activated and starts to set up an arbitrage trade. Their information will be helpful to Todd and others at the statistical arbitrage desk, who will need to rebalance their portfolio to exclude the merging stocks. The information might also be helpful to the traders at the convertible arbitrage desk, who will adjust their assumptions about credit spread and volatility, and to the traders at the options desk, who will adjust their volatility assumptions.

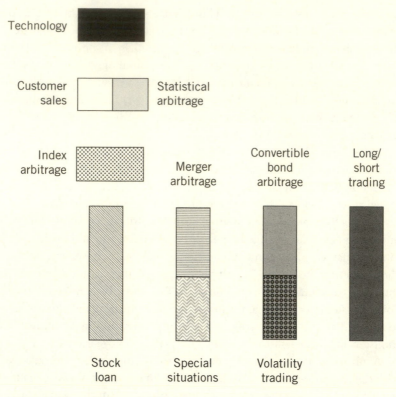

FIGURE 7.1. The trading room in 1999. In an environment of high interest rates, the stock loan desk was placed at the center of the room because of the relative importance of funding costs.

The stock loan desk may have already known that the merger announcement was coming from the tighter borrowing spreads, and once the announcement is out, merger arbitrage can help them understand changes in the spread. If the merger entails any unique provision (such as the DuPont-Conoco trade mentioned in chapter 2), the merger desk may be able to help the special situations desk. It can also assist the index arbitrage desk, as a stock will be replaced from the index (as in the case of Symantec presented in chapter 5). Finally, as Bob had explained, the long-short desk can provide the merger arbitrage desk with specialized knowledge of certain industries.

Bob's theorizing of the integration across desks went further. The various strategies in the room, he argued, belonged to one of three core categories, based on the type of knowledge they generated. The first was *fundamental* trading, involving company-specific or deal-specific research, and included merger arbitrage, stock loan, and others. By fundamental, Bob meant trading on the basis of the intrinsic properties of the listed companies. The second

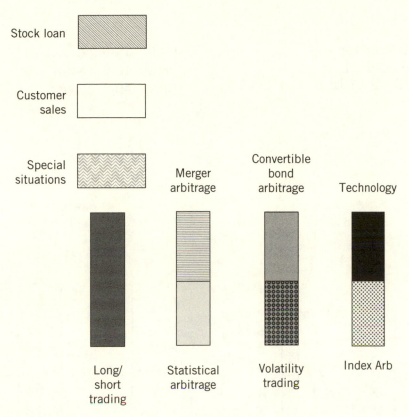

FIGURE 7.2. The trading room in 2002. In a low-interest-rate environment, the stock loan desk was moved to the periphery. Furthermore, as index arbitrage increasingly relied on speed and information technology, the technology and the index arbitrage desks were combined.

was *quantitative* trading, which included statistical arbitrage, the technology desk, and index arbitrage. In these strategies, the traders "do not know about stocks, but only about computer models and computer execution of trades." The third category was *volatility* trading, including convertible bond arbitrage and options arbitrage. These desks focused on how volatile stock price movements influenced the price of other securities such as options and convertible bonds.

The Multiple Properties of Stocks

Back at NYU, the conversation with Bob gave me plenty to consider. The presence of a phone-based desk such as stock loan within the trading room was an unexpected novelty. Bob's emphasis on how this desk was different from all the others provided supportive evidence of the arguments made by Knorr

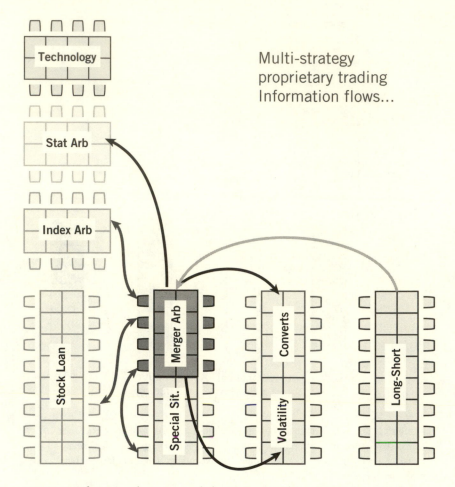

Multi-strategy
proprietary trading
Information flows...

FIGURE 7.3. Information-sharing across desks at International Securities in the event of a merger. *Source:* Bob's personal archive.

Cetina and Bruegger: as they claimed, screens had a transformative effect on the market, to such a degree that I would have to "send a clone" of myself to understand stock loan. At the same time, the case of stock loan qualified Knorr Cetina and Bruegger's findings in two ways. First, the form of embedded-ness that was found among stock loan traders did not simply entail relation-ships of trust, but a shared cultural background (Italian American), borough (Staten Island), and family (as many of them had numerous relatives in the trade). In that regard, the embedded nature of the stock loan desk was not only a network of trusted relations, as Baker described in his study, but also one that included interactions outside work, in the family sphere. A second way in which the case of stock loan challenged the depersonalization thesis developed by Knorr Cetina and Bruegger was that social ties did not appear less important at the merger arbitrage desk than at stock loan but seemed to have a different effect.

Aside from the stock loan desk, I was intrigued by the three financial properties that Bob had identified. He had taken apart, or, one might say, deconstructed, the financial value of a stock into several component aspects: fundamental, quantitative, and volatility. This was surprising to me, because I had always thought of stocks as having two basic properties: risk and return. This was based on my reading of the original research by Harry Markowitz and his seminal modeling of stock value in economic terms in 1952.[2] At the time, Markowitz's work was revolutionary for two reasons. First, he had made investors focus on the quantitative aspect of *stocks* themselves, risk and return, at a time when investors were typically tuned to the properties of the *products* that companies sold. For instance, shareholders in GM typically made investment decisions on the basis of the company's cars. Second, Markowitz showed that one could assume, without excessive oversimplification, that stock returns conformed to a Normal, or Gaussian, probability distribution, which meant they could be treated like many natural phenomena: people's height, body size, or the velocities of molecules in an ideal gas. This was critical, as it allowed investors to quantify the statistical mean and variance of stock returns, and measure risk. Before Markowitz, "risk" was an abstract and ambiguous concept; after him, it was measurable and concrete. In short, Markowitz brought numbers to bear upon financial investments, boiling the complexity of an investment decision down to two calculable magnitudes: risk and return.

Bob's traders, I now understood, were extending Markowitz's agenda: quantifying numerous other properties of stocks, beyond risk and return. Consider a company like IBM. Investment returns on shares in IBM could certainly be characterized by its statistical mean and variance, as Markowitz had established. But given the diversity of tools that had developed on Wall Street since Markowitz's time, there were many other aspects of the stock that were relevant. First, the market for corporate control that developed during the 1980s had introduced mergers into the life cycle of most companies, leading to a new property, *merger probability*, that was directly relevant to stock prices.[3] Merger probability was the bread-and-butter of Max's team at the merger arbitrage desk, but it was also relevant to other desks such as statistical arbitrage, where traders like Todd had to exclude stocks from their algorithms when they merged.

Second, the development of synthetic securities like the S&P 500 Index in the 1980s had facilitated the growth of passive investment: instead of investing in a costly mutual fund, investors could simply "buy the index" and save on transaction costs. However, the growth of index-based investments also meant that inclusion into one of these indexes had an important effect on the stock price of a company. A stock that made it to the index would suddenly experience a large bump in its price. The *probability of inclusion in the index* was thus another property that could be quantified and used for trading, as in the example of Max and Symantec noted in chapter 5.

A third financial property that had become relevant to stock prices concerned the development of strategies like merger arbitrage, which required shorting stocks, that is, betting that their price would fall. Given this practice, a stock's *ease of borrowing* became a crucial property that made the stock loan desk important.

In sum, the increasing use of financial models in a growing number of investment strategies introduced by the quantitative revolution since the days of Markowitz had produced a burgeoning of quantitative properties, including risk and return, merger probability, the probability of being included in an index, ease of borrowing, etc. In that context, Bob's decision to divide the trading room into three classes of properties—quantitative, qualitative, and volatility—suggested that the specialized knowledge generated by the traders had grown in importance, to the point of becoming an organizing device for the trading room.

Quilted Markets

One last aspect of Bob's scheme became evident a few weeks after our conversation about financial properties. I saw Bob sitting at his desk, experimenting with a Treemap visualization of the market called "Map of the Market." Treemap visualizations of the stock market were originally created by web designer Martin Wattenberg, and made available on a consumer finance website, Smartmoney.com (see figure 7.4). A Treemap typically shows the evolution of an aggregate magnitude composed of multiple parts, whether it is national voting preferences (itself made up of state-level preferences), municipal waiting times in hospitals (an aggregate of individual hospital times), or the evolution of the stock market. The Treemap shows a mosaic, made up of rectangles of various sizes and colors that correspond to the component parts. Treemaps thus reveal the difference between the aggregate trend and the subtrends that give rise to that aggregate. For instance, voters in the United States can shift their voting intention evenly or unevenly across states. An uneven shift could be entirely driven by a large movement in one or two states, or by a minor movement in many states. The same applies to stock prices and industry sectors: a rise in the S&P 500 Index can be driven by a large rise in one or two sectors, or by a minor rise in most sectors.

On the day I saw Bob use the Map of the Market, he explained that he was trying to understand whether a *quilted* market was more or less attractive than one that was not quilted (figure 7.4). I had never before heard of "quiltedness" as a financial property, but I could see Bob's point at least in visual terms: the

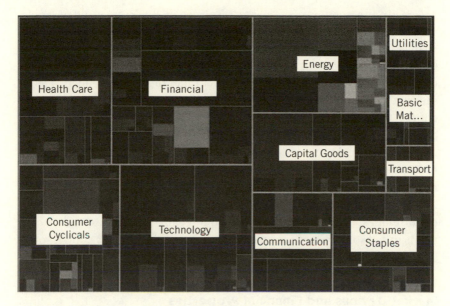

FIGURE 7.4. Non-quilted market. The Map of the Market on Monday April 4, 2005 (top) shows a visually even (not quilted) outcome, where the losses were uniformly distributed across the various markets. *Source:* www.SmartMoney.com.

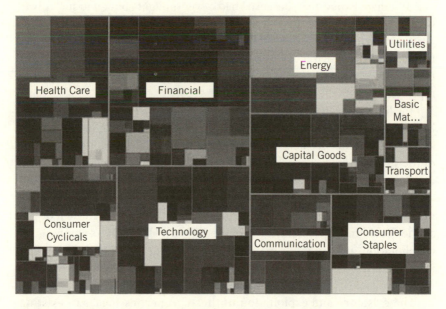

FIGURE 7.5. A quilted market. The Map of the Market from January to March 2005 (below) shows an uneven or quilted market with several large areas of green (denoting economic sectors with gains) and abundant areas of red (denoting sectors with losses). *Source:* www .SmartMoney.com.

Treemap representation of the market displayed on Bob's screen did resemble a traditional bed cover made of square layers of fabric, that is, a quilt. Bob then changed the time period he was examining, and showed that during certain time periods, the various squares in the graph had large differences in color (i.e., the market was quilted), while at other times the squares tended to be of the same color (i.e., the market was not quilted). Critically, the degree of "quilt-edness" was different from the overall direction of the market (i.e., whether the overall hue of the chart trended red or green), because a market where the S&P 500 is rising can be both quilted or not quilted, and the same applies to a market where it is falling. Bob was interested in quiltedness because he hoped to better understand the dynamics of arbitrage in the bear market of 2002. "Traders prefer a market with uneven performance, because it creates opportunities," he hypothesized about a quilted market. "For example, Todd needs to sell something each time he buys something. So, it's good if some stocks go down."

Market Devices and Financial Properties

The key lesson I derived from Bob's use of the Map of the Market concerned the relationship between the tool and the financial property it revealed. It was impossible to think of quiltedness before seeing the market represented as a Treemap. I knew that, because I had never thought about it in such a way before that day. Properties and their representations, my observation suggested, were intimately connected. Before a representation is developed, the financial property that it captures will be invisible. Only after such representation is developed will investors be able to rely on it, and if many do so, the representation might alter the price of the security.

The link between financial tools and properties had implications for how I thought about the trading room. Bob's trading room could be thought of as an assembly of specialized knowledge sets about the various properties of the stocks, based on market devices such as models, visualizations, and other quantitative technology. These properties could certainly be exploited independently, as single-strategy hedge funds and proprietary trading desks at other banks did. However, the various properties influenced each other, so they could more profitably be exploited jointly. Hence Bob's emphasis on collaboration, and especially his policy of rotating desks. Bob's policy, I realized, was ultimately an exercise in exploiting the relationship between financial models and stock prices.

The existence and exploitation of these properties speaks to existing sociological studies on market properties. Research by Michel Callon, Cécile Méadel, and Vololona Rabeharisoa argued that the characteristics of goods cannot simply be announced by their producers.[4] Such characteristics need specific measurement tools, including investments in equipment; for instance, the flavor, age, alcohol content, and origin of a bottle of wine requires the implementation of certified tests and codified measurements. Similarly, a car's road-holding, engine capacity, consumption, and comfort "are all parameters that, to be appreciated, evaluated and objectified, need a battery of tests, test benches, approved measurement instruments, documents guaranteeing traceability, etc." (p. 199). To Callon and his colleagues, the development of product tests and measurement tools was a central element in economies increasingly defined by product differentiation, that is, in the identification and measurement of the differentiating properties of a product. The result, the authors argued, was an "economy of qualities."

The concept of an economy of qualities was directly related to Bob's trading, whose various desks and tools could be considered the financial counterpart to the various tests and measures that Callon and others identified. Each desk in the trading room could be thought of as a financial equivalent of the testing, measuring or certifying units that Callon and colleagues discussed. As I understood all of this, I suddenly felt vindicated in my overall research project. Back in 1999, I had decided to focus on the tools and practices performed by the traders at International Securities, rather than on the structure of their social networks or the nature of their institutional field. In doing so, my hope was that the tools and practices would uncover the distinctive aspects of quantitative finance.

I had now hit upon one such aspect. The above-normal returns generated by Bob's trading room at International Securities might partly be due to Bob's deliberate attempt to reassemble disparate but interrelated realms of knowledge about the financial qualities of stocks, including the fundamental, quantitative, and volatility properties. Knowledge about these properties in the market was fragmented, because each property was tied to a different representation tool, and these tools had expanded dramatically following the quantitative revolution. Indeed, in the 1952 world conceived by Harry Markowitz, the only two existing quantitative properties were risk and return, and their practical significance was theoretical, because banks lacked the computational means to calculate "Beta" coefficients. By 1999, however, these and many other variables were measured. Corporations experienced disruptive events, index securities fell in and out of line with the value of their underlying stocks, and trading technology created delayed data flows. These were all measured. In this new world, then, the properties of the stocks were multiple and uncertain, and a bank could develop a better understanding than individual investors by integrating the desks that generated knowledge about them.

The contrast between Bob's and Markowitz's worlds was striking for one additional reason. The proliferation of quantitative practices and representations of the past decades could be seen as a *consequence* of Markow-itz's original efforts. New quantitative representations had led to new practices and trading strategies. In turn, these strategies often created a new financial product, and thus an opportunity for yet another representation. This was precisely the point made by MacKenzie when arguing that economic theory had been "performative." Economic theory, he claimed, had not simply acted as a passive measurement device, but as a financial innovation and engine of change.[5] For instance, as MacKenzie and Millo explained, the diffusion of the Black-Scholes equation reshaped the value of stock options. In doing so, it had also facilitated the creation of a link between the futures and the stock markets that could be exploited in the 1980s by means of a trading strategy known as portfolio insurance. But after portfolio insurance contributed to, rather than prevented, the crash of 1987, the relationship between volatility and stock prices was altered, leading to yet another property, the so-called volatility smile in the traders' charts. In sum, MacKenzie's work, including MacKenzie and Millo, established that market devices and financial properties were bound up in each other.

A Change in the Market

The rest of the year 2002 proved to be more eventful than I had expected. As the end of July arrived, I left New York City for the academic summer confer-ences and a two-week vacation. I returned to New York in September, and on my first day back at the desk I found Bob visibly upset. He had just arrived from his own vacation and had encountered a problem: "the bank's corporate managers abroad got in a panic, that's right, in a panic," he emphasized, "and forced us to sell our convertible bond position at a loss." Convertible bond arbitrage involved the simultaneous purchase of convertible bonds and the short sale of shares in the same company. The loss amounted to $30 million. Bob showed me (but did not let me keep) a chart with corporate bond prices, depicting a shaded point in time on the chart where there was a loss, followed by a rise: the typical pattern of reversion to profits that Todd also discussed with me. The pattern demonstrated that Risk Management had forced the closure of the position just before it began turning a profit. "It is a problem, because the traders are compensated based on their results, yet this decision does not come from them."

The bank's decision to override Bob's authority came in the midst of a turn toward risk aversion caused by the recent atmosphere of corporate governance scandals. The new executive at the bank's global headquarters in charge of Bob's unit feared that the convertible bonds bought by Bob's traders might become worthless. That is, he feared that the model Bob's traders were using no longer applied to the new circumstances, as investors had lost trust in the financial system, and so he thought it was better to sell. "They forced us to sell in a hurry," Bob explained. "It already happened after the 1998 Long-Term Capital Management crisis and our high-yield bonds. We could have made $30 million that we did not, but at the time I felt the problem was theoretical. After all, we might not have kept the bonds for so long, we might have sold before the peak, etc. But this time it is losses, as opposed to a forgone gain."

Bob had clearly thought a lot about this. "I understand that an organization has to have checks and balances, and that each level has to have the right to override the one below. For example, I think of the plane crash in Switzerland exactly in these terms. You have three levels of hierarchy: the plane controller, the pilot, and the automatic pilot." He was referring to the tragic crash of the Bashkirian Airlines Flight 2937 in July 2002. "Here, we have the same: business line management, risk management, and global management. Our own risk management systems did not flag this, because the losses were not large enough. They were so *afterward*, when we began to sell." The losses, in other words, were self-fulfilling: as Bob put it, "once you sell, you do it in a hurry, because that's an order. People eventually find out—you're the only one selling, and during that time the price drops lower and lower as you get rid of your holdings." In sum, the anticipation of losses by Bob's senior managers started a process that culminated in actual losses.

"You would expect," Bob continued, "that there would be less overriding the higher up you go. For example, it is normal that the head of a desk will overrule his employees daily, but I overrule heads of desks much less. My bosses are making decisions from headquarters." They should, Bob added, overrule him even less. "Otherwise, it's like Jimmy Carter trying to manage the Iran hostage crisis from the White House." The overruling, Bob added, was in part due to politics. "I have a new boss. The previous one took time to get to know me in the beginning. He flew over here [from the bank's global headquarters located outside the United States] and after meeting me he decided he was going to trust me. With time, that degree of trust grew." Now, however, Bob's boss had changed, and the management style had changed too. "In large organizations like International Securities," Bob continued, "there typically are ten people vying for promotion at the top, each elbowing the other. What the direct subordinates of my previous boss used against him was that he was a softie, too uninvolved in day-to-day management." For that reason, the new boss, who was his previous subordinate, had promoted himself as more aggressive, more focused on the details. But the end result, which was the forced liquidation of the convertible bond trade, created acute problems for Bob. "On our end, the problem is that money focuses people's minds like nothing else, and now I am $30 million short. And it's not just my traders, but also myself, because I get compensated based on the results of the floor as a whole. So how do I deal with it?"

Limits of Arbitrage

I left the conversation with Bob with an impending sense of doom. How was he going to react to his own sense of being unfairly treated? Would he leave the company and take some traders with him? Would he build an alliance with the faction that opposed the current chief executive? Back at my cubicle in NYU, I realized that the problems experienced by Bob and his traders spoke to the literature on the limits of arbitrage. This theory, formulated by economists Andrei Shleifer and Robert Vishny, argued that there are systematic constraints on the ability of arbitrageurs to conduct their trades, no matter how farsighted and correct these trades might be, and that these restrictions on arbitrageurs impose an unsurmountable constraint on arbitrageurs' ability to eliminate mispricings and improve market efficiency.[6]

While classic arbitrage requires no capital and entails no risk, Shleifer and Vishny argued, in reality, almost all arbitrage requires capital and is typically risky, creating a conflict of interests between Wall Street traders and the shareholders in their banks or funds: the arbitrageurs are risking someone else's money. This conflict means that when an arbitrage trade does not go according to the arbitrageur's plans and leads to losses, shareholders and investors who do not understand the nature of the trade may just see a risk rather than a possible opportunity. Unable to establish whether the risk is due to incompetence or to the particularities of the trade, investors will wish to reduce their exposure, and in doing so they will prevent the successful completion of the trade.

The problems created by the convertible bond position at International Securities seemed a clear case of such limits. A new chief executive was in place who no longer trusted Bob to be prudent or proficient, and a sudden change in the market environment had made losses less acceptable than before. The combination prompted the decision to force the closure of the position. The presence of limits to arbitrage was also consistent with my discussions with Bob and the traders in previous chapters: the conflicts and controversies around position closure, trading limits, etc., were all instances of limits to arbitrage.[7]

Last Months on the Trading Floor

Three months later, however, the losses in convertible bonds seemed nearly forgotten. I discussed financial results with Bob again in December 2002. The trading room, he said, "is in a good mood despite annual results that are not so good." One reason for it was the rise in market indices since October. Another reason was that, as the end of the fiscal year approached, bad news about competitors was spreading around, making Bob's traders feel relatively better. Bad news was spreading because senior executives at other banks were beginning to manage expectations in advance of paying out low bonuses. "If it is half of the previous year's, you cannot simply tell a trader, 'here's your bonus,' and then say, 'by the way, your performance was great, but it's been a difficult year.'" The trader would not take it well. "He'll say, 'what? Fuck you, you ruined me!'" Furthermore, what happened in other banks affected the expectations at International Securities. "If your neighbor is being laid off, and your other neighbor is getting no bonus, you don't need to be jealous."

A few days later, however, a conversation with Max marked a contrast to Bob's optimism. Max was concerned about the low frequency of mergers taking place, that is, the number of deals, as these were the raw material for his trades. "In terms of deals," Max said, "we are back to the 1994 recession. Saying the Dow is down by 30 percent actually misses the point. The number of deals has decreased by 75 percent, and not just that, deal quality is bad, spreads are narrow, and they have many issues." By issues, he meant reasons why these mergers might not be completed: adverse earnings, antitrust, or geopolitical risk. "So, overall, it's like that line in that movie by Woody Allen. One old lady is talking to another, and is saying, 'the food is so bad around here,' and the other answers, 'yes, and the portions are so small.'"

One novelty that Max found interesting, however, was the use of credit derivatives for betting on mergers. "Look at credit default swaps for Enron," he said. Credit default swaps, or CDS, were a derivative contract that provided protection against the possibility that a company, in this case Enron, might default on its debt. As it turned out, the price of Enron's credit default swaps (i.e., the cost of protection against Enron's bankruptcy) had begun to rise several months before Enron announced problems. "CDS have a high information content, and banks can hedge themselves against their bad loans by buying CDS." By using CDS, Max added, he could examine whether a company undergoing a merger had "any issue."

My last substantial conversation with Bob on that year took place in March 2003. At the time, the news was dominated by the prospects of a US military intervention in Iraq. The ultimatum to Saddam Hussein issued by the Bush administration had expired on the day that Bob and I spoke. In the trading room, all the television screens were turned to CNN rather than to the usual financial channel. On the screens, as I walked in, Mayor Bloomberg was giving a speech. The muted TVs showed a caption from him that read: "New York is a Target." Bob suggested we meet in his private office, which implied we were about to discuss a sensitive issue.

As we sat down, Bob smiled apologetically: things were not going well at International Securities. "Wall Street is in a depression right now, just like the steel industry was in the 1970s. Some businesses are worse than others. Investment banking, retail banking, brokerage, asset management and new issuances are terrible. I just had a meeting with my management team about this. In addition, the Street is overstaffed." This created a paradox, Bob said: he had succeeded in making his traders share information, but the trading room had lost its edge. "It took a long time to engineer respect between Max and the people from long-short. Right now, everything's perfect," he said in reference to the floor layout, "but we're just not making any money."

I also had news. I told Bob that I had accepted an academic position back in Spain, my home country. He congratulated me, although we both realized that this would put an end to my fieldwork at International Securities. Bob then changed the tone of his voice and asked me about the impending war in Iraq. "Tell me Daniel, I never asked you this sort of thing before: what is your opinion?" Bob was worried about the war. He had never seen, he said, a time in which American foreign policy, especially a war, had been so isolated and out of synch with the rest of the world. "I was in Europe in the '70s, with the Vietnam war. And I have friends from France who send me emails, and I never saw this type of divide before."

"So, what is your opinion, as a European?" Bob asked. "What strikes me most about Iraq," I ventured, "is the wide difference in opinion between the pro-war and the anti-war camps. They seem to have fundamentally different assumptions about key issues." One, for example, was whether nuclear proliferation in Iraq could be stopped by a strategy of United Nations containment. "Perhaps," I pointed out, "the Americans know something that Europeans don't." "Yes!" Bob exclaimed, interrupting me. "And, you see, here I think that they just don't." Part of the problem, he pointed out, was organizational. "The people in different units of the information agencies—the CIA, Homeland Security, the military, the White House—do not share information with each other, partly because they cannot, due to security reasons. As a result, different units develop models of reality that are not contrasted. Such as, can UN containment really work? In that atmosphere of mistrust among the different agencies, each may get more paranoid than the other." What the US agencies needed, Bob implied, was the type of integration he had at the trading room.

Trading Floors and Control Rooms

I was intrigued by our conversation, as it suggested that Bob had reflected on the importance of integration well beyond finance. Indeed, space plays a key role in the integration of knowledge in numerous settings. For instance, the control rooms of the London Underground studied by Heath and Luff allow personnel to systematically communicate information to each other and coordinate a disparate collection of tasks and activities.[8] Such integration of knowledge, Bob seemed to be pointing out, was more difficult when dealing with secret foreign intelligence, speculating that this must have hampered the US government.

That conversation was the last one we had in 2003. In May of that year I graduated from my doctoral studies. The fieldwork I had completed on International Securities, between November 1999 and May 2003, served as the basis for my doctoral dissertation. It was titled "The Social Qualities of Quantitative Finance." The first sign that the project had, for good or bad, succeeded in making unconventional claims came soon thereafter. At the graduation ceremony for doctoral candidates at NYU, the titles of the dissertations were printed in the day's program. As the other candidates and I queued up to step onto the stage and receive our degrees, the student behind me, a doctoral candidate in Finance, read the title of my dissertation. "What do you mean," he asked with barely concealed puzzlement, "by social qualities"?

Epilogue

There was a final twist to the events described above. I returned to International Securities in July 2004. I had spent a full year in Barcelona at my new academic position, and the summer recess gave me an opportunity to come back to New York for more fieldwork and to work with coauthors. I emailed Bob, asking him for an appointment. He responded right away and suggested two possible days to meet. I chose the earlier one.

Walking into the trading room in July 2004 stirred in me an odd sense of familiarity and nostalgia. Everything seemed to be as I had left it, except of course that I was no longer a regular visitor. As I approached Bob, I found him welcoming as always; however, he took me straight to the conference room next to his office, and closed the door.

"It's good that we met today," he said, "because I am leaving International Securities on Friday." This came as a shock, only made more dramatic by what he said next. "I still have to tell this to these people," pointing to the traders. The knowledge of Bob's departure was rendered all the more poignant by the glass-walled room we were sitting in. Outside that office, the traders were going about their business, speaking on the phone, buying and selling securities, oblivious to the shocking news that Bob had just dropped. Had there not been a glass wall, they would have easily overheard our conversation. Had they known what I knew just then, the trading room would immediately fill with chaos.

"How come?" I managed to ask, attempting to recover from my shock. Bob then showed me a document titled "What Is the Condition of Equity Markets?" that he had presented to others at International Securities, analyzing the overall strategy of the trading room. The point of the presentation was that the profit opportunities that had once been in equities were no longer there, and that these now lay instead in connecting stocks and corporate debt because, as Max had explained to me, the price of corporate credit default swaps seemed predictive of stock prices. However, Bob had been denied permission to do that. The refusal had come from the Risk Management department at International Securities, which Bob had once described as politically weak. "Losses give power to Risk Management." Bob said, "in addition, this is an organization, and as you know there are all these different interests going on. So, the actual opposition to us trading corporate debt came from London," he said, referring to the UK office of International Securities. "They trade credit risk."

As a result, Bob said, he had decided to resign. "It's okay for me, I'm not confrontational, so I decided to leave. We have been having this conflict since the year 2000. I feel bad for these guys," he said in reference to the traders just outside his office. "I like the people I work with. All through this year, I have been suffering. This week, there are all these things to do. I have to meet with the US Head of International Securities, and his schedule is always jumping. This is why our meeting almost got canceled." "Do you know what you're going to do?" I asked. "I don't know. I am not going to work for two years. I may not return to Wall Street. As you know, this is actually my second time here. I would like to spend time with my family. Now my pocket is fuller; I am older. Or I may do something like what Quinn did." Quinn was the doctoral student in sociology (and former banker) who had introduced me to Bob three years before. Bob was thus alluding in an indirect manner to the possibility of enrolling in a PhD program.

Strategy and Asset Classes

Bob's resignation filled me with a mix of surprise and sadness. The last thing I expected when I walked onto Bob's floor that day was learning that he would resign. Although I felt honored that he had confided his plans to me before sharing them with his own traders, I was sad to hear that the organization I had studied for three and a half years would irreversibly change. Back in my summer rental apartment in the Upper West Side, as I transcribed my notes from the meeting, I considered Bob's decision more carefully. His resignation impressed on me the extraordinary uncertainty that traders face, for even though the trading room was finally integrated, that integration did not matter in an economic context of recession, declining stock prices, and excess capacity on Wall Street.

I understood then that the strategy that Bob's managers had refused to allow was the connecting of stocks and corporate debt. Bob's goal, as Max had mentioned when discussing Enron, was to shift toward corporate credit derivatives such as credit default swaps. As MacKenzie has emphasized, corporate debt-based derivatives such as these became a highly successful asset class that should not be confused with the mortgage-based derivatives that turned toxic in 2008.[9] The very success of corporate credit derivatives was probably also the reason the London office of International Securities opposed Bob's move.

At around that time, I found news that confirmed the prescience of Bob's plan. According to the *Financial Times*, the European subsidiary of Goldman Sachs had adopted the very policy that Bob had tried to put in place, namely, combining debt and equity departments. The paper reported that, following the sharp downturn in merger and acquisitions activity, "the US-based investment bank had reorganized both research and trading, placing those who trade the same company's debt and equity in teams close to each other." The change, the newspaper added, had altered the conversation subjects among the debt traders: "while the corporate bond traders used to sit next to the government bond traders and talk about yields, *with the new seating arrangement those same credit traders were more likely to share views about the companies that equity traders were following.*"[10] The news story lent confirmation to the importance of informal conversations across trading desks, and especially among those using different strategies and representations of value. But, more important, it suggested that some such conversations were more valuable than others and that, depending on the market context, it was beneficial for a company to change the layout of the floor in order to privilege some conversations over others.

Performativity and Trading Rooms

My observations of the trading room during my last year pointed to the relationship between asset classes, arbitrage strategies, and trading rooms. One way of tying these concepts together is by analogy to an existing concept developed by the Nobel laureate economist Robert Merton Jr., the so-called financial innovation spiral. Merton posited a reciprocal influence between financial markets and financial institutions such as Wall Street banks. He started from the observation that innovative financial products were typically first offered by leading investment banks such as Salomon Brothers, and then standardized as they moved on to securities exchanges like the Chicago Mercantile Exchange, which could offer the products more cheaply. In other words, innovations were services first, then products. Once a financial product was thus commoditized, banks turned to the next lucrative innovation, thereby performing a turn in the spiral (see figure 7.6). In Merton's spiral, financial innovation contributed to a progressive reduction in uncertainty by developing more and more types of products, allowing investors to hedge against more and more types of risk. "This interaction between dynamic product-development intermediaries and markets," Merton concluded, "can be interpreted as part of a 'financial-innovation spiral' pushing the financial system toward an idealized target of full efficiency."[11] The spiral, in other words, created progress and reduced risk.

INVESTMENT BANKS   **CAPITAL MARKETS**

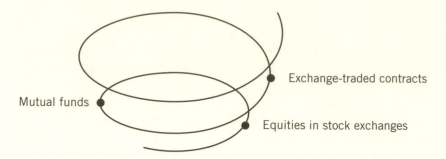

FIGURE 7.6. Merton's Financial Innovation Spiral. *Source:* Merton (1995).

As an example, Merton offered the task of providing a well-diversified port-folio of stocks for individual investors. "At one time," he wrote, "this func-tion was best served by buying shares on a stock exchange." However, there were transaction and monitoring costs that created friction. Financial markets responded with an innovation that pooled investors' capital, mutual funds, thereby reducing those costs. This led to the creation of funds that tracked the S&P 500 Index, such as those offered by the Vanguard Group. Those funds were subsequently turned into yet another financial product: futures contracts on stock indexes, such as the S&P 500 Futures offered by the Chicago Mercan-tile Exchange. These exchange contracts further reduced costs. "Thus," Merton concludes, "the institutional providers of the stock-diversification function for households were markets, then intermediaries, then markets again."[12]

Building on Merton's idea, and leveraging the concept of financial proper-ties that I witnessed at Bob's trading room, I propose a different form of spiral to represent the relationship between economic models and the properties of financial securities. In this spiral, new representations of value, typically in the form of new financial devices, tools, or economic models, lead to new investment practices. In turn, such new practices often create changes in the properties of the securities, which can themselves be represented and prof-itably exploited. In sum, there is a reciprocal influence between economic models and financial properties. Because this influence can be performative in nature (e.g., because economic models are central to the conceptualization and measuring of these properties), I refer to this as a *performative spiral* (see figure 7.7).

For an example of the performative spiral, consider Markowitz's Mod-ern Portfolio Theory and its effect on financial properties. As MacKenzie describes, Modern Portfolio Theory presented stocks in terms of two statisti-cal properties, the mean and variance of their returns, and argued that only

ECONOMIC MODELS   **FINANCIAL PROPERTIES**

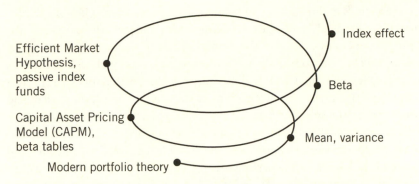

FIGURE 7.7. A performative spiral.

these properties, rather than the fundamental traits of companies (balance sheet, product offering, etc.), determined stock value. Subsequent research by William Sharpe and others built on Markowitz to develop the Capital Asset Pricing Model (CAPM), relating a stock's value to the sensitivity of its price to overall market fluctuations. Such sensitivity was called "beta," and implied that investors ought to diversify their portfolios, a message that was echoed by Eugene Fama's efficient market hypothesis. Consulting firms like BARRA or Wilshire made the use of this research practically possible by providing investors with "beta books," or lists of the beta values for different stocks, while other companies such as Wells Fargo Bank or The Vanguard Group developed passive index funds.[13] As the passive index fund industry grew in size, indexes began to shape stock prices, leading to what Maria Kasch and Asani Sarkar have recently called an "index effect," whereby inclusion into an index creates an increase in the stock price of a company.[14] Thus, the identification of the statistical properties of stocks contributed to the development of models like the CAPM and market devices such as beta books or passive index funds, which in turn created additional properties such as the index effect.

Notice that some of these properties were already in place before the market device was introduced. Such is the case of the mean and variance of stock returns; in this case, the role of the CAPM model and corresponding beta tables was not to bring the property into being, but to allow market actors to identify it. In this manner, the CAPM can be seen as performative in what MacKenzie has termed a *generic* sense: the model does not alter the properties of the stocks, but altered financial practices. In other cases, such as the index effect, the introduction of the passive index gave rise to it, so the performative mechanism can be said to be *effective*: the model altered market prices, but such change did not impact the accuracy of the model itself.

As with Merton's schema, my proposed spiral describes the evolution of quantitative finance through time. However, the performative spiral differs from Merton's in three ways. First, it departs from Merton's view of financial markets as gradually making the world less risky: the performative spiral that I propose does not make any claim about the overall degree of risk offsetting, but suggests that as some risks are addressed, new risks will appear. Second, whereas Merton's spiral is silent about the properties of the stocks, the performative spiral contends that as time passes the number of market devices and properties of the stocks will grow. Thus, while Merton sees a historical pattern of less and less risk, I propose one of more and more properties. Finally, whereas risks in Merton's spiral are external or "exogenous" to the banks and financial exchanges, in the performative spiral that I propose, risks are both external and internal to the market, as they can result from the interaction between existing models and financial properties, as in the crash of 1987.

The concept of performative spirals sheds light on the basic question that I confronted as I initiated my research: what is the point of a trading floor? Instead of creating innovative products, as banks did in Merton's model, Bob's trading room assembled a multitude of economic models and strategies within the same four walls. Each model and its associated tools generated specialized knowledge about a different property of the stocks, and interaction across desks promoted the sharing of this tacit knowledge. One way to think about the trading room, then, was as an organizational arrangement that allowed the exploitation of the performative spiral. Different desks used different market devices and properties, and physical proximity between desks allows for the exploitation of the overlaps and interdependencies between properties.

Finally, the introduction of additional devices and properties into the trading room led to changes in the physical configuration of the desks. Hence, for example, the difference between the configurations of the trading floor in 1999 and 2002. To capture this effect, I propose the term *performative trace*. By this I mean a pattern of relations of proximity across desks that changes as the market conditions change, so that integration across interrelated financial properties is made possible. Over time, changes in the layout of the floor thus tracks, captures, and traces the evolution of market properties.

The concept of performative trace differs from previous studies of social relations on trading floors by relating them to financial models. Whereas the original function of undirected communication in the trading rooms documented by Heath and others was peripheral monitoring, and while Baker's cliques on the floor of an exchange were aimed at transacting, the performative trace proposed here is based on MacKenzie's idea of evaluation practices. Such practices are path dependent and fragmented, which implies that successful interaction requires trust and frequent interaction, hence the need for proximity. Finally, the concept of performative trace offers implications for managerial practice. The study by Heath and others underscored the need for understanding peripheral monitoring before automating information exchange. Baker's study suggested that a trading group should not be too large. In turn, the concept of performative trace suggests that financial innovation calls for new patterns of relatedness on the trading floor.

Conclusion

My last months at the trading room afforded me a closer look at the people and the practices that centered my visits between 1999 and 2002. I saw new and unexpected corners of the organization such as the HR department, or Leah in the back office. More significantly, I encountered a succession of events that undid the original strategy laid out by Bob in 1997. Specifically, a change in the global CEO of International Securities meant that Bob lost a vital source of support within the bank. Furthermore, and following the burst of the Internet bubble, the US equities market entered a protracted crisis that made it impossible for the equities trading room to preserve its profitability without a change in strategy. The traders and executives confided in me their skepticism, shared their frustrations, and by 2003, even their political views.

My continued visits and conversations alerted me to the critical role of models and visualizations in forging an understanding of the market. The traders, I eventually understood, were engaged in expanding their knowledge of the various properties of financial stocks, and Bob altered the layout of the trading room accordingly. By 2004, however, Bob resigned. It took me a long time to fully understand the significance of Bob's resignation to my own study of arbitrage, but I eventually grasped it: the introduction of models in financial markets created an iterative effect between economic models and the financial properties of stocks, a *performative spiral*. Successfully exploiting the spiral entailed connecting different markets at different points in time. This, however, was precisely what the bank had prevented Bob from doing, and this was what prompted his resignation.

8

Norms

I barely saw Bob in the two years that followed his resignation from International Securities. The opportunities to meet were few, as my job in Barcelona kept me away from New York during most of the year. In 2006, however, I changed jobs and moved back to New York City for a position at Columbia Business School. Once I settled into the job, I invited Bob to speak to the MBA students I taught at Columbia. Unexpectedly, Bob's account of the culture of his former trading room cast doubts on the understanding I had developed about him and the bank up to that point.

The specific point of contention concerned the organizational integration achieved at International Securities. My fieldwork from 1999 to 2004 had led me to believe that Bob's trading room was successful because it brought together the diverse bodies of knowledge held in its various trading desks. I attributed this integration to the informal relations and open communication across desks. In turn, I accounted for these in terms of the material traits of the floor: the whiteboard, the absence of separation between traders and operations officers, the limited head count, the low-height monitors, and especially the rotating desk layout. Integration was not, in other words, the outcome of an authoritarian imposition; there certainly were two line managers, Jerry and Brian, but their primary role was to supervise and control the traders. The other middle manager, Stanley, was charged with promoting collaboration across desks. Similarly, Bob was willing to limit his own discretion in setting bonuses, committing instead to a rule-based "percentage payout" system. In sum, the floor to me was integrated, but resolutely not hierarchical.

This reading was generally supported by a vast number of studies in organizational sociology. Starting with research conducted in the 1960s by British researchers Tom Burns and Lawrence Stalker, a long-running literature has underscored the importance of non-hierarchical and non-bureaucratic structures in enabling technological innovation. Companies in new industries, Burns and Stalker found, faced rapidly changing market conditions. In such contexts, a rigid or "mechanistic" division of labor limited their ability to adapt to such changes. By contrast, innovative companies were characterized by an "organic" structure, including "fluid definitions of function and interactions that are equally lateral as they are vertical."[1] The distinction between mechanistic and organic structures proved influential, inspiring subsequent theories such as the network organization, the boundaryless organization, the flat organization, and the heterarchy. The idea of organic structure was central to how I interpreted Bob's trading room, and I took the equities floor to be proof that innovation in finance also required an organically structured floor.

A Special Visitor

My perspective was abruptly called into question in November 2007, when Bob addressed my MBA classroom at Columbia Business School. At the time, questions about trading floor structure were of secondary concern to me. As a novice assistant professor teaching three challenging MBA clusters, my attention was focused on my teaching evaluations, which left plenty of room for improvement. My difficulties in the classroom were not only due to inexperience, but also to the fact that Columbia Business School, like the business schools at the University of Chicago or New York University, was regarded as a "finance school." That is, numerous students came to Columbia with work experience on Wall Street, and an even greater number were aiming for a career on Wall Street after graduation. To some of these students, management boiled down to three things: hiring, firing, and paying bonuses. Columbia's MBA curriculum, however, included a compulsory management course titled "Creating Effective Organizations," which I taught. My classroom was thus partly populated with students who did not readily see the value of a course in management. In an effort to ingratiate myself with them, and to illustrate the relevance of management ideas on Wall Street, I invited Bob to be a guest speaker. Incidentally, I also hoped to improve my teaching evaluations.

Bob's presentation took place in November 2007, and his visit offered a great deal more than an upward tick in my teaching ratings. On the day of his session, Bob showed up to the classroom a full half-hour ahead of time, energized and self-engrossed instead of relaxed and engaging as I had always found him. As he started to address my students, he spoke with the intensity of a street activist. "I had the *privilege*," he said, "to be the laboratory rat of your professor." As he made this point, he looked in defiance at my students, as if detecting the skepticism that lay behind their blank expressions. This was met with silence. Bob continued by telling my students that he had pursued an MBA just like theirs, but that he had never collected the degree, as he had not paid the $8 he owed in late library fees. "So at the end of today, I'll pass around the hat." His academic irreverence was met with laughter. He then moved to the topic of his presentation. "Communication," he stated, "is the central driver to adding value in business." There was silence again, but now of a different kind: interested silence.

Bob then went on to talk for a half hour or so about a bank where he had worked before joining International Securities. I referred to this bank in previous chapters as Premier Financial. "Consider a classic, old-fashioned derivatives trade from the 1980s," Bob began. The Tokyo sales force, which is composed of Japanese traders, has identified that for some peculiar reason, Japanese insurance companies like the bonds of Australian companies that pay their principal in Australian dollars and the coupons in Japanese yen. "These traders," Bob continued, "want someone to provide those bonds so they can sell them to their customers and make their fee." To do that, however, they need to find an issuer, typically a US corporation that wants to issue bonds as a means of financing. This, Bob argued, placed onerous coordination demands on the bank: "the Japanese salespeople have to go to their capital markets group and persuade a company like IBM that it ought to issue bonds in Australian dollar principal and yen coupon." Doing so, however, also called for connecting different teams in the bank. "Luckily there's no language barrier for ignorant people like myself, who don't speak multiple languages," Bob added, again prompting laughter among my nationally diverse and well-traveled students. "But still, that's a time zone and two cultures away, and I don't mean Japanese and American cultures, *I mean sales and investment banking, which are universes apart.*" Bob's point was clear: the cultural gap between departments at Wall Street banks could be as wide as that between countries, leading to communication barriers that hindered business.

How, Bob asked, could a manager induce the necessary communication despite such gaps? One of my students suggested a global bonus pool. To this, Bob responded that money would seem like the logical response, "but it turns out it is dead wrong." When he ran the derivative business at Premier Financial, Bob explained, he conducted an experiment to resolve the pervasive tension between British bankers in London and American bankers in New York. "I took some American guys to London, and some Brits to New York." The result was surprising. "Three months later, some Brit in New York is telling me what a jerk everyone is in London, how they are fools, and don't know how to do business. And some American doing a phony British accent is telling me how much he hates New York." Bob drew a lesson from this: "when people sit beside each other, they like each other, they trust each other, and they share information. You move them, and the trust and friendship starts to die." Close physical proximity, Bob concluded, creates spontaneous interaction, and interaction breeds trust. Bob's solution to the problem of collaboration within his bank was rotating the teams of traders. "I moved their desks, not just once, but often, sometimes a couple times a year. It drove them crazy. But they could gripe about me, the boss, and get to know each other through their grumbling."

As I sat in the back row of the classroom, I could not help but feel perplexed. I was already familiar with the story of the relocated traders, but the novelty for me was Bob's self-presentation: his loud voice, authoritative tone, straight posture, cold-calling of some of the students, as well as his gracious replies when the answers were not what he expected. Bob owned the floor in my classroom, and no one was upset or humiliated because of it. As the session ended, a multitude of students swarmed around him with questions and comments. While I waited for the swarm to subside and take him to lunch, I could not help but question my own view of the trading room as a non-hierarchical structure. What I had just seen was an unparalleled exercise in personal energy, professional authority, and control of the audience. Bob had established his credibility among my students from scratch. Perhaps, I reasoned, this imposition of authority also took place in the trading room at International Securities *before* my study started, and I had missed that crucial part of the story. If that was the case, my view of the trading room as non-hierarchical in structure would be misplaced.

As the recognition of Bob's charisma settled in, other puzzling observations suddenly came to mind. In the summer of 2005 (that is, two years before Bob's guest lecture), I had interviewed one of Bob's former colleagues. He described Bob as a "control freak," adding that Bob's real objective in banning the stacking of monitors in his trading room was to more easily observe the traders. This was a damning charge, for if what Bob had really built was a surveillance system rather than a collaborative space, the trading room should certainly not be described as non-hierarchical. Back then, I had dismissed the colleague's comment as an overly harsh, purely provocative remark. Later that summer, I visited Bob's house and met his family, and the experience had puzzled me even further. I learned that Bob was Catholic, a father of six children, and that he lived in a well-appointed, traditionally decorated suburban house. None of these seemingly conservative traits were evocative of the organic companies described by Burns and Stalker. However, the disparity between these observations and my view of the trading room only became clear after Bob's guest lecture at Columbia.

Once the lecture had ended, numerous questions formed in my mind. What, I wondered, lay behind the seemingly relaxed and sociable atmosphere that I had seen at the trading room? Had Bob facilitated this climate by virtue of his own empathy? Or was it a product of the charisma that I had just witnessed? The question became a pressing one, not least because in those days I was also in need of finding a way to impose my own authority among my MBA students. As Bob and I left the classroom for lunch at the Faculty House (a formal restaurant on campus that Columbia reserved for academics and their guests), I decided to drop my previous plans to discuss other matters and instead use the time to query him. I wanted to hear the story of what happened in the trading room in the two years that elapsed before I arrived, including details, names, and dates. With this, I hoped, I would be able to answer the puzzle that now lay ahead of me: if the trading room could not ultimately be characterized as organic, flat, or boundaryless, how should I think about it? Similarly, if Bob's role as manager had not been that of a supportive facilitator, what had it been?

Transforming the Equities Trading Floor

The account I received from Bob over lunch was remarkably candid. Bob revealed his views on issues I had never asked about during my years at the trading room, his thinking about power, politics, authority, and coercion; as well as his own values, principles, morality, and ethics.

The harmonious trading room that I had encountered in 1999, I learned, had not always been thus. Before Bob's arrival in November 1997, the management of the bank believed there was "something wrong" with the equities floor and hired Bob to fix it. The floor was then composed of two halves that served very different and ill-fitting purposes. It contained a large international equities sales force, which served the bank's international strategy. That, according to Bob, was "a customer-driven, low-risk-taking, process-oriented business," that is, not very interesting in his eyes. In addition, the floor included a smaller group specialized in complex and lucrative Wall Street-style trading. But there was very little synergy between the two groups. Overall, "it was a poorly conceived combination of two entirely different businesses," Bob recalled. To make matters worse, the trading part of the floor was in a state of disrepair. Many of the desks were specialized in outdated activities such as market making on Nasdaq stocks, Latin American financing, or a money-losing options trading desk. In short, "it was just a mess." Bob's first year was thus consumed with closing those activities and laying off traders. He also closed the international outposts of the bank's equities division, which included an office in Canada and one in an offshore territory.

The second activity that Bob addressed during his first year was developing a firm grasp of the relations among the traders. He administered a form of network questionnaire in which he asked each trader to state who he worked for. Bob then asked the person mentioned by each trader whether he had a supervisory relationship with the respondent. As it turned out, many traders did not appear to know who they worked for. The exercise made some people uncomfortable, but it revealed the organizational confusion that was in place.

The trading room, which was initially composed of more than one hundred people, shrunk as Bob laid off or encouraged the voluntary departure of about 85 percent of the traders.

Bob's next step was to hire new traders and build up the mix of desks that I encountered when I arrived one year later. He hired Max to run the merger arbitrage desk, and two senior traders in the options arbitrage desk. Bob's objective was not only to diversify, but, as noted in the previous chapter, also to incorporate various types of knowledge into the floor, including the research-driven, trading-driven, and flow-driven properties of stocks. In parallel, Bob began a technology rebuild effort, and the transformation of the Operations department.

As part of this hiring, Bob assembled the management team that I had already met. Stanley and Jerry joined in 1998, followed by Brian in the year 2000. "All three of these guys had worked for me at Premier," he added. I was surprised to hear that Bob was only hiring previous acquaintances, but Bob's approach was consistent with an observation he had once made: showing me a detailed seating chart of the trading room, he said, "I trust this one, that one, and that one." Trust, in other words, was a scarce commodity for Bob. Jerry had worked with Bob since 1990 at Premier, and Bob described him as "my right-hand troubleshooter." Jerry was also valuable in that he was steeped in the institutional details of the market.

During our lunch conversation, Bob also revealed that Stanley did not, in the end, perform satisfactorily as broker between the desks. "His book was a failure, and I pulled it very quickly," Bob recalled, referring to the portfolio of trades, or "book," that Stanley handled. Stanley stopped playing a managerial role, becoming a trader himself, "and he was a successful trader," Bob added. Bob's perspective on Stanley's underperformance as manager was telling of Bob's own approach: "he didn't complement the culture, because he engendered mistrust." Stanley tended to engage traders by having an argument with them, but when he lost the argument, he would often use his hierarchical position. "People disliked that," Bob said, "if they've beaten you fairly in an intellectual argument, they don't want you to pull out a trump card and say, well, 'okay, never mind. I'm your boss.'"

Bob was, in other words, mindful of the limits of formal authority. For instance, he believed that formal authority biased communication. "If I needed to know the answer to something," he said, "I knew I couldn't ask the people directly, because of my position as the sole and dominant authority on the floor, which was essential for keeping order." Bob, he thought, was the law, the judge, the jury, and the person who kept peace. "But this is not compatible with true discourse. If I went to somebody and said, 'should you really be running the model?' Instead of replying, 'yes, I think I should, and here's the reason,' their first reaction was, 'do you want me to cut it, should I cut my size, how much would you like me to have in it?'" As a consequence, Bob relied on his managers for those conversations.

Bob thus had a complex relationship with authority. He combined an appreciation for power with an awareness of its dysfunctions. Partly due to this awareness, Bob refused to allow successful traders to expand their formal authority over others. "People would ask me to impose a promotion system in a hierarchy," he recalls. The argument would be along the lines of, "if I've done well trading this book, why can't I take over that guy's book and have them report to me?" However, Bob refused. In reflecting on the origin of these requests, Bob realized his traders brought these norms from other firms, "and in other firms you're acquiring kingdoms as you go up."

Two years into his job, Bob experienced a challenge to his authority. Bob had developed and communicated a specific aspect of his compensation policy: the percentage of the desk profits that traders would be paid as a bonus was not subject to year-end renegotiation. That is, this percentage was to be agreed to *before* the annual results were announced at year-end and would not be discussed again once the results were known. Having announced this, Bob found himself in a difficult dilemma when a statistical arbitrage trader named Yuris attempted to renegotiate his percentage. In March 1999, when the bank's financial results were released, Yuris learned that he had been one of the largest contributors to the profits of the floor. He was due an agreed-upon percentage of the profits he produced, but Yuris asked for a greater percentage. " 'I made so many million dollars for the floor and that guy made 10 million, and he has 14 percent, and I only have 12,' " Bob recalls Yuris telling him. To this, Bob replied that what mattered was the total bonus payment rather than the percentage. "What's the problem?" Bob said, "you did well." But Yuris was adamant that he should be paid a higher percentage of his desk's profits, and he threatened to leave.

The ultimatum put Bob in a bind. If he refused to agree to the trader's demands, Bob risked losing a crucial trader. But if he gave in and raised Yuris's bonus, the credibility of his compensation system would be fatally undermined, inviting renegotiations by the other traders. This type of dilemma is widespread in banking and has been analyzed by sociologist Olivier Godechot.[2] In such cases, managers are left with the dilemma to either pay more or risk losing the talented employee.

The decision Bob eventually made is illustrative of his overall approach to managing: Bob paid Yuris the exact bonus he was contractually due, *and then fired him*. Bob terminated the trader for reneging on an existing agreement. In other words, Bob turned the bonus ultimatum on its head: instead of a dilemma between retention and consistency, he saw it as one between principles versus interests. To Bob, the question was whether a trader should gain an exemption from the norms that applied to everyone simply because he was a star. Bob's answer to that question was "no." By refusing to budge, Bob explains, "the reputation that I developed, which I allowed to persist, was that I would burn down my own house before I would compromise with my principles or my rules."

Norms, the episode suggests, were of critical importance to Bob. "There's a thing that I really respect in your field," Bob told me in one of our later conversations about management. "There are norms that people will bind themselves to without understanding that they exist. And they're more powerful than any rational or explicit rule they think they're following." Hearing this prompted me to ask more on the topic. How, I asked, were your norms communicated on the trading room? "One very powerful way was direct conversation," Bob explained, but that was time-consuming. "The second way, since people are social and herd animals, was when they feel the emotion of the crowd. So periodically, I would speak in public. And I'm a capable public speaker."

Through his years at the bank, Bob spoke at four offsite meetings that he organized. These were presented to the traders as mandated by compliance rules. In the brokerage industry, there are regulatory requirements for continuing education, and Bob summoned employees to come to meetings on, for instance, settling and clearing trades, presenting these as part of their continuing education. "Well," Bob added with a smile, "I hijacked that process." Once at the offsite, Bob would say, "okay, this is our continuing ed. We have to do this. But let's make it worthwhile." He brought special speakers into the room, and led the discussion himself, bringing part of his vision to bear into that venue.

This was a conscious strategy. "If I had said to everyone, 'I want to give you an inspirational speech, please show up, and now open your mouths while I feed you these inspirational thoughts,' of course they'd all reject it." So instead, Bob framed the event as being about topics like trade settlement. The traders anticipated being uninterested, and resented having to attend, but they begrudged the regulator rather than Bob. Once they arrived at the venue, they received something exciting and stimulating. "Everyone in the room's laughing," Bob recalls, "they're having a good time. When they all go out, they're looking left and right and saying, 'do we like working here? Oh, we love working here.'"

Offsite meetings took place once a year, and included a mix of business presentations, socializing, one lavish dinner, and one group leisure activity such as attending a horse race. The first venue chosen by Bob was Bermuda, partly to persuade other senior managers in the bank to attend. Once the approach grew more popular, Bob progressively marched the meetings closer to home. The second venue was in Atlantic City, and the following one in an inexpensive hotel on the Jersey Shore. "It didn't matter. Once the whole offsite happened, it seemed exciting, and people were flying in from London and Tokyo to attend."

The last one was in Manhattan, at Chelsea Piers, and it included 150 people from the equities floor in New York and another 40 attendees from around the world. "In the beginning, we gave presentations on the forward curve. We'd start out with some technical stuff like that," but although Bob didn't do this part, it was his presence and enthusiasm that carried the day. "What I was doing was wrapping some technical information with my personality, how I expressed it, etc."

We had been talking for more than an hour after our lunch. At that point, Bob suddenly switched roles and turned to me. "You have the problem of getting people to come to class on time," he said. This was true. There had been many late arrivals to Bob's presentation on that morning, and in fact these late arrivals happened regularly. Because I had been flexible during the first sessions of the course, the students had become accustomed to being late on a consistent basis. Bob shared with me how he confronted late arrivals at one of his offsite meetings, recounting an incident concerning the co-head of the trading room, an international executive put in place by the bank's headquarters. "He was a good-spirited guy, but a little hierarchical," Bob recalls. The co-head and a few others were once late to one of Bob's presentations. "I had everyone come into the room, and then locked the door. People were waiting outside, and they didn't want to come in because it was too embarrassing." At that point, Bob's co-head showed up. Everyone knew he was a separate source of authority. He knocked on the door and opened it. "Bob, can we come in?" But Bob was unyielding. "No, none of you can come in. You'll have to spend time with me alone. That's your punishment." Everyone laughed at Bob's self-deprecating comment. The door closed and the twelve stood outside, including the co-head.

Bob's response had sent an unambiguous signal. Everyone was subject to the same norms of punctuality, including the co-head of the floor. Bob was willing to hold everyone to the same standard of how to behave. More important, Bob recalls, was the question of power: "how willing was I to exercise my authority? Because that's a personal moment. You know, there's this moment of tension like, jeez, that's a little hard." However, that was the message that Bob wanted to convey: "he really does have confidence. He really does feel like he's in charge." He recalls: "I really knew what I was trying to achieve in the culture there. I was working at it actively. And it was very successful."

Culture

Commitment. Authority. Emotional energy. Bob's account of his own efforts to transform the floor's culture took up our entire lunch meeting and continued in my office for a lot longer than I anticipated. Later that afternoon, once Bob left the business school and I regained the solitude of my office, I took stock of what I had learned. Bob had opened a surprising and unexpected window into the managerial work that underpinned the trust and open communication I encountered on the floor. When I first arrived at the bank in November 1999, it seemed to me as though everyone trusted everyone, and as if communication was unproblematic. There were no external signs of conflict or resistance, so I assumed that what I was witnessing on the floor was its "natural" state. This perspective now needed to be revised.

What, then, to make of Bob's transformation of the floor? His efforts speak to Mitchel Abolafia's research on Wall Street bond traders in the 1980s. The culture he identified marked a sharp contrast with the culture I encountered in Bob's trading room. Abolafia's traders represented an extreme, almost distorted, version of Max Weber's portrait of capitalism: an impersonal environment, where trust and cooperation were nearly absent. Abolafia's bond traders also exhibited a highly materialistic value orientation, to the point that the primary source of status was compensation, rather than charisma or social skills.

Despite the contrast between Abolafia's traders and those I encountered at Bob's trading floor, Abolafia's broader message is consistent with what I observed. Abolafia laid out an institutionalist conception of finance, where "economic actors construct a world of norms, scripts and strategies" that shape action. Thus, whereas a rational choice approach, as typically found in orthodox economic analyses, presents behavior as resulting from a natural drive toward individual maximization, Abolafia presented action as the result of habituation and a culturally defined toolkit. "Self-interest," he wrote, "is transformed into situationally specific, culturally proper strategies enacted from a preexisting repertoire."[3] In other words, Abolafia saw nothing natural about the celebration of self-interest he observed among bond traders, adding that it was constructed and facilitated by the "social conditions" on the trading floor.

The above accounts for the importance of the cultural norms that I saw on the equities trading floor at International Securities. The social conditions that shape behavior, Abolafia wrote, include the strength and efficacy of the reputational networks among traders, the shifts in the distribution of power among stakeholders, the existence and enforcement of institutionalized rules of exchange, and the threat of regulatory intervention. Of these conditions, the existence and enforcement of institutionalized rules was in line with Bob's initiatives such as punctuality, no stacking of monitors, and no renegotiation of the bonus. The existence and enforcement of norms is thus central in institutionalist accounts of markets, for they constrain individual behavior and make it predictable.

There were, however, several elements in Bob's account that are not readily accounted for in Abolafia's research. The institutional portrait presented by Abolafia said relatively little about how practices on the floor could be altered and transformed, yet this was precisely what Bob had achieved. To do so,

Bob had to challenge the norms and beliefs espoused by the traders, which he achieved by organizing shared experiences and rituals such as the offsite retreats in remote locations, by conveying his own emotional energy in public speaking, or by enforcing new norms in unexpected situations, as in the case of the late arrivals. In doing so, Bob seized on his role as manager, and exhibited remarkable agency in effecting change within an institutionalized setting. Thus, while Abolafia emphasized the role of norms and scripts in creating institutional stability, Bob's actions suggest that those norms could also be changed.

The central importance of norms to Bob's trading room had additional implications for my study. First, none of the aforementioned institutional dynamics had come to my attention before Bob's guest lecture at Columbia, so my realization of such a gap made clear to me that I should reconsider the rest of my certainties about the trading room. Second, while Bob's account seemed genuine, I needed to check whether it was correct. I initiated a new round of interviews with executives who were present in Bob's early months to understand if their perceptions matched Bob's account. I started by contacting Ray, an employee of the bank who had been the head of the Operations Department at International Securities during Bob's tenure at the bank. I remembered that Bob had eliminated the lounge area that separated the Operations department from the rest of the floor, but I had neither checked whether this had worked as intended nor asked to speak to the people there. I asked Bob to put me in touch with Ray, and he agreed to do so.

RAY

"And you say you teach management?" asked Ray as we shook hands at the start of our meeting, giving me a skeptical look. Ray and I met in a conference room located in Global Trust in 2008, a bank that Bob joined four years after leaving International Securities. The venue was convenient because Ray was paying Bob a social visit on that day. Ray was intrigued by my academic position and barely able to hide his skepticism. "I'd be curious to see what a person gets out of a course like that," referring to the course I taught at Columbia. I responded with a question back to him: had he encountered any really good manager through his career? "They're very few, from my perspective. Bob happens to be one of them."

I asked Ray to expand on this. How did he end up working with Bob? Ray had originally wanted to be a teacher, but his second-generation American relatives encouraged him to take a better-paid job. He ended up working at the operations department of an investment bank on Wall Street and sought advancement by taking on managerial responsibility for his team of four. "I started kind of acting as the manager," he explained, "and started liking it, and thinking to myself, 'well, gee, managing people is kind of what drove me to be a teacher, because the whole idea of teaching is to educate people.'" In opting for a management career in finance, Ray was also driven by the lack of managerial talent in his bank. "I looked around at the management of the bank, one, two, three, four levels above me, and said, 'these people are such poor managers.' No communication. No encouragement. My manager didn't even know my name. There were no staff meetings, no outings. No pizza lunches. No attaboys. Nothing." Managers would show up every day "and just kind of barked orders and yelled if one did not do the job." There had to be a better way to manage, Ray concluded.

After a succession of supervisory jobs, Ray arrived at International Securities several years before Bob did. By the time Bob arrived in 1997, Ray had taken over the Operations group there. Bob's predecessors, Ray recalls, had been "very disengaged." When Bob arrived, he told Ray that he wanted Operations to be a team effort and include him in discussions on developing new business. "It was like water in the desert," Ray recalls. He set up lunches and breakfasts for Bob and held staff meetings in which Bob came and talked to Ray's team about his objectives for the trading floor. The support staff, who previously had not received any of that information, were also invited. This was important because, before, "we were constantly scrambling, trying to catch up to what [the traders at the front office] were doing," Ray explained.

Ray and Bob soon built a solid working relationship. Ray developed a committed team, though he initially laid off sixty people out of the one hundred people he started with. Before letting an employee go, Ray gave each one an opportunity to know that there was a problem, and a proposed solution such as additional training, a change of role, etc. The employee was addressed in writing, offered counseling, the problem was documented, and the individual was sent to Human Resources. "But after six months of working with somebody, if he did not get it he would have to leave," Ray added. There were strong parallels with the work that Bob was undertaking. "Bob was doing the same at the front office," Ray adds. "We were looking for a different type of person. We were looking for people who wanted to work in that environment."

The approach eventually proved effective. Before Bob's arrival, traders were burdened with semi-clerical and semi-support tasks because they did not trust anybody in the back office. Ray insisted that Operations officials ought to be trusted to do their job: "you guys do sales and trading, okay?" he said, "we do the rest." After six months, Ray had a "Sales Trading Operations" team. "Traders felt very confident in speaking to clients about new businesses, because they knew they could toss the ball over to the other team." This change was one of several that Ray felt had contributed to the changed outlook of the equities floor at large.

Ray also changed the way he hired. Prior to Bob's arrival, Ray employed people who were career back-office officials, with no expectation of ever working in the front office. Under Bob, Ray started hiring college graduates whose goals were to be traders and salespeople. Before being promoted, they had to work for Ray first. "During that time, I assessed their character, their work ethic, whether they got along with people, their ability to absorb instructions, and their ability to learn new things." Ray then sent them to take the financial certification exam, registered them so they could be front office staff, and told them they were on the fast track. They were not guaranteed anything, but promised that when a job in the front office came up, they would be interviewed, and they would have an edge because the interviewers would be the people they saw every day. On the other side of the floor, Bob was pushing the salespeople and the traders: "if you have a choice of five people and one of them happens to be someone that works in our group, and if he's anywhere near as good as the other four, you've got to go with the inside person," Ray explained, "because that's what we were trying to create." Over a period of four years, Ray promoted more than thirty people from operations and technology into trading and sales.

Ray also decided to take over the hiring process from the Human Resources department at International Securities. "I didn't want HR involved, because they would always get the same resumes. The top kid in Yale, the top kid in Harvard, and the top kid in Columbia, and I said, 'you know what? We know those guys could do it, but that's not what I'm looking for. I'm after someone who is looking for a different way. We're not going to sit them in a hundred-thousand-dollar-a-year training program. They're going to come into my group and they'll get a lot of personal attention. I'm going to pay them $45,000. It's not Goldman Sachs. It's International Securities. It's a different environment. So, you need to look for somebody from like Penn State or Delaware, or even Albany. That's the person that we need, and we can see if that person can make it.'"

Ray's account confirmed an impression I had developed from a conversation with a trader at the technology desk in 2001 that I will call Vedish. When I asked Vedish about the traders, he replied: "many come from Operations. That's why people like to work here. They all come from the same background. There are people originally in Operations in every desk, for example, many in the sales desk. Equities is very supportive with the exam. I also took it, and my background is not in finance. These guys [pointing to the Operations Department] are all waiting to move up. For example, [name of trader] was supposed to move last month, but at the end there was no possibility." I then asked Vedish about the academic training that the promoted Operations officials brought to the trading room. Did they, for example, have graduate degrees? "Most people don't have an MBA. And it probably makes sense," he added, "because unless you are very well grounded, I guess you might have this misguided idea that you know everything. And that would be a mistake. The way it works is, Ray gets interns, and if they are good, they stay on."

Ray's pitch to the new hires was centered on the long term: "look, this is a longer road and a more difficult road, and you're not making as much money as if you'd gone to Goldman. I understand that. But you'll have people who care about you as a person and develop you as a person and watch after your interests." For Ray, the transformation of the Operations Department was a great accomplishment. "Out of almost fifteen years at International Securities, this is one of the two things I'm most proud of."

The second change that Ray introduced with Bob's support was general norms of respect for Operations officers. "I had people that came back to me and said, 'I had a bit of a run-in with somebody.'" Ray had them replay the incident and he would then follow up with the person separately. "Can I speak with you privately? Yeah. There was an exchange between you and one of the members of my staff. I'd just like to know what occurred because I don't like that sort of relationship between my staff and the traders. I need to get to the bottom of this, so can you explain?" Sometimes, Ray added, the trader might insist on his right to be demanding: "well, I want what I want, when I want it." Ray's response would emphasize the benefits of civility: "people will be as loyal and as cooperative with you as you are with them. At the end of the day, it's a two-way street. You catch more flies with honey." But if Ray thought that it was a serious enough incident, he would say so to the trader. Once, he walked up to one and said: "not allowed. Will not happen again, or I will go to HR and get you fired." But by the time things got to that point, Ray had worked for months with the trader, "because we were trying to instill a mind-set, a culture, a belief system, a way of doing things."

Toward the end of my conversation with Ray, Bob came into the conference room where we were talking. "Where's your jacket?" he asked Ray, jokingly. "I'm rebelling," replied Ray, who was not wearing one. "I'm going to have a glass of wine at lunch," he added, to which Bob countered, "I'm going to have a glass too." And then, looking at the two of us, Bob asked me, "actually, every-thing ok? Ray is an important guy from the days of International Securities. A lot of the stuff that you and I talked about, Ray and I had talked about. He shares with me, you know, the people-driven way of production."

Internal Labor Markets on Wall Street

The conversation with Ray provided me with valuable material to better understand how Bob had transformed the prevailing norms on the trading floor. I was particularly interested in the systematic way in which Bob and Ray had resorted to selection, promotion, and compensation to shape the organization. Their practice of endorsing Operations officers for promotion to trading positions seemed particularly effective. Such a policy speaks to ongoing debates over the nature of contemporary careers, and specifically the concept of "internal labor markets," which designates the use of hiring and promotion to advance existing employees in the organization. Internal labor markets were a central policy of American corporations during the postwar decades and are credited with creating employee loyalty and stimulating investments in company-specific skills. However, they came under pressure during the 1980s as the decline of manufacturing and a wave of mergers and acquisitions led companies to resort to layoffs, defaulting on their implicit contracts and undermining employee loyalty. At International Securities, by contrast, Bob and Ray were able to restore trust between operations and trading, as well as enforce norms of respect despite status differences, by creating an informal form of internal labor market. It was informal in the sense that it was unaided by the Human Resource department, but it nevertheless seemed effective.

The effectiveness of internal labor markets at International Securities is consistent with the research conducted by Abolafia, who accounted for opportunism among bond traders on Wall Street in terms of the *lack* of internal labor markets. The traders' incentive to maximize personal income and company profits, Abolafia found, was "heightened by the fact that there is no career ladder for a trader."[4] This zeal was manifested in several ways: lack of loyalty to the organization, lack of interest among the traders in moving into the management ranks, higher compensation for top traders than for managers, frequent departures to other banks by the traders, and frequent layoffs of those traders perceived by the bank to be ineffective. By contrast, the internal labor market that Bob and Ray created at International Securities was part of a broader system that promoted loyalty and sought to limit employee turnover in order to reinforce shared norms.

Ray's reliance on an internal labor market highlights another difference between Bob's trading room and others on Wall Street. Ray pressed for hiring lower-wage but perhaps humbler and more malleable recruits without elite university or graduate degrees. The goal was not simply cost reduction, but also self-selection of traders who were more receptive to the needs of the organization, as Vedish noted. It also cemented Ray's authority, as he had a say on who got promoted. This non-elite approach to hiring contrasts with the practices portrayed in Karen Ho's ethnography of Wall Street banks.[5] A Princeton alumna herself, Ho's research demonstrates the extraordinary extent to which Harvard, Princeton, and other Ivy League universities formed the core recruiting grounds for Wall Street. Undergraduate students, she reports, were constantly told by the bankers that they are "the best and brightest" (p. 11) at both recruitment events and in newcomer socialization events at the job. The elitism, when combined with the transient nature of the employment and an emphasis on extrinsic motivation, often resulted in the bankers providing merger advice to corporate clients that led to excessive organizational change, disruption, downsizing, and employee insecurity.

By contrast, Bob's trading room fostered a different set of cultural norms. Bob's floor can thus be perceived as a partial remedy to the cultural problems identified by Ho. By hiring internally, the transience in employment was reduced and employees developed commitment to the bank; furthermore, promotion could be tied to socialization into the bank's norms. In sum, by pursuing a non-elite hiring strategy, Bob also tapped into employees with a more communal and long-term outlook.

Indeed, the presence of an internal market at International Securities shed light on a puzzle that had stayed with me for several years. During my visits to the sales trading desk in 2002, I was surprised by the overall attitude exhibited by Scott, the junior sales trader that I observed. Scott was young, had recently been hired, and exhibited remarkable humility, earnestness, and pride of working at the desk. His admiration for the two senior traders at the desk reminded me of that of a younger sibling toward an older brother. I was surprised by Scott's positive attitude, and also somewhat disturbed that an employee might feel this degree of identification with his senior colleagues. At the time, I attributed it to Scott's own personality, but now I could see that such an outcome was precisely what the internal career was meant to produce, for Scott had indeed been promoted from Operations a few months before I met him.

Following my conversation with Ray, Bob's approach to managing the floor had become clearer. Even Bob's decision to make an unscheduled appearance at the end of my meeting with Ray was also revealing of Bob's approach: controlling the experience, and putting a frame, or spin, on our discussion and my takeaways from it. True to his style, Bob had remarked positively on Ray's professional worth ("he is an important guy"), done so with a sense of humor ("no jacket?"), and in a way that made his presence feel light and not overbearing.

In sum, my meeting with Ray provided evidence of Bob's efforts at effecting change on the trading floor. But as much as Ray's description of internal labor markets and norm enforcement seemed accurate, I could not shake off a slight sense of discomfort. Invocations of culture, as Ann Swidler has argued, are problematic. A long tradition of social scientists, from Harold Garfinkel[6] to Edward Said,[7] have warned against the risk of essentializing members of other cultures, that is, treating actors as cultural dopes, unreflexively playing out preexisting cultural scripts. There is, in other words, a real risk of romanticizing the role of corporate culture and concluding that one individual could truly shape it. In this regard, I wondered whether Ray was falling prey to this danger in the model for internal careers that he had described. To what extent did Bob's attempt at transforming the culture actually work? What were the downsides to it?

There was another troubling aspect to Ray's account. I recalled his remark that managing was "like teaching," and wondered whether supervising adult officers in the Operations Department should be thought of as teaching and handling students. After all, the asymmetry of knowledge between two adults, supervisee and supervisor, is not as wide as that between a teacher and a student, that is, an adult and a child. Was Ray being condescending to his own employees? And, was this not one of the risks posed by such hands-on handling of them? A final comment that seemed unusual was Ray's pitch to potential recruits: we will take an interest in you "as a person." I wondered whether the rhetoric was concealing an overly hierarchical organization, but one where power and authority played out covertly rather than out in the open.

Authority

My conversation with Ray confirmed Bob's interest in shaping organizational culture at the bank. Culture became the center of subsequent conversations between Bob and me. In our first such conversation, I asked him about norm enforcement. Two of his subordinates had once described Bob as having a "strongman approach." The term strongman designates circus performers who display feats of strength, and in the case of Bob the comment was meant to highlight his overly dramaturgical exercise of power. The comment gave me the opportunity to ask Bob about his attitude toward authority. "Would you say you were," I asked, "a strongman?"

To this, Bob replied with a rhetorical question. "Why do people put up with a boss? A boss is an impediment to one's freedom," he argued, and he's going to judge your performance. But, Bob added, there's a tradeoff. Managers provide valuable things to employees. They can save them from troubles. An employee might think, "he's going to judge me, but he is also a judge. So, when I'm in a quarrel or dispute with someone else, he's going to be a fair judge. Everybody needs a fair judge. Quarreling is very expensive, and it's fraught with risk." A manager can fulfill that role.

Another reason for having a manager, Bob argued, is protection. "I don't want people stealing what's mine, taking what's mine. The boss is going to protect me from that." And finally, the manager provides resources. "If a boss is able to be a judge, protector, and provider of resources," subordinates will naturally and willingly accept a reduction of their freedom and submit to their superior's judgment. However, a manager cannot do those things unless he is strong. If a boss appears weak, the subordinate will be anxious. " 'Oh God, this guy is supposed to provide resources, but he seems very weak. I don't know where we'll get them. How is he going to protect me from those bad guys? He seems weak. I don't know if he has the strength of character to deliver judgment when the opposing force might be very powerful.' So, the boss has to be strong."

Part of conveying strength, Bob added, was to actively show strength. Doing that took different forms in different settings. Take the trading floors, Bob said, "they house dozens, maybe hundreds of people, crowded in a tight environment, so there's a certain physical presence that has to be there." I asked him to explain what he meant by that. "You can't be tentative about where you walk or how you walk. The people have to feel like you can go wherever you want." At International Securities, he added, "there was no inch of the trading floor that wasn't mine to walk on." Bob would walk up to a group of people, sit in an empty chair, and a trader might point out that someone was sitting there: "Jack doesn't like anyone to sit in his chair," as if they were solicitous of that trader's welfare. "I'd say, 'oh well when Jack comes back, I'll get up.'"

Another form of signaling ownership of the space was by stipulating its use. "I make everyone lower the trading screens," said Bob. "Why is that? They may say, 'I don't want to lower it, I need to look at it.' And I'd say 'well, I need to look at *you*.' So, there's a little bit of personal electricity or tension." Similarly, Bob made traders occasionally clean up under their desks. "Hey, you've got a lot of newspapers under there. I want those thrown out." What was that telling them? 'That's my territory.'"

Finally, Bob added, the economic stakes involved in the traders' job made showing strength particularly difficult. The manager, Bob argued, has to build a reputation that he will harm his own interests rather than yield. "Because otherwise, any star trader will reason, 'Bob would never fire me, because I'm making $20 million, and he needs that money.'" Accordingly, the manager has to demonstrate to those people that he does not care about their profits: "what I care about is being the boss. And I can't be the boss if you hold me hostage for your money. So, why don't you go ahead and throw that money away. I don't need it. I don't need the money because I don't spend a lot of money, because I could live with very little money."

The message was surprising: less greed, more strength. Up until then I had assumed that displaying wealth in a trading room would confer credibility, but Bob claimed the opposite. "Once the traders think they hold you hostage because they are profitable, you're not the boss anymore." Furthermore, Bob's reasoning was consistent with my own recollection of him on the floor. Even on my first day at the bank, I was intrigued by Bob's reluctance to display status symbols in his personal appearance and by his rather unremarkable choice of clothes. Now I understood why: a pair of basic cotton chinos was, to Bob, more imposing than luxurious pants from a boutique.

In fact, and to my surprise, Bob was happy to be branded a strongman. "Yeah, I would hope that my subordinates thought I was a strong man," he replied, shifting from a pejorative term (strongman) to a positive one (strong [space] man). "I would like to actually be a strong person," he repeated, now shifting to the more correct gender-neutral expression (person). "But," he added, "you can't just be it, you also have to understand the theater and demonstrate it. The manager needs to convey the message he or she wants to get across, and ideally display it as much possible." There are only a few things one is allowed to hide, Bob added. "You can't pretend to be honest and be dishonest. You can't pretend to be strong and be weak. You can't pretend to be self-sacrificing and be self-dealing." However, a manager can pretend to be confident when he is afraid and be calm when inside he is very angry. Or, pretend to be angry when inside he is calm. This created a dilemma when it came to compassion: "you may actually forgive somebody already for some bad thing they've done, but you may have to show a stern and angry face. Because if you don't show them that you're angry, they might misunderstand what you actually feel. You forgive them because you know they're human, and you know they're essentially good people, but they may say oh, he didn't care about the wrongdoing. So, you have to show that too. That's the theater. The theater isn't to deny or be in conflict with fundamental character issues. The theater is to display the lesson."

Bob was, in other words, acutely aware of the interpersonal dimension to managing a trading room. "When you have a small enough organization," he argued, "status and esteem sort of become a natural tool, because people can see it. I could grant status to somebody simply by walking over to their part of the trading floor and chatting with them in the morning, with a cup of coffee. You'd see people look up and they're happy. The boss is talking. Doesn't matter what you talk to them about, sports or the weather. Everybody's happy to be talked to [by their boss]."

I then saw an opportunity to push Bob on the degree to which he was willing to exert authority. One trader at International Securities had once mentioned to me his frustration with "Bob's sobriety," adding that he missed having "arbitrage nights" out with colleagues where one could share ideas with colleagues on the trading room. At a previous bank where this trader worked, colleagues had "arbitrage nights, with umbrella golf, and push-ups against the wall." However, at International Securities there was none of this. "Could you comment on that?" I asked. Bob smiled. "Absolutely. This is going to get to the heart of it." Bob started with a detour and then returned to my question. "If you go to most modern organizations in the last fifty plus years, there's an ethic that says—and I agree with it—that people are entitled to their privacy and people should be free to behave as they choose, as long as that behavior doesn't immediately collide with the work." Coercion, Bob was saying, is a last resort, and you have to be very careful wherever you bring coercion into the enforcement of standards.

"But because I believe there are standards, it is incumbent upon me in any position of authority, certainly at work, to try to teach those standards and do everything I can to encourage people to live up to that standard." Bob explicitly rejected the relativist idea that there are no absolute moral standards for behavior. This was relevant to the question of drinking after work that another trader had mentioned. "I think drinking after work leads to many bad things. You know, I drink myself, I drink with friends. But that's a path that can lead to many bad things happening, cheating on your spouse, getting in trouble with the police. There are just a lot of bad things that can happen. Moral problems, corruption, safety, etc."

Accordingly, Bob communicated to his employees the standard he favored through his own behavior. To his surprise, it proved effective. "Without ever saying it to people, there is an element of coercion, because when I operate by that standard, I'm telling people this is what good behavior is. And if you get yourself in trouble at work as a consequence of not following the standard I've illustrated, I will not be supportive of you." For instance, a former employee of his once fell off of his motorcycle while on a work trip abroad and broke his arm. He was arrested. Bob's colleagues abroad wanted to fire him for drunk driving. "I said 'no, you cannot fire him.' We brought him back to the United States. We covered all his medical expenses, and then I fired him a year later. I was clear that I was going to, once he was back on his feet and he had recovered, because he exercised bad judgment. Not just for drinking and driving, but also for doing so when he was on an assignment with us overseas, where he knew he was going to be under great scrutiny." Even though Bob punished the trader for bad judgment, he did not personally cast off the employee: "by the way," he added, "I stayed friends with that guy. I see him periodically."

Bob's attempts at shaping norms on the trading floor extended to the structure of the floor. He was careful not to reshape the composition of the teams that made up the various desks. "The businesses were like jewels that had to be accepted on their own bases," he said of desks. "I couldn't reorganize them, change the nature of their business. I wasn't going to tell Max, 'this is the way I want you to run merger arb. Don't run it the way you used to. Run it the way I think.'" Bob felt that the profitability of the desks would be destroyed if he tampered with the composition of the traders in them. "At that operating level, the molecular level, there has to be a certain structure. It's not the same as in the whole organism." At the previous bank Bob worked for, Premier Financial, there was no integrity to the small units. There, every single person was assignable to another business. But Bob thought this was misguided. For instance, he added, "Max has worked with the same cast of characters for most of the time he has been at International Securities. I worked with Jerry and Brian for years and years. It turns out, people work better that way. They're like little families."

These tight structures gave Bob an additional way of eliciting commitment. "When somebody has a bad year and they're not going to be paid, they think, 'I'm being paid badly. I'm going to be reassigned to some junkie job. I'm going to have to work with people I don't like. All is lost. I'm desperate. I should leave.'" By contrast, Bob continued, "when they're part of a team that feels like a family, the team decides whether they should leave or stay." The trader, Bob added, might conclude, "'gee, if I leave, we don't get to work with each other.'" "Sometimes," Bob added, "the captain of the team would say to me, 'I don't get paid a bonus this year, nobody gets paid a bonus because we didn't make any money, but could you pay the junior guy, like, $25,000? Just give him a bonus.'" This, to Bob, was crucial. "There's a huge psychic reward for the leader taking care of the junior people on the team. Huge. And it binds him to the firm, to the management. Giving $25,000 to the boss wouldn't give you any loyalty, nothing. He doesn't need the $25,000. He's a millionaire already. You give $25,000 that he can hand to his subordinate, and he is justifiably proud that he did right. He'll tell you, 'that guy's twenty-six, he just got married. He's really counting on that bonus.' And so, there's this multiplier effect. The money goes a long way."

A Village on Wall Street

The conversation with Bob described above confirmed the importance he attached to controlling the organization, and more specifically to what management scholars like Gideon Kunda call "normative control," that is, control through shaping employee experiences and affective states. However, Bob seemed to hint at something more all-encompassing and profound than organizational norms. First, he insisted on enforcing norms about behavior *outside* work, such as no drinking with colleagues, even after work. His justification for it was that there were absolute standards for right and wrong, and as a manager it was incumbent on him to communicate these standards. Second, Bob sought to reinforce the hierarchical relationship between heads of desks and junior traders around the principle of family ties, giving senior traders some discretion in pay, as well as treating the desks as "jewels," that is, not amenable to his own redesign. The point of this was to achieve order and stability to induce loyalty and reduce turnover. But Bob's approach had a generally conservative orientation, not in a political sense but manifest in expressions like the "captain" of a desk, the trading room as an "organism," and the metaphor of desks as "families."

Bob's approach spoke to the concept of social structure. Originally identified with the theory of structural functionalism and associated with the mid-century sociologist Talcott Parsons, social structure has since been theorized in less deterministic ways.[8] Functionalism saw society as a complex system whose parts work together to promote solidarity and stability. Parsons begins *The Structure of Social Action* with a reference to Hobbes, the seventeenth-century philosopher concerned with the problem of social order, that is, the question of how social chaos is avoided.[9] Parsons's answer is through social structure, constituted primarily of moral consensus. Starting in the 1960s, functionalism was first criticized and subsequently abandoned for its inability to account for social change, for lacking an explanation for structural contradictions and conflict (often being derided as a "consensus theory"), and ultimately for promoting a conservative view of society that privileged stability over change. Sociologists abandoned Parsons in the 1970s, but after a two-decade hiatus, visions of social structure have reappeared in the form of neo-institutionalism and the acknowledgment that shared norms inform and regulate individual action, as seen in Abolafia's work.

Bob's thinking about the trading room appeared to be implicitly informed by an appreciation for social structure. The desks were metaphorical families and added up to a notional village of 150 people, of which Bob presumably was the chief. The relationship between the junior traders and their seniors at the desk cemented social order within the trading room, including stability in the traders' employment, widely accepted norms such as sharing information with other desks, respect for back-office officers, and a complaint-free environment at bonus time. It was also cemented by an internal labor market.

Where did Bob's interest in social structure arise from? One potential explanation can be found in the Wall Street ethnography conducted by Karen Ho, and specifically in her portrait of "liquidity," or extreme job insecurity, in the bank she studied.[10] The bankers that Ho described understood they could be laid off at any point in time, and even Ho was herself laid off halfway through her research. The resulting uncertainty colored everyone's employment experience: in anticipation of being laid off, one banker explained, "you need to be thinking, 'I'm going to get as much as I can today,'" because "tomorrow" might never arrive. Another banker, involved in advising on a merger that did not perform adequately, explained that he knew he might not be around to face the consequences. The bank, however, succeeded in rhetorically justifying such job insecurity, and to Ho's surprise, the laid-off bankers that she interviewed seemed to accept and justify this approach to careers through references to global and impersonal forces ("market instability"), or flattering imagery such as comparing their bank to a "fighter jet." All in all, employees were redeployed, moved, and relocated in order to create a seamless service for corporate clients, while marketing itself to potential recruits as global, networked, and endowed with unlimited capital and boundless geographical reach.

It struck me that Bob had experienced a similarly "liquid" approach to careers as that described by Ho in the previous bank Bob had worked for,

Premier Financial. His emphasis in ensuring social order on the trading floor might have been a reaction to the dysfunctions of the alternative, which was to treat the employment relationship as almost a spot market arrangement. In any event, as I dug deeper into Bob's approach to management, I found an organization that corresponded less and less with the organic structure that I thought I had encountered during my fieldwork. I decided to persevere in my interviews and target additional executives who had helped Bob undertake cultural change in the trading room between 1997 and 1999. I hoped they would help me answer the new question that I now faced: was Bob really a strongman?

PETER

My next meeting took place with the former head of Strategic Communication at International Securities, whom I will call Peter. He had joined the bank in 1987, ten years before Bob, and remained there until 2001, so I felt he would be able to provide context about Bob's management of the equities trading room between 1997 and 1999.

Peter started by emphasizing Bob's ability to empathize. "Bob is one of the brightest guys I've ever met and worked with. He takes time to study. He takes time to use his quality of empathy to understand the other points of view." He continued: "Bob is a curious dude. He reads a lot. He befriended you because he was curious. Most guys on Wall Street would say, 'Oh, another academic from Columbia? Thank you very much. Goodbye. I don't have time for you. You're going to teach me a new algorithm? You're going to teach me something big? Okay. Come in and sit down. And I'll pay you, by the way.' But a sociologist? 'Wrong person on my trading floor. A desk? No. You're crazy. Go away.' So, Bob has those qualities, and many of the people you see here have those qualities."

I could not help but smile at the comment. During the years I was doing fieldwork at International Securities, my friends on Wall Street exhibited the same "you're crazy" reaction when I told them I was doing an ethnographic study of a trading floor. In other words, Peter had a point: my level of access to International Securities was unusual, but I had never stopped to ask myself why Bob welcomed my presence on the floor. Now Peter had done it for me.

The combination of empathy and intellectual curiosity, Peter continued, allowed Bob to create opportunities for people to settle in a trading environment that was somewhat different from those at other banks on Wall Street. "He wasn't the Wall Street super- or hyper-macho on steroids trading floor. He had bright people who were a little different. Being a little sensitive was okay, you know? He encouraged and challenged people." Bob's ability to empathize also allowed him to be in close contact with the traders. "He was in constant meetings at the desks, wondering what's going on, what's new, making people feel comfortable." This was true especially at the beginning, Peter explained. Eventually, he would understand and trust somebody, and kind of let them go. But still, "every so often, once a day or twice a day, he'd make an excuse to sit around them." Peter emphasized another aspect. "He gives you the incentive to make money, and a lot of it in some cases. He doesn't run around shouting at people. He doesn't run around using fear as a major motivational tool. He got the best horses he could and he gave them everything that they could want or need, and he got performance out of people. So, it's a little unusual."

From Models to Norms

Taken together, the conversations with Bob, Ray, and Peter reported in this chapter shed light on a critical event that marked a before and after in my research, namely, the lecture that Bob gave to my MBA class in 2007. Before that talk, I thought of Bob's trading room as a non-hierarchical, non-bureaucratic, organic structure. After seeing Bob address my MBA students, I realized I was mistaken. Bob's performance in my classroom was a polished and tightly orchestrated one: participative but on-topic, engaging but choreographed, and with one central master frame to which everyone (students included) had to adhere. Bob's visit produced a form of role reversal in which the two of us got to better understand each other. He saw me mismanaging my MBA students at Columbia, unable to make them arrive on time to class, and I saw him micromanaging them. I not only understood the need to establish my own authority in the classroom, but also concluded that Bob must have devoted considerable time and energy to establishing his own authority at International Securities. Because I had not seen that part of the trading room's history, I understood that the picture that had emerged from my fieldnotes was incomplete.

The round of interviews that followed Bob's lecture, including those with Ray, Peter, and Bob himself, was rich in insight. The overall picture that emerged confirmed the necessity to reappraise my initial views of the trading room. Bob had led a transformation that included extensive layoffs, assembling a management team, firing a star trader, and orchestrating shared experiences through offsite events. My conversation with Ray revealed the internal labor market that Bob had introduced, and the emphasis on enforcing norms of collaboration and respect. By his own account, Bob was even comfortable with having a "strongman approach" and had introduced the rule of no monitor-stacking at least partly for the purpose of surveillance.

All these elements pointed to a clear departure from the model of a non-hierarchical organization that I had initially believed described the floor. In line with my general interest in material devices within Science and Technology

Studies, my conception of Bob's trading floor had neglected the role of humans and conjectured instead a trading room where *objects* did the heavy lifting work of coordinating people and enforcing norms. Traders, I had assumed, exhibited restraint because of the rotating desks, low-level monitors, whiteboard meeting room, and layout of the desks. I now saw the inaccuracy of such a view. It was frames, norms, shared experiences, personal energy, and other managerial elements that were equally, if not primarily, responsible for the collaboration and restraint.

Such reappraisal, as Peter suggested, did not mean that the trading floor was a rigid hierarchy or bureaucracy. Bob did not quite act like a tyrant or a despot. For instance, Bob redefined Stanley's job because he had abused his authority as minister without portfolio. Bob also refused to give successful traders control over others in order to avoid them building personal fiefdoms. Bob was willing to satisfy his curiosity to the point of accepting a researcher on the floor. In sum, as Peter explained, Bob's approach was hybrid, strong "but not macho," authoritative "but not authoritarian," and this mixed approach also described the trading floor.

This raised one final question. If neither hierarchy nor flatness defined the trading floor, what did? A more informative way of looking at Bob's trading room, I concluded, was not in terms of how much power Bob wielded, but how this power was established. Instead of relying on interpersonal conflict to shape behavior, Bob communicated general norms, and occasionally had a public conflict such as firing Yuris or leaving his co-head out at an offsite meeting. In this regard, Bob's implicit metaphor for the trading room is revealing: a notional village, populated by a notional family in each individual desk whose unity was deemed valuable as a jewel. The analogy evoked a sense of community that also brought to mind the constraints of small-town life. The private sphere, including the possibility of drinking with colleagues after work, was in fact constrained by Bob's norms at work.

As I noted the primacy on norms in Bob's trading floor, I paradoxically turned full circle in an intellectual journey that started with an interest in the material tools and devices introduced by quantitative finance. In the age of Black-Scholes and Bloomberg terminals, conceptualizing Wall Street in terms of institutions and culture seemed somehow outdated. An alternative perspective, however, was that Bob's trading floor was not old but "retro." In other words, that it sought to deliberately replicate traditional arrangements as a reaction to modern excesses. Such excesses are in fact described in the ethnographies of Abolafia and Ho, who present organizations beset by opportunism and disregard for the law (in the case of Abolafia) and by job uncertainty, organizational instability, and individual disregard for the interests of the organization or the client (in the case of Ho). The accounts by Abolafia and Ho, in other words, read like Wall Street versions of the Hobbesian problem of social order, with every banker for himself. Set against those two, Bob's trading room might appear hierarchical, paternalistic even, and seemed admittedly predicated on a conservative 1950s conception of society as a harmonious working whole, where every member has a rightful place. This, however, was Bob's attempt to avoid the opportunism and uncertainty that the Abolafia and Ho ethnographies had revealed. In sum: order versus freedom, stability versus pluralism. As I noted the choices that Bob had made in the design of his floor, I was left wondering about the full terms of such a tradeoff, and whether it was worth it.

9

Resonance

The realization, back in 2007, that the trading room was not the organic structure that I had imagined, marked a milestone in my research. I now had a better understanding of the equities floor at International Securities, less fitting with my egalitarian ideals, but more accurate nevertheless. My conversations with Bob continued through 2007 and 2008. Although he no longer worked at the bank and his trading room design had most likely been abandoned, what I had witnessed between 1999 and 2003 continued to pique my curiosity. I remained interested in two aspects of the floor. One was Bob's approach to risk: his policy of not delegating control over the traders' positions to the Risk Management department had surprised me back in 1999, but now I thought I had an explanation for it: perhaps his resistance to delegate was due to Bob's tendency toward control.

There was a second aspect that kept me intrigued. This was the traders' use of economic models, and specifically Max's use of the spreadplot and implied probability to infer market estimates of merger likelihood, the so-called process of backing out described in chapter 5. That a trader could use models to find out what his rivals were thinking without needing to communicate with them or observe their actions seemed to me surprisingly powerful. This was genuine proof of the advantage that economic models conferred to Wall Street traders, which I had long sought to witness. By the same token, however, I now wondered about the potential risks that this practice might give rise to. Existing research by MacKenzie and Millo had identified a similar process of backing out implied estimates in the context of options arbitrage, but these researchers had not established the potential dangers that such practices might pose.[1]

A subsequent lunch appointment with Bob gave me the opportunity to satisfy my curiosity. By this time, Bob was officially retired and did not have an office in Manhattan. I requested a meeting, and we agreed to have lunch at a restaurant close to Lincoln Center, half-way between my office at Columbia and Penn Station, where he would catch his train.

Non-Quantitative Risk Management

At the restaurant, and once we caught up on each other's lives, I asked Bob about his policy of not delegating control to the Risk Management department. He corrected me immediately: "I never interfered with the bank's risk management," he said. "I accepted all their reports, cooperated with them—absolute, full cooperation." Indeed, Bob's policy toward risk management was far more nuanced than I recalled: "my view on corporate risk management is that, if that's the way the executives want to monitor risk in my business, it's their decision. They can do anything they want. So, total cooperation. But I took almost none of their data as very useful to me." In other words, Bob accepted the existence of the department and complied with its requirements, but did not use its calculations.

To account for his skepticism, Bob reminded me of the way in which the Risk Management department operated. "What are they doing? They are running mathematical models based on past history, looking at boundary conditions, etc. Okay, but before *we* go into trades," he said about himself and the traders, "we're looking at that information in ways that are more robust." For instance, Risk Management had to rely on quantitative methods, "but we could do other stuff." Suppose, Bob added, a trader brought to him an idea for a trade. Bob might respond, "I never thought about it, but do you think it's influenced by oil prices? We might do an analysis that you cannot run on computers easily. We could do a hypothetical: I could take somebody and say 'hey, plot out a plausible path.' Maybe not very high probability, but reasonable, and kind of extreme. What does it look like then? Wow, that trade looks really bad." Bob's argument, in other words, spoke to the observation that quantification is limited when it comes to the future, for the future is unknown. Risk managers were forced to create backward-looking risk estimates that often failed to capture the real uncertainty ahead, but Bob and his team could exercise judgment among different possible scenarios.

Bob also believed that having a department dedicated to risk management entailed an unworkable division of labor. "One guy gets the rewards," he said about the traders, "and the other gets the responsibility," in the case of the risk managers. "One guy is the hero, the other guy is the scold, right? How the hell can that work?" By contrast, Bob's own management team was more integrated. "I worked with Brian and Jerry [Bob's management team] for a long time on risk management. We knew each other's personalities. We were aware of what each other knew, and what we didn't. We were really good at communicating. We had aligned interests, financially and personally. So, when we sat down to assess a problem, another method of managing risks, of evaluating past history, of speculating about future scenarios, and of thinking about how the different books met, we worked off each other. It was very good."

The Limits of Quantification

Back in my office at Columbia, as I reviewed my notes, I saw that Bob's concerns spoke, once again, to Knight's distinction between risk and uncertainty. Because risk management departments assessed the impact and probability of losses through quantitative means, that is, through calculation, they ended up privileging the past over the future. However, appraising the potential hazards of a trade that had not yet been executed entailed judgment, that is, careful consideration and weighting of different options.

Bob's misgivings also spoke to a growing literature on the shortcomings of quantitative risk management. In a study on Long-Term Capital Management, MacKenzie challenged the widespread view that the hedge fund's partners had blindly trusted inaccurate models. Instead, he advanced an alternative explanation for the fund's demise based on social dynamics in the securities market. One of the aggravating factors, MacKenzie argued, was the widespread adoption of model-based risk management.[2] Prevailing models such as Value at Risk estimate the likely loss that a bank or a fund can experience at any given point in time. Because of the use of Value at Risk, the increase in market volatility during the early summer of 1998 was interpreted as an increase in market risk. This, in turn, forced the funds that used Value at Risk to reduce or close their positions. Their actions widened the arbitrage spreads in existing trades, that is, increased the mispricings that Long-Term Capital Management (LTCM) was betting against, and in so doing contributed to worsening the losses experienced by the fund, draining its capital base. As MacKenzie wrote, "arbitrageurs other than LTCM fled the market, even as arbitrage opportunities became more attractive, causing huge price movements against LTCM."[3]

MacKenzie's research spoke not only to the dangers of model-based risk management, but also to the general dangers of economic models, suggesting that the success of a model can paradoxically engender its subsequent failure. This can happen when a model's success leads to widespread adoption, and such adoption alters individual market behavior so that, in the aggregate, the market stops conforming to the model's assumptions. This effect comprises two analytically distinct elements. First, the difference between *individual* and *collective* model adoption: whereas a model's assumptions may hold true when adopted by one or a few actors, they may not hold if adopted by many actors or the entire market. Second, the presence of a *feedback loop*, relating adverse environmental conditions (i.e., an increase in market risk, as measured by Value at Risk) to adverse organizational actions (i.e., reduced positions) that culminate in wider spreads.

MacKenzie's work provided me with the theoretical scaffolding to further explore the potential pitfalls of backing out implied merger probabilities, as I had seen Max do. Was there a sense to which backing out worked well when used by one trader, but failed when adopted by many? Furthermore, was there a feedback loop relating the outcome of Max's models to the estimates made by other arbitrageurs?

The answer to these questions came in a subsequent conversation I had with Max. By this time, Max had also left International Securities and had joined a hedge fund located in Stamford, Connecticut. On the day of our conversation, I told Max of my interest in understanding how Bob managed risk at International Securities without relying on indicators such as Value at Risk. Max confirmed that Bob did not use the figures produced by Risk Management, adding that Bob was not only able to manage risk, but was better at doing so than the Risk Management department. Could he, I asked, give an example? Max responded by describing the challenges he faced in August 1998, a few months after being hired at International Securities.

The Tellabs-Ciena Trade

The summer of 1998, Max recalled, was a time of unprecedented market instability. The turbulence was initially induced by the Asian crisis and the Russian bond default, and compounded by Long-Term Capital Management's impending, though not yet apparent, collapse. "During that period," Max explained, "arbitrage spreads were widening across the board." A widening of the spreads can be an unfavorable scenario for arbitrage traders, as it implies that mispricings are growing larger rather than smaller, creating unrealized losses that can trigger margin calls and that force arbitrage funds to make payments to counterparties, thereby shrinking the funds' capital base. By the middle of August 1998, the spread widening had reached such unusual proportions that it was sharply reducing merger arbitrage returns across Wall Street, as figure 9.1 shows. Furthermore, because of losses in Russia-related trades, both Long-Term Capital Management and its imitators were being forced to liquidate otherwise sensible trades in order to access desperately needed liquidity and pay for margin calls. This created a unique situation, where widespread mispricings were leading to even greater mispricings.

Situations like this, Max pointed out, can be very problematic for arbitrage traders, because their managers may ask them to reduce their positions regardless of the actual merits of their trades. "Some people have risk managers who are tapping them on the shoulders," Max explained, "because the managers of those books are saying, 'shit, this is all of a sudden not the strategy I thought

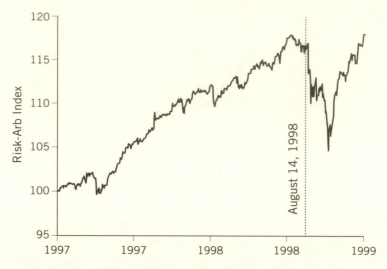

FIGURE 9.1. A diversified merger arbitrage portfolio index. This reflects the performance of merger arbitrage funds between 1997 and 1999, including the performance drop in the summer of 1998. *Source:* Chincarini (2012).

it was, and I want to cut back. And my boss in London, Tokyo, is not happy all of a sudden. So, I'm going to have to take some measures to show that I'm managing the risk, even though the right thing to do is the 180-degree opposite.'" As Max pointed out, part of the problem is that arbitrageurs are typically part of a larger hierarchy, and cannot count on their line manager or risk manager to understand their trade, much less on the divisional or global head of the business to do so.

In contrast to this unhappy scenario, Bob never forced Max to cut his positions. One specific trade was marked in Max's mind: the merger of the telecommunication equipment manufacturers, Tellabs Inc. and Ciena Corporation. Max had bet on the successful completion of the merger by buying shares in the acquisition target, Ciena. He started, as he usually did, with a small position. "I actually had 100,000 shares," he explained, "I was just screwing around. Sometimes I do that. Keeps you alert." Max had doubts about the merger due to uncertainties about Ciena's product: "they had a 16-widget splitter, so you could have sixteen conversations at once." A "widget splitter" allowed users to combine two widgets, or mechanical devices, and in the case of telecommunications equipment the splitting enabled multiple conversations. However, Max added, a competitor was already preparing the 32-widget splitter. In addition, Ciena only had four customers, one of them was responsible for one-fourth of all of the company's revenues, and its contract was due for renewal before the scheduled completion of the merger. It was, Max recalls, "the perfect storm," that is, a merger to be avoided.

Three days later, Max liquidated his position, at a loss of one dollar per share. He did so after noticing that the trade "did not sit well" with him. This liquidation was met with internal criticism: "that is such a dumb sale," the sales trader said, according to Max's recollection, noting that selling prematurely had created unnecessary losses. "Fine," Max replied. "I don't give a shit. Sell it," he added, especially given that the loss was only of one dollar a share. Later that week, Ciena's chief executive gave an optimistic speech about merger completion, but Max remained unmoved. "I don't care what the target's CEO says [in reference to Ciena's executive]. Here's how much I care about that: zero. Talk to the buyer's CEO if you want to know something."

Two weeks later, the merger was canceled following news that AT&T had stopped conducting test runs of Ciena's flagship product. To make matters worse, AT&T's decision was released just hours ahead of the shareholder vote to approve the merger with Tellabs, prompting investors to panic. Ciena's stock price fell precipitously, from $32.00 to $8.00 per share (see figure 9.2). "Not to $27.00, as people had estimated, but to $8.00," Max emphasized. Traders typically assume that the stock price of a merger target will revert to its historical pre-merger price after a merger cancellation, but in the case of Ciena the price dropped much further. While the unraveling of the deal did not affect Max's book, as he had already sold his shares, it did lead to losses of $160 million at Long-Term Capital Management and caused widespread losses among other arbitrage funds, totaling $500 million. Max reflected on how this would have affected him. "We would have been crushed. If I had had a full position—by the way, a full position for me would've been more than a million shares—I would have lost $24 million and been fired, by my contract. *I would've been fired.*"

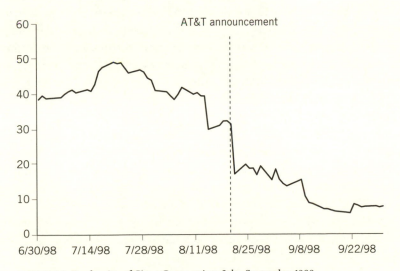

FIGURE 9.2. Stock price of Ciena Corporation, July–September 1998.

After the merger was canceled, Max saw a buying opportunity: "when that blew up, everything else widened like you wouldn't believe," in reference to the spreads in other mergers. The reason for the wide spreads, however, was not that arbitrageurs believed those mergers to be less likely, but that most arbitrageurs faced liquidity constraints after their losses in the failed Tellabs-Ciena merger. Max asked Bob for more capital to expand his positions. "Bob stayed in touch with me and tried to understand how this very unusual occurrence could be taking place, and what it meant," Max recalled. Based on their conversations, Bob understood that Max's book was composed of mergers that would be completed soon, with no more than a fifty-day weighted average maturity. "He understood the resilience of deals and the tight snapback that was going to occur, because they were convergence strategies. Not subject to the whim of the market. They had a date with destiny." Max's allusion to destiny underscored that mergers were completed or canceled with independence of the arbitrageurs' estimates. "Bob then said, 'you need additional capital,' not, 'I'm freaking out because you're losing money,'" explained Max. In other words, Bob reacted to the adverse price movements by escalating his commitment to Max's view, even if that might create an appearance of imprudence to anyone supervising Bob. The decision was successful and led to high returns in a year (1998) marked by losses among other funds.

The Limits of Judgment

The Tellabs-Ciena episode made clear that Bob prioritized judgment over quantitative rules. Once I understood this, however, I also began to wonder what potential problems an excessive reliance on judgment might create. Years earlier, my conversation with Lewis, the bank's head of Risk Management, had sensitized me to the dangers posed by situations when both a trader and his manager overlooked the same risk. These can be disastrous, because the manager will lack the ability to correct the trader's oversight. Long-Term Capital Management, Lewis ventured, had suffered from such a problem, in that the fund had escalated its commitment to loss-making trades until it reached a liquidity crisis.

I brought this up with Max. Given the absence of fixed position limits at Bob's trading room, had Bob's judgment ever proved disastrous? And if so, how had he handled it? Max proceeded to tell me about his worst loss-making trade at International Securities. The trade concerned the merger between General Electric (GE) and Honeywell International in 2001. At the time, and confident that the merger would be approved, Bob had asked Max to double his position. The merger, however, was canceled due to opposition from regulators, leading to million-dollar losses at Max's desk. Such was the size of the loss that even traders at other desks like Todd remembered the damage: "the only time

I saw Max lose money big size," Todd once recalled in a separate conversation, "was in the GE-Honeywell trade."

The story of the GE-Honeywell trade was in many ways that of a painful surprise. A lucrative profit opportunity came into view at Max's desk in October 2000. The chief executive officer of GE, Jack Welch, had announced his intention to merge the company with Honeywell International, and the merger would be completed in June of the following year. The projected synergies from the merger were significant, as the two companies had overlapping businesses in engines and services for aircraft, navigation, and other onboard equipment. The $40 billion merger was to be the largest ever between two industrial companies, and given its importance, Welch had announced that he would delay his retirement in order to oversee it. The approval of the merger, however, was complicated because it had to be authorized by both American and European antitrust authorities, as the companies were active in both continents.

Three months into the process, European regulators expressed strong reservations about the merger. At International Securities, however, Max decided to ignore the danger of a negative European ruling, and he had good reasons to do so: American authorities had already made their support clear, and American and European antitrust authorities had in the past always coordinated their rulings. In fact, never before had an American-authorized merger between two American firms been blocked in Brussels.[4] Aware of this, Max expected the European Commission to eventually come around, even if it expressed disconformity and tried to obtain concessions from the merging companies ahead of merger completion.

However, the case proved otherwise. The historical precedent was broken when the orthodox European competition commissioner Mario Monti (later appointed Italy's prime minister) issued a negative ruling on the grounds that the merger would give the combined entity an ability to engage in anticompetitive practices. The merger was effectively canceled on June 23, 2001. As news of the Commission's ruling reached Wall Street, Honeywell's stock price fell by more than 10 percent. Max lost $6 million, the largest single loss he had ever experienced. The price drop in Honeywell caused aggregate losses of more than $2.8 billion to arbitrageurs in other hedge funds, large enough to tip many of the funds' annual results into the negative. "Blood on the Street" was the graphic description given by the financial press.

Models and the GE-Honeywell Trade

The losses Max experienced led me to reflect on the dangers of economic models in arbitrage. One should naturally expect some incidence of losses in contexts of uncertainty. However, the magnitude and impact of the losses from the GE-Honeywell trade called for additional examination. Why did Max, like so many other traders, get it wrong? My analysis of the merger, presented below, suggests that the use of implied probability played a central role in aggravating the losses caused by this trade. As noted in chapter 5, Max used a model to estimate the implied probability of merger completion, that is, the probability that rival arbitrageurs assigned to it. He calculated this on the basis of the spread, or difference between the prices of the stocks of the merging companies. Max was then able to refine his own analysis of the merger by tracking the evolution of the spread over time with a tool called the spreadplot, also described in chapter 5, which allowed him to contrast his own view with his rivals' estimates, altering his exposure as his degree of certainty evolved over time.

The role of models in compounding the losses from the GE-Honeywell trade can be inferred from the evolution of Max's views about the merger. At first, Max thought that the GE-Honeywell merger was highly probable, and according to the press, his rivals were of the same opinion: as one of them declared to the financial press, "people had it among their larger positions because they thought there was a large probability the deal would get done."[5] As the months went by, however, the press began to report concerns that Monti at the European Commission might cancel the merger. In April, the *Wall Street Journal* reported that "among Mr. Monti's expressed concerns are what he calls possible 'conglomerate effects.' "[6] As noted above, Max discarded the possibility of an uncoordinated ruling because it had never happened in the past. But, critically, this was not his only reason to be confident: when Max checked the spreadplot to contrast his own view with the market's view, he found that the spread had not risen despite front-page news about Monti's opposition. This suggested to Max that his rivals felt as he did about the European Commission. Max thus concluded that he was right to ignore news about the Commission's opposition.

At this point, Bob intervened. Bob understood that Max was confident and called for an increase in Max's exposure in order to match the high degree of confidence exhibited by other arbitrageurs. In fact, I heard about this intervention directly from Bob, who explained: "I encouraged him [Max] to increase his size. You have confidence, all of your fields are fine . . . so instead of four million, I said six million." In sum, the use of models gave Max, Bob, and others false confirmation that their views were correct, thereby compounding their initial mistake.

For graphical evidence of this dynamic, consider the interplay between news and the spread between GE and Honeywell, as shown in figure 9.3. The black line plots the merger spread, which is the traders' proxy for the implied probability of merger success. The gray bars measure the number of times that the GE-Honeywell merger and Monti were simultaneously mentioned

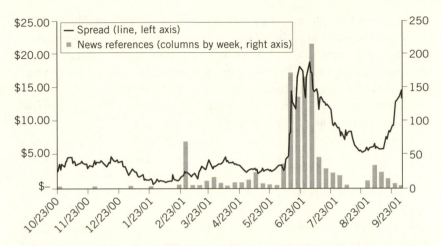

FIGURE 9.3. Arbitrageurs overlooked the danger of European opposition. Spread between GE and Honeywell (black line) against media concern over opposition by the European Union to the merger. Source: Bloomberg and ABI / Inform.

in the press; specifically, the number of weekly articles published in the *Wall Street Journal*, the *Financial Times*, and the *Economist* including in their text the words "Honeywell" and "Monti." This count is a proxy for the existence of news on European opposition to the deal. The spikes in the grey bar chart around June 2001 correspond to news of the cancellation of the merger. As is to be expected, this news led to a jump in the spread (the black line) as investors incorporated news of the cancellation in the prices of the companies.

The crucial element of the chart is the earlier spike in the grey bars, on February 27, 2001. The upsurge shows that the business media was widely reporting Monti's opposition to the deal, which in turn implies that the arbitrageurs must have known about this opposition. However, the black line in the figure, representing the spread, barely moves, suggesting that even as the media reported on Monti's opposition, the implied probability barely changed. In other words, the arbitrage community was aware of the Commission's statements, yet their estimates of implied probability suggest they did not conclude that it would translate into a negative ruling.

The above can be taken as a cautionary tale in the use of historical precedent to guide trading. But on further reflection, I concluded that the GE-Honeywell deal underscores the perils of relying on rivals' estimates via financial models and the spreadplot. When a sufficiently large number of arbitrageurs start with a similar and inaccurate perspective about the deal, the use of models may lead to disaster by giving traders misplaced confidence. As Bob admitted, the key problem in the case of GE-Honeywell was incomplete models: "everyone's database lacked a field, and the field was European regulatory denial." Max also confirmed that the use of implied probabilities created problems for the arbitrage community as a whole. Such problems typically start when numerous arbitrage funds simultaneously overlook a potential cause of merger failure. Or, as Max put it, "when there is a first impression and people don't have a basis for handicapping it properly."

How serious is the danger posed by this use of models? The question took me to the arbitrage literature in financial economics. For a few years after the GE-Honeywell blowup, I could not find any analysis of this phenomenon. In 2007, however, a study by Micah Officer coined the expression "arbitrage disasters."[7] Officer started from the observation that there was a notable correlation between losses at any given merger arbitrage desk and losses at rival desks in other banks or funds: whenever one desk lost a large amount, others tended to do so too. Officer referred to situations of widespread loss as "arbitrage disasters," defining them as instances of collective losses of more than $500 million across the arbitrage community. Arbitrage disasters, Officer argued, were created by unanticipated merger cancellations, and specifically by the cancellation of mergers that the arbitrageurs had bet heavily on. Between 1984 and 1994 there had been fifteen arbitrage disasters and they all resulted from merger cancellations (see figure 9.4). To the extent that other merger cancellations were similar to the GE-Honeywell one, arbitrage disasters can be attributed to the misplaced confidence prompted by the use of the spreadplot and implied probability.

In turn, the frequency of arbitrage disasters raised another question: when are disasters of this nature more likely to take place? A partial answer can be inferred from the GE-Honeywell case: in the deal, the problem stemmed from the combination of an unprecedented situation and the use of information technology such as models and computer databases of past occurrences. Unprecedented risks are not picked up by historical databases, as the latter only rely on past precedent. This mismatch was then compounded by the use of implied probability, because it allowed each arbitrage desk to obtain reassurance from the estimates of its competitors, yet those estimates were similarly incomplete.

Put differently, had the GE-Honeywell merger cancellation *not* been historically unprecedented, Max's databases would have picked up on the risk posed by Monti's opposition, and his reaction would have conveyed this risk to other desks, thereby averting the disaster. Conversely, had Max and the others *not* relied on implied probability to find out what their rivals were thinking—as was the case before the quantitative revolution—they would not have provided misplaced reassurance to each other, would not have increased their positions, and would not have experienced disastrous losses (though they would have nevertheless incurred some minor losses). In combination, however, the unprecedented nature of the situation and the use of databases and implied probability led to a collective disaster.

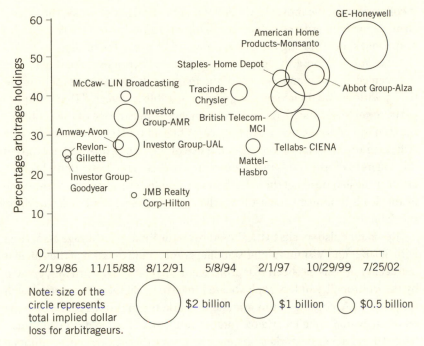

FIGURE 9.4. Merger arbitrage disasters. Total losses incurred by arbitrageurs (circle size) and relative participation of arbitrageurs (y-axis) in canceled arbitrage deals, 1986–2002. *Source:* Officer (2007: 27). Note: Size of the circle represents total implied dollar loss for arbitrageurs.

Resonance

My post-mortem analysis of the failed GE-Honeywell merger captured a remarkable instance of models and management coming together in a single disastrous outcome. It provided me with a unique opportunity to address my original interest in the dangers and possibilities posed by quantitative finance. In addressing this question, David Stark and I proposed the concept of *resonance*, which we define in this context as the amplification of error arising from a combination of cognitive similarity and confrontation with market rivals via economic models.[8]

With the expression "resonance," Stark and I sought to underscore the dangers posed by excess synchronization in finance as in, for instance, the threat created by soldiers marching on a bridge. In 1831, the Broughton Suspension Bridge collapsed when a brigade of soldiers marched across it. The accident made clear that structures like bridges and buildings, although seemingly solid and immobile, have a natural vibration within them. A force applied to an object at the same frequency as its own will amplify the vibration of such object and if the mechanical resonance is strong enough, the bridge can vibrate until it collapses from the movement.[9] Following the bridge's collapse, the British Army reportedly ordered soldiers crossing a long bridge to "break stride" so as to avoid synchronizing their vibrations and preserve the bridge.

Like soldiers on a bridge, the use of models creates a feedback loop between each trader and the rest of the market. This feedback synchronizes their positions and their views, amplifying possible mistakes.[10] Hence our use of the term "resonance." The risk of resonance is illustrative of the problems induced by economic models in finance. When all traders overlook the same risk, as in the GE-Honeywell case, the use of implied probabilities exposed the traders to disaster. This risk is greater in unprecedented situations, because arbitrage desks construct their databases in parallel, and exposure to the same history leads to similar databases, which in turn implies that all desks overlook the same risks.

Resonance also speaks to the literature on the limits of arbitrage associated with Shleifer and Vishny. A long-standing argument in defense of the efficient market hypothesis has been that arbitrageurs exploit the mispricings created by the irrationality of less sophisticated investors, thereby eliminating such mispricings. According to this argument, markets can thus be relied on to be efficient, even if not all market actors are rational.[11] Shleifer and Vishny challenged this defense of market efficiency by noting that arbitrageurs cannot be relied on to exploit all mispricings, as their ability to withstand adverse market movements is limited in time. Eventually, they run out of capital. Markets cannot thus be assumed to be efficient simply by virtue of having arbitrageurs.

The concept of resonance adds to the limits of arbitrage literature by highlighting one additional constraint faced by arbitrageurs. A key source of high returns in arbitrage is the use of models and tools. However, the effectiveness of these tools is limited: the ability of arbitrageurs to eliminate mispricings only works in situations for which there is a historical precedent. By contrast, in a truly new and unprecedented situation, the use of models will not eliminate mispricings and may well compound them. In this sense, resonance can be seen as a form of material limit to arbitrage, distinct from and complementary to the behavioral limits identified by Shleifer and Vishny.

There was an intriguing end to the GE-Honeywell trade. According to the *Financial Times*, in 2001 the New York-based hedge fund Atticus Global Management undertook a successful contrarian strategy.[12] Atticus anticipated the arbitrage disaster resulting from the GE-Honeywell merger, and bet against it. As the article noted, while most fund managers followed their usual strategy of going long Honeywell and short GE, Atticus shorted Honeywell and longed GE, making a 10 percent return on a very quick investment. Atticus's success suggests that resonance might provide grounds for a contrarian trading strategy. Such strategy would be premised on the dangers of using economic models to calculate implied magnitudes such as implied merger probability.

From Judgment to Intuition

Finally, the GE-Honeywell trade also points to the dangers inherent in the use of judgment. Relying on his own judgment, Bob advised Max to double the size of his position, thereby compounding Max's losses when the merger was canceled. When I asked Bob about this, he openly admitted to doing so, and provided his own reasons for prodding Max. Bob felt that Max had been too prudent on previous occasions: "one of the things about Max is, he runs less capital than you think he should by conventional evaluation. Any outsider, including me, would think the guy should run twice as much." This extreme prudence was compounded, according to Bob, by Max's tendency to exit too quickly: "when there's a problem, he gets out," Bob said, "and he locks in losses and seems to sacrifice gains." Thus, Bob attributed Max's resistance to increase his exposure to excessive risk aversion.

An equally notable aspect of the episode is that Bob admitted his own responsibility. "I had no way to compensate Max for that loss," Bob admits. "The loss, which was a consequence of me pressuring him to trade outside of a pattern he developed over twenty years, was going to come out of his pocket and the pocket of his team. So, it's a threat to my authority as a manager, because the natural reaction from Max and his team should have been, 'hey boss, this is your problem. We wouldn't have done this without your pressure, and you were wrong.'"

After the GE-Honeywell trade, Bob became a lot more careful about interfering with the decisions of his traders. He became interested in the academic field of "naturalistic decision-making," which explores the ways in which intuition operates, as well as how professionals sometimes develop correct "hunches" that they cannot explain. Bob pointed me to a monograph by psychologist Gary Klein, *Sources of Power*.[13] In one of the book's examples, Klein follows a fire crew into several emergency calls. During one of those calls, the fire crew lieutenant enters a one-story house where there is a fire. At first it seems a conventional blaze with the usual danger, so the lieutenant sends the crew in. However, he suddenly decides to order the crew out. Immediately afterward, the floor collapses. As it turned out, the house had a basement that the lieutenant had not been told about. The entire crew would have been dead had he not immediately ordered them out. The key question that Klein asks is, how did the lieutenant suddenly know about the basement? The lieutenant— and this is the point of Klein's account—did not know *how* he knew. Once the fire was extinguished, however, the lieutenant understood: given the amount of visible flames, the temperature outside the house should have been hotter. The lieutenant, Klein concludes, *decided that things were not normal*. He had no new data, other than the fact that he lacked what he expected to find. But he knew that instinctively, and acted on it.

"This story stuck with me forever," Bob told me after recounting it to me. The use of models in trading, he thought, required a similar sensitivity to the emerging impression that "things are not normal." The problem, Bob realized, was that such sensitivity could be hampered by managerial supervision. If Bob asked traders to spell out what they're doing, he said, his personal experience suggested that their intuition might be dampened: "if you ask people to articulate in advance what they are going to do, they do it worse," Bob explained. "They create a model in their head, instead of allowing the real complexity of the situation to drive the decision-making." In actual decision-making, Bob added, the trader should not let the model dominate his thinking. "He's really *using* the model. His model is a way of evaluating something. But it doesn't really decide for him."

As a result of the GE-Honeywell trade, Bob became reluctant to interrogate his traders about the bases for their decisions, as he feared that if they articulated their approach, they would do a worse job. The change suggests a shift in Bob's approach from judgment to intuition. Judgment denotes a balanced weighing up of evidence to form a decision or opinion. As noted in earlier chapters, the importance of judgment in markets was underscored by Frank Knight, who counterpoised it to calculation. Intuition, by contrast, describes the ability to acquire knowledge without proof or without understanding how the knowledge was acquired. Intuition, as Bob used the term, is not only a cognitive mechanism, as it includes the emotional reactions that are experienced by the user of the model. It does not amount to building an additional representation to rival the original model, leveraging instead the decision-maker's sense of how the model should work when it does so correctly, in order to be able to identify situations when it does not. Using intuition is complicated and cannot be boiled down to building a "model of the model." In other words, it cannot be reduced to calculation. "Everyone hates intuition," Bob noted, "because it sounds like guesswork or whatever." But intuition, he added, may be another way to say: things that are difficult to express in simple forms still have validity.

Relying on intuition in arbitrage introduces an additional layer of complexity. For intuition to operate effectively, the model, the trader, and the trade itself need to be treated as an effective unit, an assembly of parts that cannot be taken apart for the purpose of auditing and supervising. For instance, examining how the trade and the model fit with each other would require the supervisor to ask the trader about his opinion and affective reaction. In this sense, an appreciation for intuition also hints at the presence of limits to the engaged approach to managing the floor that Bob had put in place at International Securities. The manager's answer to the limits of calculation should no longer be a simple reliance on judgment and conversations with the traders, but a more delicate balancing act between demanding reasons and allowing the traders to evolve in their reasons for acting.

There is one final twist to the story of the GE-Honeywell trade. I revisited the trade in two conversations with Max, and his recollection of it, even years after the event, was crystal clear: "Bob came by and told me to buy more the day before. He thought I was being too chickenshit." However, Max adds, "I still made money that month." How come? Max loaded up in his other trades, because he knew he might be taking a bad hit on Honeywell, "and Bob was supportive." In a sense, then, Bob's use of judgment contributed to reducing the negative impact of Bob's insistence that Max increase the position. Interestingly, the episode did not diminish Max's appreciation for Bob. He appreciated Bob's honesty in admitting he interfered. "It is amazing," Max said. "Most people are not honest about it, and they can't help interfering," but Bob was the exception.

Managing Risks in Quantitative Finance

The conversations described above with Bob and Max provided fertile ground to reflect on the various strategies for monitoring and controlling losses on the floor. Taken together, the failed mergers of Tellabs-Ciena in 1998 and GE-Honeywell in 2001 offered contrasting pictures of the tradeoffs involved in relying on judgment, models, and intuition.

One conclusion that emerges from the two trades is that the limits of arbitrage can be overcome by relying on managerial judgment. In the summer of 1998, Max closed his position in Tellabs-Ciena at a loss because it was not "sitting well" with him. By using judgment in this manner, Max avoided a $24 million loss. Later that summer, Bob's support of Max's strategy despite the market turbulence illustrates the benefits of managerial judgment: by engaging Max directly rather than simply relying on quantitative indicators of market risk such as Value at Risk, Bob correctly concluded that he should encourage Max to increase his exposure to several merger trades. The positive results experienced by International Securities in the summer of 1998 contrast with losses at Long-Term Capital Management and suggest that the limits of arbitrage experienced by other funds can in turn be exploited. For this defiance of the limits noted by Shleifer and Vishny to be possible, the management of the floor needs to be willing to distinguish between a widening of spreads due to genuine market uncertainty and one that simply results from a spike in Value at Risk.

An additional conclusion that emerges concerns the limits to managerial judgment, and the importance of intuition. In the case of the GE-Honeywell trade in 2001, Bob made a qualitative assessment of the possible risks entailed in the merger, as well as of Max's own track record, and told Max to increase his position. The resulting losses were thus a partial outcome of Bob's reliance on his own judgment. Following the GE-Honeywell disaster, Bob increased his awareness of the dangers of second-guessing his traders and balanced his reliance on judgment with an appreciation for the traders' intuition, that is, their sense that something might not be quite right. From the standpoint of a manager, engagement involved developing social proximity to the desks on the floor, listening to the traders' reasons, and empathizing with their choices. By contrast, appreciating the traders' intuition called for accepting their actions and inactions with less intense scrutiny, given the impossibility of eliciting their rationale without altering their intuitive ability.

Resonance as Material Phenomena

Finally, our proposed concept of resonance illustrates the advantages of emphasizing technological elements in the study of markets. Resonance, or the danger that financial models might amplify a trader's mistakes, reconciles the existence of financial disasters with a conception of traders as reflective and mindful individuals. To appreciate the significance of this, consider an alternative account of financial disaster: the concept of the "Black Swan," as developed by Nassim Taleb.[14] According to Taleb, the use of models leads traders and regulators to underestimate the danger of high-impact, low-probability events such as wars or other crises. This effect, the argument goes, results from an uncritical use of models that are based on a Normal probability distribution. Such distributions are thin-tailed and underweight the probability of extreme events. Taleb thus warns against "the psychological effects of statistical numbers in lowering risk consciousness and the suspension of healthy skepticism."[15] Taleb's account, however, presents financial actors as unaware of the limitations of their own models, implying that traders either ignore what any observer can readily see (i.e., that extreme events happen) or lack the reflexive capacity to act on this observation. By contrast, resonance presents traders as reflexive individuals that are aware of their own fallibility. Indeed, resonance takes place precisely *because* traders use the spreadplot and implied probability to question their own fallible estimates. Such devices for doubt, however, fail when most arbitrageurs overlook the same risk, leading to disasters.

Furthermore, resonance illustrates the need to rethink the meaning of "social" in financial markets dominated by economic models and introduce the role of material objects. To appreciate why this matters, consider the prevailing account of sociality in behavioral finance, the so-called herding effect whereby investors court disaster by mechanically imitating each other. In the original account of Scharfstein and Stein, herding takes place when incentives and uncertainty push actors to imitate others.[16] Consider two salespeople who must choose whether to sell wine in the east or west end of a city. There is uncertainty as to how much demand for wine there is on each end, and each salesperson has private information about it. Scharfstein and Stein argue that if these salespeople are paid a percentage commission on their sales, each of them will end up in whichever side of town they believe will have greater demand. The private information, in other words, will be put to good use. However, the authors add, if the salespeople are paid according to a comparative scheme (for instance, if the second person's bonus is based on performance relative to the first), the second salesperson will often find it to be in his best interest to simply follow the actions of the first, even if his private information would suggest otherwise. The reason is that doing so allows the second person to avoid the worst-case scenario, namely, one where the first person is lucky to find demand and the second one is unlucky. In this worst-case scenario, the second wine salesperson would receive a double penalization: a lower bonus for his low sales, and an even lower one because the first salesperson did well. Imitation, in other words, protects against bad luck. This form of imitation, herding, is socially undesirable because it implies that the second salesperson is ignoring his private information.

While herding succeeds in introducing social dynamics into accounts of financial markets, it neglects the feedback loops and interdependencies between investors that financial models introduce. The widespread adop-tion of models, as the case of Max suggests, creates a vicious cycle whereby a trader's estimate enters the calculations of other traders. In this regard, models introduce a relational effect into financial markets that does not result from social conformity (as the case of herding evokes) but from model-induced interdependence.

In sum, the concept of resonance illustrates the advantages of a turn to objects and tools in the study of finance. The first is to move from a "human error" perspective of quantitative finance, where traders are presented as bliss-fully unaware of the faulty assumptions of their models, to a "joint error" per-spective in which problems arise from failures in the modeling practices put in place by mindful traders. The second turn is from a "lemmings" problem created by imitation and conformity to a material and calculative version of group-think, where the model creates cognitive interdependence across the market. In sum, while existing accounts of financial disasters often present investors as naïve users of models or mindless imitative lemmings, my pro-posed concept of resonance explains arbitrage disasters without any need for such characterizations and describes arbitrageurs that are reflexive and tech-nologically equipped.

10

The Global Financial Crisis

I did not see Bob again for several months after his presentation at Columbia in 2007, but I knew what kept him busy. A few months earlier, he had intimated that he might go back to work. The American division of an international bank, which I will refer to as "Global Trust" (pseudonymous), had expressed an interest in hiring him to run one of its subsidiaries. This would include overseeing the equity derivatives business, as Bob had managed at International Securities, in addition to fixed income. In other words, it included the bank's entire securities business, a step up from Bob's previous job. In the late spring of 2008, Bob emailed to let me know that he had accepted the position and that he would start in July. I wrote back to congratulate him and express my interest in studying his new bank. We agreed to meet at the end of August once he had settled into the new position.

Global Trust

My first visit to Bob's new bank took place at the end of August 2008. Unlike International Securities, the company was located in an iconic skyscraper in Midtown Manhattan, which lent further novelty to the occasion. Once inside the building, and after several twists and turns, I ended up in an entrance that was blocked by a security guard. Standing next to him was a familiar face that welcomed me to the bank. "Daniel! It's good to see you again." The person greeting me was Jenn, Bob's former executive assistant at International Securities. I was relieved to see her, as I had gotten lost in the labyrinthine layout of the skyscraper. Luckily, someone at the bank had anticipated this possibility and sent Jenn to find me. I was, in other words, clearly back in Bob's world, among familiar faces and, as he once put it, in the "people-oriented way of production."

I met with Bob in one of the bank's conference rooms, a simple and functional meeting space. He shared with me the story behind his appointment. Bob had been brought into the bank by his old boss at International Securities, Jack Schneider (pseudonymous), who had worldwide responsibility for both fixed income and equities at Global Trust. The bank had several subsidiaries in the United States, and Bob was the CEO of its securities subsidiary. Bob's mandate was to build a new unit on the basis of the existing one, with the added complexity that the business had been underperforming in the past.

Given the limited time that Bob had spent at the job, the rest of our conversation centered on his plans for the future, rather than actions so far. "I'm quite curious about one aspect of the challenge," he explained. "How do you build a securities firm in this day and age, essentially from scratch?" The answer, he reasoned, could not simply be "by copying what is already in place elsewhere." However, this is not how most people saw things. "People are prisoners of what the final product looks like. So, if you ask somebody, they'll begin to describe for you what Morgan Stanley looks like today. So, if Morgan Stanley has 1,000 fixed income salesmen, we need to hire 1,000 people to sell bonds."

However, Bob added, purely replicating the present overlooks the importance of informal relations, and the fact that they can only be built up over time. "It would be like saying, 'oh, how do you have a 50-foot oak tree? Let's put a 50-foot oak tree.' No, there's roots, you know?'" Furthermore, Bob believed that replicating history's path was not sufficient either. "One thing you can do is, you can say, 'well, let's look at the history of Goldman and recreate that.' Unfortunately, what they did in 1920 or 1950, or even in 1980, is not particularly relevant, because things have changed." A securities firm, according to Bob, should be "organic." In light of this, the questions he asked himself centered on establishing priorities. "What sequence would provide a healthy development over the next five years?"

I was intrigued by Bob's word choice—*organic*. It was the same as the term used by the original academic proponents of the non-bureaucratic organization, Burns and Stalker.[1] Recalling my research at International Securities, I asked Bob how his new project related to the previous one. "A lot of the stuff we worked on at International Securities is at the back of my mind. Some of those principles overlap, the information flow and cooperation, etc. But this is a broader scope. The question now is, if you had the whole firm, what would you do?"

As a first step, Bob was planning on introducing an open-plan layout. This made a great deal of sense to me, because I had already gotten lost in the building. Bob explained that the bank's architecture was "the opposite" of conducive to information flow. It was divided into two separate floors of the skyscraper, the eighteenth and tenth. Furthermore, these were not accessible by the same elevator. To get to the trading floor on the tenth from Bob's office, he had to take the elevators, change, go through a locked door, walk across a hallway, and walk through another locked door. There, in a dark corner, sat thirty-five people in a cramped space. Things were no better on Bob's floor: first there was security, then one executive office, two additional offices, and a meeting room. There were fifteen people in that room, another fifteen people in the room next to it, and then twenty-five more, all of whom were working behind closed doors. It was, Bob said, "the most ill-conceived structure and office that you can imagine." But there was more: "when I saw this," Bob added, "I said, 'well, how unfortunate. They'll squeeze people into whatever.' Then I discovered, that no, it wasn't unfortunate. They had recently spent $6 million to renovate the office. *They even wanted it.*" To put things in perspective, Bob concluded, the cost of all the renovations that he had ordered at International Securities totaled $1 million over the course of seven years. The layout at Global Trust, Bob had concluded, was so terrible that it could not be fixed. His plan for the bank was to leave the building and move to a new one.

Crisis

As our meeting drew to a close, I left the bank with a reassuring sense of validation. Bob continued to espouse the key organizational goal I had documented at International Securities: integration. Proof of this was his concern for architecture, as well as for organic growth. My plan was to return to the bank the following week and start interviewing the traders. Bob's new challenge, managing an entire securities firm (including stocks as well as bonds), was an exciting one, and his insistence on organic growth would surely provide interesting material.

Nine days later, however, my plans were turned upside down by the eruption of the global financial crisis. On September 6, 2008, the American government placed the government-sponsored enterprises Fannie Mae and Freddie Mac into conservatorship, a temporary form of nationalization. One week later, on September 14, Bank of America announced its plans to acquire Merrill Lynch, thereby saving the latter from an insolvency crisis. On September 15, Lehman Brothers filed for Chapter 12 bankruptcy protection. On September 16, the Federal Reserve prevented the collapse of the insurance company AIG with a secured credit facility of up to $85 billion. On September 21, the Treasury announced the creation of the Troubled Asset Relief Program, a bailout fund aimed at rescuing the financial industry. Finally, on September 22, Goldman Sachs and Morgan Stanley announced their conversion from investment banks into bank holding companies, thereby gaining access to the funding provided by the Federal Reserve.

The unprecedented sequence of events that took place in September 2008 left me with an acute sense of dissonance. Media reports presented daily news of reckless activity on Wall Street, including mortgage lending to penniless home buyers, billion-dollar losses from derivatives trades, and lavish bonuses paid to the banks' executives. Mismanagement on this scale was difficult to reconcile with the reasonably prudent, seemingly conservative, and for the most part sound organization that I had seen at International Securities four years before. My perspective on Wall Street, I then realized, had ultimately been colored by a moral assessment of a single subunit, Bob's equities floor. As I mentioned in chapter 1, such dependence on a single case was perhaps inevitable for an ethnographer like myself, but it nevertheless put me in an uncomfortable position, for I could not make sense of the crisis. Was the trading room that I had studied an exception to an otherwise corrupt industry? Or, had Bob and his traders managed to dupe me for the duration of my studies, and they were in fact as corrupt as the bankers appearing in the news? Neither option seemed credible.

In search of answers, I asked Bob for another meeting. I had in fact already emailed him one week after our conversation in late August, but, understandably, he had not replied. The crisis was keeping him busy. I thus wrote to Bob again at the end of September, once the $700 billion bailout package had been announced, and the sense of capitalist cataclysm had subsided slightly. In his reply, Bob apologized for not answering earlier, and suggested we meet in early October. I immediately accepted.

As the day of my meeting with Bob approached, developments in Washington, DC were making investors anxious once again. On September 29, the Treasury's bailout plan was rejected by the House of Representatives, prompting an unprecedented selloff in the stock market, and causing a drop of almost 9 percent in the S&P 500 Index. "For stocks," the *New York Times* wrote after the market closed, it was the "worst single-day drop in two decades."[2] As my meeting with Bob drew closer, the sense of uncertainty thus returned to Wall Street.

When I arrived at Bob's office, I found him in the midst of a tense phone conversation. I stood at the entrance of the room, unsure of what to do, taking in the space. Bob's office was a large but sparsely furnished executive suite with two windows, a desk, and a small meeting table. Without interrupting his call, Bob beckoned me to enter. I sat, and suddenly saw something that startled me: pasted on the wall behind Bob, there were two large organizational charts with signs that read, "Lehman, equities" and "Lehman fixed income." Under each of these, there were about two hundred boxes with names in them and a web of arrows connecting them. Lehman's traders, whom I thought would be stigmatized after the bank's bankruptcy, had become sought-after job candidates barely fifteen days after the bank's bankruptcy.

On the phone, Bob was losing patience with someone. "What's up? What's up? I'm really under the gun here," he shouted. "I don't give a fuck, we just gotta keep moving." He was, I later found out, speaking with a headhunter. A competing bank had just hired a nine-person team from Lehman. The decision had come directly from the bank's global headquarters, without even consulting the relevant bank division. "People are diving with their fists, grabbing whatever they can," Bob explained. He too was under pressure to hire. He wanted to start building the securities firm without waiting for the right market conditions, because if these did not materialize the bank would never put his ideas to the test. Hence the need to move fast.

The ambitious plan drawn by Bob and his former boss to modernize Global Trust was a fragile one, because neither of them were close to the bank's headquarters nor its center of power. Both Bob and Jack knew they faced an internal power struggle. None of this, however, mattered to Bob when he took the job. "I felt the need to work," he confessed. As he said this, Bob suddenly caught a glimpse of his Bloomberg terminal. "My God. Market's down by 4 percent," he said. He interrupted our conversation to check the screen.

Once he finished, we turned to the bailout. To my surprise, Bob was against it. "The irony about the plan is," he said, "there is no plan. They made it bigger. It is now 200 pages, but the first three are unchanged. It's just more and more pages wrapped around nothing." Bob also disagreed with the pro-bailout argument that a drop in stock prices indicated that a bailout was needed. "Let's say the car companies ask for a bailout. You see workers saying, 'this is terrible for the American economy.' But we know [that] what they're really saying is, 'I'm worried about my job.' So, no one says, 'oh I need to ask the auto union for a true opinion on what the collapse of the auto industry would mean.' Yet we give Wall Street the ability to do that." Bob was thus opposed to the very principle that financial regulators should take stock prices into account. If not bail out Wall Street, I countered, what should the US government do? Bob favored the plan put forth by the Nobel laureate economist Joseph Stiglitz: a government recapitalization of the banks, similar to what Warren Buffett had done with Goldman. "The government could easily take 25 percent of all banks. This would be enough to recapitalize them."

There was something unusual about the debate on the bailout, Bob added. In other historical crises, the interests of the various social groups in the country had led to different policy prescriptions. As he put it, "the elites have one voice, the people have another voice, and the market is actually an independent voice." But this time, the media, the politicians, and Wall Street were all speaking with a single voice, and that voice affirmed the need for a Wall Street bailout. Indeed, Democrats in Congress were voting in support of a plan created by a Republican Secretary of the Treasury, and that would help Wall Street. How was that possible? Even more puzzling, the only politicians that had opposed the bailout were Republican congressmen, many representing constituents in the American Midwest. However, the mainstream media was portraying these congressmen who rejected the bailout as anarchists and nihil-ists, thereby taking sides with Wall Street. Again, a very puzzling situation.

Bob's explanation for this paradox was identity. "What you see is a cultural breakdown of positions along the same lines as cultural issues, with Fox and the Internet on one side, and the mainstream media on the other." This divide explained the reaction of the anti-Wall Street House Republicans. These sena-tors, Bob argued, were not familiar, and did not identify with, Wall Street. "They are saying to the bankers, 'Who the fuck are you?'" To Bob, the crisis had altered the axis of the country's political debate, and it now fell along a local-cosmopolitan divide instead of a right and left axis. On one side of the new divide there were "transnationals," such as a female worker from Bombay at a Pepsi factory in Ohio ("her identity is with the transnationals, regardless of the blue-collar status"), as well as bankers on Wall Street ("the bulk of them are not paid that well, but their stability comes from their education, so their identity is tied to the job, and they are also transnationals"). Then there were "locals": "a colonel in the army; he is highly educated but he does not iden-tify with the transnationals." Finally, Bob came to us, whom he classified as transnationals. "You and I, my friend, I'm afraid we cannot avoid being in that camp." As he said it, however, I could sense that he was not too proud of his category membership. Bob's comment was the second political remark I had heard from him in our nine years of acquaintance, the first one being during the Iraq war. It was so unexpected that I could barely react to it.

I was equally surprised to hear Bob's views on what the crisis meant for Wall Street. The last three standing investment banks, Goldman Sachs, Morgan Stanley, and Merrill Lynch, had abandoned their legal status as investment banks a few days before. "Is this," I asked him, "the death of Wall Street," as some newspapers were asserting? Bob's response caught me unprepared: "the Wall Street that I knew when I came in 1982," he replied, "is now dead. But that's been going on for twenty-five years. All those famous names, Kidder Peabody, E. F. Hutton, are gone. But that is not the death of markets. There are far more asset classes, and for far more things than ever before, especially with the growth of derivatives. It comes down to the meaning of Wall Street. Wall Street is now a metaphor for rich and overpaid people."

Wall Street Is Dead

Wall Street was dead, replaced by markets. What did that mean? At the time, Bob's comment struck me as either a misunderstanding on my part or an impossibly glib remark on Bob's part. He was the chief executive of a bank on Wall Street; was he calling himself a fat cat? I kept the question to myself in order to let Bob continue with his account.

Regulatory changes over the past four decades, Bob continued, had made the capital markets less and less manageable. In addition to the repeal of Glass-Steagall, commercial banks used to be connected to the regulator by a structure of informal social relations that created further checks. The ten largest banks in New York, the so-called money center, were carefully monitored by the New York Fed. When the economy overheated, it would informally ask banks to raise their lending requirements. Before globalization, Bob pointed out, this informal approach might have worked. "The complexity was manageable. But this is not true anymore," he added. "It is too complex for Paulson," Bob noted, in reference to Secretary of the Treasury Hank Paulson. For example, "what exposure do you think there is in Morgan Stanley's books to Russia?" I ventured a guess, based on their percentage of the world economy. "Five percent?" Fine, Bob replied, let's say it's 5 percent. In fact, the Russian economy is far smaller than that. This would yield $500 million. They actually have $4.5 billion."

I paused as I grasped the implications of Bob's words. The banks, he implied, were out of control. "I had a far rosier picture of Wall Street," I confessed, "based precisely on my study of *your* trading room." "You had a false understanding," Bob replied. "We had a simple business at International Securities. We marked to market." In other words, because there was a market for the derivatives that Bob's unit traded, their value was always clear, and managing their risks was simple. "One need only look at the new CDOs," Bob added in reference to the asset class on everyone's lips, collateralized debt obligations. He went on to describe in detail one recent CDO that he had looked into. "Much of what goes on is opaque."

There was another way, Bob added, in which CDOs were different from the arbitrage trades that I had seen at International Securities. "Merger arbitrage is the closest there is to real arbitrage, because there's a boundary where you can exit the trade, capturing the value," Bob said. This exit was the merger completion date, when the deal either happens or does not happen, regardless of what arbitrageurs expect. "Most trading does not have that exit hatch, so the model becomes very important." In the absence of a clear date with destiny, there was no agreed-upon external reference for market participants to value the assets. As a consequence, marking positions to a model led to more complex and potentially more dangerous dynamics. Bob added, "if the only thing that links everybody is the model, then there is something else entirely going on. The more everybody's using the same model, it's really just a way of guiding everyone's behavior to behave like each other."[3]

As the conversation continued, a new and more pessimistic view of Wall Street gradually sank in for me. Before leaving, I asked Bob about the personnel charts of Lehman on the wall. "I have this for theater," he said with a smile. "When people come in, I make them sit here, just in front of it, and I can look at their face when they see it. But in fact, I don't need it. I have my own headhunter working for me. He's the person I was talking to on the phone when you came in."

Rethinking Wall Street

As I typed my notes back in my office at Columbia, I reflected with perplexity on the conversation I just had. Bob's reading of the crisis called into question the optimism I had developed toward financial markets, thanks to his own trading floor. Wall Street, I now understood, was a darker place than I thought. Bob had made that clear in his talk at Columbia back in 2007, but the message was hitting home only now. Far from being *representative* of other Wall Street banks, his trading room at International Securities was *illustrative* of how Wall Street banks might have been, or could be in the future, had they been organized differently. Instead of a microcosm, a miniature version of Wall Street from which I could learn how the larger industry worked, Bob's original trading room was its negative image. To learn about Wall Street on the basis of it, I would have to proceed by way of contrast: behind each unique element in the trading room's design, there was an implicit critique of some aspect of Wall Street.

This shift in perspective called for rethinking several of the core beliefs I had held up to that point. First and foremost, Bob's interpretation of the crisis called for reconsidering the narrative of progress associated with the trends that had shaped Wall Street until then, and especially quantification. Within economics, this was particularly clear in Robert Merton's financial innovation spiral, discussed in chapter 7. Sociologists of finance, myself included, had made extensive use of research in Science and Technology Studies to account for the purported advantages of quantitative finance. The introduction of information technology in trading, according to some accounts in this literature, allowed for less dependence on fragile social networks, provided greater geographical reach, and offered expanded cognitive possibilities.

Those accounts, I now saw, had not grappled with the institutional and organizational framework that lent durability to the system, the disappearance of which Bob now lamented. Bob's reference to Kidder and Hutton alluded to the investment banking partnerships that dominated the industry thirty years before. Prior to 1970, the New York Stock Exchange prohibited the incorporation of "member firms," that is, those that could trade on the floor. This implied that investment banks could not be corporations. Once it relaxed its rules to allow corporate ownership, its member firms gradually abandoned the partnership form. The firm Donaldson, Lufkin & Jenrette went public in 1970, Merrill Lynch went public a year later, in 1971. Lehman Brothers did so when it was acquired by a publicly listed company in 1984, Bear Stearns went public in 1985, Morgan Stanley followed suit in 1986, and Goldman Sachs maintained its partnership structure until 1999.[4]

Second, I was surprised to hear Bob's views on the investment banking partnerships. For him, Wall Street was defined by the partnership structure. But for me, who arrived on the scene in 1998, the names of the last remaining partnerships only evoked vague memories of privilege, old white men in suits, and the occasional scandal, as in the case of Kidder and its jailed bond trader, Joseph Jett. My critical perspective on partnerships was echoed by literature in economics that has presented their disappearance as the efficient outcome of better risk management technology. According to economists Alan Morrison and William Wilhem, going public gave investment banks access to a larger capital base, which helped them respond to the competition of large international banks entering the business.[5] It also allowed these partnerships to fund their growing activity in proprietary trading. Morrison and Wilhem also took the view that risk management did not need to suffer from the transformation of partnerships into corporations, as there was new quantitative risk management technology available.

Having heard Bob, however, and in the wake of the global financial crisis, Morrison and Wilhem's argument seemed less compelling. For one, the core innovation in risk management technology to which these authors pointed, Value at Risk, had not only failed to prevent banks from accumulating toxic assets on their balance sheets, but had actually *encouraged* them to do so, as the triple A rating of the senior tranches of the toxic derivatives called for lower regulatory capital needs to satisfy Basel II requirements, thus encouraging the banks to load up on such toxic assets. Furthermore, when the investment partnerships went public there was also a change in incentives taking place, as senior executives no longer had their capital tied to the firm in the same way that partners once did. Beyond incentives, partnerships also had institutionalized rituals such as the partners' meetings that contributed to create shared norms and values, and those disappeared as well.

Instead, Bob's perspective echoed the historical research conducted by Philip Augar, a former banker, on the disappearance of the old merchant banks in the City of London following the deregulatory "big bang" of 1986. This historical event brought dominance of the City of London to the large Wall Street banks. Augar contends that the displacement of the merchant banking partnerships altered the logic of the City's institutions, from cultural norms to material incentives. "In the old broking firms, career structure was straightforward. The goal was partnership," he writes. The adoption of corporate form through acquisition by international banks, however, led the merchant banks in the City to abandon the partnership structure. "Once this was removed," Augar adds, "status was dethroned and cash became king."[6]

There was a third aspect of my conversation with Bob that proved surprising. He claimed that avoiding over-the-counter derivatives in his trading room at International Securities had created a simpler and safer organization. As an example, he noted that merger arbitrage lacked the dangerous self-referential dynamics that characterized credit derivatives such as CDOs. The circularity that Bob talked about was not unlike the "beauty contests" that John Maynard Keynes denounced in the 1930s, in which investors picked stocks by trying to guess which stocks other investors would pick.[7] Models were supposed to change those dynamics, grounding valuation in hard data and logical arguments. But, as Bob explained, over-the-counter derivatives had brought self-referential dynamics back to Wall Street, this time in the choice of model. In the old beauty contests, the question was, "which stocks will other investors choose?" In the new ones, the question was, "which model will other investors choose?" In sum, there was a significant part of Wall Street that, unbeknownst to me, was dangerously self-referential.

The circularity of credit derivatives has in fact been documented in MacKenzie and Spears's investigation on the role played by "Gaussian copula" models in the crisis. The formula, originally developed by the statistician David Li in the year 2000 to estimate the probability distribution of losses on a pool of loans or bonds, had been credited by journalist Felix Salmon with bankrupting the American financial sector.[8] "The Gaussian copula became so deeply entrenched," Salmon wrote, "that warnings about its limitations were largely ignored." MacKenzie and Spears challenge Salmon's conclusions, showing instead that the adopters of the Gaussian copula used it for many different purposes: not simply in credit rating, but also in communication, compensation, and risk management. Such users were painfully aware of its limitations, uncomfortable with its use, and skeptical about its output. The real question, MacKenzie and Spears add, is why such inadequate device was so widely adopted. The answer they provide is that it was a useful form of convention,[9] confirming Bob's point. As they observe, "all shared models in derivatives trading in investment banking are resources for coordinating action" (p. 13).

The final and least expected aspect of my conversation with Bob was his rejection of Wall Street's bailout. I had naïvely expected Bob's position to be colored by his own self-interest, perhaps not his direct self-interest (since his bank would not have received any bailout funds) but the self-interest of his broad group, chief executives of Wall Street banks. However, Bob had not only disregarded his economic self-interest, but also pointed to a paradox I had missed: most progressive politicians and media seemed to favor the bailout. Bob attributed that support to their transnational identity. Bob's comment put me in the spotlight, because it captured my own views regarding the bailout with such accuracy. As much as I opposed the moral hazard that the bailout created, I was persuaded of the practical need to have one. My view, I now understood, had been colored by my own cosmopolitan identity as a Spanish graduate student living in Manhattan, as well as by my researcher's proximity to Wall Street. More important, Bob's comment alerted me to the political realignment that the crisis had created.

November 2008

My next meeting with Bob took place six weeks later, in November 2008. During those six weeks, developments on Wall Street had been consistently negative. I found Bob visibly concerned. "We're still in a state of great disorder in this firm and in the market," he said. "There's definitely an end of the old order." A number of banks, Bob added, would be leaving the securities business. For instance, on that very day a US federal grand jury had indicted the former supervisor of a whistleblower at the Swiss bank UBS, presaging difficulties for the institution. UBS, Bob thought, will not have the financial wherewithal to absorb a multibillion-dollar fine. "It will have to exit the leadership race for the securities business."

The crisis, Bob told me, had unleashed a fierce political struggle inside the banks. The credit derivatives business was widely expected to shrink radically. Surviving firms would have to shift to other businesses, but their chief executives needed to be careful in steering this shift. "You may have very angry departures from high-performing people, who break their connection to the firm." If that happens and the structural shift does not materialize as expected, "you're stuck with a bunch of overpaid guys in dull, low-yield businesses." Uncertainty about the future thus called for chief executives to be careful in their strategic changes. Everyone in the banks had a strong incentive to argue their own case. "There's a lot of tension, even in the firms that are not experiencing mergers."

Closer to home, the crisis had created a major threat to Bob's position. The bank had agreed to a deal that would ensure the survival of an American bank damaged by the crisis, which I will refer to as Northfield Financial, a pseudonym. At Global Trust, the decision to enter the deal with Northfield had not been made by Bob; the negotiations had been handled directly at the bank's headquarters abroad, and the idea had not even been developed internally. "It's not clear if it was Northfield's CEO, or [Hank] Paulson who called Global. But whoever it was, it was not Global reaching out," said Bob. "They're on life support," he said about Northfield, "and we are the kidney dialysis machine."

The situation posed a serious danger to Bob, for it left him without a strategy. The deal with Northfield would effectively generate Wall Street-type revenues for Global Trust, just as Bob had planned to do by growing an in-house securities business. As a consequence, the acquisition rendered Bob's plans redundant, and by extension made Bob's position at Global Trust untenable. Was his perspective, I asked, biased by his own interests? "Of course, we have a view," said Bob, referring to himself in the first-person plural. "Under one point of view, we don't really need the new securities company," he said about his original plan. "But under another perspective, we should just let them go down, rather than drag us with them," he said about Northfield. "It's not self-serving. It's what I came here for. They can fire us [Bob]. But now [the contract] it's on paper, so they'd have to pay us. And I could always go back to retirement. You could say we are conflicted, but in fact we are less conflicted than others who have been here forever, because we came with a perspective on what should be done."

The situation, in other words, was extremely challenging for Bob. For this reason, he had not lost any time in growing the securities company. He had already hired various former employees from International Securities. "Todd works here," he remarked, "he's the head of Risk Management, because we didn't have any statistical arbitrage to do. He was very explicit about constantly questioning his model." Jerry, Bob's former lieutenant, had also been hired. Bob had also hired two senior traders from the program trading desk at International Securities, as well as someone from the customer sales desk.

Our conversation shifted to the public debate on the global financial crisis. At the time, some commentators were pointing to the risk management function as the cause for the crisis: given the relatively low status (and pay) of risk managers within top management teams at Wall Street banks, the argument went, the position attracted less talented executives. Was bad risk management, I asked Bob, the root of the crisis? "Wait a minute," Bob responded. "The one thing you've got to remember is, top risk management executives make a couple million dollars a year. Only on Wall Street would you look at a guy who's making $750,000 a year because he's the number four in risk management and say, 'he's not very well paid.'" Bob had a different perspective. "*The management failure is a CEO-level failure.* The CEO decides whose view he is going to give weight to in any given year. Do I need to listen to my CFO, my head of retail sales, my institutional sales guy, my proprietary trading person, or my risk management guy? There's always tension, as people are pursuing their strict area of responsibility. The CEOs chose to give lower weight to risk management."

In other words, Bob emphasized the CEOs' responsibility. He also underscored their continued need to rely on their own judgment in relation to their subordinates. "Take Joe Cassano," said Bob in reference to the CEO of AIG Financial Products, the company whose losses would have bankrupted the insurance company AIG, had it not been rescued. As it turns out, Cassano and

Bob had crossed paths a few years before. Cassano had originally worked for Howard Sosin in the 1980s when the latter created AIG Financial Products. "AIG got really sick of Howard," said Bob. "He cut himself a very sweet deal. And then he went out and pioneered the 30-year interest rate swap market, which was improperly priced. He put AIG in the center of that market, a triple A insurance company. He made a ton of money, personally. They had to pay him out several million dollars when they finally got rid of him."

I knew much of this to be true. According to press reports, Howard Sosin had struck a famously lucrative deal with AIG, and received a very generous compensation package when AIG decided to stop working with him. Bob continued: "Joe Cassano was his number two, kind of the bookkeeper. And AIG, instead of saying, 'we need to get rid of this Sosin and his number two,' ended up doing a search, including talking to *me*, and gave the job to Cassano. He [Cassano] then repeated the same basic problem with the credit default swap business, bad models. Everybody loved having AIG's triple A credit rating as counterparty. He sold the hell out of these things. Blew up the firm."

The account of AIG's demise that Bob had offered was one that I could not take lightly. It would take some time to check and triangulate but, if true, Bob's story had one important advantage relative to the various theories being put forth: simplicity. As Bob finished telling his story, our meeting came to an end and I left for the subway.

Moral Judgment

Back in my office at Columbia, as I transcribed my notes I realized that my conversation with Bob had surprised me yet again. I was alarmed by Global Trust's decision to enter into a deal that might make Bob redundant, barely three months after he had accepted the position. Bob, who seemed extraordinarily skilled at organizational politics, appeared to have been blindsided by the bank's decision to acquire Northfield Financial. He seemed to be engaged in a losing political battle within the bank that was not quite in keeping with my recollections of him at International Securities.

I was also struck by Bob's views about whom to blame for the crisis. He placed the responsibility squarely with the chief executives of the banks, who he expected to show better judgment: CEOs were responsible for what to prioritize, who to listen to, and who to bring into the bank. In the case of AIG, Bob felt that the company's experience with Sosin should have been enough of a red flag for the firm not to promote Cassano to CEO of Financial Products. Existing accounts of Sosin's work in AIG Financial Products provided some confirmation.[10] At the core of Sosin's derivatives strategy for Financial Products was selling financial protection in the form of swaps, backed by AIG. These swaps were lucrative because AIG's triple A rating allowed Sosin to inexpensively hedge their risk, but they were also a threat to AIG, leaving it exposed to impossibly large payouts in case of default. For instance, despite Sosin's best efforts to hedge all possible risks, a transaction in 1993 with a Canadian conglomerate called Edper led to a $200 million unhedged exposure that revealed the magnitude of the risks for AIG. The exposure alerted the CEO of AIG, Maurice ("Hank") Greenberg to the risks that he was running with Financial Products, culminating in Greenberg's demand that Sosin leave.

In choosing a successor, Bob contended, Greenberg should have antici-pated that Cassano, Sosin's subordinate, would exhibit a similar lack of good judgment, which he did. To Bob, then, responsibility for the losses created by Cassano sat squarely with the CEO of AIG, Greenberg, who promoted Cassano after Sosin's departure. Responsibility lay at the top, Bob argued, it entailed judgment calls, and to a large extent judgment calls about character. The cause of the crisis, Bob seemed to imply, was management failure, and responsibility for the crisis remained with a few chief executive officers. I found this account surprising, as it marked such a stark contrast with that put forth by MacKenzie. The latter did not clearly attribute moral shortcomings to any actor in particular and instead emphasized the complexity of modeling credit derivatives.

My meeting with Bob produced a third, perhaps even more puzzling, observation. In evaluating who was responsible for the crisis, Bob seemed to be in favor of combining economic and moral judgments. Bob's assessment of Howard Sosin as greedy, for instance, seemed to be bound with Bob's dis-approval of the models Sosin used in the 30-year interest swap market, and Bob had even alluded to Sosin's "messy divorce." This moral undertone was not unlike the reactions that some politicians and public commentators had expressed toward Wall Street bankers. Once again, Bob sounded more like a member of the outraged public than a Wall Street elite, though in this case Bob's outrage might have been made worse by the fact that Sosin's protégé beat him out for a job.

February 2009

I saw Bob again three months later, in February 2009. By the time we met, Bob was even more pessimistic than he had been in November of the prior year. The deal with Northfield had gone forward, and Global's top management were predictably stalling on whether or not to continue with the securities firm that Bob had been hired to build. Bob's response to the indecisiveness was to forge ahead rather than wait for approval. He offered an analogy from a management article he remembered from his MBA studies: "organizations write rules, and then people get around the rules." The article described a company with a rule that employees could not spend more than $50,000 without requesting approval. Nevertheless, one of its employees built an entire factory by having vendors sell him bricks in $48,000 increments. "So that's what I do," added Bob, smiling. In his case, the equivalent of buying bricks at small increments was hiring older employees to whom he could disclose the nature of the challenge he was facing, which was none other than building a securities firm without authorization from headquarters. This meant, in many cases, hiring people he already knew.

Bob likened his predicament to the game of "red light, green light." The original children's game is a race in which participants can only move when a judge in charge says "green light." As soon as the judge says "red light" everyone has to stop, and any player caught moving is penalized. "So, we play red light, green light," Bob confessed. "Essentially, the organization is constantly watching us to make sure we don't do anything new. So, we take a complex exercise, break it up into single steps and execute it one step at a time, but only in the intervals when the organization effectively is not directly observing us. And then when they turn around, 'did you move?' 'No.' 'It looks like you're in a different spot.' 'Well, I think I'm in the same spot.' 'It looks a little different.' 'I don't think so.'" As he said this, I could not help but acknowledge Bob's talent for metaphor. "It's really bizarre," Bob acknowledged, "but we do it every day. We have a new trading floor. In our new businesses, we have regulatory signoff. We're really making progress. It's strange. But in the environment we're in, it's no stranger than anyone else. It's just a different form of strange."

I was surprised to hear that the bank had obtained a regulatory license. Back in the summer of 2008, Bob had given himself a time frame of two years to obtain regulatory signoff, but as soon as his bank agreed to the deal with Northfield, the regulators approved his plans. I was less surprised to hear that the bank did have a new trading floor, as he had already told me of his plan to do so. Bob had managed to move to a different floor of the same building, and he took me on a tour of the changes he had introduced. Each of the different departments of the firm—internal auditing and compliance, fixed income origination, bond trading, and investment banking—had a slightly different setup. Compliance relied on cubicles, and Bob had lowered the employees' partitions to develop what he now referred to as "open horizon view." Employees did not like it, however. Originations had a see-through glass wall that acted as a Chinese Wall, but employees complained that clients would not find it confidential enough. The Fixed Income trading room had the classic setup like that of International Securities, but the desks were narrower because they were designed for flat screens.

I asked Bob about the situation in the finance industry. "It's horrible," he confessed, with no attempt at qualifying his concern. "It's the end of the world as we know it." There had been a sharp consolidation of the banking industry after the crisis. JP Morgan had acquired Bear Stearns and Washington Mutual.

Bank of America had acquired Merrill Lynch. Wells Fargo had acquired Wachovia. The crisis had thus given rise to a new entity, the conglomerate Wall Street bank, which the press sometimes referred to as the "megabank." Bob feared that this consolidation would reverse a hundred years of antitrust enforcement in the United States, turning Wall Street into a collection of even less manageable banks than before the crisis.

The problem with such a scenario, Bob argued, was the complexity involved in managing those large banks. In the past, regulatory restrictions "had the unintended consequence of keeping most institutions operating at the complexity horizon of a single smart executive. Even in large banks, because it's not that complicated. We need to make commercial loans. We do it in this region. We have this bond trading operation, and we do municipal bonds. There's a scope. So, a guy, by the time he's fifty, can do it." However, this did not work for the newly merged Wall Street banks. These institutions required their chief executives to think through the deposit cycle in every country in the world, factoring in regulatory restrictions, trading operations, and the bank's lending practices. "No single executive, arguably no team of executives, can understand that within their capacity for complex thinking. So, what happens is, they use mechanistic approaches to decision-making. There will be a model for every decision. How do we measure deposits? Well, we have a model. How do deposits work in Indonesia? And the trading risk? We have a Value at Risk model. And the lending cycle? We have the creditworthiness rating." This system can be further mechanized, Bob added. For instance, the traders can put in hedging instruments. "And soon enough what is being managed is not the *bank* but the *model*, which ultimately is a hypothesis about how the bank works. It's rigid and brittle, but it's big." There are few situations that are bad enough such that a model like this would not apply. "But when you hit them, it's impossible."

Why impossible? "Take Value at Risk," said Bob. This indicator was (and is) used by banks and regulators to gauge the capital needed to cover potential losses at a given point in time. "Suppose someone were to come to me and ask, 'tell me about the trading risk,' I'd say, well, 'it's not simple.' 'No, simplify.' 'I can't.' How is it going to work when the market goes down? Well, you know, is Jack sick or is he at work? Because it's going to make a difference.'" By contrast, the risk manager who relies on Value at Risk can make far more certain statements: "when the market goes down, *this* will happen across the whole portfolio. Why? Because he simplified everything artificially so he can move one piece. And because it's mathematically defined, he knows the answer to every question. What happens if the correlation widens between these two? *That* happens." Compare this, Bob insisted, to managing the bank without the model. "What happens if the correlation widens? 'I don't know.' Now, one can ask, which of the two is right?" Bob continued. The right answer is, he added, "I don't know." The problem, he concluded, is that "*the simple and more appealing answer* [i.e., the one given by the model] . . . *is also the wrong one.*" The use of models, Bob argued, creates an illusory simplification that is attractive but misleading.

There were, furthermore, self-serving reasons for turning to models. The pretense of knowledge provided a justification for organizational growth. "If you're in management and you're trying to grow your company, the right answer ["I don't know"] is not the answer that will allow you to grow the company, because if you accept that we don't actually know, then why are you betting more and more of the shareholders' capital? But Value at Risk gives you a clear answer, so it justifies more and more investment."

Bob was not implying that models should never be used. His point was instead that the user of the models should be able to understand events independently from the model, in order to decide if the model is working. This was difficult in a complex organizational context. "The essential decision in model-based trading is, 'is the model working?' That's why you have a human being." However, Bob added, the situation changes when the model is used in an organization, with bosses and subordinates, because the model is simultaneously being used to manage the subordinates and the bank. "The manager needs to be very careful about letting subordinates override the model. The more complex the organization, the more the model becomes written down as a rule, and you're not allowed to break it. 'Who the hell exceeded our risk guidelines?' 'Who did this? Who did that? Who's responsible for breaking those rules?' [You cannot say] 'Well, I had an intuition it was time to get out.' You can't do that in a complex organization."

Ultimately, Bob concluded, models suit the interests of bank executives rather than those of the bank itself. The idea that a very large bank can be managed, which presumes that model-based risk management is possible, creates the conditions for aspiring managers to line up, whether they are able to do the job or not. "If banks pay well enough for the position of CEO, there will be no honest self-selection. There will be nobody who says, 'I don't really want that job because I'm not a genius-savant-charismatic-guy.' Who wants $48 million a year compensation? I mean, anybody will say, 'I'd like that. Yeah, that's neat. I can do it for two years. Just pay me $50 million a year.'"

Our time, I soon realized, had come to an end. I expressed my interest in coming back soon, and Bob said he was amenable to it. "Hopefully we'll be doing more business," he said, "but it doesn't matter. We're playing red light, green light at a furious pace."

The Limits of Models in Organizations

Back in my office at Columbia, I took stock of what I had heard during my visit. The conversation had uncovered a major surprise: Bob had decided to create his securities firm without top management consent. The combination of the crisis and the acquisition of Northfield had rendered Bob's original plan obsolete. In response, Bob was going around the bank's rules to deliver on his plan, but such circumvention seemed dangerous. Bob's decision was remarkable in that it seemed inconsistent with the image of a conservative and discreet executive I had in mind.

A second surprise was Bob's opposition to risk models. The use of models in risk management, Bob claimed, had promoted growth at Wall Street banks to the point that their users, risk managers and CEOs, lacked any ability to ascertain whether the model worked or not. They had lost an ability to independently check, calibrate, and validate the model. This challenge was compounded by the hierarchical structure of the banks: when the model was used by a single individual, Bob believed, that person could always rely on personal judgment and depart from it. When used by someone under the supervision of someone else, the model set a normative expectation for the correct course of action. If the employee decided to depart from the model and the outcome was unfavorable, such departure would immediately come across as incompetence rather than random misfortune. This created pressure on employees to follow the model.

I was intrigued by Bob's perspective. It not only challenged an abundant economic literature on the benefits of quantitative risk management, but also offered a critique based on power that differed from sociological arguments about the performativity of economic models. In Bob's view, risk models were *political*. They sustained a large organizational size and allowed for the accumulation of power at the head of the organization.

July 2009

My last conversation with Bob in 2009 took place in July when he returned to Columbia as a guest speaker for another MBA course. By this time, the consolidation of existing banks into megabanks had already taken place. The crisis had led to a severe slowdown in economic activity, a sharp decrease in stock prices, and a rise in unemployment and mortgage foreclosures. The content of Bob's talk was exactly the same as his previous one, but given the challenging economic environment, the students' questions centered on the shocking events of September 2008.

After the lecture, Bob and I headed back to my office for some informal conversation. He reflected on a question one of my students had asked. The man had probed Bob about the performance of his trading floor at International Securities. Bob had picked up on the skepticism in the student's tone. "It's not a stupid question, not even the wrong question," Bob said to me, "but his body language was like, 'well . . .' So, I tried to answer factually." Bob had given the students the relevant figures and moved on to the next question. But as Bob and I talked about it in my office, Bob formulated a different response: "the right answer is, '*all the best performers from 2001 to 2007 were the businesses that got destroyed in 2008*. Destroyed. UBS fixed income, Merrill Lynch fixed income, unbelievable performers, money-spinning engines. Destroyed their firms.'"

Bob's comment piqued my curiosity. A related point had come up one week before, as I had conducted a case discussion on Merrill Lynch with the same MBA class. A different student had argued that it was unfair to judge the performance of Stan O'Neal, Merrill's CEO in 2006, with the information we had in 2009. This was of course a reasonable point, but as I thought about it I also worried that the argument could be misused to justify reckless management. I put the question to Bob: what did he think? "Here's where this gets really interesting," he replied. "Take the medical profession, and the old way of diagnosing patients. They smell their breath. Smell their urine, look at their skin, etc. Those were the diagnostic tools doctors would use. And as the scientific method comes along, they can replace that. We don't need to look at whether there's sugar. We don't need to see if ants will eat the urine. We can do a diabetes test that measures glucose exactly. OK, great. But here's the thing. The totality of information embodied in traditional diagnostic methods may exceed the tools we have today."

Drawing an analogy between medicine and finance, Bob added that he had come to believe there was more information available to chief executives on Wall Street than that offered by their modern tools, that is, the models. For that reason, he concluded that the problems with the subprime mortgages could have been anticipated. "If you go back to 2006, *Stan O'Neal could have known*. But he wouldn't have known using any toolkit that was given to him by the guild. He couldn't have measured it, quantified it, or shown it as a performance model. The way he would have known is by using the other set of things: 'I don't like the way those people talk to each other, talk to me, talk about their craft, see themselves, engage in the company. I'm nervous, and I want to take away their capitalistic tools.'" And, Bob added, there is an even bigger paradox: even if Stan O'Neal had wanted to stop things, "he could not do it. He wouldn't be allowed. The board might fire him."

Moral Intuition

Once Bob left my office, I took some time to reflect on our conversation. It had left me somewhat dispirited, for Bob had simultaneously offered a reason why the crisis might have gone undetected at Merrill, provided an alternative approach, and concluded that this alternative would have been unfeasible anyway. Bob's diagnosis of Merrill's failure was similar to his views on AIG: the chief executive had morally misjudged his subordinates. The general point was that chief executives ought to draw on their intuition and complement the numbers produced by their models. This included making moral judgments about the subordinates' behavior.

Years earlier, Bob and I had talked about the use of intuition in relation to the challenges of evaluating whether a model was right or wrong. Intuition alerted traders when "something was wrong" in a trade, even if they could not properly articulate what that was, allowing them to reconsider the use of the model. What Bob now seemed to be advocating was the use of *moral intuition*, that is, relying on ethical judgments of subordinates' behavior for the purpose of deciding whether to continue using the model that subordinates advocate.

The conversation recounted above was the last I had with Bob for several years. Taken together, my visits and exchanges with Bob between 2008 and 2009 speak to a growing literature on the organizational and sociological dimension of the global financial crisis. At risk of oversimplifying, this literature has presented two competing perspectives based respectively on organizational structures and individual morality. On the one hand, the analysis by MacKenzie and others attributes the crisis to structural silos within the rating agencies, which Wall Street banks exploited by creating toxic assets that subsequently contributed to their ruin. I shall refer to this as the "structural silos" hypothesis. On the other hand, a number of studies, including those by Fligstein and Roehrkasse; by Pernell, Jung, and Dobbin; as well as by Carruthers, point to morally questionable behavior such as alleged fraud (predatory lending and concealment of lower underwriting standards) and a form of moral licensing wherein banks with a chief risk officer reduced their policing of their own risky behavior. Understanding the significance of my conversations with Bob calls for a brief detour into these accounts.

The Structural Silos Hypothesis

MacKenzie's analysis directs the analytical focus away from the well-known scandals at Bear Stearns and Lehman Brothers, turning instead to one specific class of financial assets, "ABS CDOs," or collateralized debt obligations (CDOs) whose underlying assets are asset-backed securities (ABS), often mortgages. These derivatives of mortgage-based bonds are the "toxic asset" that threatened to bankrupt the US financial system. At aggregate losses of $290 billion, ABS CDOs made up the largest single portion of the total losses generated by the financial crisis, which totaled $1.4 trillion. Indeed, half of AIG's losses came from selling insurance against the failure of ABS CDOs, and the holdings of ABS CDOs on the books of Wall Street banks led to much of the losses at Citi, Merrill Lynch, UBS, Bank of America, and Morgan Stanley.

Why, MacKenzie asks, did Wall Street banks accumulate so much of this toxic asset? His answer starts by challenging a prevailing explanation of the crisis, that is, perverse incentives and moral shortcomings. After all, he argues, the banks themselves decided to keep the senior tranches of the ABS CDOs on their books. In light of this crucial observation, MacKenzie argues that "the assumption of amoral calculators," that is, of reckless bankers who knowingly sank their institutions, is "invalidated."[11] Instead, MacKenzie claims, scholars need to examine the social process by which investors came to mistakenly believe that ABS CDOs were safe. In other words, the crisis needs to be seen as "a problem in the sociology of knowledge." MacKenzie's contention is supported by the institutional analysis conducted by Kim Pernell-Gallagher. The latter concludes that "by 2006, it was clear that CDOs had achieved widespread social acceptance," and that bank CEOs came to believe in the value and safety of these derivatives through a process of learning from the positive stock market reaction to the CDO underwritings of their rivals.[12]

In accounting for the way in which organizational structures, rather than opportunism, created the crisis, MacKenzie draws an analogy to the field of the social studies of science. As sociologists of science have established, scientific practices vary to a remarkable degree across disciplines such as physics or chemistry, and even within disciplines. As with science, MacKenzie argues, financial innovation in the 1980s and 1990s led to distinct social worlds in Wall Street banks and rating agencies. One such world was comprised of specialists in securitization, who had developed an expertise in bundling mortgages into bonds. This world was heavily influenced by the rating agencies and was historically focused on the "prepayment risk" carried by mortgages, that is, the danger that if home owners pre-paid their mortgages when interest rates turned in their favor, the bank would stand to lose money.

The second social world involved in the creation of toxic assets was composed of derivatives traders who used models to back out market estimates. They proceeded as Max did in the case of merger arbitrage, using this practice for the purpose of trading credit derivatives. These traders had historically emphasized default risk rather than prepayment risk, because they came from the world of corporate debt rather than mortgage-based bonds. Unlike standard American mortgages, corporate bonds ran a high risk of default, so default risk had to be factored in. These two worlds, mortgage and derivatives specialists, formed distinct communities; their practitioners sat in different teams at the rating agencies, they rarely spoke, and often did not get along.

The two worlds described above came into contact in the 2000s when Wall Street banks extended the use of CDOs to mortgage-based bonds, that is, ABS CDOs. Within the rating agencies, the teams that covered ABS CDOs were the derivatives teams. But instead of evaluating directly the risks of the underlying mortgage bonds, these teams decided to rely on ratings from the mortgage teams in the same agency, created by their ABS specialists. The agencies, in other words, used a two-step process for evaluating ABS CDOs, not unlike preparing a meal by combining different precooked components.

The process described above made mortgage derivatives vulnerable to inaccuracies in the ratings of the mortgage bonds, setting off a mechanism that culminated in the accumulation of toxic assets on the books of Wall Street banks. This mechanism can be summarized in three conceptual steps. *First*, MacKenzie argues, the use of credit ratings for mortgage-based bonds led investors to establish a rough equivalence across asset classes: a triple-A mortgage-based CDO was perceived as having the *same* risk as triple-A corporate bonds, for they were both rated "triple A," even though they pertained to different assets. This equivalency led to a clear strategy for banks: buy inexpensive ABS, package them as ABS CDOs, sell them, and capture the difference. This was a form of "ratings arbitrage," although of course a misleading version of arbitrage, in that the equivalence was not real but simply based on the terminology of credit ratings. ABS CDOs thus gave rise to the exploitation of a misplaced mechanism of equivalence created by the rating agencies.[13]

There was a *second* step in the banks' path to ruin. The ABS CDOs turned out to be riskier than expected, because the default rates of the securities within them were more correlated than originally estimated. However, MacKenzie insists, the correlation among mortgage-based assets was not at first easy to ascertain. Unlike corporate bonds, mortgage-based bonds lacked associated stock prices that could be used to estimate default correlation. Such correlation was initially estimated by the agencies to be 0.3 (that is, 30 percent), partly for consistency with previous practices, though arguably also for self-serving reasons: a correlation of 0.5 would not have allowed them to turn triple B–rated bonds into triple A–rated derivatives. Nevertheless, MacKenzie insists, the choice of 0.3 seemed *conservative* at the time, because the correlation coefficients coming out of econometric studies (albeit with admittedly short historical time series) were as low as 0.06. The assumption of low correlation, however, proved fatal for banks and investors, as in retrospect the actual coefficient turned out to be as high as 0.8.

The *third* and last step outlined by MacKenzie is paradoxical in nature. Banks ended up holding an extraordinary number of super-senior tranches of the toxic ABS CDOs. The reason resided in the governance role that regulators have historically accorded to credit ratings, allowing banks to hold fewer capital reserves against assets with high credit ratings. In effect, regulators were relying on the models used by the rating agencies to ensure that banks had enough capital reserves. When those models proved to be inadequate, so were the banks' reserves. Thus, in a strangely circular twist of fate, the banks that most clearly gamed the ratings system ended up keeping the largest volumes of toxic assets on their books, thereby suffering the strongest losses.

In sum, rating agencies did not correctly model subprime mortgage derivatives, banks created an extraordinary number of them, and banks kept a large proportion of them on their books. Things went downhill from there. The value of ABS CDOs dropped quickly once house prices stopped rising. The owners of subprime mortgages, incapable of reselling their houses whenever they missed their mortgage payments, started defaulting at record rates. The rate of events-of-default of ABS CDOs was high in 2005, higher in 2006, and reached an unprecedented 80 percent in 2007. In turn, these defaults triggered the bankruptcy of two hedge funds associated with Bear Stearns in 2007. When Merrill Lynch seized $850 million of the funds' assets, the bank found that it could only sell them at 20 percent of their face value, triggering a repricing of CDOs around the world. This repricing then initiated a sequence of margin calls that culminated in the downfall of Lehman Brothers.

Overall, MacKenzie's analysis focuses on the problems created by the coexistence of path-dependent evaluation practices in different corners of the rating agencies. The problem is thus a lack of organizational integration. Journalist Gillian Tett has advanced a similar, anthropologically informed account of the crisis.[14] The structural silo hypothesis thus offers a surprisingly sober diagnosis that resists the temptation to voice moral outrage. It stresses ignorance rather than twisted incentives, incompetence rather than immorality, and impersonal structures rather than specific individuals.

Norms

Other sociologists have presented an alternative account of the crisis, based on alleged fraud and moral licensing. Among them, Fligstein and Roehrkasse see a deliberate strategy of opportunism among America's largest financial institutions. The authors draw on out-of-court settlements between regulators and financial institutions over alleged bank malfeasance, using such data to develop a proxy for alleged fraud, that is, alleged manipulation or falsification of information for gain. While the banks did not admit to any wrongdoing in their regulatory settlements, the authors argue that "the enormous size of the settlements in our sample, and the significant financial and legal power of large banks, support the assumed relationship between settlement and culpability."[15] Fligstein and Roehrkasse locate such settlements in predatory mortgage lending, where mortgage originators allegedly deceived borrowers about loan terms and eligibility requirements; and in loan issuance, where banks that packaged mortgages into securities that allegedly misrepresented the quality of the loans and the extent of their due diligence, simultaneously betting against the mortgage-based securities they issued. As many as thirty-two out of the sixty largest financial institutions in the sample had incidences of alleged fraud. In sum, the analysis by Fligstein and Roehrkasse contends that the financial crisis had a moral, and not simply technical, dimension. As the authors write, their analysis "advances a theory of systemic fraud in the context of historic financial crises."[16]

Lack of restraint, in the form of "moral licensing," is at the center of a related account of the crisis put forth by Kim Pernell, Jiwook Jung, and Frank Dobbin.[17] The authors examined the elevation of compliance specialists to chief risk officers at American banks. They contend that such promotion of risk management had two effects. First, having a "CRO" shifted the bank's risk management agenda, from one based on avoidance of financial calamities to a riskier approach that sought to balance risk and return. Second, the presence of chief risk officers encouraged managers in trading floors to relax their monitoring of risk, in the belief that this was being done elsewhere. As a result, during the years 1995 to 2007 the banks that appointed a chief risk officer ended up with a greater adoption of risky over-the-counter derivatives over other forms of derivatives.

Crisis, Models, and Morals

My visits and conversations with Bob in 2008 and 2009 provided me with an admittedly partial and limited window into the global financial crisis, albeit one that speaks to the debate described above. My data reveal the views and assessments of the CEO of a Wall Street bank, in real time, and in the context of a long-running relationship of mutual trust. Bob's views and reactions to the crisis speak to the sociological debate over the mechanisms that culminated in the global financial crisis.

Consider first the structural silos hypothesis. This account is in many ways consistent with the observations at International Securities reported in the previous chapters. The central message that emerged from my fieldwork at Bob's equities trading room during 1999–2004 was the importance of integration across the various desks. Indeed, MacKenzie drew upon this research to illustrate his argument on the credit crisis. "In their analysis," he writes of an article that David Stark and I wrote, " 'the friction among competing principles of arbitrage' is productive: it 'generates new ways of recognizing opportunities.' " In other words, MacKenzie presents the communication across desks that took place at International Securities as a practice that might have mitigated the crisis. Had the ABS desk been located at one end of an integrated trading room like Bob's, while CDO traders sat at another, the disaster might have been avoided, because a company organized in this way would have seen the danger and rated the ABS CDOs differently.

Bob's perspective of the crisis, however, departs from MacKenzie's with regard to the importance of moral and institutional norms in the crisis. In his guest lecture in November 2007, Bob predicted the demise of two large Wall

Street banks, as they were too large and complex to be well managed. Bob's pessimism, I later found out, centered on model-based risk management, Bob added, with tools such as Value at Risk that had allowed Wall Street banks to grow beyond the point where their complexity could be managed.[18] Their size made it impossible for a competent and experienced chief executive to exercise judgment over the output of the various models governing the banks. Furthermore, growth was not an unintended outcome of the new quantitative tools, but a deliberate strategy that advanced the bankers' interest in empire-building. Indeed, Bob claimed in September 2008 that Wall Street was already "dead" before the crisis, because the structures and informal regulatory networks that promoted restraint had disappeared due to deregulation and consolidation. Finally, Bob was clear in that the responsibility for the problems faced by the banks lay with their chief executive, and this responsibility was not limited to crunching risk numbers but included making ethical judgments about the CEOs' subordinates. In this regard, my visits and interviews with Bob lend support to the emphasis on moral norms by Fligstein and Roehrkasse, by Pernell, Jung, and Dobbin, as well as by Carruthers.

Conclusion

The events that occurred during 2008 and 2009 were among the most difficult of my entire research project. The global financial crisis questioned the trust in the financial system that I had developed through my years of fieldwork at International Securities. From 2003 to 2008, I had rejected the charge, often voiced by institutional theorists and political economists, that my perspective (and more broadly, that of the social studies of finance) was overly agnostic about the social consequences of derivatives, unconcerned about power on Wall Street, and generally cavalier about the ethical dilemmas of financial capitalism. The crisis revealed that such concerns were not unwarranted. The cynical assessments that Bob and other Wall Street insiders often made of the chief executives of the large banks were not based on prejudice, but on repeated exposure to behavior that they perceived to be morally lacking. To them, Wall Street was a dark place. I had finally understood their reservations and empathized with their mixed feelings. Now I needed to fully comprehend the nature of such darkness.

11

Scandal

The financial crisis brought to the fore something that my original fieldwork had not quite captured: the dark side of Wall Street. The dysfunctions of the financial industry, so exhaustively captured by media reports after September 2008, seemed prominent in Bob's mind, but I was not able to grasp them simply by referring back to my fieldwork between 1999 and 2003. After all, what I had observed at International Securities was an attempt to avoid the problems that had surfaced at other Wall Street banks, so my fieldnotes contained no evidence of those problems. I eventually understood that I needed to adapt my research design, and shift from participant observation to oral history in order to capture what went wrong on Wall Street. What I needed, I resolved, were tape-recorded interviews with Bob and others, aimed at probing into the past rather than the present, and into Wall Street at large, rather than International Securities. I asked Bob to set aside some time, so that I could elicit what qualitative researchers call the "grand tour" of his Wall Street career.[1] Bob's account, which I present below, revealed a dimension of him that I had not previously heard, or for that matter, imagined, providing me with invaluable context to understand the elusive dark side of Wall Street.

"Please start from the very beginning," I instructed Bob on the day we met. Bob explained that he was born in Omaha, Nebraska, in the late 1950s. His father was a career military officer in the US Army Corps of Engineers, in a unit responsible for the construction of fortifications and managing the American defense system. At home, Bob was exposed to his father's interest in engineering, as well as his appreciation for technology and mathematics. "A cavalry officer could be dumb as long as he was brave," Bob explained, but an engineer like his father "had to be educated." Indeed, Bob was born in Omaha because his father was stationed there in order to supervise the construction of the headquarters of the missile defense system, the so-called Strategic Air Command. The facility was a gigantic underground construction in Lincoln, Nebraska, "dead center of the United States," because the location was deemed safer from the Soviet threat. "In the days of fighter bombers," Bob added, they "would have to fly over the whole bulk of the United States to get there."

As the son of a US Army officer in the 1960s, Bob gained an early exposure to international affairs and organizational politics. Shortly after Bob was born, his father was reassigned to the German town of Hanau, and the family followed. At the time, the Berlin wall was being erected amidst extraordinary geopolitical tension. Hanau gained a US military base because it was close to the so-called Fulda Gap, the opening in the Vogelsberg Mountains that the Red Army would have to cross in the event of war. In the following years, Bob's family kept relocating as his father kept being reassigned. In 1962 they moved to Framingham, Massachusetts, just outside of Boston, and in 1967 they moved again to Mechanicsburg, Pennsylvania, where the navy had a large supply base to take advantage of a confluence of railroads. "Acre after acre of warehouses," Bob recalled, "surrounded by fences, and a little tiny housing complex tacked on the corner, where the officers lived." Bob's father was by then Inspector General, and as an *army* officer reporting on a *navy* base, that is, in a different part of the military, he was perceived as an outsider. The children of navy families made Bob's life difficult, but it was during this time that Bob learned about corporate politics. "The army in peacetime is a bureaucracy. So, my father would talk to me a lot. How do you work within bureaucracy? I learned most of that from my dad," he explained.

Bob's involvement with financial markets was an unintended outcome of the recession of 1981. Bob pursued a college degree in international affairs. He graduated from a prestigious university in Washington, DC in the midst of the recession of 1981 and, given the limited career opportunities available at the time, he enrolled in a business school in New York City to pursue a part-time MBA. He entered Wall Street in 1982, joining one of America's largest banks to work in a group that specialized in privately placed debt. The group was responsible for making loans to Latin American countries, and as part of this activity, "the bank fell by accident into interest rate swaps." A swap, which is explained in more detail below, is an agreement to exchange income streams, and is widely seen as the origin of the extraordinary growth in the over-the-counter derivatives industry during the 1980s. It was thus that Bob ended up in the over-the-counter derivatives business.

While the expression "over-the-counter" conjures up images of worktops and face-to-face exchanges of money for paper certificates, the central characteristic of these markets is that buyers and sellers transact privately with a Wall Street bank (the "dealer") rather than through a public bourse or financial exchange. As MacKenzie wrote, if a participant wishes to transact, "he must directly contact the dealer in question, normally by telephone, and after receiving a definite bid or ask price, the deal is agreed to verbally, and an exchange of paperwork or electronic confirmation follows subsequently."[2]

Riding the Derivatives Revolution

The use of derivatives on Wall Street, Bob pointed out, resulted from the banks' attempts to circumvent financial regulations. The derivatives business began in 1982 with the issuance of Eurobonds, or dollar-denominated bonds in American corporations issued in European countries. That market, Bob explained, was a way of "getting around" Glass-Steagall. "*And when I say getting around*," he emphasized, "*that is what they wanted to do*." Glass-Steagall made it illegal for large commercial banks like JP Morgan or Chemical Bank to raise debt for large corporations in the United States, as only investment banks were allowed to perform this function. Commercial banks thus turned to the Eurobond market to do so.[3]

As part of their services, these banks started offering their corporate clients a new product, interest rate swaps. Swaps are complex financial instruments that involve an exchange of streams of payments. While a regular loan entails the exchange of one large payment for a single stream of smaller ones, a swap entails two different streams, with money flowing in both directions, and with recurring obligations for both parties. The purported benefit of swaps was to protect corporations from so-called market risk, or the risk of fluctuations in the market price of securities or commodities that threatened businesses during the unprecedented inflation and high interest rates of the 1970s and 1980s. Swaps also protected against credit risk, or the risk that a borrower may not repay a loan.

The first highly publicized swap took place in 1981 between IBM and the World Bank. The World Bank needed to borrow German marks and Swiss francs to finance its international operations, and IBM needed US dollars whenever interest rates rose. The two organizations thus swapped their streams of debt payments, with IBM exchanging its francs and marks for the World Bank's dollars (see figure 11.1). The success of this swap lent legitimacy to this derivative contract, prompting its diffusion. Aside from the exchange rate convenience and ability to protect against risk, one key reason for the attractiveness of swaps, Bob adds, was that they were over-the-counter agreements, that is, privately conducted between two corporations and thus "did not show up on their balance sheets." In other words, swaps made possible the type of opaque off-balance sheet entities, credit default swaps, that played a central role in the 2008 financial crisis.

In 1984, Bob changed jobs as the team he worked for was hired by the New York subsidiary of a British merchant bank, and he moved with the team. Soon

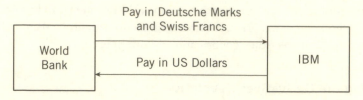

FIGURE 11.1. Schematic representation of currency cash flows in the World Bank's swap agreement. Adapted from Bock (1984).

afterward, a large British "clearing" (i.e., retail) bank acquired this merchant bank, and Bob decided to move again. "I didn't want to be part of them," he said in reference to the retail bank. Bob changed jobs once again in 1987, joining a large American commercial bank that I will refer to as Premier Financial, and he stayed there until 1995. "A phenomenal experience," he recalls. The bank was one of the leading derivatives firms on Wall Street. "A very exciting firm, staffed by really, really smart people. Men who held themselves to very high standards and very high values. Honest, high-integrity people."

By then, swaps had become the dominant type of derivatives contract, and Premier was a leading participant in the interest rate swaps and currency swaps markets. From 1987 to 1995, Bob adds, the derivatives business not only experienced phenomenal growth, but also an expansion into multiple asset classes (see figure 11.2). "Equity derivatives, commodity derivatives, credit derivatives, insurance derivatives," Bob recalls, "the absolute globalization of the business, and the increase in complexity, all that took place in an extraordinary cycle." Premier was at the heart of it. "It was the innovation firm. They were in the vanguard of the derivatives revolution, thinking of organizing around rational, mechanistic structures, and imagining how well ordered it would be."

What placed Premier in such an enviable position? The bank, Bob explains, had paradoxically benefited from being absent in the traditional investment banking businesses, which freed up resources for its derivatives division. Its leading proprietary trading business also gave it a head start, helping the bank specialize in the use of economic models. "If I had to identify a hedge fund that was most like Premier," Bob says, "it would have been Long-Term Capital. A securities firm most like Premier would have been Bear Stearns. Firms that loved model-based trading." Existing accounts of Premier confirm this point. An article written in *Euromoney* in the early 1990s (which I will paraphrase rather than quote literally to preserve confidentiality) remarked on how Premier had transformed itself from a second-rate, ill-focused, near insolvent commercial bank into a dynamic, well-capitalized, highly profitable bank.

Bob rose quickly through Premier's ranks. By 1992, he was one of the two or three senior executives responsible for derivatives trading. "I was in charge

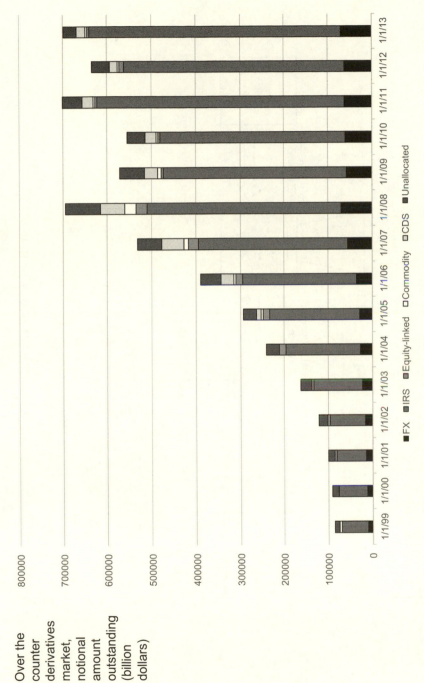

Over the
counter
derivatives
market,
notional
amount
outstanding
(billion
dollars)

FIGURE 11.2. Notional amount of outstanding over-the-counter derivatives, 1998–2010.

Source: BIS.

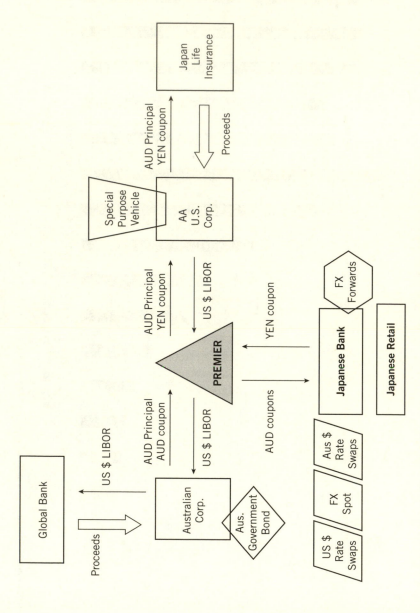

FIGURE 11.3. A typical interest and currency swap agreement at Premier Financial in the mid-1990s.

of the most glamorous, most profitable, fastest growing, most innovative business, and I ran the trading side globally," he recalls. Although he was only thirty-two years old, he was already part of the bank's management group, together with the chief financial officer, chairman, vice chairman, and a few others. "I was, without question, one of three or four people at Premier that would have been on track to run the company. A powerful executive. Global responsibilities, hundreds of people working for me."

As an illustration of the work that Bob's subordinates did, consider a typical swap designed by Premier in the 1990s. A Japanese life insurance company wants to buy bonds in Australian dollar principal and yen coupons (figure 11.3). To serve that demand, Premier needs to find a US corporation such as IBM and persuade it to issue bonds in yen coupon and Australian dollars principal. The US corporation then needs to swap that bond, because it will have to pay bondholders in Australian dollars and Japanese yen, and it does not have these currencies. To perform that additional operation, Premier will issue a *second* swap agreement that will accept Australian dollar principal and yen coupons. Alternatively, Premier could also create a special-purpose vehicle. As Premier does not really have a use for those currencies either, it will have to find an Australian corporation that wants to match those flows, or some portion of them, through Premier's investment banking team in Australia. In turn, the Australian corporation will typically be looking to borrow money, not do swaps, so Premier's traders will have to ask its loan desk to arrange a syndicated loan. Alternatively, Premier could leave the Australian corporation out, and head directly for the Australian government bond market.

The need for this swap agreement, which remained in place for more than ten years, was ultimately driven by retail customers in Japan, who had a peculiar love for Australian-dollar, Japanese-yen risk, which they would embed into their deposits. But what this trade illustrates is the complexity of swap agreements: as figure 11.3 shows, there were a large number of organizations involved, as well as numerous parts of Premier, globally, that had to collaborate. Furthermore, the agreement was not arranged for a single time period, but for a number of them: it was an agreement to exchange *flows*. The swap tethered together multiple organizations, through multiple periods of time, creating interdependencies between companies and their subunits, and accumulating complexity within Premier.

As I considered Bob's professional journey, I was intrigued by its peculiar path and trajectory. He had progressed from a military family in the years of the Cold War to financial derivatives in the 1980s, and from the American Midwest and a small town in Germany to Washington, DC and New York City. Such overlap between economics and the military has been noted by economic historian Philip Mirowski. In *Machine Dreams*, Mirowski argues that the roots of contemporary economics and its emphasis on information processing and computer metaphors can be found in the development of the field of operations research at the RAND Organization, the American defense and policy think tank founded after World War II. As he writes, "the Pax Americana had much to do with the content of such abstruse and formal doctrines such as linear programming and game theory."[4]

Bob's account of the early growth of the derivatives industry also speaks to research by Russell Funk and Daniel Hirschman, whose history of interest rate and foreign exchange swaps documents that these instruments undermined the separation of commercial and investment banking established by the Glass-Steagall Act of 1933, even as explicit political action failed to do so. Swaps, these authors conclude, illustrate how "ambiguous innovations may disrupt the regulatory status quo."[5]

Scandal

The success of Premier, however, was jeopardized by a succession of scandals that, beginning in the early 1990s, originated in its derivatives division. The first of these scandals took place at an international subsidiary of the bank that was part of Bob's responsibility. Bob was in charge of *derivatives sales* in a small unit abroad. "A tiny office," he said, and certainly not the focus of his attention. "I spent most of my time worrying about Hong Kong and New York and London and Toronto and Sidney." The office in question was staffed by twenty-five derivatives salespeople, sitting across from the commercial banking division of Premier, and separated from it by a glass wall that also divided legal responsibilities, in line with local regulation akin to Glass-Steagall. Bob had no authority over the employees of that division, which specialized in *commercial banking*, and sat across from his people. "None," he emphasized, given the laws of that country, which were "strictly enforced."

The bank's problems started when some of Bob's subordinates in New York tried to sell more lucrative products than Bob was willing to allow. These subordinates circumvented Bob and turned directly to the commercial banking unit at Premier. "They flew over and dealt with the bank people [Premier's commercial bank division], and they sold toxic derivatives to customers in that country." One of these customers was a large local investment bank, and the derivatives blew up. "But," Bob insists, "they weren't my salespeople. They were the [commercial] bank's salespeople." As I heard this, I naturally wondered whether Bob was being self-serving in his recollection. Did he *really* have nothing to do with the scandal? I will come back to this point below.

Once the scandal hit, however, Premier did not have anyone to handle the problems with its affronted corporate customers, so the task came to Bob. He negotiated a solution with the customers. "I resolved every dispute and all the customers were satisfied in the end." The settlement, however, cost Premier millions. Back in New York, Bob was criticized by the bank's top executives because they did not want to settle with the customers. "They felt the customers had signed the contracts, so the customers should pay. My view was, the customers did not fully understand what they were doing. Premier had obligations too. And so, I negotiated a compromise, as you do in these things." Brokering such a compromise proved to be extraordinarily difficult, and a time of burnout for Bob.

Having settled the problem, Bob confronted an additional challenge: how to ensure that it did not recur. He listed the structured derivatives, exotic derivatives, and derivatives that had hidden risks in them, and created an acronym: ROLEX. "Each letter stood for a different type of problem you could have in a customer trade." Bob printed these words on two laminated sheets of paper, had them bound in red notebooks, and required everyone on the floor, "all forty in total, including traders and salesmen," to attach the notebook to their desk with a chain, "so that it couldn't go anywhere but the top of their desk."

"They couldn't throw it out," Bob recalls, "they couldn't put it in the drawer. It had to sit there." The red book only had two pages in it. The first one said "ROLEX" and listed the various types of problems that could ensue. The second page stipulated what to do for each of them. "Essentially, you consult, right? If it fits there, you have a conversation. That was the only rule. Pretty straightforward." Bob laid out this rule for everyone, and occasionally walked around the floor and asked traders to rehearse the acronym. "I'd be like, 'ROLEX, what does it stand for?'" and the bankers had to recite the words that made up the acronym in their rudimentary, non-native English. "I kind of made it fun, but everyone had it there." Sometimes, however, Bob found resistance. He would walk to someone's desk and the red binder wasn't on it. This tended to happen with the English-speaking expatriate traders. "Some guys were like 'hey, I don't want to put this thing on my desk.'" And Bob's response was equally clear: "get that thing out. Chain it to your desk, or I'll send you back to New York." The scandal was thus addressed. "We poured concrete over that problem, and sealed it," Bob recalls.

In the ensuing years, Premier and several other banks experienced an explosion of unrecognized customer risks, resulting from the same type of security that created problems for Bob, over-the-counter derivatives (see table 11.1 for a list of the most notable of these scandals across different banks, which may or may not include Premier). The most notorious of these, as portrayed on the cover of *Time* and *Businessweek* magazines, took place when Wall Street banks were accused of taking advantage of unsuspecting American companies like Procter and Gamble and Gibson Greeting Cards (see table 11.1). Bob's foreign subsidiary, however, did not have any further problems. It was, Bob says, "an island of tranquility and peace."

Other units at Premier, however, were seriously affected. The scandals were particularly damaging because of Premier's atypical uncompromising approach. Whether for cynical or enlightened reasons, Bob notes, most of

TABLE 11.1 Derivatives Scandals, 1964–2002

Year	Affected company	Derivative family	Description
1964	Citibank	Forwards	A single Belgian trader bet that the British pound would not devalue. Company incurred a loss of $8MM (close to 10% of the company's $94MM consolidated operating profit).
1991	Allied Lyons	Options	Treasury department bet (via currency options) that US dollar–British pound exchange volatility would subside during the Gulf War. Company incurred a loss of $285MM.
1993	Metall-gesellschaft	Futures	Sold forward contracts to deliver oil to distributors at fixed prices over 10 years. Hedged by rolling stacks of near-term futures contracts. Could not fund margin calls when energy prices fell. A group of banks saved the company from bankruptcy in a $1.9B bailout.
1993	Shell Showa	Forwards	Hedged currency exposure with dollar forwards. Loss-averse traders rolled over dollar forwards to conceal and avoid settling cash losses, eventually amounting to $1.07B.
1994	Bank Negara	Forwards	Took a large-scale speculative position in currency markets by buying British pound forwards, and incurred losses of $3.16B.
1994	Procter & Gamble	Swaps	Purchased two leveraged interest rate swaps from Bankers Trust in hopes of reducing the company's cost of financing. Incurred a loss of $152MM, but a lawsuit settlement allowed the company to pay a reduced $35MM.
1995	Barings	Options	Trader in Singapore concealed losses on Nikkei 225 index futures in a secret error account. Barings eventually collapsed due to estimated losses of $1.4B.
1995	Gibson Greeting Cards	Swaps	Purchased two leveraged interest rate swaps from Bankers Trust in hopes of reducing the company's cost of capital. Company accumulated losses of $27.5MM.

TABLE 11.1 (*continued*)

Year	Affected company	Derivative family	Description
1995	Orange County	Swaps	The County treasurer used leverage and interest rate derivatives to run the municipal investment pool like a hedge fund, in hopes of increasing returns. Resulted in a $1.5B loss and subsequent bankruptcy.
1995	Sumitomo	Futures	A chief copper trader cornered and squeezed the copper market to keep the price of copper high and generate large profits. After regulators intervened, the company incurred a loss of $2.6B.
1998	Long-Term Capital Management	Swaps	A highly leveraged hedge fund that made convergence trades to take advantage of arbitrage between US treasuries. The fund incurred large losses due to the Asian financial crisis and Russia's bond default. The New York Federal Reserve Bank called on Wall Street firms to rescue the hedge fund in a $3.6B bailout.
2002	Allied Irish Bank	Options	Currency trader speculated on yen appreciation through forward contracts. Concealed losses by writing deep-in-the-money options. US subsidiary Allfirst Financial Inc. incurred a loss of $691MM.
2008	AIG	Swaps	Sold credit default swaps and did not have appropriate reserves to pay for future losses. Required a $150B bailout by the US federal government.
2008	Société Générale	Options	Trader built large positions in stock index futures, and circumvented trading limits by booking fictitious trades. SocGen lost $7.4B.

Source: Jacque (2010).

Premier's rivals did not want to fight with their customers. "They had a different mentality," Bob explains. "They wrote checks. They gave money, they compromised, they settled." But Premier would not settle with its customers. "The bank said, 'you're big boys, you signed the contract. If you didn't understand the risk, that's your problem. Pay us.'" Premier's customers were outraged. One of them sued the bank. Others filed complaints with the regulators. As a result, regulators ended up negatively predisposed against Premier.

Premier's approach, Bob believes, was the consequence of a reductionist perspective on the part of its management, exclusively based on the legalities of the agreement. "The management was not corrupt. They were personally very honest, did not pay themselves excessively, didn't even pay themselves well relative to Wall Street standards. Personally, very honest, but they were prisoners of this way of thinking. They were unyielding to the customers, and they were unyielding to the regulators." As Bob sees it, at the core of Premier's approach lay a fundamental view of the economy: "the top managers in Premier believed in financial models and the rationality of human beings." They had faith in their own ability to improve the profitability and risk exposure of their clients through carefully thought-through models. The flip side of that belief in rationality, Bob adds, was an expectation that customers would also be up to Premier's standards of understanding and sophistication, leading Premier's management to hold the customer completely accountable for the terms of the contract.

"That legalistic idea about your relationship with your client," Bob adds, is symptomatic of a larger problem, which was that the derivatives business lends itself to predatory behavior. "You're taking apart a structure and creating a new one, and your profit comes from understanding that there's hidden value locked up in the old one." A standalone corporate bond has some value, but has more value if restructured with a derivative attached to it. "You are the genius who figured out the hidden value. Now you have to decide how much of it to share with your customer. Should you tell him, 'hey, there's a hundred cents of hidden value, I'm keeping ninety cents of it and you can have a dime?' Well, you could, but human nature being what it is, the client would say 'no, let's split it fifty-fifty.' So, the natural tendency is to discover hidden value, not disclose it, and give only what you have to in order to induce the client into the trade. That's not unique to derivatives, but it's exaggerated in derivatives." Over-the-counter swaps, in other words, were an asymmetric form of innovation, with disproportionate benefits to the bank.

Ultimately, the downfall of Premier's top management did not directly result from the derivatives scandals. The bank solved those, but it came out with a strained relationship with the regulator.[6] However, a second scandal followed the first. It was completely unrelated to derivatives, but was serious enough to prompt regulatory accusations of fraud. Bob was drawn into this

as well, because once there were indications that the regulator was consider-
ing criminal charges, the sales managers that were involved started quitting.
"They weren't even going to be there when the investigation started," says
Bob, "they just got new jobs."

Bob ended up heading the discussions with the regulators. As they went
through the records, they found Bob's red binder with the ROLEX acronym. They were impressed, but also asked pointed questions: "you did the
prudent thing," they said, "but the bank didn't do what you did. Why did
you not try to implement your system globally?" Bob's answer was that his
system was not really scalable. In the first instance, "I had people in an office
that physically saw me every day. This is a really good system for that kind of
office. But we had five hundred employees in the derivatives business, and they
interacted with another 2,000 wholesale bankers. That was not a good system
for 2,000 people." Bob faced one important challenge at this time: although he
was not in charge of the area affected by the scandal, he had to explain what
had happened to the regulators. "As you can imagine," he explains, "that created tension between me and management. They needed me to make a good
defense of them, but they resented the fact that I was being held up as this
model of clean-hands management."

The combined effect of the derivatives scandals and fraud charges proved
too much for the top management of Premier. The fraud charges took up all
their energy. "By the time they finished settling that," Bob recalls, "they were
shattered. *Shattered*. The derivatives scandal was like a stroke, and the fraud
charges, which were settled, was like cancer. Management was on their last
legs." A management change took place, but it made things worse for Bob. As
much as Bob objected to his previous bosses, he was in good standing with
them. "I liked them personally, and I admired their integrity and their honesty.
I was loyal to them." Their replacement, however, was different. The new chief
executive did not trust employees from the derivatives division, such as Bob.
The feeling was reciprocal. "I did not like him," Bob explains. "I did not admire
him. He did not like me. And at the very first opportunity, he fired me." Bob
received a generous severance package. "I was fired," Bob says, "the way you
get fired on Wall Street." He left the bank in 1995.

Bob shared an anecdote that illustrates the problem that arises from
the worldview of the original top managers at Premier. In the early years of
derivatives, bank documents stipulated that if a client that had received a loan
defaulted anywhere in its global operations, it would count as a default against
the bank in the United States. This contingency was known as a cross-default.
If the subsidiary of a company in, say, Brazil, went into default, the contracts
of the New York-based holding company with any bank would be affected. This
provision, which made sense for the purpose of bank loans, ended up shaping
the language of derivatives contracts, and opened the door to customer abuse.

When currency swaps were first introduced, Wall Street banks borrowed the language of bank loans, including the cross-default provision. "And the one thing about bank lending language is, the bank never owes the customer money, right? Of course, it's the customer who owes the bank money. That is obvious and mutually understood: the bank is lending money, so the customer has to give it back." But in a currency swap, whether the bank owes money to the customer or whether the customer owes money to the bank depends on which way currency has moved over the course of the years. "It could go one way or the other. So, it's unusual. It's not the same as a loan. Loans are always one direction." Currency swaps operate in two directions, yet the language did not reflect that. And the contract stipulated that if there was a cross-default, the bank could terminate the currency swap with no further payments.

Premier then exploited this clause to profit from a customer. Back in the 1980s, a large American company experienced a technical default. By "technical," Bob meant that the company was not insolvent and no debtor had lost any money. "They weren't really in default. Everyone got a hundred cents on the dollar. They went through a default bankruptcy as a means of restructuring the company." However, Premier invoked the "default" clause. The bank owed the customer around $10 million from a currency swap. "So, the bankers went to the chairman of the bank to say 'hey, technically they're in default and we can keep the $10 million,' and the chairman of the bank said hey, 'how much money do we make from that relationship every year? So, let's say half a million dollars? That's sixteen years of revenue. Yeah, call them in default. Cancel the trade.'" Of course, Bob adds, the company was outraged. " 'Why would you do that? We're not in default. We're your customer.'"

The anecdote, Bob concludes, illustrates a shift in ethical standards at Premier during its embrace of derivatives. "It's legal, [but] is it moral? Buyer beware. We're all intelligent players here. You know, we all look out for ourselves." The bank, Bob adds, carried that mentality into the derivatives business, externally with its customers as well as internally to its employees. What is notable, Bob added, is that Premier was a very well-behaved bank in most other respects. "It just wasn't corrupt in the way people think. It was corrupted by an ideology, fascination with a science experiment, innovation, libertarian rationality. It was really in the thrall of a mechanistic view of how to run things."[7]

Risk Management

Looking back, Bob points to a range of problems that made him vulnerable to being fired. By 1995, he had a strained relationship not only with top management, but also with his own subordinates and peers. The reason, he argues, was that the derivatives business was morphing and growing more complex.

In addition to customer disclosure problems, Bob was combating growing complexity in the trades. "We struggled with properly valuing the books, with properly hedging them," he noted. Bob took over books that were created by other people, and had to clean them up. "And these were not regulatory problems. They weren't customer problems. But they were money-losing problems."

However, Bob adds, and in contrast with numerous characterizations of Wall Street traders, this growing complexity and risk was not rooted in bonus payments. Unlike International Securities, Premier did not have a percentage payout policy in its derivatives business. Bob's traders, however, were profit-oriented. The root of Bob's difficulties, he explains, was that his traders booked profits according to their own models. "And sometimes they were the only ones who understood the model." This, he argues, is the key problem in over-the-counter derivatives. As the manager, Bob often found himself denying the traders the bonuses that they thought they deserved, because he did not believe the profits were real. "On other occasions I trusted the models, but I did not like the risk profile." Having that much risk, Bob thought, was detrimental to the firm, "and certainly it was not worth paying the trader many millions of dollars for putting so much risk into the books."

Keeping Bob's traders in line proved extraordinarily difficult. There were a hundred and fifty of them, spread globally. "They were constantly seething, wanting to be better paid for the profits they were reporting, for taking new and complex structures into the book, and for taking on more risk." They were not just motivated by a desire to make more money, "they also wanted to make money for esteem reasons. That's really powerful." In some cases, this surpassed compensation as the explanation of behavior. "Even if you tell a guy, 'I'm going to pay you $2 million no matter what,' he will still like to show a $50 million profit and not $10, because $50 million means he's a rooster. He can walk through the hen house as the biggest rooster."

Far from having a stabilizing influence, competition with other banks made things worse. Bob's competitors were taking risks that Bob refused to take and thereby winning business from his customers. The bank's salespeople complained: "why are your traders so cowardly that they won't take this big trade?" If a competitor agreed to do a complex, difficult-to-value trade that Bob did not allow, the salespeople would also object: "this customer just did a deal with [name of a competitor] and we wouldn't even price it. We say, 'that's not priceable,' 'that's not hedgeable,' but they did it." The competitive drive to add risk and new, difficult-to-value attributes to the trades was intense. "My traders were pushing against me. The sales managers were pushing against me, and senior management was pushing against me, because they wanted growth in profits."

What to do? Bob had a strong, trust-based relationship with the bank's top executives, and he shared these problems with them. "My president and chairman said, 'we hear you, we appreciate the problem. We have the solution.'" Premier had developed sophisticated methods for managing risk. The bank had created a comprehensive mathematical risk management system that would improve on the rudimentary controls of lesser firms. To do so, Premier had empowered its head of Risk Management. "Brilliant guy," Bob recalls. "He had straight access to the chairman and the president, and the cutting-edge mathematical models. And he would be the counterweight to those traders and salespeople." Bob handled the introduction of the system, introduced the risk management personnel, and coordinated regularly with the head of Risk Management. "So, I watched," Bob continued, "I participated. I helped. We were both going to the same president. We both liked him, loved him, good man. Talked to each other, very, very collegial."

Nevertheless, the system had the opposite effect from what Bob had hoped for. The bank's risk management allowed it to aggregate risks across different units of the bank. "So, you may think you're taking too much interest rate risk, because you think that rates will be dropping, but maybe proprietary trading has the opposite [position]. 'Even though you're nervous about your risk, don't scale back because the other side may be compensating. So, Bob, what's your problem? Step on the gas.'" By aggregating risks across divisions, in other words, Risk Management called into question Bob's intuitive sense of what was prudent.

A second challenge was the effect of the risk management system on the traders. They disliked risk management. "They absolutely hated it. They were just as smart as risk management; you would get a PhD in flow physics, or chaos theory. So, what do you think my traders did? They spent all day examining the risk management system, finding its intellectual deficiencies, and using those deficiencies to attack Risk Management, to humiliate them and criticize them and claim that they were doing a bad job, and to drive around that barrier."

Premier and the 2008 Financial Crisis

As Bob spoke, I was struck by the parallels between the 1990s scandals at Premier and the global financial crisis of 2008. It seemed as if the credit crisis of 2008 was an echo of the derivatives scandals of the mid-1990s. I asked him, "How is it possible that history would repeat itself?" Bob's answer was simple but no less surprising: events in 2008 were not a repetition of history, but a *continuation* of it. "In fact, it never stopped. The derivatives crisis that got on the cover of *Fortune* and *Time* didn't end. They didn't fix the problem, and no one changed anything." Or, Bob added, they did fix one of the problems, but left another one unaddressed. The regulatory response to the mid-'90s scandals, he argues, was to focus on customer disclosure, but not on trading risk. Banks were required to convey the risks of their products, but they did not have to change the products they sold. There was a reason for this: at the time, Bob added, trading risks were not disproportionate. "I sell you a stock in a small start-up, and you're an elderly person, and I don't explain to you the risk. That's a classic problem with the securities business." Regulators addressed this problem with the frame they had used for eighty years since the unscrupulous sales of penny stocks in the Crash of 1929: "did you disclose to your customer the risk?" But regulators did not examine a different problem: is the risk manageable? Or, as Bob put it, the regulators could have asked the trader selling the product: "do you know how to manage these risks *yourself*?" The two types of risk run hand in hand: the more complex the product was, the more challenging customer disclosure became, and the more difficult risk management was internally. But disclosure and complexity were different problems. "They didn't touch that problem," he says in reference to complexity.

Could Bob give examples? "Let's start with one that is easy to hedge and easy to explain," he said. "A five-year interest rate swap is blindingly easy to hedge. But it can be complex to explain to a customer who's not familiar with it." The difficulty lies in the fact that a swap is a combination of elements of other asset classes. A company entering a swap agreement is committing to make payments over time, so there is a credit risk; as in a loan, the other side can default. However, the payable amount is not fixed, as it would be in a loan, but depends on something else, as in a futures contract.

How about, I asked, a derivative that is easy to explain but hard to hedge? Bob had to think for a second. "Ok. A *rolling Libor*, which is Libor-set at the beginning or the end. Easy to hedge, very hard to explain, right? Clients will not understand the risk to it. You're going to screw the client every time." How, I asked him, did he know that? "I invented this trade," he answered. I expressed my surprise. "Oh yeah. I invented the trade knowingly, eyes wide open, and I drew a chart for my people saying, 'why are you so squeamish?' These are big boys. It's their job to understand it. So, not my proudest moment. I was twenty-seven, you know?" I could not help but pause at hearing this. That a twenty-seven-year-old man could design derivative contracts that misled corporate customers was worrying. That he would have meetings to try and persuade reluctant salespeople to disregard their ethical objections was positively shocking. Most importantly, that this twenty-seven-year-old would be someone with the integrity I now saw in Bob was truly disturbing, because it suggested that anyone on Wall Street, not just the least scrupulous members of society, might find themselves doing it.

Our discussion of Premier brought us back to the global financial crisis. My view before this conversation was that the core problem was in collateralized default obligations, or CDOs, of asset backed securities, or ABS. However,

Bob's account alerted me to the significance of the other three-letter acronym made infamous by the crisis, credit default swaps, or CDS. These derivative instruments enabled market participants to transfer or redistribute the risk that an entity might default, as well as to bet on the future of the housing market. Between 2001 and 2008, the size of the CDS market grew at an extraordinary pace, from $0.6 to $62.4 trillion in 2007.[8] This growth, combined with the opacity that stemmed from the over-the-counter nature of trading in this market and the concentration of holdings in a few large actors, led to a situation of financial interconnectedness that forced the bailout of AIG. Thus, while the root of the losses in 2008 was the toxicity of CDOs of subprime assets, such losses might not have translated into an economy-wide systemic risk had financial organizations not been interconnected through CDSs. Remarkably, at the core of this web of vulnerability lay the derivative instrument that Premier helped diffuse in the 1990s, the swap.

Bob also corrected my impression that Wall Street's problem during the 2008 crisis lay exclusively in credit derivatives: it was not just credit derivatives, he argued, but many others. "Fixed income derivatives, equity derivatives, commodity derivatives, they'd *all* gotten out of control," he said. The problem was worse than in the 1990s, because credit derivatives were different. Almost all credit derivatives, Bob added, entail correlation rather than convergence trades, which implies that banks cannot perfectly cover their exposure. "They can be priced, but they can't be hedged. Those are different beasts altogether." "So, it is an enormous problem," Bob concluded. The root of the difficulty with the existing regulatory supervision, Bob went on, is that regulators mistakenly believe their supervisory practices are enough to manage the banks' derivatives. But, paradoxically, those supervisory techniques rely on the same risk management techniques as those used in the banks. "Regulators are still full of hubris, the kind of hubris they despise in the banks."

Once Bob left Premier in 1995, he gave himself two years before looking for another job. "I thought I was not going to work on Wall Street at all. I felt like I'd seen enough." But when he went back on the job market, the position that attracted him the most was again in finance, at International Securities. He liked it for two reasons: it did not involve over-the-counter derivatives, but listed, liquid products. Furthermore, it entailed proprietary trading: "no model-based pricing, no customer derivative business at all," Bob recalls. "I did not have to deal with any of the challenges that I had found so destructive. I didn't have to fight with my traders about pricing, valuation, etc. Didn't have to deal with customers."

Bob's move to International Securities in 1997 can thus be seen as an indictment on the model of banking that marked his ascent to top management at Premier. In particular, Bob points to the ethical stance of Premier's top management. Such management, he said, did something paradoxical: while their own behavior was constrained by morality, the system they envisioned only constrained people's behavior by mechanistic rulemaking. To justify the inconsistency, they attributed their own good behavior to rational motives only. "They weren't sufficiently self-aware," Bob said, "to realize that what was guiding their behavior was a set of moral standards that were not in fact rooted in any sort of rational, logical analysis." Furthermore, top management did not trust their subordinates. Even though they understood that they themselves were willing to behave in a moral fashion, they weren't willing to expect or aspire to that from other people. *"They didn't have a sufficient respect for their fellow man,"* Bob summed up. In other words, a focus on rationality that overlooked the moral and non-cognitive aspects of human nature led Premier's top management to conclude that their subordinates could only be managed by rules. And, in turn, the inevitable limitations of the effectiveness of those rules enabled the reckless behavior they had been designed to avoid.

Morality and Premier

Morals. Ethics. Lack of respect for others. Back in my office, as I analyzed the transcripts of my discussions with Bob, it struck me that his reflections on morality were an unexpected finale to a conversation that had started with one of the most lucrative innovations in financial history, over-the-counter derivatives. The conversation, however, had proved revelatory. To begin with, it addressed a question I had often asked myself: how did Bob end up on Wall Street? I now had an answer, and it revealed the connections between his personal trajectory and the broader economic milieu. Bob's family origin had provided him with an appreciation for technology, for international affairs, and for organizational politics. Nothing in this trajectory said "finance." However, by the time Bob graduated from university in the 1980s, American manufacturing was already in decline, financialization was starting to take hold, and the most lucrative employment opportunities were increasingly found on Wall Street.

My conversation with Bob also shed light on the origins of his moral awareness. The scandals at Premier, I concluded, had made him more mindful of his role as manager. This was clear from Bob's rejection of the moral worldview expressed by Premier's top management. Here, I was surprised to note that Bob's disapproval was remarkably close to the classic sociological critique of so-called *homo economicus*, that is, of rational economic models of decision-making. Sociologists have long faulted these models for being unrealistic, devoid of social context and moral grounding, and Bob expressed similar objections to his bosses' ideology. Bob's rejection of economic reductionism, however, was not aimed at the theory but at its application. He claimed that the combination of financial theory and an ideology of amoral decision-making had eroded the ethical standards at Premier. Financial derivatives, he argued,

were a celebration of logic and reason, but for that reason also an encouragement for bankers at Premier to exclude social or moral considerations from
their behavior. Furthermore, Premier's chairman relied on a narrative that
presented bank managers, their employees, and their clients as calculating
and self-interested actors. This justified the bank in excluding moral considerations from its business decisions, including the bank's decision to refuse
sharing responsibility for derivatives losses. Paradoxically, such inflexibility
laid the groundwork for regulatory antagonism and the harsh penalties in the
subsequent scandal that Premier encountered.

At first, I was unsure of just what to make of Bob's emphasis on the moral
shortcomings of Premier's top management. Part of my perplexity stemmed
from my own lack of familiarity with morality as an object of inquiry. Morality had not been part of my own academic research, so I was not comfortable
theorizing about morally right and wrong behavior. I was particularly keen
not to come across as *moralizing*. For some time after 2008, I thus ignored
Bob's repeated allusions to morality, attributing them simply to a conservative
ideology. Eventually, however, I realized I had to confront such allusions if I
wanted to fully understand the dark side of Wall Street that Bob had seen, and
that he blamed for the global financial crisis.

As it turns out, I was not alone in my discomfort with moral theorizing.
According to a recent analysis by Steven Hitlin and Stephen Vaisey, over the
past few decades sociologists have moved away from their long-running interest in morality.[9] Morality was very present in the work of the founding fathers
of sociology such as Emile Durkheim, and also at the core of the dominant
sociological theories of the 1950s, particularly of Talcott Parsons's structural
functionalism. Parsons's paradigm emphasized the role of moral norms and
moral consensus as the key structure that bound society together.[10] Parsons,
however, was criticized in the 1960s and '70s for presenting social actors as
uncritically adopting prevailing cultural norms. The actors that Parsons had in
mind were, according to Garfinkel, "cultural dopes," that is, slavish followers
of the cultural scripts given by their culture, while in practice people tend to
be reflective and critical of their cultural surroundings.[11] It is in that sense that
Dennis Wrong famously wrote that Parsons's actors were "oversocialized,"
that is, excessively shaped by their social context.[12] The demise of Parsons
and structural functionalism also led to a reduction in sociological interest in
moral norms.[13]

That sociologists had lost some interest in morality as a research topic only
made Bob's insistence on it more intriguing. Before I could give Bob's positions
on morality more serious consideration, however, I realized that I needed to
corroborate the information I had received from him about Premier. Unlike
my previous research, this time I had not directly observed the company and
the people that Bob had described, so I needed to understand to what extent

Bob's account was colored by his own bias. This was particularly important because, as the story of the rolling Libor contract suggested, he was perhaps still making peace with himself for his own work at Premier.

I went out on a limb and contacted Quinn, the former executive who had originally put me in touch with Bob back in 1999. I knew that Quinn had worked with Bob at Premier Financial, so he might be able to provide me with a way to contrast Bob's claims. I had not spoken to Quinn since 2008. I did not, in fact, know what had become of him. A quick web search, however, revealed that he had joined a private equity fund after completing his PhD, and that he continued to live in New York. He was in fact the chief executive of this fund. I emailed him, and to my surprise he agreed to talk.

Quinn

Quinn and I met two months later. As I arrived at the office of the fund he ran, I was asked to sit in a well-appointed conference room. As soon as Quinn walked into the meeting room, I was reminded of his imposing physical appearance. Mindful of the need to establish rapport, I started by asking him about his current position before posing questions about his former work at a Wall Street bank. To my surprise, Quinn cut to the chase and emphasized the differences between his work, private equity, and his previous jobs on Wall Street. At the private equity fund, he said, "we don't just interface with other finance people. We have a long, seven-year horizon. People here are more heterogeneous than in hedge funds." At the private equity fund, he added, they thought in terms of consumer behavior, not of interest rate differentials. They were a provider of capital, and "the money went back to the economy." To fully make his point, Quinn turned to technology: "*I don't have a Bloomberg,*" he noted. Quinn seemed to want to dissociate himself from mainstream finance. This could be, I reasoned, because of the stigma associated with Wall Street after the financial crisis, but I wondered whether it had something to do with his work at Premier decades ago.

The conversation then shifted to Premier and his knowledge of Bob. "You know, the first time I met Bob was not at Premier." The two had met in 1985 while working for different banks. "We were a bunch of twenty-three-year-olds, very young for our positions, and it was my first business lunch. At a French restaurant." Quinn and Bob subsequently worked together at Premier. "I co-ran the trading floor when Bob was running the derivatives team. He was smart. We both disliked the same people."

I asked Quinn about the bank itself, Premier. I wanted to know whether it was really marred by ethical shortcomings, as Bob had suggested. Quinn's answer corroborated Bob's view: "I left in '92. And I told the president, 'you are letting people with no ethical values in your business. It's all about the money for them. They're short-term-oriented.'" And indeed, Quinn felt, his concerns had proved him right: "that's what happened," he added, in reference to the bank's demise. "Culture of money. They just lacked self-awareness." What, I asked, led to the bank's demise? "Bad relations with clients," Quinn replied, leading to scandals. "Two or three bad client relations. That's all you need." As he said this, however, Quinn realized he might have sounded too negative. "To be fair with Premier," he added, "at the time the asymmetry in skills was really extreme. You could buy something for a million, and a few years later it was worth 25. That does not happen these days. Even in the case of the CDOs, it was not risk-free for the banks to make money. But at the time [in reference to the 1990s], you could actually structure something that was literally risk-free."

My meeting with Quinn offered many other insights. He was surprised to hear that I had at first thought of Bob's trading floor as an organic structure ("Yes . . . but come on, for a long time his favorite book was about war"). Quinn also took issue with Bob's insistence on loyalty. "See," he said, "again that is Bob's thing. I'm not worried about loyalty. It implies a degree of emotional involvement that is not even necessarily good." Finally, Quinn confirmed that Bob was very careful about the group of traders that reported to him and were affected by the first of the derivatives scandals. "He was paranoid about his group. He would not expose himself." I asked Quinn, what do you mean? "Not hire laterally, not enter into projects that he wasn't sure of, or that were new."

Most importantly, Quinn lent support to the thesis that ethics had contributed to Premier's downfall. A similar message, however, came across from my own search in the financial press. The material I found confirmed the core themes that Bob pointed to, including the bank's remarkable rise and fall. In the mid-1980s, for instance, the *New York Times* praised the work of Premier's chairman, referring to his vision for the bank as industry "leadership." In the early 1990s, *Fortune*'s account concurred with the *Times*'s assessment, underscoring the role played by over-the-counter derivatives in Premier's success. However, the magazine also raised questions about Premier's ability to handle its own risks. After the scandals of the mid-1990s, the *Economist* noted that the clients' interests often appeared to come second to Premier's own interests. In sum, the overall portrait of the firm emerging from the financial press points to the role of derivatives, opportunism, and scandal in the rise and fall of Premier Financial, thereby confirming the broad outlines of Bob's account.

Morality on Wall Street

I left my conversations about Premier with Bob and Quinn with a feeling of accomplishment. I now understood the dark side of Wall Street. I could see that Bob had been silently reacting to the dysfunctions he had seen at Premier Financial since the beginning of my fieldwork in 1999. The problems that bedeviled Premier, or at least Bob's experience of them, held the key to under-standing Bob's own pessimism about Wall Street. At its core, Bob's objection to Premier, also confirmed by Quinn, came down to morality—specifically, to the recognition that Premier Financial had indirectly but systematically enabled misconduct.

A long-running academic literature in economic sociology has debated the relationship between morals and markets. This literature builds on the seminal research by Viviana Zelizer, which has shown that the customers of the life insurance industry in nineteenth-century America expressed moral objection to receiving money following the death of a spouse. Only after the insurance salesmen reframed insurance payments in morally palatable terms (e.g., pre-venting a "pauper's burial," protecting orphan children, etc.) did potential widows find life insurance acceptable.[14] More generally, Zelizer has shown how establishing boundaries, organizing relations, and defining objects and people as sacred or profane can make market transactions morally acceptable. These sustaining mechanisms are most clearly visible in non-conventional markets such as those for life insurance, organ donation,[15] or trade in human cadavers,[16] which require active work on the part of participants to be made viable. Four-cade and Healy have described this approach as a "moral project" perspective on markets, in which the ethical or unethical nature of a market is contingent on the frames, practices, rituals, and other arrangements put forth by market participants.[17] Of particular interest is Zelizer's emphasis on preserving the quality of the social relations. For instance, Zelizer has considered the nuanced ways in which various forms of intimate relationships are differentiated from one another, underscoring the importance of the *form* that economic outlays can have in whether they are seen as payments, gifts, or entitlements.

In the context of Wall Street, research in institutional sociology by Mitchel Abolafia has provided an account of unethical behavior centered on the ero-sion of existing mechanisms of restraint. In his view, markets are stable and orderly arrangements where economic actors construct a world of norms, scripts, and strategies that shape action.[18] Attitudes like extreme materialism or opportunism are not innate to the traders, Abolafia argues, but are the out-come of strategic choices within a bounded menu. Changes in the institutional environment shape behavior precisely by altering that menu. These institu-tional changes include the severity of regulatory penalties, or the presence of organized exchanges that demand transparency in transactions.[19] Research by Karen Ho has complemented Abolafia's work by pointing to other organi-zational factors that induce or relax institutional restraint, including transient employment and elitism. But while both Abolafia's and Ho's accounts have shed light on the role of institutional factors on the erosion of restraint, neither has examined the moral consequences of using economic models, derivatives, and risk management.

In elucidating the interaction between moral norms and economic models, I turn to two concepts from research in social psychology: *organizational justice* and *moral disengagement*. While the expression "justice" normally refers to the administration of fairness at a societal level (i.e., what judges do), over the past three decades an established literature in social psychology has used the term organizational justice to denote the ways in which employees judge the behavior of the organization, and especially the effect that these judgments have on employee attitudes and behaviors.[20] Following the seminal research by Jerald Greenberg, scholars have distinguished between distributive and procedural justice.[21] Procedural justice denotes the fairness of the process that leads to an outcome, while distributive justice relates to the process by which surplus is allocated.

Building on the above, research by Albert Bandura has argued that a perception of organizational injustice can alter the employees' normative stance.[22] Specifically, unfairness can lead to moral disengagement, that is, to the detachment of immoral behaviors from the habitual self-condemnation or other negative emotions that typically prevent individuals from behaving unethically. Moral disengagement suppresses the activation of self-sanction, facilitating the practice of unethical behavior without a feeling of distress. Furthermore, such disengagement is thus not simply an abstract cognitive process, but entails the suppression of concrete bodily reactions to counter-normative behavior such as digestive dysfunctions, accelerated pulse, etc. Some of the ways in which individuals manage to suppress self-sanction include displacement of responsibility, or dehumanizing those that are mistreated.

One last conceptual move is called for in order to relate the problems of organizational injustice and moral disengagement to the use of economic tools: the concept of *economization*, an expression developed by sociologists of markets to denote the process by which markets expand their presence in society. Economization, Caliskan and Callon argue, takes place when behaviors, organizations, and institutions are "constituted as economic" by market actors and social scientists.[23] One way in which this happens is when such entities adopt the capability to calculate.

Building on the concepts of moral disengagement and economization, my analysis of Premier identifies four levels in which the introduction of an economic model and related discourse reshaped entities within the bank, culminating in weaker self-sanctions and moral disengagement (see figure 11.4). Premier introduced the ability to calculate discussed by Caliskan and Callon by developing a revolutionary way to measure the cost of risk through a version of the Value at Risk formula.[24] These had multiple consequences at the level of the bank's strategy, discourse, the role of its middle managers, and its handling of customers.

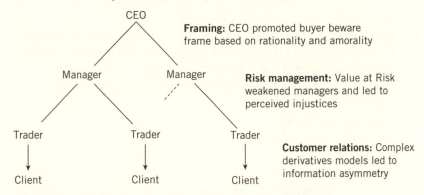

Strategy: Risk calculations led to weaker corporate relations and funding through capital markets

CEO

Framing: CEO promoted buyer beware frame based on rationality and amorality

Manager   Manager

Risk management: Value at Risk weakened managers and led to perceived injustices

Trader   Trader   Trader

Customer relations: Complex derivatives models led to information asymmetry

Client   Client   Client

FIGURE 11.4. Financial models and the reconstitution of strategy, organizational frames, manager-trader, and trader-customer relationships at Premier Financial.

Consider first the bank's *strategy*. The introduction of risk management models at Premier led to a fundamental change away from banking relationships and toward securities trading, isolating the bank from the repercussions of reputational loss in the event of a scandal. More specifically, Premier's risk management system relied on a version of Value at Risk that calculated the risk-adjusted return on capital. An extension of this approach prompted the bank to conduct a strategic assessment of the costs involved in making corporate loans. This was done after the insolvency crisis of corporate America in the 1980s, which bankrupted many of the banks that lend to corporations.[25] In this exercise, Premier concluded that corporate loans carried a higher risk than previously expected, resolved that relational banking was not worth the risk, and decided instead to shift into transactional banking, that is, trading. In turn, doing so eroded one institutional constraint on unethical behavior, namely, the danger that reputational threat might make existing customers leave the bank.

Second, consider the *discourse* mobilized by Premier's top management team. These managers reframed their own moral attitudes and those of the bank's employees and customers as self-interested, contributing to the erosion of self-sanctioning in the event of customer losses. This reframing was coupled with a celebration of economic rationality associated with the use of innovative derivatives such as swaps. Swaps had disrupted the institutionalized practices in the industry, opened up new profit opportunities, and led to extraordinary returns. The perspective taken by the bank's CEO was that if a corporation was willing to enter a swap agreement (and sign a "big boy" legal clause in the process), it should be knowledgeable enough to watch out for its interests. Taken together, the presumption of opportunism, the celebration of rationality, and the attitude of "buyer beware" culminated in inflexibility toward customers who misunderstood the complex derivatives contracts they had agreed to, and who had incurred extraordinary losses. In this regard, Bob's willingness to pressure the bank's salespeople to overcome their own moral misgivings in selling complex derivatives suggests the existence of a concerted, top-down, organizational process to produce disengagement.

Third, the role of divisional *managers* like Bob was altered by the introduction of risk management models. By limiting the managers' ability to rely on their own judgment about what excessive risk was, risk models changed the relationship between managers and their traders. The managers' discretion was diminished, and so was their authority. Furthermore, by adding a hard limit to each of the traders' positions, the model displaced the existing relationship between the trader and the manager based on norms and personal obligations, turning it into one where the manager simply administered the model's dictates. Finally, the imperfect nature of Premier's risk management model (a version of Value at Risk) meant that traders were sometimes erroneously forced to close a position, experiencing losses that were subsequently demonstrated to be unnecessary. When that happened, the traders were left with a perception of injustice that led to moral disengagement, and that provided a retaliatory justification for questionable behavior such as purposely undermining the risk management system. As Bob explained in a previous conversation, when employees feel mistreated, "they often go on to mistreat the organization."

Finally, at the level of *customers*, the introduction of complex models also altered how the bank conceived the actors that paid for its derivatives. Corporate customers were viewed as counterparties, that is, the other part to the derivative contract agreements established by the bank. In contrast to the advisory role played by many commercial banks, Premier was not bound by any duty of care to its counterparties. This shift was legitimized by the observation that derivatives contracts are a zero-sum gain (one party's gain comes at the expense of the other). As part of this adversarial relation, Premier did not disclose the dimension of the bank's profits from the contracts it was signing with corporate customers. As Bob pointed out, the traders' temptation was to hide these gains in order to be able to capture almost all the value created. The bank thus had an incentive to preserve opaqueness, reveal as little as possible to the customer, and design overly complex trades to perpetuate such opaqueness.

Taken together, the strategic, discursive, managerial, and commercial consequences of the introduction of models at Premier reconstituted the entities and social relations within the bank, from being constrained by norms, to being shaped by legal rules and economic incentives. The combined effect of models impacted the bank's corporate strategy, espoused values, control mechanism, sales tactics, and ultimately, ethical stance. At the center of this process were economic models, coupled with perceptions of injustice, leading to moral disengagement.

A telling sign of the importance of models in driving opportunism is that, years later, when Bob took charge of International Securities, he not only relied on a different narrative and rhetoric than those he saw at Premier, but also on different economic models and trading strategies. Bob did not make use of model-based risk management on the grounds that it had been gamed by Premier's traders; he avoided over-the-counter derivatives that had invited abuse at Premier; and he insisted on managing a single floor rather than a sprawling bank division covering several continents, because such distance had created opportunities for mis-selling derivatives at Premier. None of these measures would have been necessary if opportunism had been purely a function of symbols and narratives. Economic models, in other words, were central to the problem of moral disengagement at Premier.

Models and Morals

My inclusion of models into an explanation of opportunism at Premier complements existing accounts of morality on Wall Street offered by Abolafia and Ho. Like the institutionalist explanations offered by Abolafia and Ho, my account points to the role of discourse, frames, and scripts. At the same time, it differs from those by grounding the symbols, narratives, and beliefs in the adoption of hard economic models, which led to a celebration of innovation, disruption, and rationality. For instance, the use of complex derivative contracts such as swaps reinforced an elitist conception of banking that legitimized managers' decision to ignore the losses experienced by corporate customers with lesser quantitative competence, presenting them as less deserving of consideration. In this, elitism had a morally disengaging outcome, as Ho found in her study of bankers in mergers and acquisitions departments, but while Ho's case concerns the effect of Ivy League qualifications, the mechanism I outlined above was driven by having a superior understanding of derivatives models.

My analysis also contributes to a growing literature in critical accounting that underscores the compliance-oriented and ineffective nature of risk management. Early critics of risk management such as Michael Power have noted that the effectiveness of risk management was greatly limited because it took place "in a climate of organizational defensiveness and a logic of auditability" where the emphasis rests on avoiding institutional sanctions by creating an audit trail rather than addressing excessive risk.[26]

In a related analysis, Kim Pernell, Jiwook Jung, and Frank Dobbin have demonstrated that the appointment of chief risk officers in banks during the 1990s and 2000s was associated with a greater reliance on over-the-counter derivatives such as over-the-counter swaps, which subsequently proved to be fatally risky for many banks. In other words: *the appointment of chief risk officers led banks to take greater risks.*[27] The authors provide two causal explanations for this puzzling finding. First, the new risk officers may have displaced the goals of the risk management function, from minimizing the risk of catastrophic failure to balancing risk and return. Second, a form of organizational licensing may have taken place, whereby the appointment of a chief risk officer persuaded managers in the bank's trading floors to worry less about risk, because someone else is doing so already. My account of Premier is in line with their findings, though the precise causal mechanisms is different. Instead of a mechanism of compliance-driven goal displacement, Premier points to the moral effect of imperfect models such as Value at Risk. Instead of organizational licensing, the case of Premier also suggests a form of organizational disempowerment of floor managers like Bob, for even if floor managers had wanted to reduce risks, they would not have been able to do so once the decision was taken on the basis of a model.[28]

The Dark Side of Wall Street

Taken together, the case of Premier proved richer and more instructive that I initially anticipated, as it revealed the dark side of Wall Street that had eluded me during the years of my fieldwork at International Securities. The darkness that Bob was reacting to, I now understood, exceeded the usual critique of Wall Street and its focus on short-termism, greed, or individualism. What Bob had seen at Premier was a more widespread, unyielding, and dangerous problem, not simply related to the ideas, but to the very tangible tools that the traders worked with, and the mechanisms of control that shaped them. The darkness was not only projected from the top downward, but also radiated from the core outward, stemming from the very models for valuation and risk management that the bank had developed, mastered, and exploited during the 1980s and 1990s. These tools had partly grown out of mistrust of the bank's ability to enforce norms of prudent decision-making, but had paradoxically ended up undermining those very norms.

12

When All Is Said and Done

That quantitative finance might have eroded the already precarious state of ethics on Wall Street during the 1980s and 1990s was at this point only a tentative hypothesis, based on accounts from two former employees in a single bank, Premier Financial, described in the previous chapter. Establishing the validity of this thesis required additional research, and at least for the purpose of my study, providing answers to two questions. First, was this consistent with what I had seen during my fieldwork at International Securities? Second, how did it relate to the developments that anteceded the global financial crisis? In order to answer these questions, however, I would need to speak again with my protagonists.

My conversations with Bob, Max, and others had concluded in the summer of 2009. In September of that year I had moved from New York to London for a position at the London School of Economics. This made my regular face-to-face conversations with Bob unfeasible, and other research projects took priority. That state of affairs changed abruptly in June 2012, however, with the eruption of the Libor scandal, placing ethics front and center of the financial reform debate. The Libor, or "London Interbank Offered Rate," purported to measure the rate at which banks were willing to lend or borrow capital in the interbank market and was the dominant global benchmark that anchored interest rates in a wide array of loans and derivatives contracts. The Libor was calculated by taking the average of the rates submitted by a panel of different banks established by the British Bankers' Association. Doubts about its integrity began to surface in 2008, and in 2012 it became known that some banks had manipulated their Libor submissions to influence interest rates or increase the value of their holdings to their advantage. The seriousness of the case prompted the eventual conviction of a trader at UBS, Tom Hayes, the resignation of the chief executive of Barclays Bank, and a reform of how the Libor rate was calculated.[1]

The scandal was particularly damaging to the public perception of the financial industry, especially because the legal settlements and fines paid by Barclays and UBS came to light in 2012, well after the financial reforms bills had been enacted, giving an appearance that the Libor misconduct was taking place *despite* the reforms. The latter, however, had actually been enacted after the misconduct had taken place, and were in many ways an important legislative achievement. In the United States, Congress passed the Dodd-Frank Wall Street Reform and Consumer Protection Act in 2010. Its key provision was the Volcker Rule, which prevented deposit-bearing institutions (i.e., banks) from engaging in proprietary trading. Another key provision of Dodd-Frank was the creation of a Consumer Financial Protection Bureau. In the UK, the Financial Services Act of 2012 restructured the entities that regulated financial activity, and the Bank of England announced plans to separate, or "ringfence," the investment banking operations of British banks from government-insured retail banking. In the rest of the European Union, bonuses were capped in 2014 at twice the total annual salary. Internationally, the Basel Commission was working on Basel III rules on bank capital. There had been, in sum, intense regulatory activity, but the expected improvement in the legitimacy of the financial system was compromised by the onset of the Libor scandal. Wall Street's problems, Libor suggested, ran deeper than the structural reforms put in place by regulators.

Meeting in 2013

Soon after the Libor scandal, I contacted Bob ahead of a trip I had scheduled to New York City in 2013. I would be interested in receiving an update on his job at Global Trust—would he have time to meet? His reply caught me by surprise. "I left Global Trust eleven months ago. I have been full-time president of Baxter [pseudonymous], a public-interest law firm." Bob went on to explain that Baxter's core activity was to sue the government for encroachments on constitutionally protected liberties. "I travel a lot—down to [Washington] DC frequently or around the country," he added. "It is quite entertaining for me, since I believe strongly in this issue and I find the change of activity stimulating."

The news was shocking. The Wall Street protagonist of my doctoral dissertation had just left Wall Street. As soon as I recovered from the news, several questions came to mind: why had Bob left Global Trust? Was it because of exhaustion with corporate politics? Was it due to the failure to realize his strategic plans? Leaving aside events at Global Trust, Bob's decision to join a public-interest law firm—an activist organization—was also striking; after all, I had always pictured him as a bank executive. A quick Internet search revealed that Baxter was a controversial organization, faulted by some online commentators for advancing an overly conservative ideology.

Bob agreed to meet and suggested we do so in the coffee shop of the Morgan Library on 34th Street. I arrived for our appointment ahead of time, and spent a few minutes admiring the Old Masters' paintings. Bob appeared soon afterward. He looked remarkably rejuvenated, casually dressed and equipped for mobile work with an iPad and a detachable keyboard that he used with dexterity to check facts and figures while we spoke. We started by discussing the work he was doing at Baxter, but I did not press him on the politics of the organization.

The conversation soon turned instead to the challenges posed by financial reform. How could regulators avoid a repetition of the global financial crisis? Bob's experience as chief executive had alerted him to the powerful levers that large banks, including his own, had at their disposal. Once Global Trust agreed to acquire part of Northfield Financial, US regulators had been only too willing to shorten by two years the license-approval process that Global had applied for. The implication was that in the absence of more stringent capital requirements for larger banks, small banks had little chance of posing a threat to their larger competitors. Without some form of compensatory effect, the playing field would not level, and the small banks would never pose a moderating influence on the large ones.

Culture Wars

The meeting with Bob did not last long, as he had a pending appointment. We shared a taxi ride to Penn Station and parted ways. Back in my hotel in Midtown Manhattan, and after another web search, I realized that Bob's new job at Baxter was not entirely unrelated to my project. Baxter, a newspaper charged, was rekindling "the culture wars of the 1980s." The expression culture wars, coined by sociologist James Davison Hunter, denotes the conflict between traditional and liberal values that played out in the United States during the 1980s, with battles waged over abortion, gun laws, global warming, or the separation of church and state. By connecting Baxter with America's culture wars, the newspaper headline made clear the centrality of values to the organization that Bob was now running. It suggested that norms and values were key to Bob's priorities and, by extension, to the way he had run International Securities.

The newspaper headline, however, raised additional questions. As I became aware of the depth of Bob's conservatism, I wondered whether I should revise my views about International Securities. Specifically, to what extent was Bob's emphasis on norms the product of values such as the importance of authority, rather than an answer to his bank's problems? Indeed, perhaps I had been insufficiently critical of what I had seen on my visits to International Securities.

After all, the mechanistic structures that Bob decried in Wall Street banks had also given employees in Western societies a great deal of political freedom during the twentieth century. More personal approaches to managing organizations might turn companies into oppressive small towns, where employees with values and norms that differ from those of their managers are rejected for not being "team players."

Last Visit, 2015

I saw Bob one last time. By 2015, the policy debate on financial reform had progressed further, and interest in the problem of "bank culture" had gained prominence. Several government-sponsored reports in the United States and United Kingdom had pointed to values, norms and, more specifically, bank culture, as a contributory factor in the global financial crisis and a key problem to address. For instance, in 2010 the chief executive of the UK Financial Services Authority had remarked on the need to improve the culture of British banks and financial institutions.[2] Similarly, in 2011 the US Financial Crisis Inquiry Report found "a systemic breakdown in accountability and ethics" in American lending institutions.[3] In 2012, the Kay Review of UK Equity Markets and Long-Term Decision Making found that "a culture of trust relationships [. . .] has been displaced by essentially a culture of transactions and trading."[4] In 2013, the Salz Review of Barclay's Business Practices identified an "entitlement culture" within the bank. Even more significantly, in October 2014, the president of the New York Federal Reserve, William Dudley, organized a closed-door meeting with the chief executives of Goldman Sachs, JP Morgan, and other large banks titled "Workshop on Reforming Culture and Behavior in the Financial Services Industry."

In sum, after enacting the necessary legislation to promote *structural* reform in the form of the US Dodd-Frank Act and the UK Financial Services Act, regulators across the Atlantic had turned their focus on *cultural* change, that is, on norms and values in the financial industry. Because of the centrality of organizational norms to my own conversations with Bob, the Fed's new policy agenda raised the stakes of my own study. What implications, I wondered, did my analysis have to offer to the financial reform debate?

With this question in mind, in the winter of 2015 I organized a final round of face-to-face meetings with the key informants of my research project. This included Bob, as well Todd, Max, and others. My first priority was to triangulate: I needed to establish the extent to which Bob's account of events at International Securities was shared by others. This was of particular importance, because I knew that I had missed the cultural transformation that Bob undertook at International Securities in 1997–1998. I thus wondered whether Bob's strategy of integration across desks was as central as I originally thought it was, or whether it was an excuse to exert power over the traders and give importance to his own role as manager. In other words, did the traders believe, as Bob seemed to, that integration and attention to moral norms were critical to the success of the equities floor at International Securities? Conversely, was quantitative risk management the fatal problem that Bob claimed it was?

I was also interested in professional trajectories of the traders I had encountered at International Securities. The last time I had spoken to Todd was in 2003, and several years had also elapsed since I had spoken to Max. Traders like them had experienced a cataclysm in their industry of historical proportion, and I was keen to know how they thought about the global financial crisis. Furthermore, by now they would also be experiencing the impact of the Dodd-Frank Act, so it was important for me to find out as well how financial reform had affected their careers. Finally, I was curious to hear their own reflections about the crisis of 2008 and subsequent events. What did they make of it? The passage of time often brings clarity, and by 2015, seven years would have elapsed since September 2008. I expected the traders would have settled on an informed perspective of what had happened. I thus wondered, would their diagnosis of the crisis be the same as mine? Would it be compatible with the lessons that I derived from my fieldwork?

In this regard, my research interests paralleled those of anthropologist Hirokazu Miyazaki. Miyazaki conducted substantial research on arbitrage traders in Tokyo during the late 1990s and returned to them soon after the crisis of 2008 to ascertain what had become of the traders' visions of economic, social, and personal transformation that brought them to the financial industry. By 2008, he discovered, the traders he had come to know had all left the Japanese finance industry and had also abandoned the hopes and aspirations that took them there. They had given up on "the energy, speed, and utopianism of financial innovation."[5] These former traders, Miyazaki added, recognized that "the fraudulent nature of finance had been disclosed" in the financial crisis, and that "no further innovation in financial technologies would be possible."[6]

TODD, REVISITED

The weather in New York was predictably cold in the days of March that I had chosen for my research trip. I had booked a return economy ticket from London to New York, an inexpensive hotel room on the Upper West Side, and had contacted the traders in advance of the trip to arrange as many meetings as I could. My first appointment was with Todd. I had located him through a search on LinkedIn, and he had responded to my message within a day. Over email, Todd had explained that he now worked for a financial data company, and that his current job involved the development of "new and custom products" for the firm, as well as in-depth product support to internal sales staff and clients. In other words, Todd had left Wall Street and had become an IT specialist at a large financial media company.

On the morning of my first day of interviews, I took the subway to Midtown Manhattan and headed for a tall corporate tower where Todd's company was headquartered. The receptionist on Todd's floor asked me to wait in a smart, minimalist meeting room. While I waited, I reflected on the fact that I had not seen Todd for thirteen years. Would I recognize him? Would he recognize *me*? What type of rapport would develop between us? As soon as he walked in, however, I was relieved to find that his old cordiality was still there. Todd retained the polite demeanor, the cautious responses, and the engineer's penchant for irony.

I asked Todd to recount his entire time at International Securities, even before Bob's arrival, and then work his way up to the present. Todd had arrived at International Securities in 1991, he explained, and persuaded the bank to let him trade with economic models in 1993. Our conversation moved to the time we first met at International Securities in the year 2000. His view of Bob's time at the bank was a prosaic version of what I already knew. Bob arrived at International Securities in 1997, four years after Todd. "He fired a few people when he got there," Todd explained, as "he had no tolerance for stupidity or dishonesty." Bob then "turned the floor into a hedge fund," refocusing it around proprietary trading, and hired new traders to run additional strategies. In this regard, Todd's strategy was valuable to Bob, because its returns were negatively correlated with those of another desk, options arbitrage.

What about Bob's management style? To my surprise, Todd did not admit to remembering much on this front. "I probably recall more the statistical and mathematical aspects of my job," he replied. But Todd did offer new information about Bob's departure. "Bob's secret was diversification. But in the early 2000s, every strategy turned negative and correlated. Top management interfered and forced a cutback in the convertible bond book to halt the losses. The bank placed executives on the floor that sent to headquarters daily accounts for why the traders made or lost money—we called them *the daily excuse.*" The frequency of the scrutiny, Todd added, was so high that the bank's management was chasing noise. "If you take risks, there will be uncertainty, so you cannot evaluate strategies on the day, but through longer time periods," he said. That the bank chose a daily frequency "shows that they did not understand." In response to the monitoring pressure, Todd agreed to reduce the size of his trading positions whenever he experienced losses. Bob, however, did not find a similar accommodation for himself in the new environment, and resigned from International Securities in 2004 after the arrival of a new executive from the bank's headquarters abroad. "That same guy eliminated my job," Todd added, "*and in fact closed down all equities trading to move all the activity into fixed income.*" Todd left the bank in 2006.

"I hope you appreciate the humor of what happened next," he noted. "*I joined Bear Stearns.*" Todd went on to provide his own version of Bear's demise. "The bank wasn't well supervised. The two hedge funds that got the firm into trouble lost so much capital that you would have been better off putting your money with Madoff," he said, in reference to the infamous fraudster Bernard Madoff. "At least in his case you could go into the apartment and sell the artwork." The two funds that Todd was referring to were the infamous "High-Grade Structured Credit Fund" and "High-Grade Structured Credit Enhanced Leveraged Fund," which Bear sponsored and which lost nearly all of their value amid a rapid decline in the market for subprime mortgages in July 2007.

To this, I replied with the inevitable question: why such disastrous performance? The executive running the firm, Todd said in oblique reference to Warren Spector, was personal friends with a salesman at the bank, and this salesman expressed an interest in managing capital for Bear. Todd seemed to be alluding to Ralf Cioffi, but did not explicitly name him. "Because he [Spector] did not trust him [Cioffi], he put him in charge of an external fund, thinking that there wasn't much damage he could do there. And then he forgot he was there, and failed to supervise him." I found the story shocking, but it is public information, though not often emphasized or told in this manner.[7]

Todd's next move proved equally informative. "I then went to work for Global Trust." He arrived to the bank (again) a few months before Bob. Shortly after Bob arrived, Todd added, the bank "was intimidated" into doing a deal to help another Wall Street firm that was in trouble. Global Trust agreed to the deal in exchange for regulatory support in a pending matter. But this called into question Bob's original project of starting an equity derivatives operation. "The parent company was in two minds as to the convenience of running an equities trading floor and never actually authorized it. *I believe they eventually fired Bob.*"

Fired. The news was shocking. I had until then assumed that Bob had resigned of his own will. I kept quiet, however, and let Todd continue talking. Todd moved on to discuss how his job as trader had been eliminated by the Volcker Rule. "The things I was doing in International Securities are no longer in demand. The thinking is that banks should not be running their own prop trading, but also that they should not be committing much capital to facilitate customer activity." This, Todd felt, was not a good solution to the crisis, and created its own problems: "the result is no losses, and thinner markets." Regulators, in other words, had reduced the overall level of risk, but at the cost of making markets less effective. It had economic implications for traders as it called for the increased use of deferred compensation. "The other day," he added, "I bumped into an old friend. He put it well: 'they pay less, and it's no longer cash.'"

I seized the opportunity to ask him about his current relationship with his former peers, especially in light of his new status as an outsider to Wall Street. "Do you," I asked, "keep up with the people from International Securities?" "When I bump into them, I do," Todd answered, suggesting that he did not really keep up, but that he was not on bad terms with them, either.

Vulnerable Careers

Back in my hotel, as I transcribed my fieldnotes, I reflected on the outcome of my conversation with Todd. The meeting had been more revelatory than I had anticipated. I was saddened to hear that the entire equities floor at International Securities was disbanded in 2006, especially as it seemed to be for the worst possible reason: to chase a bubble in fixed income. A quick Internet search revealed that the fixed income division at International Securities did enter the subprime mortgage securitization business, and that although it remained a small participant in the business, the bank experienced subprime losses in 2007 that were nearly six times its revenue. The incursion into fixed income had proved to be a misstep.

Todd also impressed on me the vulnerability of a trader's career. His trajectory after we parted ways in 2003 looked like a sequence of impossible assignments: three different companies, International Securities, Global Trust, and Bear Stearns, all of them marred by turmoil in the top management team, outside Todd's control, and leading to short tenures. Todd's case thus spoke to the transience of employment relations on Wall Street, as discussed by Karen Ho,[8] but it added a twist. Whereas Ho's analysis found that job insecurity prompted bankers to act irresponsibly, Todd's account suggested that the traders were also harmed by mismanagement among top executives in the banks. Indeed, Todd's difficulties spoke to classic managerial shortcomings: favoritism and lack of competent bosses in the case of Bear Stearns, and misguided changes in strategy at International Securities.

I was equally struck by Todd's hazy recollection of Bob's efforts at International Securities. That he would have so readily forgotten Bob's policies cast doubt on their success. At the same time, however, Todd's forgetfulness could be due to an unwillingness to speak ill about Bob, perhaps for fear that I might relay this back to him. Finally, it was possible that Todd's quantitative training might have blinded him to issues such as informal relations and group dynamics on the trading floor, and that Bob's attempts at integration across desks truly came across to Todd as diversification. In any event, I made a note to find out more about this.

Finally, I was startled to learn that Todd was not enthusiastic about Bob's overall performance. As much as Todd had always been the most ironic observer on the trading floor, his lukewarm recollection raised a troubling question: was Bob really the highly successful executive that I had pegged him for? I also could now see that Bob had on occasions been stubborn and overly strategic. He had insisted, for instance, on preserving proprietary trading at International Securities, to the point of resigning over it. He pushed for having a securities unit within Global Trust, well after corporate headquarters had discarded the idea. Hence, was the synergy that Bob had purportedly created at International Securities an outcome of the integration of the trading strategies, or (as Todd put it) diversification? And ultimately, was Bob an exceptional executive, or an average one? These questions stayed on my mind as I prepared for my subsequent meetings.

MAX

My upcoming meeting with Max called for extra preparation. I had spoken to him on the phone in London and he had been receptive to my request to meet, even suggesting that we do so for lunch. However, he then added that he preferred not to agree on a specific time for the meal because he was going through a divorce and had already "dropped the ball on several appointments." Best if I called him one hour before lunch, he concluded. I learned something else during that phone call: as it turned out, Max had started his own hedge fund, and things had not gone as expected. "I always enjoyed our conversations," he said, "but I was somewhat distracted by running a book at the same time. *Now that won't be a problem, because I'm closing down my fund.*" Max had suffered sizeable losses and the main investor in his fund had pulled out his capital. "I never had an event go wrong before," he said. "My investor misunderstood an opportunity for a problem." The closure of the fund had made Max recall, even in the short space of our phone call, his time at International Securities. "This," he added, "never happened with Bob. He understood the strategy."

Max's fund was located at one of the emblematic corporate towers of Midtown Manhattan, featuring a midcentury-style lobby, tall ceilings, and marble walls. I gave my name to the concierge and took the elevator to Max's floor. As I arrived, I spotted a large sign behind the receptionist with the names of numerous funds, including Max's, Sharper Investments LLC (pseudonymous). As it turns out, I was in an office for hedge funds, a facility in which the owners of small hedge funds could rent space and share the receptionist and other facilities, a so-called hedge fund hotel.

I found Max far more engaging than I originally remembered. "Daniel!" he exclaimed when he saw me arrive at the reception desk, shaking my hand. "You're not looking a day older." This was untrue, for my hair had turned gray in the twelve years that had elapsed since we had last seen each other. But I appreciated the urbane manners. Max looked older, but he also seemed energetic. We walked to his office and he introduced me to his two remaining employees, who were leaving the fund on that day. We then headed out for lunch. Max had a specific restaurant in mind, so I simply followed him. On our way, he began an account of his situation. "It's tough to wind down a hedge fund. You have to deal with numerous vendors. SEC files. Keep the material. One of the hardest things."

The restaurant was an offshoot of one of New York's classic establishments. Max was warmly greeted by the maître d', who took us to our table. Max ordered the branzino (European sea bass), the most expensive dish on the menu, and a glass of white wine. On a whim, I decided to go for the same. "Very good choice," Max remarked approvingly. Before I had the chance to ask questions, Max told me about his divorce. The split included a difficult post-nuptial settlement. This was problematic, he added, because Max was in his mid-fifties and had limited time to rebuild his wealth. "I thought I could set aside money for my brother [. . .] Now none of that is possible."

As our main course arrived, we shifted to Max's family origins and professional career. Max was born to a comfortable middle-class Jewish family in the New York area. His father was a psychiatrist. Max knew of the risk posed by the stock market because his grandfather had lost his life savings during the Great Depression after investing in a Brazilian tractor company. "So, I guess I was trying to avoid that happening to me—to build Fort Knox. Protect my family, etc. But I did not take care of myself," he explained, in reference to the divorce.

After graduating with a degree in mathematics from one of the country's elite universities, Max started working at a small partnership on Wall Street, a "merchant bank" that invested in technology companies. "It was a much better system than nowadays," Max explained. "Back then, culture was taught. There were two-year rotations. You had to dress properly—wear an undershirt for work, even in the summer. Polished shoes." Max started at $19,000 a year and had to invest in a Brooks Brothers suit that proved expensive. "The setups were also far more luxurious. On a good day, the managing director would treat us to lobster and filet mignon." To Max, the partnership model seemed ideal. "The partners did two things that people don't do these days: they did their own risk analysis, and they criticized each other's risk positions at the partners' meetings." In fact, Max said, what inspired Bob at International Securities were the investment partnerships. "Bob's policies did not come from nowhere. They were an attempt to replicate this culture in a subset of the bank."

Max's own experience at the investment partnerships pointed to the ways in which these organizations instilled norms of responsibility. Max experienced his first sizeable investment loss when he was twenty-two years old, working at a mid-sized investment partnership on Wall Street. "I was bearish on the Adams computer, which Warner Communications was buying at the time. I was right to be bearish, but wrong in the trade." He had used the wrong type of stock option, and his position was down by $500,000 (around $1 million in 2015 terms). "For a young guy," he recalls, "it was huge." At that point, Max had a choice: he could either keep the position and hope it would improve (though it could also worsen) or realize the loss. "I remember going around to the different traders, kind of saying, 'I lost $500,000 on this trade. What should I do?' And they treated me like I had a communicable disease." None of his colleagues would give him an answer. One of them, however, said something that Max would subsequently remember. "If you're asking me that question, you should not be in the stock." That, Max felt, was wise advice. "I got out of it, and it hurt like hell to take the loss onto the books. Having done that, I think, was probably the single most important lesson I've ever had as a trader. Take the loss and move on. Very hard, if not impossible, to teach that to someone in any abstract way."

Max received a second lesson soon afterward. Such was the size of Max's loss that the Wall Street partnership could not keep Max as a trader. The partners offered to move him into equity research. Max, however, wanted to be in trading. He had received a competing job offer and again confronted a dilemma: should he stay or go? He turned to a senior trader in the fund and explained to him that he had the decision to make, so that in a sense "the ball was in his court," Max admitted. What should he do? "He took his glasses off his head," recalls Max. "I remember it like it was yesterday. And stuck one of the ends in his mouth, and said, '*the ball's always in your court.*'" Max felt that the partner's answer spoke to the importance of being responsible for one's own actions.

The partnerships, Max admitted, were not perfect. The partners taught Max to be risk averse, but the firm went bankrupt in the 1987 crash due to excess leverage. Max went to work for another partnership, run by a Jewish investor. "A Zen Buddhist and vegetarian, but that did not stop him from taking the helicopter to the Hamptons." He also "donated money to the Center," said Max in reference to New York's Jewish Center, a well-known Orthodox synagogue. "The view was spectacular, and the risk arbitrageurs ran everything, just as with Gus Levy at Goldman." From that fund, Max moved to a family office and stayed in it for twelve years. "A very discreet fund, owned 100 percent by two families. No 20 percent ownership there. I started at $30,000, the following year I got a raise to 45 and the following year to 60. There was no way I was going to go to business school," implying that he was too financially successful to invest in a graduate education.

As we finished our fish, the waiter came to take our dessert orders. "Do you have any of your cheesecake?" Max asked. They did not, the waiter replied apologetically. Max insisted on paying for my lunch, and I decided I should let him do it. We had not yet finished our conversation—we had barely gotten to the topic of Bob at International Securities—but Max had to leave for an appointment. We shared a taxi to the Upper West Side. I asked him if we could meet again, and he suggested lunch in his office two days later. I offered to bring sandwiches.

The Institutional Structure of Restraint

Back in the hotel, as I worked on my notes, I reflected on the unusual state in which I had found Max. He seemed stressed, his hedge fund was closing, and he was going through a divorce with financial disputes. He even appeared to be unable to keep appointments. I was surprised by how much work and life had changed for him. When I first met Max in the year 2000, he was the star trader of the floor, confident in his mathematical skills. I had marveled at the quantitative sophistication of Max's strategy, and especially at his ability to infer collective beliefs from prices, checking and double-checking his own inferences against those of his rivals. Fifteen years later, and following a succession of jobs in companies that had either closed down, been reorganized, or simply disappeared, Max was closing his own fund.

Max's account of his early years at an investment partnership had proved intriguing. His description confirmed the significance of the incentive structure that characterized investment partnerships: joint interdependence, deferred rewards, and limited mobility. However, Max also pointed to another aspect that made partnerships unique: the way in which risk-taking was defined through social standing in a web of hierarchical relations. Losing money was bad, but being treated as "having a communicable disease" must have been a lot worse. Indeed, it appeared that prudent risk-taking was defined in vividly remembered face-to-face encounters. As a result of these, young Max experienced a lesson for life, and moderated his risk-taking. Furthermore, and as part of such interactions, the partnership mobilized status symbols such as luxurious offices and extravagant meals, which might be interpreted as a celebration of the existing hierarchical order, and a promise of future wealth for those who accepted it. In this regard, Max's account spoke to Abolafia's argument that there is nothing natural or unavoidable about opportunism on Wall Street, because self-interest is culturally defined by the institutional environment. The rituals, symbols, interactions, as well as sanctions and incentives at Max's partnerships, shaped how he defined self-interest. This structure of restraint was partly what Bob had tried to replicate at International Securities by insisting on engaging the traders, setting norms, recreating a career structure, and not delegating risk management.

SECOND MEETING WITH MAX

As planned, my second meeting with Max took place two days later. I arrived at his office with turkey and mayonnaise sandwiches from a nearby deli, just as he suggested. He greeted me in a summer jacket that seemed out of place in the freezing winter weather, matched with wrinkled blue cotton chinos. He also looked like he was not sleeping well. "I'm on LA time," he admitted. We ate the sandwiches in his office, and drank free soft drinks from the hedge fund hotel. The lunch gave me precious minutes to ask a number of pending questions: how was Bob as a manager? How did politics at International Securities shape events on the equities floor? Finally, was risk management effective, or an exercise in compliance?

I started by asking about Bob: how would Max summarize his approach to management? "Best manager I ever had," he replied. "I would go over the top for him." Max appreciated Bob's insistence on a small trading floor. "He kept the floor at some level of homeostasis, *the 150-people Mennonite village.*" But what Max appreciated most was Bob's approach to risk management, "especially given the dysfunctions of the environment around us. He did a lot of tackling to protect us." Max went into the details of how risk management was practiced at International Securities. Before Bob's time, the bank had experienced losses of several billion dollars in commercial real estate investments in the late 1990s, so there was little appetite for risk.

At that point, Max and I were interrupted. A young woman with great poise entered the room and asked Max a question in a low voice. She was a personal assistant he had hired for a week to help with the closing of the fund. Her job was, among others, to place the documents that had to be preserved in boxes. "Shall I have the boxes sent to your apartment or a storage facility?" "You know what," Max replied, "let's send them to a storage. What my friends have suggested is, the apartment is now looking very nice, and I don't want to spoil it with boxes." To this she replied, "I called the movers. They can do this week. Friday?"

As the assistant left the room, Max returned to his account. The Risk Management department was not effective in instilling restraint. "It should really be called risk *measurement,*" Max quipped. The core of what they did was keep records of the traders' positions over time and use a custom probability distribution to evaluate whether the losses were normal or exceptional. Personally, Max got along well with the head of Risk Management, Lewis Cabot, who was "very professional and knowledgeable. He had a PhD in some natural science." Each month, Lewis and Max would "have a constructive conversation." Max's own risk avoidance was given by the maximum loss the bank was willing to take from him, $10 million, which made him limit the size of his total positions to $600 million. However, "Bob always wanted me to go to one billion."

Bob, Max continued, could be temperamental. Max proceeded to recount a crucial meeting that he and Bob had with a senior executive in 2002. At the time, and as a result of the scandals in Enron, WorldCom, and others, low prices of corporate bonds were unusually low. Max thought about entering stressed debt. Bob was tasked with allocating new strategies among existing desks, and it was by no means clear that the business should go to Max, for while the junior tranches of corporate debt do become equity, the senior tranche remains a bond, so the business could be thought of as both. "Oh, come on Bob," Max pleaded, "give it to me." Bob invited him to attend a meeting with a more senior executive in the bank. "Bob told me, I am going to go ballistic after twenty minutes." In the meeting, the executive asked Max about the size of the position that he wanted. "Five hundred million," said Max. "That's too much," the executive replied. "We could start with fifty and gradually grow," Max countered. "No, the executive said again," as that would not be large enough to make a difference. At that point Bob started complaining in an aggressive manner. "'You don't know how to run an equities business," Max recalled him saying, "you don't know how to run a fixed income business . . . you are just saying this because you are unqualified.' *It was the verbal equivalent of grabbing the guy by the lapels.*" Once Bob finished, the executive said: "thank you very much, this meeting is finished." All along, Max knew that Bob was planning to "go ballistic." When the two of them left, Max asked Bob why he had done that. "Now they owe us one," he said.

There were, Max added, other instances in which Bob was temperamental. "Bob got very upset when he found out that Jerry [one of two middle managers] failed the Series 55 exam." He was referring to the license that entitled employees to actively participate in equity trading, also called the Equity Trader Qualification Examination. "In fact, Bob started taking bets on the result of the exam, effectively "making a market on the probabilities of various exam results," Max added. "With this, he intimidated the hell out of people," Max added. "Another intimidation technique he had was to send people home instead of firing them. Sometimes it was for a day, sometimes for a week." What type of things, I asked, would merit being sent home? "Not being a team player could be one. Another one was the stacking of monitors."

As we finished the sandwiches, I put on the table two portions of cheese-cake I had brought from the deli. Max's face lit up at the sight of it. "You thought like an arbitrageur. You noticed I asked for it at the restaurant," he said. His comment gave me the perfect opening: what did he mean by thinking like an arbitrageur? "You buy the stock at $10 and by the end of the morning it is $19 and you expect it to go up to $20. The arbitrageur is the guy who buys it at $19 and sells at $20, and does it correctly." In other words, a speculator who bought at $10 on a hunch or a tip would lack the skills or tools to know whether the price will rise from $19 to $20, but the arbitrageur has them. Arbitrage, Max implied, was about putting things together. "It is not at all a sales culture." In fact, he noted, "prop trading has always been the bastion of wit," he added. "Films like *Trading Places*, *Arbitrage*, or *The Wolf of Wall Street* have nothing to do with anything that goes on in my world."

Once dessert was finished, Max glanced at his watch and suggested we conclude. I realized we had not yet discussed the financial crisis, or Max's career prospects. He offered one last opportunity to see him that week. "Let's meet in my apartment," he suggested. He gave me an Upper West Side address, and a time.

Normative Control

Back at the hotel again, I considered my conversation with Max. I was particularly surprised by Max's expression, "the Mennonite village." This casual utterance, entirely unprompted on my end, was a crucial confirmation of my own recollection of Bob's trading room. Against Todd's view that the "secret" to Bob's success was diversification, Max's perspective pointed to knowledge integration and shared norms as the core of Bob's approach. Max also seemed to be highly appreciative of Bob's general approach. I looked up the expression that he used, "going over the top," and found that it dated back to World War I and was used to convey loyalty, as in conquering the top of a hill that is held by the enemy.

Max's account of Bob's handling of politics at International Securities was striking, for two reasons. First, it revealed a tough version of Bob that I had not seen first-hand. The meeting he recounted was one of several key encounters that persuaded Bob he would never be able to expand into fixed income and culminated in his leaving the bank. Max's account also confirmed Bob's impression that risk management played a largely symbolic role at International Securities.

The conversation had also revealed Max's motivation for working on Wall Street. As Bob had described, the money was not irrelevant. After spending time with Max, however, what stood out about him was his general pursuit of *worth*, including the Ivy League education, or the fine restaurants. The core value that Max appeared to live by was doing excellent work, meeting outstanding people, and enjoying fine things in life. It certainly included materialism, but reducing it to the pursuit of luxury would overlook that Max seemed to value material for its symbolism of professional and intellectual excellence. Max was, in other words, more in line with the elitist investment bankers described by Ho than with a purely materialistic investor in an economics textbook. This appeared to confirm Bob's insistence that social factors like "status and esteem" were as important as the annual bonus.

Third Day

My third and possibly last opportunity to speak with Max came two days later. After the previous two meetings, I had ticked off several items from my list of pending questions, but we still had not discussed the global financial crisis and its effects on Max's career. On the actual day of our meeting, it was pouring rain in Manhattan. The elegant lobby of Max's apartment building proved a welcome relief from the rain and cold on the street. I gave my name to the concierge, but he informed me that Max had called to warn that he was having trouble finding a cab and would be a half hour late. He suggested I take a seat and wait, pointing to a comfortable leather couch beneath an elaborate light fixture. I settled in on the couch and took the opportunity to survey the lobby. For thirty minutes, a succession of middle-aged residents walked in alone, mostly women in undyed gray hair, bundled up in dark down coats and sneakers. The doorman opened the door for each with a courteous smile, greeting them by the name. Many had specific requests for the concierge: had a certain package arrived? Was so-and-so home already? By the time Max arrived, the elaborate social system of a doorman apartment building in New York City had been played out in front of me, conveying what Peter Bearman's ethnography of the profession called "the expressive nature of distinction, social distance, and social class."[9]

Max finally walked in. As we shook hands, I commented positively on the lobby decoration, but he was dismissive: "this is not where I used to live." He had moved into the building one year before, following the divorce. For the previous twenty-five years, he had lived in a large penthouse overlooking Central Park. We went up to his apartment, which turned out to be a well-appointed one-bedroom unit, and sat around the kitchen island. I asked him to finish the account of his career. The equities trading room at International Securities, Max explained, closed down in 2007. "I was the last man standing," he added. From there Max moved to Sapphire Partners (pseudonymous), a hedge fund located outside Manhattan. "It was great," Max said, but the fund was closed after regulators conducted an aggressive investigation that did not subsequently lead to any conviction. "A clear case of prosecutorial excess," Max added.

Shifting to the future, I asked Max about his job prospects. These were very much constrained by the Volcker Rule, he explained. The rule stipulated that deposit-bearing institutions could not engage in proprietary trading. "Because of it, people are being given the choice to move to Toronto, Tokyo, or somewhere else. But those who have wives who work in the city, or kids in school, do not want to move. So, they're looking around for jobs. The environment is competitive." Max was looking at foreign bank subsidiaries that did not do traditional deposit banking in the United States, which meant they could do proprietary trading. There seemed to be one bank where he could count on a job.

I then asked about the financial crisis. Why, in his view, had it happened? Max was critical of the structure of the mortgage industry, in which banks were able to distribute the loans they originated and were left with no incentives to be prudent. "You should read the reports from Warren Buffett, going all the way back to the eighties. He's furious with the fact that the banks are giving out mortgages and not keeping any of them." Closer to his world, Max was also critical of regulatory changes in the late 1990s. "The structure of Wall Street was wrong. Glass-Steagall should have never been repealed. I hate the Volcker Rule and the way it's implemented, but most people are crappy at risk management. *Mommy and daddy are not really driving the car*." What did he mean by that? "The senior managers," he explained, "cannot be assumed to really put the bank's best interests first. One just cannot count on the company being well run."

We had been talking for more than two hours. At this point, just as Max had already anticipated, his yoga instructor arrived at the apartment for a personal class. She was a petite, middle-aged woman with a bright smile. Max introduced me to her, and even took the trouble to explain to her that I was an academic in the field of the sociology of finance. "And what is that?" she asked with puzzlement, and perhaps some curiosity. "Not stacking up rows of monitors," was Max's reply.

Mismanagement on Wall Street

I took some time to order my thoughts after the visit to Max's apartment. He had not only been generous with his time, but also willing to meet with me in a very personal setting. I was somewhat taken aback to hear that Max saw regulation such as Glass-Steagall as necessary, despite the constraints that the Volcker Rule imposed on himself. This, I felt, was another instance of Max's reflexiveness. But more striking than his acceptance of the Volcker Rule was the reason why Max thought that it was needed: individual traders could not be counted on to adequately moderate their own risk-taking, and the managers who were supposed to help them had a conflict of interests, so they did not ultimately put the interests of the bank first. The individual trader, as Max put it, is like a helpless child in the back seat of a car, who realizes that the adults in the front seat are not his parents, and that they cannot be trusted. Managers, Max concluded, were the ultimate problem on Wall Street.

BOB

The last of my meetings on this trip was with Bob. He suggested we meet at his house, which was fortunate because this would give us time for the many questions I had for him. My meetings with Todd and Max had produced somewhat inconsistent accounts, so one of my goals was to resolve the discrepancy. Was Bob excessively controlling, or simply careful? Were his designs for International Securities a solution to Wall Street's problems, or a product of his conservative politics? Was his attempt to shape norms on the floor effective, or a shiny gloss on a more mundane diversification strategy? Finally, I was also keen to ask about the internal politics at International Securities, and to better understand the "tackling" that Max said Bob did for him.

I had an early wakeup on the day of our meeting. I took the 8:21 am train from Penn Station to Pendle, New Jersey (a pseudonym), and found Bob already waiting for me outside the station, sitting in an old sport utility vehicle. As he drove to his house, I mentioned my meetings with Max, which Bob had facilitated. "I was glad to hear he was willing to meet with you," he added, "because it might remind him of better times." I also told him I had spoken with Todd, a meeting that I had not asked Bob to facilitate. Bob liked Todd, he said, "but he was never very profitable." We drove through Pendle's town center and continued through suburban streets lined with elegant old houses surrounded by tall trees. "This area is very different from Westchester and Long Island. If you go in that direction, the landscape is flat and sandy. Here, it has forest. That's why New Jersey is called the Garden State." As it turns out, Pendle used to be one of the first vacation destinations around New York City. The large houses, Bob explained, were one reason why Bob and his wife had moved there.

We arrived at Bob's house, which I already knew from two visits a decade earlier. This time, however, it struck me as smaller than the surrounding mansions. There were two other sport utility vehicles already parked in the garage. "I see a predilection for SUVs," I remarked casually. "In a family of six children," Bob replied somewhat defensively, "they're people movers, and as you can imagine I don't much care for the theories of environmentalists."

We settled in Bob's study, a spacious home library with a large conference table in the middle, and French windows that opened up onto a garden. The walls were covered with bookshelves from floor to ceiling. Among Bob's many books, I saw a good number of monographs on conservative political theory. On the shelf nearest to where I was sitting, for instance, there were works by Friedrich Hayek, Gertrude Himmelfarb, Thomas Hobbes, Richard Hofstadter, Samuel Huntington, and Roger Kimball.

Our conversation began with small talk about Quinn, the banker who first introduced me to Bob in 1999. Quinn and Bob had kept in touch over the years, though only sporadically, and they had recently met for dinner. "For those who have worked on Wall Street," Bob commented, "there are lots of people to keep up with." "Why is that?" I asked. The intense consolidation of the industry during the past three decades, he replied. "It hasn't been neat and orderly, like taking small boxes and stacking them together. It's happened by bloodletting." Consolidation started in the 1980s, and was driven by deregulation, Glass-Steagall, and the removal of barriers to interstate banking. It was compounded by the shift from partnerships to corporations, which allowed securities firms to have a bigger scale as their capital structure became more

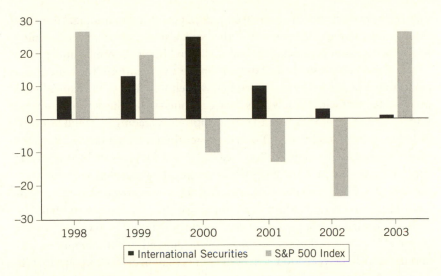

FIGURE 12.1. Returns at the Equities Division of International Securities and of the S&P 500 Index. *Source:* International Securities.

stable. "So that's why careers are so tangled," Bob concluded, "consolidation put a lot of turbulence in them."

I then brought up the first of several sensitive topics I had on my list. I first wanted to confirm the performance figures for the equities trading room at International Securities. My numbers were correct, Bob said (see figure 12.1), and he offered his interpretation. "The first six months we improved performance by cleaning up, doing some rationalization. Ninety-eight was a strong year. Ninety-nine was a very strong year. Two thousand, when the market was getting hammered, was another very strong year. And then, March of 2001 to March of 2002 were very difficult years." Bob had a serious illness, and September 11 naturally had a negative impact on results. "The markets were very unfriendly."

I then asked Bob about his relationships with the top management of International Securities. In what ways did they influence the strategic choices he made? When Bob arrived at International Securities in 1997, he explained, he had been hired by two New York-based executives and the bank's subsidiaries had nearly complete independence from global headquarters. Bob anticipated that he would operate with significant freedom, but within six months the bank had switched to a matrix structure, giving the global heads of product control over the "regions," including the United States. As a result, Bob found himself unexpectedly reporting to the global head of Equities. However, he added, "the handoff was successful." That year, 1998, was marked by the Long-Term Capital crisis, which prompted executives at the bank's headquarters to publicly announce that they would stop doing proprietary trading. "But they didn't," Bob added. "They kept us." The bank also said it would stop signing percentage payout contracts, but it also allowed Bob to continue doing so.

How did Bob persuade his bosses to make an exception? The concession came after a highly emotional meeting in which Bob flew to the bank's headquarters to meet with his new boss. Bob explained to him his position: he had joined International Securities to run a proprietary trading unit, and he could not give up prop trading now. Bob's manager then got up on the whiteboard and explained *his* position. As Bob recalls, "this is the pressure he was under: the CEO had announced no proprietary trading, he was obliged to work with the CEO, etc." The boss then proceeded to show Bob how to rename groups from proprietary trading into something else. "And then," Bob added, "he imposed on me an obligation: '*don't lose money*. Don't be reckless in your trading.'" Bob agreed to the terms. He was allowed to continue in his job, and in the ensuing years Bob delivered results that made his boss successful.

In 2001, however, there was a second management change, bringing in new bosses at the product and regional levels. The new management was even more uneasy than the previous one about proprietary trading and percentage payouts, because by then these practices were completely anomalous in the rest of the organization. As a result, they forced Bob's unit to cut a convertible bond position in the middle of a market downturn. "We gave up tens of millions of dollars by cutting at the low," Bob recalls. Although Bob managed to develop a good personal relationship with the new bosses, they could not ultimately agree to what Bob wanted, proprietary trading. Part of the reason was the broader environment on Wall Street: following the crash of the Internet stocks, the fixed income bubble that years later culminated in the 2008 crisis was already beginning to form, and Bob's new boss in equities was losing power to their counterparts in fixed income. Bob held his position and tried to reverse the situation through 2003, but found it impossible. "I negotiated my exit and left in July of '04," Bob concluded.

Our conversation moved to Bob's time at Global Trust. Bob started with his motivations for joining the company. The first one was loyalty to his former boss, who recruited him. A second reason was the compensation: "I was going to be paid well, by Wall Street standards. By normal standards, a lot." And, last but not least, Bob was ready to return to work. "I thought, 'this will be good for my younger kids who hadn't seen me working. I'll put on a suit and tie. I'll go work.'" The contract negotiations between Bob and the bank started in mid-2008. Bob had been waiting for the credit bubble to subside. "I was like, 'this thing's never going to melt down.' My pessimism was sort of wilting. So, I took the job. And it melted down."

Bob's involvement with Global Trust was almost entirely defined by the global financial crisis, which compounded the company's own debate as to whether or not to open a securities firm in New York. There was a political struggle between executives who had invested their reputations in the securities firm and its buildout, and those who had not. Bob took sides in this debate. "My job became to build a securities firm. So, I built a securities firm within the constraints Global gave me, which were tremendous. But we were profitable, growing, and we found a niche. We did it." It was a very conventional business, he added. "We just ran it very carefully, with a lot of old and experienced people who were prudent, kept expenses low, were very efficient with the technology." Bob's traders liked working there, given the uncertainty and lack of alternatives created by the crisis. He didn't overpay anyone. "We weren't allowed to do proprietary trading. I didn't want to do any derivatives, and we couldn't in New York anyway. It was pretty routine stuff."

Time had flown. It was now lunchtime, and we faced a time crunch. Bob had made a reservation for lunch in an upscale restaurant in Pendle, but we both realized it would be far more productive to stay in his study, where I could continue taking notes and use the digital recorder. Bob canceled the restaurant reservation and went off into the kitchen. In short order, a domestic helper brought a large tray with freshly brewed coffee, four types of bagels, hummus, cream cheese, salmon, and sliced cucumber and tomatoes: a New York version of English high tea, improvised for lunch.

Cycles of Opportunism and Restraint

Bob's account of his own challenges with the top management of International Securities spoke to Abolafia's concept of "opportunism cycles." Abolafia built on Karl Polanyi's observation that the reforms that restrained the free market excesses of nineteenth-century England (factory laws, tariffs, social insurance) were quickly followed by liberalization after World War I, as the country pursued growth and postwar reconstruction. The free market creates social unrest and ends up being reined in, Polanyi concluded, but as soon as the problem is addressed, the restraint is removed. Abolafia posited a similar dynamic in financial regulation: the introduction of restraint on Wall Street curtailed excesses, but eventually gave rise to pressures to reduce such restraints.

Abolafia's cycles offer a potential reading of Bob's challenges at International Securities. By the time Bob left Premier Financial in 1996, Wall Street had been beset by scandals related to over-the-counter derivatives, what Abolafia would call a stage of opportunism. Bob chose to join International Securities in 1997 because the company did not do any over-the-counter derivatives or any significant customer business—what Abolafia would call restraint. In 1998, however, the Asian crisis and demise of Long-Term Capital Management (widely perceived as engaged in excessive risk-taking) contributed to delegitimizing proprietary trading, to the point that International Securities announced a global commitment to stop prop trading (in other words: restraint). Bob managed to preserve proprietary trading on his floor, but only because of the personal trust of the bank's chief executive. Once that CEO was replaced in 2002, proprietary trading became unviable for Bob (another instance of restraint), prompting his resignation. Bob's challenges, in other words, can be seen as part of the dialectical tension between opportunism and restraint theorized by Abolafia. In contrast to the latter, however, who presented this dynamic as purely iterative, Bob's experience suggests that these cycles include innovation in strategies and asset classes, from over-the-counter derivatives in the mid-1990s to proprietary trading in the early 2000s.

Trading Room Behavior

As Bob and I finished lunch, I decided to bring up a slightly controversial topic. I had given plenty of thought to the prank that, back in the early 2000s, Joe at the sales desk pulled on a Jamaican caller. At the time, it seemed inappropriate, and at the risk of appearing sanctimonious, I wanted to know Bob's perspective: had he seen it, and if so, did he do anything about it? I described the scene to Bob. "That was very classic trade floor behavior," he said, but he did not recall being there. What would he have done, had he been present? "If I had been involved in that one, I would have laughed, and then I would have made them correct what they did. And then, I would have demonstrated to them why that guy was human, why it wasn't so funny for him, etcetera. Everybody would have enjoyed it, and then they would have got the message."

Bob's reaction seemed to me consistent with his emphasis on ethics on the floor. However, what he said next was surprising: "I kept those sales guys close to me [Bob was sitting only meters away from them] but that was because, you know, I was nervous about their compliance and I wanted to be able to hear what they were doing." Indeed, Bob said, there seemed to be a tension between traditional surveillance and the sophisticated rotation of the various desks based on work complementarity. "It was expensive real estate," he said of the location of the sales desk, "because I could have benefited from having other people sit close to me, but I didn't want to let them out of my sight. I had had my problems with regulators already," he added, in reference to his time at Premier Financial.

Looking Ahead

We moved on to the debate on financial reform. To what extent, I asked, was the equities trading room at International Securities a useful template for other Wall Street banks? Bob was guardedly optimistic. "The operation I was running was too small to serve as a guide. But many of the principles certainly could be used on a bigger scale." For instance, the personal trust generated in a 150-strong organization disappears beyond that size, but in an organization of 15,000 people there are other ways of creating trust. Similarly, "status and esteem is a public thing." For 150 people, Bob added, the interaction happens in one room; for 1,500 people, it's an amphitheater. "The boss gets up in the front, has a big speech, and maybe he calls Daniel: 'Come on up. *Do you realize what Daniel did for the team this year?*'" By the time you get to 15,000 people, Bob continued, it can be a Skype call. "Essentially, it's a theater, where the interaction is what creates the recognition."

What about the compensation formula that Bob fought so hard to retain? In most jobs, Bob admitted, percentage payout contracts do not work. "One would not want to have them for tax collectors, for instance, and certainly not for doctors." However, Bob thought they made sense in a trading room. "The reason I used percentage payouts is that I was also unhindered by other rules. So, that was the one rule I followed like a gold standard. Like, the money was sound. And then, everything else was judgment: I had the power to fire a person on the spot. *Hard standard, wrapped by judgment,*" Bob summed up.

I countered that this was the opposite of the practices at numerous large banks, which determine compensation by relying on subjective measures such as cultural fit. Whereas Bob combined a fixed rule with his own judgment, the large banks used hard rules that were made up of aggregate judgments. Bob expressed skepticism about such attempts to explicitly target cultural fit and reward it, a practice that numerous scholars refer to as "alignment," or designing incentives to reinforce norms. "The desire to have the compensation system line up with the objectives in the organization, that's a big mistake." It ignores, Bob added, all the other ways in which managers can convey value. It amounts to piling up on one lever all your aspirations, one channel where all things go. "It creates a very lopsided structure."

I then brought up the partnership system. Was it, as Max said, a better way to organize trading? "So, pause there," Bob interrupted. "Old men—Max and I are old men now, right? Old men have a habit of looking back to the past and saying 'oh, we should go back to it.'" This could be because of the wisdom that comes with time, but it could also be the weakness of old age. "With the partnerships, is that weakness or wisdom? We don't know." Partnerships, Bob added, were a particular case of a more general phenomenon: "attention to human nature using human character attributes, honesty, modesty, etc. The old partnership style was more attentive to that. They were smaller." In the early 1980s, for instance, a normal-sized securities firm totaled two thousand employees; Goldman only had about 3,500 people.

One clear feature of the partnerships was their reduced employee turn-over, which was both positive and negative. "You couldn't get out as fast. You couldn't take your capital unless they gave it to you." To what extent,

I asked, were the current clawback provisions on bonuses similar to partnership arrangements? Here, Bob was adamant that the two were not the same. "You can leave a clawback in a heartbeat," Bob replied. Just go to another firm, negotiate out. Restricted stock, he added, was just as ineffective. In any event, Bob added, the partnerships were not perfect. They did not last. They opened and closed in extraordinary succession. Furthermore, the partners had a very personal relationship to the employees. They typically hired them, and there was some prior relationship. "When they see the shoeshine, they're personally connected to him. It may be a little old school and patronizing."

I did not ask Bob whether he had been, as Todd said, fired from Global Trust. My interest lay instead in Bob's views on the rest of Wall Street. It seems, I noted, that nobody now has a compelling or attractive and inspiring vision for the future. "There really is an alternative," Bob responded emphatically. Deregulation and information technology, he added, had changed Wall Street. "You can do things with finance that you couldn't do before, and create gigantic firms," he said in reference to conglomerate banks like JP Morgan or Citigroup. But these megabanks are not really necessary, he added. The two reasons given for their existence are diversification and the provision of global solutions to multinational corporations. "They say 'well, we have a ten billion financing need for AT&T. So, we have to be JP Morgan to handle that.' But that's absolute nonsense."

The arguments in favor of the large banks, Bob added, failed to hold in light of the success of online crowdfunding platforms like Kickstarter, which were no more than online versions of the nineteenth-century bank underwriting syndicates. As far back as the 1800s and early 1900s, investment partnerships managed to coordinate activity despite being small and fragmented. One can tell, Bob said, from looking at the so-called tombstones, or notices that a transaction had taken place: along with the name of the company that had done the transaction, they also showed the syndicate of banks that had advised it. "If you look at a tombstone, what is Kickstarter or any kind of online auction but a method of organizing the syndicate?" This had important implications. "You could shatter all the financial services firms into small pieces, and AT&T could still go to one and say, 'I want you to be my underwriter' and hand over the job to that one firm, which could be thinly capitalized but intellectually prepared."

The second justification that was often given for large banks, Bob continued, is global presence. "We have to operate globally," Bob paraphrased. "I may be in the Philippines one day and in Indonesia on the other." However, the experience in other industries such as Silicon Valley cast doubt on this argument. The case of Uber, for example, had persuaded Bob that operating globally could be done in a distributed fashion. "Uber's in every country in the world. What could be more particular or local than a car service, with all the regulations and cultural and insurance differences? So, the proposition that if Monsanto wants to do trade financing in both Indonesia and Holland it can only get that accomplished with a global bank like Citi, regulated, capitalized, and present in both Indonesia and the Netherlands, is absurd."

But if the large banks were not necessary, what was the alternative? The answer, Bob stated, was to recognize that the technological changes in the 1980s had not stopped, and that technology had kept moving. Technology, Bob argued, not just the computer and the phone but the combination of all the various elements, including the software, the cloud, and all the new ways of interacting, "is transforming industries all over. Yet it's not transforming Wall Street. Why not? Why, after the crisis, do the governments in Europe and the United States choose not to go that way?" After all, financial crises are usually accompanied by hostility toward capitalism, and hostility manifests as breaking up in the consolidated firms or nationalization. "In the United States, there was a reasonable chance that a regime, left or right, Democrat or Republican, could respond by saying 'hey, we don't like the trusts. We're going to smash these firms up. We're going to go back to no interstate banking. We're going to go back to Glass-Steagall. We're going to force the firms to break apart.'"

But, Bob added, that's not what politicians did. "They showed an absolute lack of confidence in technology, in the broadest sense of new ways of organizing knowledge, capital, and information." Politicians rejected that, he added, "and they rejected the idea that smaller, disaggregated organizations are safer. *They essentially did the Siamese twin of the error that brought down the big banks.* They criticized the hubris of the banks, which assumed that their model-based management would be a good mechanism for controlling risk. Having criticized the firms for their failure, they adopted the exact same mechanism for protecting the financial system. So, now they have model-based, rule-based structures that they've imposed. And of course, those are extremely unwieldy."

Regulation, Bob concluded, does not give real control but an illusion of it. Regulators do not have any more control than the chief executives at Morgan Stanley, Goldman Sachs, JP Morgan, or Citi. "They couldn't possibly be better informed, more mathematically sound, and have greater control over pay and promotion and status and esteem" than their chief executives. Take, for instance, the chief executive of Citi: "he has enormous leverage over his organization," Bob said. "It is a single company, so there's friendship and loyalty. He pays the big bonuses. He promotes people. He tells the other peers who's a good person and who's bad. He has all those tools, and yet he can't control his company in a crisis. Why would the regulators be able to do it, when there's a sense of animosity between the regulator and the regulated? They can't control compensation. They can only interfere with it periodically. They can't control promotion. And they cannot grant status and esteem. So, they're, like, wearing mittens and they're trying to control these big firms with the same tools that big firms used and destroyed themselves with. It's absurd."

Regulation, Bob noted, was the reason why Wall Street banks had survived the disruptive possibilities of information technology. But the danger, he added, is that technology's potential would be realized *within* the banks, as opposed to outside. If that happened, it would only advantage the large institutions. "You wouldn't want to let the transformation take place inside of that protected environment," he said, "it'd be as if we allowed Google, Facebook, and Apple to develop, but only if IBM, GE, and General Motors could control every single aspect of them." It would not produce real innovation, and the benefits would be reaped by the existing firms, rather than the customers. "GE would just be a mega-profitable organization that would have information technology in every appliance in your house. They would own all the data. They would own all the appliances. They would own the financing of them." This would be disturbing, Bob added, if it happened as a consequence of market forces. But if it happened because GE had been able to outlaw the use of technology by anyone but them, one would denounce it as crazy. "But that's what we have. We're going to get Kickstarter for finance, but Goldman's going to run it."

Why was such a terrible scenario a plausible one? Wall Street had enough resources to make politicians regulate the system to preserve the status quo. Bob's evidence came from *his* own bank, Global Trust, which had been advantaged by regulators—granted full regulatory licenses in one month rather than the usual time line of two years—as a reward for helping regulators prevent the failure of another financial institution. How, then, to avoid a complete dominance by the large Wall Street banks? "My view is, just dust off the antitrust law and break them up. Change the capital structure in the financial industry to force them to break themselves up, and then promise deregulation at the other end." In other words, Bob thought banks should be broken up *before* being deregulated. "This is 'deregulate second, deconglomerate first.' I think you'll have a constituency for deregulation once you deconglomerate it."

Finally, what type of Wall Street would emerge from this plan? Bob confessed he did not go that far in his thinking. All he knew is that the present arrangement was flawed, down to its philosophical underpinnings. "One of the problems with systems that believe they're based on rationality is that it's very hard to attribute any rational value or basis for love and esteem," he said. Such systems force those out. "Okay, nothing here. That's love, put it away. That's friendship, put it away. That's esteem, put that away. Status, envy, strip all those out. But there are reasons for this reductionism. Logical models are given power if they can eliminate the non-rational."

However, Bob did not have concrete solutions to introduce a more rounded system. "How do you," he asked rhetorically, "as a sociologist, describe, quantify, measure, standardize, and test these types of things?" He did not know. "It's like when I went to Barcelona," he continued. "I saw, like, a temple, a church." He was referring to La Sagrada Familia, the Art Nouveaux cathedral and crowning achievement of Catalan architect Antoni Gaudí. "I loved that, of course. Everybody does, because the different styles, all that organic stuff, is very strange. It defies conventional categorization as an architectural work. And yet, there's integrity to it." Bob then concluded: "so, how would you build an organization based on these principles? I don't really know."

As I paused to take all of this in, I noticed it was already 4:30 pm. Bob and I had been talking nonstop for about seven hours. I was exhausted. He had family obligations to attend. I thanked him, expressed my satisfaction with the material I had collected, and he offered to drive me back to the train station. During our car ride, Bob returned to a topic that he had casually mentioned several times: the standardization of the curriculum in American public schools, and the prevalence of moral relativism. For that reason, he sent his kids to Catholic school. His daughter's school was girls only.

Break Up the Banks

The train ride from Pendle back to Manhattan was more scenic than I remembered from my previous visit, with a layered view of large houses, woods, and the skyline of Lower Manhattan along the journey. Despite my fatigue, I began to jot down ideas from my day-long conversation with Bob. The most surprising remark had been Bob's ultimate prescription for financial reform: *break up the banks*. This was truly shocking. Bob actually favored dismembering the very companies he had devoted his life to running. His view illustrated just how far the policy debate had come after the financial crisis. Wall Street banks seemed to have lost legitimacy even among their own insiders. I had come upon many paradoxes in the course of my research on International Securities, but this one took the prize.

What to make of Bob's call to break up Wall Street? At a basic level, it seemed to align Bob with a populist, bust-the-trust agenda. The banks, according to this perspective, had grown large enough to be the new oil companies, too powerful to allow for the benefits of market competition. There was certainly truth in that claim, as the mergers that had taken place after the 2008 crisis had increased the market share of the largest four megabanks, JP Morgan, Bank of America, Citigroup, and Wells Fargo, to as much as 40 percent of all US deposits in 2015. The problem, according to Bob, was not simply the size of the banks, but their ability to obtain regulatory favor, as he himself had experienced when Global Trust regained the missing banking license two years ahead of time, as a reward for its assistance in rescuing Northfield Financial.

At another level, however, Bob's concern was not about competition but about the effect of economic models on the banks. Large banks were problematic because their managers relied to a far greater extent than in small ones on the use of economic models. This was the core reason Bob was skeptical about Value at Risk: when managers use models to supervise their subordinates, deviating from the model's prescriptions becomes counter-normative, creating pressure on subordinates to act as the model states. However, because models are imperfect representations, those subordinates will end up pressured to go along with the model even when it is inaccurate. This pressure will be greater the bigger the size of the organization.

This dynamic speaks to the problem of power, and more specifically to the sociological literature on *governmentality*, which has explored the techniques and strategies by which a society or organization is rendered governable. As originally noted by philosopher Michel Foucault, power is far more nuanced and pervasive than the hierarchical, top-down authority typically attributed to absolutist rulers. One key element in the attainment of control is the production of knowledge and technologies that make such control possible. In this regard, Peter Miller and Nikolas Rose have shown that the neoliberal shift to privatization in the 1980s was made possible at the British National Health System through monetarization, that is, the translation of medical services into monetary costs and the elaboration of standard costs for these services, so that budget deviations could be identified. Monetarization, they establish, was followed by a change in the rhetoric around health services, from "collective provision" and "market solidarity" to "consumer choice" and "market competition." Thus, the possibility for control at a distance happens when the governed develop the necessary technology for the center to exert it. As Rose and Miller observe, the key to power lies in "the humble and mundane mechanisms by which authorities seek to instantiate government: techniques of notation, computation and calculation."[10]

In the case of Wall Street, the quantitative revolution produced a new technology for control at a distance: economic models. As the case of Premier Financial shows, the adoption of Value at Risk models allowed the bank to grow and diversify into multiple markets and asset classes without appearing to lose its ability to quantify and aggregate the various risks it entered into. This allowed the bank to combine risks and returns into a single strategic goal, risk-adjusted returns. Risk management, in other words, was the Wall Street equivalent to the standardized costs that Rose and Miller identified at the NHS. The problem, as Bob emphasized, was that Value at Risk oversimplified risks. It enabled growth, but only by endangering the bank's health. In light of the above, the breakup of the banks as Bob advocated would not only moderate the lobbying power of Wall Street, but also constrain their reliance on model-based control. This in turn would make them more responsive to unanticipated contingencies and interdependencies.

In sum, there were two potential reasons why Bob favored a breakup of the banks. One was a traditional antitrust argument: to promote competition, limit rewards to lobbying, and free up innovation. The second was a more unconventional argument, based on materiality: models lead to large banks that oversimplify complexity. Bob's injunction to break up the banks thus relates politics and market technology, as the effect of a technology such as risk models on banks formed the basis for Bob's political argument for breaking them up.

The second surprise from my day-long interview was Bob's lukewarm attitude toward investment banking partnerships. Based on my previous conversations with Max, I expected Bob to be a radical proponent of these partnerships, yet he was not. The partnership culture that Bob took inspiration from at International Securities, he argued, was no utopia. Many partnerships were short-lived, undercapitalized, or took excessive risks, as in the case of Max's first employer. Along these lines, Bob's remark that partnerships were old-fashioned and patronizing spoke to the sociological literature on patrimonialism. This expression was first used by Max Weber to denote a form of traditional domination, different from rational or charismatic domination. Patrimonialism involves an expansion of the patriarchy, that is, the authority of fathers within families. Patrimonial structures, as seen in medieval monarchies or feuds, take place when the patriarchy is expanded into non-family relations.[11]

One sign that the old investment partnerships were a form of patrimonialism lies in recent research by Megan Neely on patrimonialism in contemporary hedge funds. Hedge funds differ from the old partnerships in their reliance on leverage and limited liability, but hedge funds arguably constitute the organizational structure on Wall Street that comes closest to the investment partnerships. According to Neely, hedge funds rely on patrimonial rather than bureaucratic structures because of the uncertainty faced by these organizations. In the absence of clearly stipulated rules for how to respond to market contingencies, hedge funds turn to judgment and trust in subordinates. However, such an approach "restricts access to financial rewards and facilitates the reproduction of the white male domination of this industry," thereby contributing to social inequality.[12]

In sum, Bob had serious concerns about the Wall Street megabanks that emerged from the global financial crisis, but was also skeptical of the traditional investment partnerships. What alternative was there? Bob's answer to this question was my third surprise of the day. Despite his skepticism about Value at Risk, Bob believed that the solution to Wall Street's problems would require *more* rather than less technology. Supervisory interactions, Bob added, could be internally leveraged at various levels within the bank, thanks to technology. But this, he added, should reinforce and extend these interactions, rather than erode them as Value at Risk did. Bob was particularly sensitized to the importance of attending to the complexity of the traders' motivations, as well as the importance of social dynamics on the floor: the power of "status and esteem." Appreciation, in his view, emerged from the interactions between managers and their subordinates, the "theater." An adequate organization would incorporate those. In this, Bob reminded me of the arguments made by E. F. Schumacher, the celebrated author of *Small Is Beautiful*.[13] Despite the title of his book, Schumacher wrote, his real goal was not to ban large companies but to "achieve smallness within a large organization."

At the level of the industry, Bob argued that technology could play a role in enabling a networked conception of Wall Street based on smaller organizations. Drawing an analogy to the investment banking syndicates of the early twentieth century, Bob noted that a network of organizations could achieve a similar level of capital access or geographical reach as a single large organization. Recent changes in information technology, from the Internet to social media, had led to companies like Uber or Kickstarter that relied on technology to connect their employees or so-called partners with customers (at the time of our conversation, Uber had not yet been stigmatized by scandals, leading to the resignation of its chief executive in 2017). Bob's argument spoke to the growing importance of the fintech industry, a designation that refers to the cluster of start-up companies seeking to integrate digital technology and finance.

My final observation related to morality. Bob finished our conversation with a reference to a cathedral, the *Sagrada Familia*, in Barcelona. I was quite familiar with the monument, for I had lived in that city for eight years, not far from the cathedral itself. Religion, and the use of religion-inspired organizational practices, had been a recurring theme in my conversations with Bob. Early in my research, I had learned that his trading room had been partly inspired by the Mennonite communities to which Bob's ancestors belonged. (Incidentally, this may have explained Bob's practice of sending traders home: Mennonites also relied on "penitence," which separated the person from the community and then allowed the individual to come back gradually.) Bob, however, was not Mennonite himself, but a Catholic, and had embraced the Catholic faith because he felt that it was the only one strong enough to withstand the pressures of modern life.

In this regard, one remaining puzzle was the relationship between religion and Bob's reliance on norms on his trading floor. For instance, I had been struck by Bob's repeated denunciations of moral relativism. "There is absolutely a right and wrong about many, many, if almost all, human behavior," he told me when discussing his objections to drinking with colleagues after work. "It's not always easy to discern, but the standard is there." An important reason why Bob sent his daughter to a private Catholic school was that state school curricula included moral relativism. Why, I asked myself, did Bob object so strenuously to moral relativism?

I eventually found an answer in Gabriel Abend's research on morality in business. Abend's study developed the concept of *moral background*, which denotes the underlying set of moral concepts, methods, reasons, and objects that support and enable morality in a society. Abend assembles a history of business ethics in the United States from the 1850s to the 1930s, including Protestant ministers, business associations, and business schools. His analysis revealed two types of internally consistent moral backgrounds. The first, which he labels "Standards of Practice," is characterized by a "scientific worldview, moral relativism, and emphasis on individuals' actions and decisions."[14] The second, which he denotes by "Christian Merchant," is characterized by "a Christian worldview, moral objectivism, and conception of a person's life as a unity."[15] Abend's distinction clarified my own thinking about Bob's insistence on norms, religion, and moral objectivism, suggesting that Bob's views conformed to a Christian Merchant moral background, and that his thinking hailed from the tradition that included Charles Rhoads, Henry Boardman, or Richard Steele. As Abend explains, the Christian Merchant is aptly illustrated by the title of Boardman's seminal book, *The Bible in the Counting-House*, a juxtaposition that was not unlike the idea of a Wall Street bank as a "Mennonite Village."

Abend's taxonomy also speaks to the related debate over financial reform and the need to improve "bank culture." Having understood that Bob's views entailed a Wall Street instantiation of the Christian Merchant, I asked myself about the other moral background that Abend identifies, the Standards of Practice. What shape and form did the Standards of Practice take on Wall Street? I eventually realized that this background might describe the regulatory agenda to improve "bank culture" promoted by regulators at the Federal Reserve Bank of New York. For instance, when journalists pressed William Dudley, President of the New York Fed, to better explain what he meant by "culture," his response was that "culture is too broad [. . .] I think, reflecting on it, it's really about ethics and conduct." If Dudley's goal was moral improvement, why call it culture? One potential answer is that doing so provides regulators like him with a measure of moral relativism that accommodates pluralism and lends their agenda broader appeal on Wall Street. An additional sign that the bank culture agenda conforms to a Standards of Practice background is the very name given to the British organization set up by Parliament to enhance bank culture, the UK Banking *Standards* Board.

Conclusion

The return flight from New York to London gave me plenty of time to reflect on my week-long visit. The meetings with Todd, Max, and Bob were of great value in relating my original fieldwork to the crisis of 2008. My pursuit of the chief protagonists of my time at International Securities, well after the crisis had taken place and a good twelve years after my fieldwork concluded, parallels Miyazaki's revisit of the Japanese arbitrageurs he followed before the global financial crisis. However, several differences stood out between the arbitrageurs that I followed and those followed by Miyazaki. The latter had exited the financial industry, and concluded that arbitrage, at least in the way they conducted it in Japan, was fraudulent and unviable, casting doubt on the visions of reform that brought them to the industry in the first place.

Like Miyazaki's arbitrageurs, two out of the three financiers I spoke to during this trip had left the financial industry, but skepticism about their original visions was far more circumscribed. Todd lamented the regulatory changes and managerial incompetence that had pushed him out of the market, but continued to espouse faith in his approach: bringing technology into finance. Max's skepticism centered on human limits to manage risk, and on the twisted motivations of managers at Wall Street banks. However, Max remained nostalgic about Bob's management style and had preserved his belief in the possibility of excellence through mathematical sophistication in arbitrage. Finally, Bob had become markedly skeptical of the rationalist vision that informed derivatives traders and model-based risk management at Premier. Bob, however, had an alternative vision for Wall Street, based on technology, small organization, and a social and moral conception of trading. I realized that Bob's ultimate vision might have been one of moral betterment all along, or at least since his departure from Premier in 1996. Moral betterment had been key to International Securities and had been even more central to Baxter, the public-interest law firm that he now ran. Taken together, the contrasting visions for finance, computers, mathematics, and morality, of the protagonists of my book encapsulated the themes that have informed my study. Whereas Miyazaki's arbitrageurs seemed to inhabit "the end of finance," the three financiers I spoke with presented a more ambivalent stance. Part of their original vision had certainly proved disappointing, but other elements continued to attract their energy. It was now up to me to discern what their ambivalence meant.

13

Conclusion

The central argument presented in this book concerns the relationship between economic models and morality in financial organizations. It joins a debate initiated by the official reports and reviews of the global financial crisis, and especially their emphasis on the need to better integrate morality into financial markets, both in theory and practice. In providing a sociologically informed account of how this might be accomplished, this book has sought to go beyond over-socialized conceptions of morality such as shared norms and all-encompassing values, addressing instead two core questions. The first concerns the diagnosis of the crisis: if not through materialistic values such as greed or impatience, how is morality related to adverse economic outcomes in financial organizations? The second centers on the prognosis for financial reform: given the limits of values-based reform initiatives, how to improve the moral standards on Wall Street? In light of the importance of economic models in contemporary finance, this book has addressed these questions by turning to the interplay between morality and economic models. It asked, what effect did the introduction of economic models have on morality on Wall Street?

Models and Morals

The analysis presented in the preceding chapters argues that the introduction of economic models for the purpose of organizational control impairs self-sanctioning behavior, leading to moral disengagement. I refer to this process as *model-based moral disengagement*. The social-psychological concept of moral disengagement was developed by Bandura to describe situations where the self-regulatory function of individuals ceases to apply. In such cases, individuals

275

become freed from self-sanction and the guilt that accompanies behaviors that violate their own ethical standards, leading to unethical decisions. Building on this seminal idea, other social psychologists found that moral disengagement is more likely when individuals are less aware of the needs and feelings of others, when they have less empathy, or are more cynical.

My study extends Bandura's work by identifying organizational and material conditions that lead to moral disengagement, highlighting the use of models for control as one such condition. Model-based moral disengagement takes place at various levels of a bank. At the top, disengagement is created when the chief executive presents market actors as rational and self-interested, justifying a narrow legal definition of responsibility and eschewing broader moral obligations. In the area of strategy formulation, disengagement can take place when the use of risk management models to decide what sectors to enter and exit leads the bank to abandon relational banking and embrace trading in capital markets, conceiving of its customers as counterparties, that is, as a form of economic adversary. In the case of divisional managers, disengagement takes place when the use of model-based risk management reduces the need for managerial judgment, redefining the managers' role vis-à-vis the traders. In addition, the use of model-based position limits can lead to disengagement if it creates a perception of injustice among traders, especially when the models prove inaccurate and make the traders feel unjustly restrained. Finally, the use of complex models in over-the-counter derivatives can lead to disengagement by creating an asymmetry between the bank and its customers, allowing the former to keep almost all the value it creates, thus encouraging further complexity. Taken together, discourse, strategy, supervision, and commercial relations are four different mechanisms that reinforce each other.

The provocative idea that a lifeless and inanimate object such as an economic model might impact the ethics of Wall Street traders builds on Caliskan and Callon's concept of *economization*. Economization is the process by which behaviors, organizations, institutions, or objects are constituted as economic, and it takes place when organizations adopt a capability to calculate.[1] My study documents how economization took place at one large Wall Street bank, Premier Financial, through attempts to bring risk within the realm of the economic. The use of a version of Value at Risk allowed the bank's executives and traders to quantify the cost of risk in financial decisions at multiple levels such as strategy formulation, supervision of traders, and the design of customized swap agreements. Such pervasive introduction of calculation, coupled with a discourse that promoted a calculative, profit-maximizing orientation, comprises the combination of tools, practices, and ideology that Caliskan and Callon denote by economization.

By relating moral disengagement to model-based control, my analysis speaks to a long-running debate over the origin and social consequences of financialization. Sociologists like Greta Krippner and Gerald Davis have used the term financialization to denote the growing weight of finance, financial markets, and financial institutions in the economy.[2] Political economists such as Gerald Epstein have related financialization to the ascendancy of shareholder value as a mode of corporate governance, as well as to the growing dominance of capital market financial systems over bank-based financial systems.[3] Epstein's arguments have subsequently been mobilized to account for the excesses of the financial industry in the global financial crisis. For instance, the official reports and reviews of the 2008 crisis attribute banks' losses to a lowering of the ethical standards in the financial sector and explain such lowering to a shift from a "banking culture" to a "trading culture" that took banks away from trust-based relationships, and toward short-term transactions.

However, and as MacKenzie has noted, invoking culture to explain behavior in financial markets is fraught with conceptual difficulties. Attributing financialization to the rise of trading culture is problematic, whether the term "culture" is used in its anthropological or sociological sense. If used in the broad, older sense employed by midcentury anthropologists such as Clifford Geertz (i.e., the entire way of life of a people), the diagnosis of the problems posed by bank culture become so diffuse that a solution becomes unviable.[4] If, on the other hand, culture is used in the narrower but equally old usage employed by midcentury sociologists such as Talcott Parsons (i.e., culture as shared values), the result is equally problematic. Given contemporary skepticism that values can be easily internalized or uniformly shared by the members of a collective, it is difficult to see how trading culture might have, by itself, driven opportunism.

My analysis addresses these difficulties by offering an alternative mechanism that relates an expansion of the economic with a change in morality. Model-based moral disengagement proposes a concrete and material account, the introduction of economic models, which led to a change in self-censorship. It invokes morality, rather than culture, to account for opportunistic behavior in banking, offering an account based on distinctions between right and wrong or good and bad, rather than on cultural symbols or vehicles of meaning. Finally, model-based moral disengagement suggests a specific way in which a change in moral action takes place: disengagement. Rather than positing a change in the moral meaning of certain practices, I present a number of model-related processes that led to disengagement: the traders felt unfairly treated when the models led to decisions that arbitrarily reduced their bonuses, they concluded that customers who were less familiar with economic models were undeserving of consideration, and the bank managers who were expected to discipline the traders' behavior lost their authority and prestige following the introduction of risk management models.

Proximate Control

This book outlines a possible solution to the problem of model-based dis-engagement. It proposes the concept of *proximate control* to denote a set of choices in the areas of strategy, discourse, structure, and supervision, that can limit model-based moral disengagement (see figure 13.1). At the level of strat-egy, proximate control includes explicit measures that eliminate or reduce the potential for abuse, avoiding calculative asymmetries between the organization and its customers or stakeholders. In terms of discourse, proximate control is reinforced by a rhetoric that avoids celebrating the mechanisms by which model-based reconstitution operates, whether it is rationality, innovation, calculativeness, or disruption. Instead, proximate control involves a rhetoric that, while unable to replace the employees' values, can provide symbolic pointers in a context of uncertainty and radical change. Such discourse can reinforce organizational norms by drawing on symbolic sanctions of behavior that disregards the law, such as neglecting official certifications and exams.

I identify two additional elements of proximate control. In terms of struc-ture, proximate control reinforces organizational relations and stability as countervailing forces against the disruption posed by market uncertainty or by the rival authority of star performers. This can be accomplished through practices that stimulate informal interaction, whether on the floor or outside it, as in corporate retreats. A related organizational element is internal labor markets, which contributes to promoting cohesiveness. Perhaps most impor-tant, control is exercised through symbolic work at the interpersonal level in the form of face-to-face meetings with the head of the unit or its middle managers. For the managers, this includes the display of approval or disap-proval in line with the subordinate's conformity or disconformity with existing organizational norms. The ultimate outcome of proximate control is to avoid perceptions of organizational injustice and the moral disengagement that fol-lows. This can partly be accomplished by ensuring that managerial decisions are made with sufficient contextual knowledge, something that model-based control typically lacks.

The proposed concept of proximate control stands in direct contrast to what governmentality scholars like Rose and Miller have called "governing at a distance." Instead of relying, as their example of the British National Health System illustrates, on a combination of remoteness, monitoring technology, cost data, and a calculating orientation, proximate control relies on mecha-nisms of vicinity in supervision. This includes face-to-face evaluations, per-sonal judgment, the use of intuition, or a reliance on interpersonal trust. In other words, proximate control avoids technologies for control at a distance such as risk management models. At the same time, proximate control is com-patible with economic models in general, that is, with equations, visualizations,

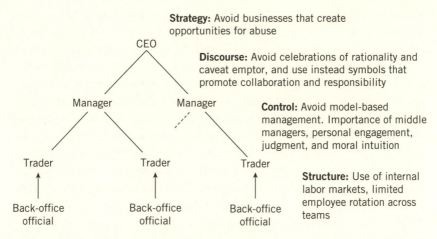

FIGURE 13.1. Proximate control at International Securities.

and trading terminals, as long as they are used for the purpose of evaluating external objects such as a stock or bond, rather than members of the organization. Put differently, my findings suggest that the use of models in financial organizations typically fails when the organization turns them *on itself*.

Indeed, proximate control can benefit from objects and artifacts that reinforce the formal or informal organizational structure such as the layout of the desks, height of the monitors, or areas for brainstorming. In sum, proximate control is a form of organizing that uses models and tools in a way that complements, rather than substitutes for, management. It identifies models and morals as two spheres to be recombined rather than as "hostile worlds," to use Zelizer's expression. Conversely, proximate control is incompatible with model-based measures of organizational control such as rating agencies or capital requirements. Relying on proximate control under such regimes would require establishing an alternative basis for according value that differs from the dominant metric, is internal to the organization, non-calculative in nature, and decouples internal decisions from the external governance regime.

Proximate control speaks to the current interest on the investment banking partnerships of Wall Street before the 1980s. Following the financial crisis of 2008, disillusionment with the corporate bureaucracies that dominate Wall Street has prompted a nostalgic reappraisal of the merits of the partnership form. These merits are often formulated in cultural terms such as the "partnership culture," but the precise components of such culture are often articulated in terms of incentives, whether in the form of ownership rights, legal liability, length of tenure, or supervision. Used in this manner, "partnership culture" becomes no more than a cultural label used to describe economic processes rather than cultural ones. Incentives, payoffs, and rational choice are wrapped in images of tailored suits, elaborate meals, and wood-paneled offices. Evocative as these images are, in the absence of a specifically cultural account of the mechanisms that create restraint, it is unclear which cultural elements were responsible for it: was it the formal dress code, the epicurean meals, or the status symbols? Furthermore, by tying financial restraint to a particular time and place such as Wall Street before the 1980s, the celebration of a partnership culture may hinder appreciation for new organizational forms that incorporate technology into trading and that do not look like a traditional partnership. My concept of proximate control addresses some of the problems of the expression "partnership culture" by identifying the moral and material mechanisms that created restraint in the partnerships, generalizing from a particular recreation of the partnership culture on Wall Street that I observed in the early 2000s, the equities floor of International Securities.

Morality and the Social Studies of Finance

Over the past two decades, an emerging body of literature known as the social studies of finance has developed a novel and original perspective on financial markets, drawing from research in sociology, science studies, anthropology, management, accounting, and other social sciences.[5] This novel perspective provides an alternative to orthodox financial economics and its microfoundations on rational choice, as well as to behavioral economics and its psychological emphasis on biases and heuristics in decision-making. It focuses on the effect that material tools such as economic models, trading terminals, or matching algorithms have on financial markets. Such emphasis builds on Callon's seminal concept of performativity, which contends that market devices shape economic action. The material equipment of market actors, Callon notes, can even turn them into entities that resemble the decision-makers posited by economics, or *homo economicus*.

Partly because of this interest in the material, social studies of finance scholars have barely engaged with moral phenomena. My study addresses this gap by providing a material account of morality on Wall Street. Specifically, my proposed concept of model-based disengagement accounts for the dangers inherent in the use of models for the purpose of control. In doing so, it builds on sociological research that differentiates between two possible uses of models—valuation and governance. MacKenzie and Spears have argued that what actually "killed Wall Street" in the financial crisis was not the use of David Li's Gaussian copula for valuation purposes, but the embedding of the Gaussian copula in governance via ratings, which led to "the large-scale 'gaming' of them and of the other models employed by the ratings agencies."[6] That is, an otherwise harmless valuation model was used for the purpose of governance, with fatal consequences. My concept of model-based moral disengagement extends this argument by emphasizing the ethical dangers of model-based control *within* the banks, and not simply of regulatory control *of the* banks.

Model-based disengagement also speaks to a growing skepticism among accounting scholars about quantitative risk management. Enterprise risk management, Power has argued, amounted to the risk management of "nothing" during the financial crisis, in view of the audit logic in which it takes place.[7] In her ethnographic study of risk managers, Mikes identified the existence of "quantitative skeptics" that treat Value at Risk figures with healthy caution and disbelief. These skeptics, she writes, "credited these numbers only with indicating the underlying risk trends, not with capturing the risk profile in any absolute sense."[8] My findings add to the skepticism voiced by Power and Mikes by exploring its implications beyond risk management and suggest that it should apply to any form of model-based control. Furthermore, my findings cast doubts on the extent to which quantitative skeptics can persevere in their disbelief. Because model-based control typically leads to the calculative reconstitution of the bank at multiple levels, individual resistance will be difficult and may come at the cost of organizational survival.

A number of theoretical implications follow from the concept of proximate control. In recent years, there has been a move toward expanding the social studies of finance beyond materiality so as to integrate phenomena like identity, affect, or embeddedness into material accounts of markets. As part of this, Callon has proposed a broad conception of material markets often known as *homo economicus 2.0*. Callon's proposal advances a model of the individual decision-maker that, unlike the traditional *homo economicus*, is not an individualist profit-maximizer but "engages in strategic activities and interacts with other agents." To live and flourish, Callon adds, this decision-maker "draws on diverse material and emotional resources and relies on interpersonal networks."[9] Callon's new conception of markets is summed up by the notion of *habilitation*, an expression that evokes contemporary remedies to the limitations faced by disabled people. Traditional approaches to disabled care can be seen as *prosthetic*, that is, based on introducing rigid attachments to objects (prostheses) or to other people, such as carers, that compensate for maladjustment to the environment. The alternative, i.e., habilitation, entails a restoration of agency by intervening on the environment in which the handicapped individual operates. Habilitation may involve constructing a combination of ramps, elevators, and alternative routes so that individuals with limited mobility can more easily access a given building. Habilitation thus reconfigures that environment to "put the handicapped person in a position to define her own projects."[10] By shifting attention away from an exclusive focus on tools, habilitation opens up possibilities to combine tools and social relations, tools and affective attachments, or tools and identities.

Proximate control speaks to Callon's concept of *homo economicus 2.0* by introducing the realm of morality in a material account of markets. Indeed, some analyses of the global financial crisis implicitly treat bankers as morally handicapped and seek to remedy their moral deficiencies through intervention on the person. This can be seen in new initiatives to introduce moral improvement based on the introduction of monitoring and decision-making constraints. From a Callonian perspective, these compliance artifacts can be considered prosthetic attempts to cure the morally disabled. Like any prosthesis, these attempts are often characterized by rigid attachments and maladjustment to the choices and dilemmas that arise in actual practice. Conversely, the concept of proximate control implies an alternative approach to financial reform that is based on intervening on the traders' environment, including their supervisory relations, bank strategy, choice of products, corporate symbols, rhetoric, and identity. Put differently, my proposed concept of proximate control can be considered as a way of habilitating the exercise of ethical choices through the creation of an environment that is conducive to them. In that sense, it illustrates the gains from combining a material and moral approach to the study of markets.

Performative Spirals

A second theme explored in this book concerns the effects of economic models on financial markets. It asks, how did the introduction of models impact the organization of trading? Based on my analysis, I proposed the concept of *performative spiral* to describe the reciprocal influence between economic models and the financial properties introduced by these models. In developing this concept, my argument proceeded in several steps. I suggested that modern arbitrage can be viewed as the use of models to isolate, quantify, and bet on specific *financial properties* of stocks and bonds rather than making general claims about their overall value. Examples of these properties include mean-reversion, implied merger probability, or "quiltedness." Because many of these properties have no existence outside the models used to quantify them, arbitrage can be regarded as performative, in the sense that the economic models used to quantify the financial properties of interest are an integral part of the calculative infrastructure of arbitrage. Over time, and as the returns from betting on established financial properties are competed away, traders develop new models and properties, which in turn will eventually become established and be less lucrative. As a new model is developed, however, the old ones remain in use, leading to an overlap in financial properties and interdependencies across models. I refer to this iterative dynamic as a *performative spiral*, a term that contrasts with Robert Merton Jr.'s idea of a financial innovation spiral.[11]

There are several differences between Merton's spiral and the performative spiral. While Merton's spiral emphasizes Wall Street's role in providing increasing protection against risk, the performative spiral highlights the growing diversity of economic models and tools developed on Wall Street, as well as the growth in financial properties that these models enable. Unlike Merton's spiral, which depicts financial markets as unambiguously progressing toward a safer and less risky world, the performative spiral that I propose points to greater knowledge, but also to novel sources of risk. Given the overlap between new and existing properties, new models not only create new possibilities for investors but also lead to new interdependencies that need to be managed, and new financial properties that have to be taken into account. Merton's world, in sum, gets progressively safer thanks to financial innovation, while in the performative alternative that I outline the world becomes more equipped with models, tools, and equations, but also becomes exposed to new risks.

Finally, the analysis presented in this book also proposes the concept of *performative trace* to denote a changing pattern of social relations across trading units that are specialized in related financial properties, in response to the evolving models and properties in the market. The performative trace is an organizational counterpart to the performative spiral and offers a conceptual platform to examine the changes in trading room layouts within Wall Street.

Finance as Science

The proposed concepts of performative spiral and performative trace speak to a flourishing sociological literature on performativity in markets. Over the past two decades, and following the seminal study by MacKenzie and Millo, the idea that models can shape rather than describe markets has firmly established the social studies of finance within economic sociology. My concept of performative spirals contributes to this literature by extending MacKenzie and Millo's findings beyond a single performative turn. The spiral considers not only the consequences that arise when a single model such as Black-Scholes is introduced, but also what happens when that model is subsequently adopted, diffused, commoditized, and eventually replaced by a different one as traders search for ever-higher returns. The spiral posits a temporal schema that brings together successive performative turns, leading to a gradual proliferation of economic models and financial properties. Put differently, whereas MacKenzie and others have considered the effects of performativity one model at a time, the performative spiral envisions the cumulative effect of a sequence of models, each one adding to the previous rather than replacing it. The resulting lamination of models, practices, and properties can lead to gaps and silos in the modeling process, as documented by MacKenzie. In that sense, the performative spiral combines Callonian performativity with the economic idea that market actors compete with each other, so that market outcomes are the combined effect of an actor's actions and his competitor's response.

The performative spiral is also illustrative of the theoretical agenda that marked the development of the social studies of finance in its origin, back in the late 1990s. As established science scholars such as MacKenzie and Knorr Cetina entered the study of finance, they brought with them the methods and theories used to study scientists such as mathematicians or high-energy particle physicists. From its inception, then, the social studies of finance exhibited an interest in what Knorr Cetina described as " practices, arrangements, and mechanisms bound together by necessity, affinity, and historical coincidence that, in a given area of professional expertise, make up how we know what we know."[12] Scholars in the social studies of finance have thus focused on the epistemic nature of financial activity, that is, on its relationship to knowledge, and to how knowledge is created. The performativity spiral, as well as the related idea of financial properties, is part of this epistemic turn.

Specifically, the performativity spiral advances the metaphor of finance as science by inviting an understanding of quantitative finance around visual entities such as price charts, spreadplots, or treemaps. Financial properties rely on what science historian Peter Galison has described as the "material culture" of images in science.[13] In his study of experimental physicists, Galison identified two major subcultures, one centered on the use of devices to produce elaborate pictures of particle interactions, and another dominated by measurement devices that produced numbers and figures. A similar reliance on images can be found on Wall Street. While traders have traditionally been associated with models and numbers, trading rooms are also populated by a wealth of graphical representations of visual significance. These images capture something about financial properties that numerical tools and models possibly miss. The production of images on trading floors is supported by a large number of interactive designers, graphic artists, and PowerPoint specialists, whose Wall Street career and market influence deserve more academic study.

Paralleling the success of the social studies of finance, a related literature known as valuation studies has explored the material dimension of consumer and producer markets beyond finance, whether in food retailing or wholesale energy production.[14] The epistemic approach adopted in this book has strong parallels with valuations studies. In their study of the "economy of qualities," for instance, Callon, Méadel, and Rabeharisoa present contemporary product markets as knowledge-producing devices. The value of a bottle of wine, a box of orange juice, or a new car model, they argue, is nowadays defined by tests, scores, and standards that rely on technology to establish worth.[15] Beyond producing in greater quantities, modern economies increase the value of what they produce by finding ways to better measure, appraise, and communicate the qualities of their products. This activity, they add, accounts for much of what marketing campaigns, retailing strategies, or certifying authorities do. In this regard, the financial properties that I identify can be seen as the Wall Street counterpart of the economy of qualities that Callon and colleagues identify. The parallel suggests that the spiraling trend toward greater complexity introduced by financial models is not unique to Wall Street, but part of a broader knowledge-based economy.

Turning to the performative trace, this concept speaks to the literature on performativity by relating performative processes and mechanisms to ongoing debates in organization theory. At the core of the concept of performative trace is the question of how to organize economic modeling when the models are performative. After all, established organization theorists such as Burns and Stalker have long claimed that the effective organizational structure is contingent on a firm's relationship with the environment. In the case of innovative firms operating in uncertain environments, organic structures are more suitable; for less innovative firms in more stable environments, mechanistic structures are preferable. This suggests that the optimal organization of economic modeling may well be contingent on the use and impact of the economic models: depending on whether models are descriptive or performative, a different organization will be needed. The literature on modeling, however, presents a gap in this regard. While most studies of performativity are conducted at the level of markets, the practical use of models that results in performativity is actually supervised by partners, senior traders, or managing directors; in other words, it takes place in organizations.[16] Modeling, in other words, happens in a corporate context of formal roles, reporting structures, subunits, etc., but little of this context is captured by market-level studies of modeling that use aggregate variables or cross-company data. As a result, the existing literature lacks guidelines for how to organize modeling when these models are performative. (One partial exception to this gap is MacKenzie's study of the global financial crisis, which explicitly considered how modeling was structured in organizations such as banks or credit rating agencies; however, MacKenzie's study does not explicitly incorporate the performative possibilities of the economic models.)

The proposed concept of performative trace addresses this gap by providing management scholars with a frame to conceptualize the organization of modeling in banks and funds when the models are performative.[17] It suggests that when the use of models is performative, the modeling process needs to be accompanied by periodic internal reorganizations in response to the various turns of the performative spiral. Conversely, when the use of models is external to phenomena of interest (and provided that such phenomena remain stable), organizations might not need to alter their organization of the modeling process over time.

Seen in this light, the performative trace speaks to a growing interest in the management literature on performativity.[18] Most of this literature has not considered, as Callon did, the role of calculative devices in markets, but reached back instead to the original philosophy of Austin, positing various ways in which utterances and actions in organizational contexts are capable of intervening rather than merely describing. The performative trace relates instead performativity in markets to the organizational literature by building on midcentury contingency theorists such as Paul Lawrence and Jay Lorsch.[19] The latter highlight the problem of integration, that is, of "achieving unity of effort among the various subsystems" in organizations. That same problem, integration, also lies at the center of the performative trace. Whereas integration was presented by contingency theorists as a remedy to the problem of the *division of labor*, a performative trace can be considered an integrative solution to the related problem of the *division of modeling*, i.e., the parceling of modeling tasks into different subunits on the trading floor. Indeed, performative traces are arguably relevant beyond financial organizations, as more and more companies rely on model-based representations of their markets through tools such as social media or algorithms.[20]

Resonance, or the Dark Side of Models

The global financial crisis has sparked scholarly interest in the dysfunctions of financial markets. This book contributes to this literature by pointing to the dangers of financial models in modern arbitrage. In this regard, David Stark and I propose the concept of resonance to denote the amplification of error that arises from the use of economic models in a context of cognitive similarity.[21] Resonance speaks to a literature in the social studies of finance that has shown how models create feedback loops and contribute to financial crises. These loops typically arise when the actions of a trader have an effect on other traders, and the actions of those other traders feed back into the original one. Loops arise, in other words, when the widespread diffusion of an economic model creates interdependencies. Examples of such loops, as documented by MacKenzie, include the liquidity problems posed by Value at Risk during the Russian default crisis in 1998, or the role that, according to official reports, portfolio insurance played in the market crash of 1987.[22] In these two cases, the nature of the feedback was financial, that is, driven by the losses experienced by some traders and their impact on other traders. The concept of resonance adds to this literature by presenting a feedback mechanism in which the interdependence is cognitive rather than financial, that is, induced by the effects of one trader's actions on the other trader's estimates, and transmitted via the use of an economic model. Taken together, the recurring incidence of model-based feedback loops and crises is illustrative of the dangers posed by quantitative finance, dangers that are captured in the concept of a performative spiral.

Resonance also echoes a key contention of the social studies of finance, namely, that material tools in financial markets create effects that are overlooked by orthodox or behavioral economics. In particular, resonance illustrates how the introduction of models has altered established mechanisms of imitation on Wall Street. Scholars such as Scharfstein and Stein have traditionally conceptualized imitation as herding, that is, as instances when actors ignore their own private information to avoid an inferior relative performance. By contrast, resonance takes place when arbitrageurs use models to test their beliefs against each other. Put differently, herding arises from the use of less information than is available, while resonance arises from using as much information as possible. As a result, imitation patterns in quantitative finance such as arbitrage disasters need not be the result of lemming-like behavior, but of reflexive action. Furthermore, addressing the risks posed by resonance might call for different policies than those aimed at herding.

Finally, resonance speaks to the fallibility of arbitrage and quantitative finance. A growing literature on prediction markets has pointed to the remarkable ability of markets to anticipate uncertain events such as election outcomes.[23] In this vein, the introduction of quantitative tools in finance would appear to increase such predictive accuracy even further. By contrast, resonance suggests that the introduction of models only creates greater accuracy at the expense of the occasional disastrous mistake. Indeed, while the use of models in arbitrage has repeatedly led to more accurate and stable predictions, it has also given rise to arbitrage disasters that were nonexistent before models were introduced. My analysis confirms that models prove helpful for pooling the collective knowledge held by market actors, but whenever market actors collectively lack a crucial piece of knowledge, the models can also give market participants a misplaced sense of confidence, potentially leading to disaster. A classic example of such a pitfall is political risk: when economic developments are shaped by historically unprecedented political forces, the key variables are typically not present in the traders' databases, as was the case in the GE-Honeywell trade. The use of models thus creates a distinct risk of resonance. Future studies could further elucidate the relationship between resonance and political risk by exploring investors' failure to anticipate the financial crisis of 2008, the Brexit referendum, or the outcome of the American presidential elections in 2016.

The Global Financial Crisis

How do my findings shed light on the global financial crisis of 2008? Two competing sociological perspectives have accounted for the crisis. MacKenzie or Tett have explained the growth in toxic mortgage derivatives in terms of organizational silos in the banks and rating agencies, that is, in terms of fragmentation in the modeling process. MacKenzie even warned against ret-rospective accounts that attribute the creation of toxic derivatives to "amoral calculators." By contrast, other sociologists have explained the crisis in terms of opportunism. Fligstein and Roehrkasse pointed to abuses on the part of American banks, while Pernell, Jung, and Dobbin documented self-serving investments in derivatives within banks.

Was the financial crisis an outcome of fragmentation, or opportunism? The analysis presented in this book develops a third perspective that has elements of both. My analysis explains the global financial crisis in terms of a secular reorganization of the industry, partly induced by the arrival of economic mod-els. Between 1981 and 2007, Wall Street experienced fundamental change: trad-ers adopted quantitative tools and models, the investment partnership form was abandoned, and the industry became deregulated. My analysis contends that such reconstitution impaired Wall Street's ability to self-regulate, in two ways. Model-based moral disengagement may have given rise to opportunistic investment in derivatives or abusive practices in mortgage origination. Fur-thermore, and as the concept of performative spiral suggests, the development of new models entailed new financial properties and interdependencies among existing properties. However, these properties were insufficiently well used or understood by traders, as their adoption of new models was unaccompanied by a reorganization of the modeling process. In other words, the account of the global financial crisis that emerges from my study underscores the impor-tance of economic models in creating the epistemic and moral preconditions for its occurrence.

My findings address a second question: what did the crisis mean for Wall Street employees? Few ethnographic studies have considered the effects of the 2008–10 recession on Wall Street employees. Yet it is important to understand how bankers and traders experienced the crisis, how they made sense of it, and what their interpretation implies for existing academic narratives. In this regard, Miyazaki's study of Japanese arbitrageurs after 2008 has pointed to the doubts his subjects harbored about the legitimacy arbitrage in Japan, and more broadly about the future of the financial industry in that country.

By contrast, my conversations with Todd, Max, and Bob in 2015 suggest that the problem does not lie in financial markets but in mismanagement within financial organizations. Thus, Todd emphasized the poor administration that he encountered at International Securities after Bob left, as well as the mis-management he confronted again at his subsequent job at Bear Stearns. Max was critical of the Wall Street managers and investors he had recently worked with. He also manifested appreciation for his former bosses at the investment partnerships he worked for in the 1980s and praised the partnership-like orga-nization that Bob put in place at International Securities. Finally, Bob's experi-ence of the crisis reinforced his prior view that Wall Street banks were "too large, too complex, and not well managed." The crisis made Bob even more pessimistic about the financial industry, for he believed that the government bailout of Wall Street banks would ensure the survival of the large banks as well as the problems associated with them. The common theme that ran through my subjects in 2015 thus points to mismanagement on Wall Street. This emphasis on badly run banks challenges competing theories of the crisis centered on models, regulation, or the price mechanism, and reinforces instead the need for more research on the organizational dimension of Wall Street.

Morality on Wall Street

Over the past decade, a new sociological literature on morality has reinvigorated academic interest on the topic. The so-called new sociology of morality differs from the traditional literature in its rejection of the Parsonian emphasis on shared values and moral consensus. As Hitlin and Vaisey put it, the new sociology of morality "is no longer wedded to the assumptions about universal internalization and unproblematic consensus that doomed functionalist theory."[24] This new literature does not rely on a fixed, substantive definition of the moral, focusing instead on the determinants of what a society, group, or organization deems moral. As Abend notes, such a methodological approach does not necessarily imply a substantial position of moral relativism. Consistent with it, the literature on morals and markets developed by Zelizer and others has demonstrated how practices, framings, and boundary-drawing activity can address moral objections to economic transactions.

My study speaks to the new sociology of morality, and specifically to the morals and markets literature, by considering the case of derivatives traders in financial markets. It relates a change in moral behavior, i.e., a surge in customer abuse in over-the-counter derivatives in the mid-1990s, to a sociotechnical process, the introduction of model-based control. By leveraging the social-psychological concept of moral disengagement, my study avoids a researcher-imposed definition of what is morally acceptable, presenting instead a change in moral behavior relative to the actors' own standards. One limitation of this approach is that it does not consider whether the moral meanings might have changed as well. For instance, the traders engaged in customer abuse at Premier Financial might have genuinely believed their actions were ethically sound. Future research on morality on Wall Street would do well to complement my emphasis on disengagement with an examination of the impact of economic models on the prevailing moral concepts, methods, reasons, and objects in the large banks.

My research also speaks to the new sociology of morality by offering an empirically grounded framework, proximate control, that can guide current efforts to make financial markets morally acceptable. In line with Zelizer's treatment of life insurance, proximate control points to the need to draw boundaries between the acceptable and the unacceptable. As part of this, some activities may be regarded as almost sacred, as in treating desk compositions as "jewels" (to use Bob's own words), while other practices may be treated as profane; at International Securities, these included drinking with colleagues after work, stacking monitors, renegotiating bonuses, or ignoring regulatory licenses.

Furthermore, my research echoes Abend's sociology of morality by illustrating how his moral categories apply in a financial setting. Abend's recent history of business ethicists coined the concept of moral background, which denotes the context underlying everyday morality: what moral concepts exist in society, what moral methods can be used, what reasons can be given, and what objects can be morally evaluated. Abend identified two distinct backgrounds, the Christian Merchant and the Standards of Practice.[25] My findings speak to this taxonomy, in that Bob's discourse and actions seem to clearly conform to the Christian Merchant. Bob embraced Catholicism but sought inspiration in the Mennonite communities that his ancestors belonged to. Unlike other Anabaptist communities such as the Amish, the Mennonites that Bob studied made use of technology, but also put in place a concerted effort to prevent technology from reconstituting their communities.

Finally, Abend's distinction illuminates the ethical challenges that Bob encountered as a manager on Wall Street. Such were the profits generated by his traders that Bob, as indirect beneficiary of them, found himself in a bind: the slightest slip into instrumentality in his norm enforcement posed a fatal danger to his managerial credibility. The solution that he adopted was a complete rejection of instrumentality, and the effort to build instead a reputation that he would "burn" his house before compromising on his norms. Another element of the Christian Merchant that was prominent in Bob's case was his rejection of moral relativism. He not only developed an articulated opposition to relativism, which he often expressed, but also learned that as a manager he needed to make it compatible with societal demands for moral pluralism in the workplace. In the case of his rejection of drinking with colleagues after work, the solution he implemented was to lead by example.

Models, Morals, and Financial Reform

My investigation into morals and models speaks to the policy debate on financial reform that has followed the global financial crisis. In recent years, regulators across the Atlantic have complemented structural reforms such as the 2010 Dodd-Frank Act with an interest in improving the ethical standards on Wall Street and the City of London, a policy agenda often known as bank culture.[26] In practical terms, regulators at the New York Federal Reserve and officials at the UK Banking Standards Board have sought to integrate ethical concerns in financial organizations through high-profile seminars, conferences, and employee surveys that measure organizational traits such as competence, reliability, responsiveness, and resilience. In doing so, they have promoted the importance of ethical standards in the public policy agenda.

The bank culture agenda has been further advanced by a growing activity within compliance departments in Wall Street banks. In effect, the bank culture agenda has often been delegated to the area of compliance, turning this functional area into one of the fastest-growing businesses on Wall Street.[27] Banks have made extensive use of information technology to document, assess, and potentially intervene on the norms and values espoused by their employees. The growing list of tools used to that end includes PowerPoint presentations, key performance indicators, or web-based videos with mandatory tests attached to them. These efforts are typically led from a service department such as compliance, rather than through the line of command.

My analysis in this book speaks to the bank culture agenda, pointing to the limitations of such an approach. Consider first the values-based view of morality that is implicit in numerous compliance interventions. This view of morality arguably invites interventions at the level of the symbolic, including speeches, workshops, or breakout groups, yet such initiatives run the risk of proving too general to have a concrete bearing on trading practices. In addition, attempts to instill different values in bank employees overlook the fact that values are not easily internalized and that, in any event, as Swidler established, values are not a particularly powerful determinant of action. Furthermore, because norms and values are not often shared among most members of a collective, including banks, organization-wide initiatives led by compliance or other service departments may prove too generic to effect change.

The perspective presented in this book complements the bank culture agenda by offering an alternative conception of morality and a different avenue for change. When stripped from the jargon and the technical language, the core insight developed herein boils down to a simple recipe for improving the financial sector: *better management*. This seemingly obvious point gains significance when contrasted with the bank culture approach. Unlike the distant form of control attempted by regulator-hosted workshops or behavioral surveys, banks already possess a mechanism for improvement, that is, their own hierarchical structure. Banks, like other Weberian bureaucracies, are formal control systems that send information upward and exert authority downward. Furthermore, the supervision put in place by hierarchies is spread through the organization in the form of close supervision: because each manager is in charge of the officials below, supervision is conducted with a higher degree of proximity than that conducted by compliance departments. Such proximity in turn provides the necessary contextual knowledge to evaluate and sanction with fairness. In sum, proximate control complements the bank culture approach by providing a mechanism for updating or enforcing ethical standards through proximity rather than distance.

Beyond morality, proximate control speaks to other aspects of Wall Street's evolution with regard to changes in size, strategy, discourse, and technology since 2008. Consider first the structure of the industry. It is no secret that the banking industry as a whole has experienced substantial consolidation since 2008. From the standpoint of model-based disengagement, this is a cause for concern as greater bank size creates a need for more models, which in turn may give rise to moral disengagement. But while the large banks have become larger, recent years have also witnessed the growth of the alternative finance industry, including hedge funds, private equity firms, as well as boutique mergers and acquisitions advisors. The small size of these companies relative to Wall Street banks suggests a lower risk of model-based moral disengagement. Naturally, and as research by Neely among others has suggested (see the methodological note below), the alternative investment industry faces its own challenges.[28]

Consider now the recent changes in bank strategy. A centerpiece of financial reform in the United States has been the enactment of the Volcker Rule, which prohibits proprietary trading in commercial banks. Some banks like UBS or Credit Suisse have gone beyond the Volcker Rule and divested or sharply reduced the size of their Fixed Income, Currencies and Commodities (FICC) divisions following the Libor scandal in 2012. These decisions can be understood from the standpoint of orthodox economics in terms of avoiding misaligned incentives. An alternative interpretation, based on proximate control, stems from the recognition that controlling employees through personal supervision rather than quantitative metrics is unavoidably costly. For that reason, conflict-prone business areas create a burden on bank managers who wish to ensure that subordinates act ethically. The overriding goal of proximate control is thus not to create an organization where the alignment of incentives is such that supervision is not needed. (Given the uncertainty and ambiguity that characterizes trading, the scope for differences in interpretation and unforeseen contingencies is such that a conflict-free Wall Street bank simply does not exist.) The objective of introducing proximate control is instead to create a financial organization in which supervision is effective, and not overwhelmed by the sheer number of clashes, tension, and struggles between traders and their managers. Banks can attain this outcome by adopting strategies that avoid these businesses, and the Volcker Rule arguably helps in this regard.

Consider the discourse on ethics put forth by proponents of bank culture. Given the current context of structural reform and technological change on Wall Street, discourse can contribute to improvement in two ways, even if none realizes the Parsonian goal of instilling better values among the employees. First, and as Swidler pointed out, discourse on moral norms and values can be helpful as long as it is accompanied by changes in business practices. To that end, discourse is a communicative device that signals a broader set of transformations and flags the need for employees to develop new strategies of action. This is particularly helpful in situations of what Swidler called "unsettled lives,"[29] that is, large-scale change such as Wall Street is arguably undergoing following Dodd-Frank. Furthermore, such discourse can draw on the use of communication tools, such as social media platforms and mobile applications, to extend its reach.

There is another way in which discourse can advance financial reform. From the standpoint of proximate control, attention to discourse provides a managerial device to gauge the moral world of subordinates. Managers can ask, how are their subordinates talking about customers? How are they referring to their own subordinates? How do they refer to the bank as a whole? By examining discourse in their organization, managers can develop a moral sense of their subordinates and draw on it to evaluate their proposals for uncertain financial trades, sensitive products, or other innovations, technically complex as they might seem. This can be done through intrusive means such as reading the employee's email correspondence or social media postings, but such challenges to employee privacy would give rise to perceptions of injustice. Alternatively, managers can rely on what they hear and overhear in their conversations with others, as Bob often did.

Finally, technology can be used on Wall Street in ways that are compatible with proximate control. The emergence of technological start-ups in finance over the past years in the form of the so-called fintech industry offers new opportunities for navigating the tradeoff between scale and proximity in control. Start-up organizations in fintech have the opportunity to avoid model-based disengagement by relying on information technology to create networks of small companies that act collaboratively and without a need for a large size. The outcome of such an approach could be large inter-organizational structures that can enjoy the advantages of scale while relying on proximate control. Certainly, this is not the first time that the network form is presented as the solution to the hierarchy. More than three decades ago, Michael Piore and Charles Sabel called for American mass manufacturing to seek inspiration in the flexibility of networks of collaborative small firms.[30] This approach, however, is the opposite of the strategy adopted by Wall Street banks, which proceeded instead to consolidate and become megabanks. In the current post-crisis environment, the network form may have greater success, as regulators see in the fintech firms a potential ally to promote financial reform through technological disruption.

METHODOLOGICAL NOTE

This book is based on a mixed-method research design, structured in two different parts. The first reports on the ethnography I conducted on a Wall Street trading room between 1999 and 2003. The second adds to the first with a combination of ethnographic revisits and interviews conducted between 2004 and 2015, in the spirit of what Michael Burawoy calls a "punctuated revisit," where the researcher returns to the original site over a time period spanning at least ten years.[1] The combination of these two approaches gave me the opportunity to reconsider my original findings in light of the financial crisis, and to address new problems such as the relationship between models and morals, the causes of the global financial crisis, and the debate on financial reform.

Specifically, the first half of my study was conducted in the equity derivatives trading room of International Securities, the US subsidiary of a global investment bank located in New York City's Lower Manhattan. My study joins a tradition of ethnographies of financial institutions such as those conducted by Abolafia, Ho, and Lépinay.[2] Between 1999 and 2003, I conducted a total of sixty-five visits to the equities floor of International Securities lasting between one and seven hours, observing and interviewing twenty-five traders in total. Beginning in June 2002, I had my own desk and computer, my own magnetic access pass, a login for the corporate Intranet. Through this period, I observed the work of traders at three desks, interviewed three middle managers, and spoke casually to numerous other employees that I met along the way, including administrative personnel, operations officers, and others. I did not tape record my interviews, taking handwritten notes instead. After each visit, I returned to my office at the business school to transcribe the material before the end of the day. A typical visit would yield between five and ten pages of single-spaced typewritten notes.

In this initial phase of the project, I was fortunate to have an inspiring and supportive coauthor, David Stark. Between 1999 and 2003, we analyzed the fieldnotes from every single one of my visits. David joined me in five of my visits to the bank. After each visit, I emailed my fieldnotes to David, met with him soon afterward, and wrote a memo summarizing the theoretical themes emerging from our discussion in order to structure my subsequent observations. Unlike with some ethnographies, every one of my visits was preceded by an analysis of my observations in the preceding visit. Our conversations were captured in more than 120 typewritten memos that track, as Agar wrote, the beguiling "movement from breakdown to resolution to coherence."[3]

Work on the book project actually began well before I set foot in International Securities, for it took me a full year, and two failed attempts, to make a successful entrée into the field. I gained access to International Securities thanks to an introduction made by a fellow graduate student I met at a PhD seminar in Economic Sociology at Columbia University. In line with other ethnographers in the social studies of finance, the primary focus of my fieldwork was not the bank's culture, structure, or strategy. Instead, my goal was to document and analyze the mediating effect of market devices such as economic models or electronic visualizations on valuation. In this, I followed a rich tradition in Science and Technology Studies that focused on the content, rather than the social context, of scientists' work. I relied on the "flat description" techniques proposed by Latour and Woolgar in *Laboratory Life*, documenting the ways in which the traders themselves established and understood associations within the trading floor, rather than imposing my own categories such as "network ties" or "top management teams." I also focused on content of the value claims made by the traders rather than on the social context of their work.[4] The findings from my fieldwork were published in five articles coauthored with David Stark, the first of which received the Richard Nelson Award by the Institute of Management, Innovation, and Organization in 2009; and the Outstanding Paper award by the Communication and Technology division of the American Sociological Association in 2005.[5]

Revisits

The second half of my study builds on interviews and site visits that took place once I left the bank in the spring of 2003 and consists of twenty-three follow-up visits and interviews with the key actors I followed at International Securities. At first, my revisits were not part of an established plan. I left New York City in June 2003 for an academic position at Universitat Pompeu Fabra in Barcelona, and the geographical distance from New York City helped me appreciate the privileged nature of the access that I had gained at International Securities. In the summer of 2004, I returned briefly to New York and again visited International Securities; I then learned about Bob's impending resignation. During another short trip to New York in 2005, I spent a day at Bob's family residence, and had lunch with him, his wife, and their children. In 2006, back in New York for an academic position at Columbia Business School, I conducted an extended interview with Bob in which I found out about his role in the loss-making trade in GE-Honeywell in 2001. In 2007, I invited Bob to speak at my

MBA class, and on hearing his critical views of Wall Street, I refocused my subsequent conversation with him around organizational norms in his former trading floor. I also interviewed Max in 2006 and corresponded with him via email on several occasions.

Starting in 2008, I initiated additional revisits to the protagonists of my original fieldwork, but this time with the explicit objective of assembling material for a monograph. I resumed a calendar of meetings with Bob at a different bank, Global Trust, where he was CEO. After September 2008, our conversations went back and forth between his daily challenges and his reactions to the financial crisis. I met with Bob again a total of seven times in the months after September 2008, including a follow-up meeting in 2013 once he had already left Global Trust. Finally, in 2015, I conducted one last round of interviews that included Bob, Todd, Max, Ray, and one former trader outside International Securities who had worked with Bob in the past. All these interviews were taped and transcribed in their entirety.

As I reencountered the protagonists of my trading room in 2015, I asked them about their past and specifically the time before we met in 1999. I inquired about the traders' careers, prior jobs on Wall Street, and about the differences between Wall Street in the 1980s and the 2000s. As I did so, I straddled the methodology of the ethnographic revisit and oral history. My motivation for doing so came from Bob's claim in 2008 that deregulation and consolidation had meant the death of Wall Street. I was also curious about Bob's comment that he had replicated some organizational elements of the investment banking partnerships of the 1980s at International Securities.

My questions also became more general than in my initial ethnography. For instance, instead of probing traders about their practices, I asked them about their views on the Volcker Rule. My goal in doing so was to learn about the traders' own answers to the questions I myself was hoping to answer, that is, to engage with the traders as "coanalysts, cointerpreters, and cotheorists of economy and society, and even as cocritics of capitalism," as Miyazaki wrote of his own approach to studying Japanese arbitrage traders after the global financial crisis.[6]

The combination of two distinct approaches to data collection, fieldwork, and interviews described so far allowed me to reformulate the conclusions of my original fieldwork in light of the financial crisis of 2008. This conforms with Burawoy's "punctuated revisit," which is in part designed to reveal historical change. My design differs from Burawoy's scheme, however, in that I did not return to the physical site of my original fieldwork. The equities division of International Securities closed down in early 2007 and its traders were disbanded. Nevertheless, my repeated returns to Midtown Manhattan and my visits to the homes and new workplaces of the protagonists of the original site approximate a return to it.

Finally, why revisit? That is, why interview ethnographic informants once the fieldwork is over? One might argue that such interviews can never match the richness of the original data, and that they can only produce idealized myths and stories of the past. I would argue otherwise. While there were limitations to what I could gain from my revisits, there were three unique advantages. First, I learned about aspects of the organizational context that I missed in the early 2000s. After all, what I saw back then excluded the strategic discussions, debates, and controversies among the bank's the top management. Years later, as I looked back on those years in my conversations with Bob, Max, or Todd, I could probe them about difficult events, controversial decisions, or even significant mistakes that would have been too sensitive to discuss in real time. Revisiting my protagonists allowed me, for instance, to fully understand why Bob resigned in the summer of 2004.

A second benefit of my revisits was triangulation. My revisits allowed me to establish when and whether a given event had taken place, and especially what it had meant for others. I understood, for instance, that the Asian crisis and failure of Long-Term Capital Management in 1998 contributed to delegitimization of proprietary trading at the headquarters of International Securities, culminating in Bob's departure six years later. I also understood just how powerfully the symbolic decisions made by Bob had resonated among the traders' understanding of what was expected of them.

Finally, my revisits allowed me to pose new questions that problematized my original findings. For instance, I was able to ask about the ways in which Bob's trading room prevented the dysfunctions that other banks subsequently fell prey to. Similarly, I could ask the traders about their views on arbitrage after the financial crisis. The benefits from my revisits are again captured by Burawoy's words: revisits allowed me "to extract the general from the unique, to move from the 'micro' to the 'macro,' and to connect the present to the past."[7]

Of course, no research design is perfect, and one limitation of the present monograph is that I do not discuss the events around September 11. Because of its location in Lower Manhattan, the bank was seriously affected by the terrorist attack. Luckily, none of the traders working on the equities floor lost their lives, but the people on the trading room were temporarily displaced for several months before returning to their original floor. I decided not to include September 11 in this book for two reasons. First, the literature and theories that my analysis of September 11 speak to, centered on organizational resilience, reliability, and responsiveness to disaster, are too different from the debates over arbitrage and economic models to make for a coherent monograph. Second, the terrorist attack also calls for an appropriate tone that is difficult to reconcile with abstract debates about valuation and materiality. Life, death, and the threat to the American way of life are not easily integrated within discussions of merger spreads and arbitrage returns. The readers who wish to know more about the response that International Securities put in place to the tragic events of September 11 are welcome to read my published research on the topic.[8]

Gender on Wall Street

In recent years, there has been increasing academic interest in the role of gender in organizations, including gender differences in career outcomes, the effects of balancing work-life obligations, and the ways that gender dynamics play out in teams.[9] In the financial industry, the role of gender has attracted particular interest since 2009, after EU Competition Commissioner Neelie Kroes claimed that the crisis would not have happened as it did if Lehman Brothers had been run by women, that is, if it had been "Lehman Sisters." To the extent that female company directors can be assumed to be more risk-averse than their male counterparts, Kroes reasoned, increasing board diversity in banks would lead to different and potentially better board dynamics.[10]

The experience of women on Wall Street has also been the object of an anthropological study by Melissa Fisher.[11] In her study, Fisher documents the experience of the first generation of women that established themselves as professionals on Wall Street. In response to discrimination, these female employees created informal networks and associations to promote each other's careers, leading to what Fisher describes as a form of "market feminism" that "aligned feminist ideals about meritocracy and gender equality with the logic of the market." In a more recent sociological study, Neely has argued that the prevailing organizational practices in the hedge fund industry, including hiring practices, grooming protégés, or obtaining seed funding, lead to the patrimonialism in the sector. The resulting structures, activated through trust, loyalty, and tradition, end up contributing to gender discrimination. As Neely puts it, patrimonialism "restricts access to financial rewards and facilitates the reproduction of the white male domination of this industry."[12]

Unfortunately, my study did not originally aim to analyze these topics. One limitation of this book is that it does not sufficiently engage with gender on Wall Street, nor does it provide a detailed portrait of women on the trading floor. As I reexamined my fieldnotes from International Securities, I was struck by the limited extent to which women appear in them. Furthermore, the women that do appear did not hold high-ranking positions. It is my hope that future ethnographic research on Wall Street builds on the work of Fisher and others, explores the role of gender in finance, and improves on the limitations of my own study.

NOTES

Chapter 1. Introduction

1. Financial Crisis Inquiry Commission (2011: xi); cited in Abend (2014).
2. See Dudley (2014).
3. See Salz (2013).
4. Kay (2012). See also Augar (2014); Spicer et al. (2014); Lambert (2014).
5. Millman (2015).
6. Millman (2015).
7. Parsons, Shils, and Smelser (1966).
8. Swidler (1986: 275).
9. See Guiso, Sapienza, and Zingales (2006: 60).
10. Lo (2015).
11. O'Hara (2016: 15). Quote on p. vii.
12. Zelizer (1983).
13. Anteby (2010).
14. Fourcade and Healy (2007).
15. Abolafia (1996: 171).
16. Ethnographic monographs on the organizational culture of investment banks and exchanges include Zaloom (2006), Ho (2009), and Lépinay (2011).
17. Callon (1998: 2).
18. Callon and Muniesa (2005).
19. Callon (1998: 2).
20. MacKenzie and Millo were careful not to ignore the moral component of the options market, and documented the moral arguments made by the lobbyists hired by the options exchange in order to countervail the perception of stock options trading as speculation. However, their treatment separates licensing from trading, and morality from the mediating effect of models on financial valuation.
21. MacKenzie and Millo (2003: 107).
22. Knorr Cetina and Bruegger (2002).
23. See Knorr Cetina and Preda (2006).
24. See for example Latour (1984).
25. Latour (1994).
26. Callon (2008).
27. See Beunza and Stark (2004).
28. Burawoy (2003).
29. Burawoy (2003: 645).
30. Bandura (2016).
31. MacKenzie (2011b).
32. Mackenzie (2008B: 21).

33. MacKenzie (2011b); Tett (2009, 2015); MacKenzie and Spears (2014a, 2014b); Pernell-Gallagher (2015).

34. Fligstein and Roehrkasse (2016); Pernell, Jung, and Dobbin (2017); Carruthers (2013).

Chapter 2. First Impressions

1. Hayek (1945: 521).
2. Abolafia (1996: 15).
3. Baker (1984: 775).
4. Heath, Jirotka, Luff, and Hindmarsh (1994).
5. Heath et al. (1994: 6).
6. Heath et al. (1994: 11).
7. Knorr Cetina, and Bruegger (2002: 906).
8. Zaloom's (2006) research also speaks to the tension between social interaction on an exchange floor and trading on electronic terminals, comparing the floor of the Chicago Board of Trade with a London-based investment fund that used terminals. Zaloom reports that the design of the terminals purposefully excluded social cues in order to focus attention on prices and order sizes, suggesting that the shift from live floors to electronic markets was not purely shaped by technological capabilities, but informed by an economic conception of markets as impersonal entities.
9. Knight's (2012) distinction was introduced in economic sociology by White (2002) among others.
10. This concern with communication and knowledge flow between the front and back office is also discussed in Lépinay's (2011) ethnography of a French investment bank, and in Muniesa, Chabert, Ducrocq-Grondin, and Scott (2011: 20).
11. Gladwell (2006).
12. Dunbar's Number was first proposed in the 1990s by British anthropologist Robin Dunbar, who found a correlation between primate brain size and average social group size. By using the average human brain size and extrapolating from the results of primates, he proposed that humans can comfortably maintain only 150 stable relationships. See Dunbar (1992).
13. See also Miyazaki (2007).
14. Burns and Stalker (1961: 6).
15. Dunbar (1992).

Chapter 3. Trading Robots and Social Cues

1. The expression "robot" was the native word that Todd and Bob used at the time to refer to the trading algorithm. For the purposes of this book, "robot," "algorithm," and "computer program" are used interchangeably.
2. MacKenzie (2000).
3. See Preda (2017).
4. See Lowenstein (2000).
5. Greenberg (1987).
6. Nader (1972: 05).

Chapter 4. Animating the Market

1. Heath et al. (1994: 5).

Chapter 5. Models and Reflexivity

1. Miyazaki (2007).
2. Overall, studies have found that risk arbitrage generates substantial excess returns. For example, Dukes, Frohlich, and Ma (1992) and Jindra and Walkling (2004) focus on cash tender offers and document annual excess returns that far exceed 100 percent. Using a stock and cash mergers sample, Baker and Savaşoglu (2002) conclude that risk arbitrage generates annual excess returns of 12.5 percent.
3. Mitchell and Pulvino (2001).
4. MacKenzie and Millo (2003: 125).
5. Muniesa, Millo, and Callon (2007).
6. MacKenzie and Millo (2003).
7. Zaloom (2009).
8. Knorr Cetina and Bruegger (2002: 994).
9. See Jetley and Ji (2010).
10. Jetley and Ji (2010: 54), emphasis mine.
11. Ferreira and Bousarsar (2014).
12. Ferreira and Bousarsar (2014: 4).
13. Callon (1998).
14. Callon (2008).
15. Callon (2008).
16. Knorr Cetina and Preda (2007).
17. Beunza and Stark (2012).

Chapter 6. Managers

1. Power (2009); quote on p. 849.
2. Danielsson, Shin, and Zigrand (2012).
3. Guill (2016).
4. See Tett (2009) and MacKenzie (2013).
5. The hard limit, whether in the form of risk management, innovation, or road maps for venture capital investors, is a deceptively useful policy to rein in constructive processes. Garud and Karnøe (2001) have explored this in the context of innovation.
6. That the fund's models were fundamentally correct, MacKenzie argues, is demonstrated by the fact that the fund, once recapitalized by the consortium of Wall Street banks, ended up turning a profit. Instead, a number of constraints including lack of liquidity, internal controls, and even imitation by rivals, came into play to prevent Long-Term Capital Management from continuing trading. MacKenzie's analysis thus suggests that excess faith in faulty models was not the cause for Long-Term Capital Management's demise, and that this part of Lowenstein's book is mistaken.
7. Browning (2001).
8. Patterson (2010).
9. O'Higgins and Downes (2011).
10. Abolafia (1996: 116).
11. Knorr Cetina (2009: 67).
12. Baker (1984).
13. Burt (1992).
14. Abolafia (1996).

Chapter 7. Performance Spirals

1. In this text, I am not reporting on the effect of the terrorist attacks of September 11 on the trading floor (see methodological note). For a published account of the impact of September 11 on the equities floor of International Securities, see Beunza and Stark (2003, 2005).

2. Markowitz (1952).

3. According to Davis (2009), mergers, acquisitions, or divestments are no longer exceptional but systematic, to the point that the market for corporate control has arguably eroded the corporation as a social institution.

4. Callon, Méadel, and Rabeharisoa (2002).

5. MacKenzie (2008b).

6. Shleifer and Vishny (1997).

7. Shleifer and Vishny (1997).

8. Heath and Luff (1992).

9. MacKenzie (2011b).

10. Cohen (2004: 17), emphasis mine.

11. Merton (1995: 27).

12. Merton (1995: 27).

13. MacKenzie (2008b: 85).

14. Kasch and Sarkar (2012).

Chapter 8. Norms

1. Burns and Stalker (1961: 6).

2. Godechot (2008).

3. Abolafia (1996: 174).

4. Abolafia (1996: 33).

5. Ho (2009).

6. Garfinkel (1967).

7. Said (1978: 325).

8. Hechter (2008).

9. Parsons (1949).

10. Ho (2009).

Chapter 9. Resonance

1. MacKenzie and Millo (2003).

2. MacKenzie (2004a, 2003).

3. MacKenzie (2003: 349).

4. Bary (2001: 43).

5. Sidel (2001).

6. Murray (2001).

7. See Officer (2007).

8. Beunza and Stark (2012).

9. Howell (2013).

10. For a discussion of the tension between resonance and dissonance beyond a financial setting, see Stark (2011).

11. Shleifer and Vishny (1997).

12. Clow (2001).

13. Klein (2017).
14. Taleb (2007).
15. Taleb (2007).
16. Scharfstein and Stein (1990).

Chapter 10. The Global Financial Crisis

1. Burns and Stalker (1961).
2. Bajaja and Grynbaumsept (2008).
3. See MacKenzie and Spears (2014a, 2014b).
4. Morrison and Wilhelm (2007).
5. Morrison and Wilhelm (2007).
6. Augar (2008).
7. Keynes (2016).
8. Salmon (2009).
9. MacKenzie and Spears (2014a).
10. Boyd (2011).
11. MacKenzie (2011b: 1788).
12. Pernell-Gallagher (2015) adds that one can also retrospectively see that such learning was "superstitious," in that it focused only on the positive market reactions and excluded the negative ones. In any event, the superstitious nature of the learning does not invalidate the claim that CEOs believed ABS CDOs to be safe.
13. Even more perversely, bonds based on riskier subprime mortgages were often *preferred* over bonds based on prime mortgages, because they had lower prepayment rates: subprime buyers could hardly pay their interest payments, so they could hardly prepay the principal. Crucially, prepayment risk was the only risk that securitization teams focused on, for they had historically ignored default risk as they assumed that it was idiosyncratic and could therefore be diversified by including mortgages from different regions in the securities.

For complementary accounts of the role of rating agencies, see Carruthers (2010) and Rona-Tas and Hiss (2010).
14. Tett (2015).
15. Fligstein and Roehrkasse (2016: 638).
16. Fligstein and Roehrkasse (2016: 619).
17. Pernell, Jung, and Dobbin (2017).
18. In an elaboration on the problem of financial interdependence, Marc Schneiberg and Timothy Bartley have suggested that future financial crises might be averted by redesigning the financial architecture so as to reduce its complexity and interconnectedness. Schneiberg has made the case for non-corporate organizational structures in finance, or what he denotes a "Jeffersonian" financial system based on a mistrust of concentrated power, as characterized in the thinking of American Founding Father Thomas Jefferson.

Chapter 11. Scandal

1. Spradley (2016).
2. MacKenzie (2012: 340).
3. See also Huault and Rainelli-Le Montagner (2009).
4. Mirowski (2002).
5. Funk and Hirschman (2014).

6. An independent report on the bank's over-the-counter derivatives commissioned by the Federal Reserve and other regulatory agencies concluded that while the institution did not disregard its duties, deficiencies in the management and control of the derivatives personnel at Premier allowed certain individuals to engage in conduct that warranted severe criticism.

7. The role of language and knowledge flow in the derivatives industry has also been discussed by sociologist Lépinay (2011). In his ethnography of a French derivatives bank, tellingly titled *Codes of Finance*, he not only confirms the problem of customer disclosure discussed by Bob, but adds that this difficulty even took place between various departments of the bank. "Traders and engineers," Lépinay writes, "do not share the computer codes of their *pricers* with the salespeople [. . .] Salespeople do not share with the back-office manager the detailed history of the deals" (2011: 16). Lépinay's analysis, in other words, confirms the presence of a systematic tendency to exploit information asymmetries, even through the use of language, in the derivatives business.

The ambiguity of swap agreements has also been examined by sociologists Russell Funk and Daniel Hirschman. The authors argue that swap agreements were a financial innovation of an ambiguous nature, partly a futures contract and partly a loan, and add that this led to jurisdictional disputes among regulatory bodies that contributed to regulatory inaction, letting commercial banks circumvent the separation between commercial and investment banking introduced by Glass-Steagall, and rendering such legislation obsolete. This process culminated with the repeal of Glass-Steagall in 1999.

8. Terzi and Ulucay (2011).

9. Hitlin and Vaisey (2013).

10. Parsons, Shils, and Smelser (1965).

11. Garfinkel (1967).

12. Wrong (1961).

13. Hitlin and Vaisey (2013).

14. Zelizer (2017).

15. See Healy (2004).

16. See Anteby (2010).

17. Fourcade and Healy (2007).

18. Abolafia (1996).

19. Ho (2009).

20. Greenberg (1987).

21. Greenberg (1987).

22. Bandura (1990).

23. Caliskan and Callon (2010).

24. Caliskan and Callon (2010).

25. This shift was thoroughly documented by Davis and Mizruchi (1999).

26. Power (2007). In an updated analysis after the global financial crisis, Power highlights the role of risk management in precipitating the catastrophe. Since risk management does not address the interconnectedness between financial institutions in a situation of liquidity crisis, he argues, "the security provided by enterprise risk management is at best limited to certain states of the world, and at worst it is illusory"; see Power (2009: 879) and Mikes (2009).

27. Pernell, Jung, and Dobbin (2017).

28. Nevertheless, the mechanisms of risk intensification in place at Premier are ultimately compatible with those identified by Pernell, Jung, and Dobbin, because Premier was one of the earliest adopters of risk management and therefore different from the average bank considered by Pernell et al.'s study. As other institutionalist studies have shown, the reasons for adoption shift along the adoption curve.

Chapter 12. When All Is Said and Done

1. MacKenzie (2008a).
2. Sants (2010a, 2010b).
3. The Financial Crisis Commission (2012: 4).
4. Kay (2012)
5. Miyazaki (2012: 4).
6. Miyazaki (2012).
7. See Cohan (2010: 281).
8. Ho (2005).
9. Bearman (2005:4).
10. Rose and Miller (1992: 183).
11. A telling difference between patriarchy and patrimonialism is that in the latter, the chief or ruler has employees that aid in his administration of power. As Weber (2012) writes, patrimonialism emerges when the patriarch takes on staff, and takes place "when the ruler's household expands with the household administration giving rise to governmental offices. All officials are personal dependents or favorites of the ruler, appointed by him."
12. Neely (2018: 366).
13. Schumacher (2011).
14. Abend (2014: 281).
15. Abend (2014: 26).

Chapter 13. Conclusion

1. Caliskan and Callon (2010).
2. Krippner (2001) and Davis (2009).
3. See Epstein (2005).
4. See Geertz (1973).
5. See Knorr Cetina and Preda (2012).
6. MacKenzie and Spears (2014a).
7. Power (2007, 2009).
8. Mikes (2009: 286).
9. Callon (2008: 31).
10. Callon (2008: 43).
11. Merton (1995).
12. Knorr Cetina and Preda (2007: 67).
13. Gallison (1999).
14. Helgesson and Muniesa (2013).
15. Callon, Méadel, and Rabeharisoa (2002).
16. The literature in management has not considered the performative effect of economic models on markets and its implications for management, but a growing literature has explored other forms of performativity. See for instance Gond, Cabantous, Harding, and Learmonth (2016); and Spicer, Alvesson, and Kärreman (2009).
17. Lépinay (2011).
18. See Ferraro, Pfeffer, and Sutton (2005); Gehman, Treviño, and Garud (2013); Gond, Cabantous, Harding, and Learmonth (2016).
19. Lawrence and Lorsch (1967).
20. See Healy (2015). Also see Orlikowski and Scott (2013).
21. Beunza and Stark (2012).

22. MacKenzie (2008b).
23. Wolfers and Zitzewitz (2004).
24. Hitlin and Vaisey (2013: 53).
25. Abend (2014).
26. See Dudley (2014).
27. Millman and Rubenfeld (2014).
28. Neely (2018).
29. Swidler (1986: 278).
30. Piore and Sabel (1986).

Methodological Note

1. Burawoy (2003).
2. See Ho (2009) and Lépinay (2011).
3. Agar (1986: 23).
4. Latour and Woolgar (2013).
5. See Beunza and Stark (2003, 2004, 2005, 2012, 2013).
6. Miyazaki (2012).
7. Burawoy (1998: 5).
8. See Beunza and Stark (2003, 2005).
9. Fernandez-Mateo and Kaplan (2018).
10. Adams (2016).
11. Fisher (2012).
12. Neely (2018: 365).

BIBLIOGRAPHY

Abend, G. 2014. *The Moral Background: An Inquiry into the History of Business Ethics*. Princeton, NJ: Princeton University Press.

Abolafia, M. 1996. *Making Markets: Opportunism and Restraint on Wall Street*. Cambridge, MA: Harvard University Press.

Adams, R. B. 2016. Women on boards: The superheroes of tomorrow? *Leadership Quarterly* 27(3): 371–386.

Agar, M. 1986. *Speaking of Ethnography*. Beverly Hills, CA: Sage.

Anteby, M. 2010. Markets, morals, and practices of trade: Jurisdictional disputes in the US commerce in cadavers. *Administrative Science Quarterly* 55(4): 606–638.

Augar, P. 2008. *The Death of Gentlemanly Capitalism: The Rise and Fall of London's Investment Banks*. London: Penguin UK.

———. 2014. Investment Banking: The Culture of a Casino or of Profession? Lecture at the House of Common Westminster.

Bajaj, V. and Grynbaumsept, M. 2008. For stocks, worst single-day drop in two decades. *New York Times*, September 29.

Baker, M. and Savaşoglu, S. 2002. Limited arbitrage in mergers and acquisitions. *Journal of Financial Economics* 64(1): 91–115.

Baker, W. E. 1984. The social structure of a national securities market. *American Journal of Sociology* 89(4): 775–811.

Bandura, A. 1990. Mechanisms of moral disengagement. In *Origins of Terrorism: Psychologies, Ideologies, States of Mind*, edited by W. Reich, 161–191. New York: Cambridge University Press.

———. 2016. *Moral Disengagement: How People Do Harm and Live with Themselves*. New York: Worth Publishers.

Bank for International Settlements. 2010. OTC derivatives outstanding. Accessed January 2018, from https://www.bis.org/statistics/derstats.htm.

Bary, Andrew. 2001. Deal me out. *Barron's* 81(26): 43.

Bearman, P. 2005. *Doormen*. Chicago: University of Chicago Press.

Beunza, D. and Stark, D. 2003. The organization of responsiveness: innovation and recovery in the trading rooms of Lower Manhattan. *Socio-Economic Review* 1(2): 135–164.

———. 2004. Tools of the trade: the socio-technology of arbitrage in a Wall Street trading room. *Industrial and Corporate Change* 13(2): 369–400.

———. 2005. Resolving identities: successive crises in a trading room after 9/11. In *Wounded City: The Social Impact of 9-11 on New York City*, edited by N. Foner, 293–320. New York: Russell Sage Foundation.

———. 2012. From dissonance to resonance: Cognitive interdependence in quantitative finance. *Economy and Society* 41(3): 383–417.

———. 2013. Seeing through the eyes of others: dissonance within and across trading rooms. In *Oxford Handbook of the Sociology of Finance*, edited by K. K. Cetina and A. Preda, 203–223. Oxford: Oxford University Press.

Bock, D. 1984. Currency swaps: a borrowing technique in a public policy context. Staff Working Papers No. 640, World Bank, Washington, DC.

Boyd, R. 2011. *Fatal Risk: A Cautionary Tale of AIG's Corporate Suicide*. Hoboken, NJ: Wiley.

Browning, E. S. 2001. Stocks plunge as heavy selling hits all sectors. *Wall Street Journal*, April 4, C1.

Burawoy, M. 1998. The extended case method. *Sociological Theory* 16(1): 4–33.

———. 2003. Revisits: An outline of a theory of reflexive ethnography. *American Sociological Review* 68(5): 645–679.

Burns, T. and Stalker, G. M. 1961. *The Management of Innovation*. London: Tavistock.

Burt, R. S. 1992. The social structure of competition. In *Networks and Organizations: Structure, Form and Action*, edited by N. Nohria and R. Eccles, 57–91. Cambridge, MA: Harvard Business School Press.

Caliskan, K. and Callon, M. 2009. Economization, part 1: shifting attention from the economy towards processes of economization. *Economy and Society* 38(3): 369–398.

———. 2010. Economization, part 2: a research programme for the study of markets. *Economy and Society* 39(1): 1–32.

Callon, M. 1998. Introduction: the embeddedness of economic markets in economics. *Sociological Review* 46(S1): 1–57.

———. 2008. Economic markets and the rise of interactive agencements: from prosthetic agencies to habilitated agencies. In *Living in a Material World: Economic Sociology Meets Science and Technology Studies*, edited by T. J. Pinch and R. Swedberg, 29–56. Cambridge, MA; London: MIT Press.

Callon, M., Méadel, C., and Rabeharisoa, V. 2002. The economy of qualities. *Economy and Society* 31(2): 194–217.

Callon, M. and Muniesa, F. 2005. Peripheral vision: economic markets as calculative collective devices. *Organization Studies* 26(8): 1229–1250.

Carruthers, B. G. 2010. Knowledge and liquidity: institutional and cognitive foundations of the subprime crisis. In *Markets on Trial: The Economic Sociology of the US Financial Crisis: Part A*, 157–182. Bingley: Emerald Group Publishing Limited.

———. 2013. From uncertainty toward risk: the case of credit ratings. *Socio-Economic Review* 11(3): 525–551.

Carruthers, B. G. and Kim, J. C. 2011. The sociology of finance. *Annual Review of Sociology* 37: 239–259.

Chincarini, L. B. 2012. *The Crisis of Crowding: Quant Copycats, Ugly Models, and the New Crash Normal*. Hoboken, NJ: Wiley.

Clow, R. 2001. Atticus Global finds its strategy paying off. *Financial Times*, August 30, p. 25.

Cohan, W. D. 2010. *House of Cards: A Tale of Hubris and Wretched Excess on Wall Street*. London: Allen Lane.

Cohen, N. 2004. Goldman moves to combine equity and debt coverage. *Financial Times*, May 25, p. 17.

Danielsson, J., Shin, H. S., and Zigrand, J. P. 2012. Endogenous and systemic risk. In *Quantifying Systemic Risk*, 73–94. Chicago: University of Chicago Press.

Davis, G. F. 2009. *Managed by the Markets: How Finance Re-Shaped America*. Oxford: Oxford University Press.

Davis, G. F. and Mizruchi, M. S. 1999. The money center cannot hold: commercial banks in the US system of corporate governance. *Administrative Science Quarterly* 44(2): 215–239.

Dobbin, F. and Jung, J. 2010. The misapplication of Mr. Michael Jensen: How agency theory brought down the economy and why it might again. In *Markets on Trial: The Economic Sociology of the US Financial Crisis: Part B*, 29–64. Bingley: Emerald Group Publishing Limited.

Dudley, W. 2014. Enhancing financial stability by improving culture in the financial services industry (No. 147). Federal Reserve Bank of New York.

Dukes, W. P., Frohlich, C. J., and Ma, C. K. 1992. Risk arbitrage in tender offers. *Journal of Portfolio Management* 18(4): 47–55.

Dunbar, N. 2000. *Inventing Money: The Story of Long-Term Capital Management and the Legends Behind It*. Chichester: Wiley.

Dunbar, R.I.M. 1992. Neocortex size as a constraint on group size in primates. *Journal of Human Evolution* 22(6): 469–493.

Engelen, E., Erturk, I., Froud, J., Leaver, A., and Williams, K. 2010. Reconceptualizing financial innovation: frame, conjuncture and bricolage. *Economy and Society* 39(1): 33–63.

Epstein, G. A., ed. 2005. *Financialization and the World Economy*. Cheltenham: Edward Elgar.

Fernandez-Mateo, I. and Kaplan, Sarah. 2018. Gender and organization science: introduction to a virtual special issue. *Organization Science*. Published online in Articles in Advance, October 29. Accessed November 2018, from https://doi.org/10.1287/orsc.2018.1249.

Ferraro, F., Pfeffer, J., and Sutton, R. I. 2005. Economics language and assumptions: how theories can become self-fulfilling. *Academy of Management Review* 30(1): 824.

Ferreira, P. and Bousarsar, M. 2014. Ride the M&A wave with merger arbitrage. *Alternatives Insight. Research from Lyxor Managed Account Platform*. Société Générale Group. May 5.

Financial Crisis Inquiry Commission. 2011. The financial crisis inquiry report, authorized edition: Final report of the National Commission on the Causes of the Financial and Economic Crisis in the United States. Public Affairs.

Fisher, M. S. 2012. *Wall Street Women*. Durham, NC: Duke University Press.

Fligstein, N. 2010. Response to Kenneth Zimmerman. *Economic Sociology The European Electronic Newsletter* 11(2): 53–54.

Fligstein, N., Stuart Brundage, J., and Schultz, M. 2017. Seeing like the Fed: culture, cognition, and framing in the failure to anticipate the financial crisis of 2008. *American Sociological Review* 82(5): 879–909.

Fligstein, N. and Roehrkasse, A. F. 2016. The causes of fraud in the financial crisis of 2007 to 2009: evidence from the mortgage-backed securities industry. *American Sociological Review* 81(4): 617–643.

Fourcade, M. and Healy, K. 2007. Moral views of market society. *Annual Review of Sociology* 33: 285–311.

———. 2016. Seeing like a market. *Socio-Economic Review* 15(1): 9–29.

Funk, R. J. and Hirschman, D. 2014. Derivatives and deregulation: financial innovation and the demise of Glass–Steagall. *Administrative Science Quarterly* 59(4): 669–704.

Galison, P. 1999. *Images and Logic: A Material Culture of MicroPhysics*. Chicago: University of Chicago Press.

Garfinkel, H. 1967. *Studies in Ethnomethodology*. Englewood Cliffs, NJ: Prentice Hall.

Garud, R. and Karnøe, P. 2001. Path creation as a process of mindful deviation. Path dependence and creation. In *Path Dependence and Creation*, edited by R. Garud and P Karnøe, 1–38. Mahwah, NJ: Lawrence Erlbaum Associates.

Geertz, C. 1973. *The Interpretation of Cultures* (Vol. 5043). New York: Basic Books.

Gehman, J., Treviño, L. K., and Garud, R. 2013. Values work: a process study of the emergence and performance of organizational values practices. *Academy of Management Journal* 56(1): 84–112.

Gladwell, M. 2002. *The Tipping Point: How Little Things Can Make a Big Difference*. New York: Back Bay Books.

Godechot, O. 2000. Le bazar de la rationalité. Vers une sociologie des formes concrètes de raisonnement. *Politix* 13(52): 17–56.

———. 2008. "Hold-up" in finance: The conditions of possibility for high bonuses in the financial industry. *Revue française de sociologie* 49(5): 95–123.

Gond, J. P., Cabantous, L., Harding, N., and Learmonth, M. 2016. What do we mean by performativity in organizational and management theory? The uses and abuses of performativity. *International Journal of Management Reviews* 18(4): 440–463.

Greenberg, J. 1987. A taxonomy of organizational justice theories. *Academy of Management Review* 12(1): 9–22.

Greenspan, A. 2008. Hearing by the Congressional Committee for Oversight and Government Reform on the role of federal regulators in the financial crisis. Preliminary hearing transcript, Washington, DC.

Guill, G. D. 2016. Bankers Trust and the birth of modern risk management. *Journal of Applied Corporate Finance* 28(1): 19–29.

Guiso, L., Sapienza, P., and Zingales, L. 2006. Does culture affect economic outcomes?. *Journal of Economic Perspectives* 20(2): 23–48.

Hayek, F. A. 1945. The use of knowledge in society. *American Economic Review* 35(4): 519–530.

Healy, K. 2004. Sacred markets and secular ritual in the organ transplant industry. In *The Sociology of the Economy*, edited by F. Dobbin, 308–331. New York: Russell Sage Foundation.

———. 2015. The performativity of networks. *European Journal of Sociology* 56: 175–205.

Heath, C., Jirotka, M., Luff, P., and Hindmarsh, J. 1994. Unpacking collaboration: the interactional organisation of trading in a city dealing room. *Computer Supported Cooperative Work (CSCW)* 3(2): 147–165.

Heath, C. and Luff, P. 1992. Crisis management and multimedia technology in London Underground Line Control Rooms. *Computer Supported Cooperative Work (CSCW)* 1(1–2): 69–94.

———. 2000. *Technology in Action*. Cambridge: Cambridge University Press.

Hechter, M. 2008. The rise and fall of normative control. *Accounting, Organizations and Society* 33(6): 663–676.

Helgesson, C. F. and Muniesa, F. 2013. For what it's worth: an introduction to valuation studies. *Valuation Studies* 1(1): 1–10.

Hitlin, S. and Vaisey, S. 2013. The new sociology of morality. *Annual Review of Sociology* 39: 51–68.

Ho, K. 2005. Situating global capitalisms: a view from Wall Street investment banks. *Cultural Anthropology* 20(1): 68–96.

———. 2009. *Liquidated: An Ethnography of Wall Street*. Durham, NC: Duke University Press.

Holzer, B. and Millo, Y. 2005. From risks to second-order dangers in financial markets: unintended consequences of risk management systems. *New Political Economy* 10(2): 223–245.

Howell, E. 2013. Why do soldiers break stride on a bridge? *Live Science*, May 22. https://www.livescience.com/34608-break-stride-frequency-of-vibration.html.

Huault, I. and Rainelli-Le Montagner, H. 2009. Market shaping as an answer to ambiguities: the case of credit derivatives. *Organization Studies* 30(5): 549–575.

Hull, J. 2007. *Risk Management and Financial Institutions*. Hoboken, NJ: Wiley.

Jacque, L. L. 2010. *Global Derivative Debacles: From Theory to Malpractice*. Singapore: World Scientific.

Jetley, G. and Ji, X. 2010. The shrinking merger arbitrage spread: reasons and implications. *Financial Analysts Journal* 66(2): 54–68.

Jindra, J. and Walkling, R. A. 2004. Speculation spreads and the market pricing of proposed acquisitions. *Journal of Corporate Finance* 10(4): 495–526.

Kanter, Rosabeth Moss. 1983. Change masters and the intricate architecture of corporate culture change. *Management Review*, October: 18–28.

Kasch, M. and Sarkar, A. 2012. Is there an S&P 500 index effect? Federal Bank Reserve of New York Staff Report No. 484. November.

Kay, J. 2012. The Kay review of UK equity markets and long-term decision making. *Final Report*, 9.

Keynes, J. M. 1936. *General Theory of Employment, Interest and Money*. London: Palgrave Macmillan.

King, B. G. 2015. Organizational actors, character, and Selznick's theory of organizations. In *Institutions and Ideals: Philip Selznick's Legacy for Organizational Studies*, 149–174. Bingley: Emerald Group Publishing Limited.

Klein, G. A. 2017. *Sources of Power: How People Make Decisions*. Cambridge, MA: MIT Press.

Knight, F. H. 1921. *Risk, Uncertainty and Profit*. New York: Houghton Mifflin.

Knorr Cetina, K. 2007. Culture in global knowledge societies: knowledge cultures and epistemic cultures. *Interdisciplinary Science Reviews* 32(4): 361–375.

———. 2009. *Epistemic Cultures: How the Sciences Make Knowledge*. Cambridge, MA: Harvard University Press.

Knorr Cetina, K. and Bruegger, U. 2002. Global microstructures: the virtual societies of financial markets *American Journal of Sociology* 107(4): 905–950.

Knorr Cetina, K. and Preda, A. 2006. *The Sociology of Financial Markets*. Oxford: Oxford University Press.

———. 2007. The temporalization of financial markets: from network to flow. *Theory, Culture & Society* 24(7–8): 116–138.

———. 2012. *The Oxford Handbook of the Sociology of Finance*. Oxford: Oxford University Press.

Kraatz, M. S., ed. 2015. Institutions and ideals: Philip Selznick's legacy for organizational studies. In *Institutions and Ideals: Philip Selznick's Legacy for Organizational Studies*, p. iii. Bingley: Emerald Group Publishing Limited.

Kraatz, M. S., Ventresca, M. J., and Deng, L. 2010. Precarious values and mundane innovations: enrollment management in American liberal arts colleges. *Academy of Management Journal* 53(6): 1521–1545.

Krippner, G. R. 2011. *Capitalizing on Crisis*. Cambridge, MA: Harvard University Press.

Lambert, R. 2014. Banking Standards Review. Retrieved December 20, 2014, from https://www.thepfs.org/knowledge/policy-and-public-affairs/articles/banking-standards-lambert-review-final-report/30421

Latour, B. 1984. The powers of association. *Sociological Review* 32(S1): 264–280.

———. 1994. On technical mediation. *Common Knowledge* 3(2): 29–64.

Latour, B. and Woolgar, S. 2013. *Laboratory Life: The Construction of Scientific Facts*. Princeton, NJ: Princeton University Press.

Lawrence, P. R. and Lorsch, J. W. 1967. *Organization and Environment: Managing Differentiation and Integration*. Cambridge, MA: Harvard University Press.

Lépinay, V. A. 2011. *Codes of Finance: Engineering Derivatives in a Global Bank*. Princeton, NJ: Princeton University Press.

Lo, A. W. 2016. The Gordon Gekko effect: the role of culture in the financial industry (No. w21267). *Economic Policy Review*, Federal Reserve Bank of New York, August 17–22.

———. 2017. *Adaptive Markets: Financial Evolution at the Speed of Thought*. Princeton, NJ: Princeton University Press.

Lounsbury, M. and Hirsch, P. M., eds. 2010. *Markets on Trial: The Economic Sociology of the US Financial Crisis* (Vols. 1 and 2). Bingley: Emerald Group Publishing Limited.

Lowenstein, R. 2000. *When Genius Failed: The Rise and Fall of Long-Term Capital Management*. New York: Random House.

MacKenzie, D. 2000. Long-term capital management and the sociology of finance. *London Review of Books*, April 13, 1–5.

———. 2003. Long-Term Capital Management and the sociology of arbitrage. *Economy and Society* 32(3): 349–380.

————. 2004a. The big, bad wolf and the rational market: portfolio insurance, the 1987 crash and the performativity of economics. *Economy and Society* 33(3): 303–334.

————. 2004b. *Mechanizing Proof: Computing, Risk, and Trust*. Cambridge, MA: MIT Press.

————. 2008a. What's in a number? The importance of LIBOR. *Real-World Economics Review* 47(3): 237–242.

————. 2008b. *An Engine, Not a Camera: How Financial Models Shape Markets*. Cambridge, MA: MIT Press.

————. 2011a. Evaluation Cultures? On Invoking "Culture" in the Analysis of Behaviour in Financial Markets. Unpublished manuscript, University of Edinburgh, Retrieved July 2015, from http://www.sps.ed.ac.uk/__data/assets/pdf_file/0007/64564/EvalCults11.pdf.

————. 2011b. The credit crisis as a problem in the sociology of knowledge. *American Journal of Sociology* 116(6): 1778–1841.

————. 2012. Knowledge production in financial markets: credit default swaps, the ABX and the subprime crisis. *Economy and Society* 41(3): 335–359.

————. 2013. The magic lever: how banks do it. *London Review of Books* 35(9): 16–19.

MacKenzie, D. and Millo, Y. 2003. Constructing a market, performing theory: the historical sociology of a financial derivatives exchange. *American Journal of Sociology* 109(1): 107–145.

MacKenzie, D. and Pablo Pardo-Guerra, J. 2014. Insurgent capitalism: island, bricolage and the re-making of finance. *Economy and Society* 43(2): 153–182.

MacKenzie, D. and Spears, T. 2014a. "The formula that killed Wall Street": the Gaussian copula and modelling practices in investment banking. *Social Studies of Science* 44(3): 393–417.

MacKenzie, D. and Spears, T. 2014b. "A device for being able to book P&L": the organizational embedding of the Gaussian copula. *Social Studies of Science* 44(3): 418–440.

Markowitz, H. 1952. Portfolio selection. *Journal of Finance* 7(1): 77–91.

Merton, R. C. 1995. A functional perspective of financial intermediation. *Financial Management* 24: 23–41.

Mikes, A. 2009. Risk management and calculative cultures. *Management Accounting Research* 20(1): 18–40.

Millman, G. J. 2015. Why bank culture is not the problem. *Wall Street Journal*. Retrieved May 2015, from https://blogs.wsj.com/riskandcompliance/2015/03/18/why-bank-cultures-not-the-problem/.

Millman, G. J. and Rubenfeld, Samuel. 2014. Compliance officer: dream career. *Wall Street Journal*, January 15. Retrieved January 2015, from http://online.wsj.com/articles/SB1000142405270 2303330204579250722114538750.

Mirowski, P. 2002. *Machine Dreams: Economics Becomes a Cyborg Science*. Cambridge: Cambridge University Press.

Mirowski, P. and Nik-Khah, E. 2007. Markets made flesh: performativity, and a problem in Science Studies, augmented with consideration of the FCC Auctions. In *Do Economists Make Markets?: On the Performativity of Economics*, edited by D. MacKenzie, F. Muniesa, and L. Siu, 190–225. Princeton, NJ: Princeton University Press.

Mitchell, M. and Pulvino, T. 2001. Characteristics of risk and return in risk arbitrage. *Journal of Finance* 56(6): 2135–2175.

Miyazaki, H. 2007. Between arbitrage and speculation: an economy of belief and doubt. *Economy and Society* 36(3): 396–415.

————. 2012. *Arbitraging Japan: Dreams of Capitalism at the End of Finance*. Berkeley: University of California Press.

Mizruchi, M. S. 2013. *The Fracturing of the American Corporate Elite*. Cambridge, MA: Harvard University Press.

Morrison, A. D. and Wilhelm Jr, W. J. 2007. *Investment Banking: Institutions, Politics, and Law*. Oxford: Oxford University Press.

Muniesa, F. 2014. *The Provoked Economy: Economic Reality and the Performative Turn*. Abingdon: Routledge.

Muniesa, F., Chabert, D., Ducrocq-Grondin, M., and Scott, S. V. 2011. Back-office intricacy: the description of financial objects in an investment bank. *Industrial and Corporate Change* 20(4): 1189–1213.

Muniesa, F., Millo, Y., and Callon, M. 2007. An introduction to market devices. *Sociological Review* 55(s2): 1–12.

Murray, M. 2001. GE's Honeywell deal is more than sum of airplane parts. *Wall Street Journal*, April 6.

Nader, L. 1972. Up the anthropologist: perspectives gained from studying up. In *Reinventing Anthropology*, edited by D. Hymes, 284–311. New York: Pantheon.

Neely, M. T. 2018. Fit to be king: how patrimonialism on Wall Street leads to inequality. *Socio-Economic Review* 16(2): 365–385.

Officer, M. S. 2007. Are performance-based arbitrage effects detectable? Evidence from merger arbitrage. *Journal of Corporate Finance* 13(5): 793–812.

O'Hara, M. 2016. *Something for Nothing: Arbitrage and Ethics on Wall Street*. New York: Norton.

O'Higgins, M. B. and Downes, J. 2011. *Beating the Dow Completely Revised and Updated: A High-Return, Low-Risk Method for Investing in the Dow Jones Industrial Stocks with as Little as $5,000*. River Valley, NJ: Harper Collins.

Orlikowski, W. J. and Scott, S. V. 2013. What happens when evaluation goes online? Exploring apparatuses of valuation in the travel sector. *Organization Science* 25(3): 868–891.

Parsons, T. 1949. *The Structure of Social Action* (Vol. 491). New York: Free Press.

———. 1951. *The Social System*. Glencoe, IL: Free Press.

Parsons, T., Shils, E. A., and Smelser, N. J., eds. 1965. *Toward a General Theory of Action: Theoretical Foundations for the Social Sciences*. New Brunswick, NJ: Transaction Publishers.

———. 1966. *Societies: Evolutionary and Comparative Perspectives*. Upper Saddle River, NJ: Prentice Hall.

Patterson, S. 2010. *The Quants: How a New Breed of Math Whizzes Conquered Wall Street and Nearly Destroyed It*. New York: Crown Business.

Pernell, K., Jung, J., and Dobbin, F. 2017. The hazards of expert control: chief risk officers and risky derivatives. *American Sociological Review* 82(3): 511–541.

Pernell-Gallagher, K. 2015. Learning from performance: Banks, collateralized debt obligations, and the credit crisis. *Social Forces* 94(1): 31–59.

Piore, M. J. and Sabel, C. F. 1986. *The Second Industrial Divide: Possibilities for Prosperity*. New York: Basic Books.

Power, M. 2007. *Organized Uncertainty: Designing a World of Risk Management*. Oxford: Oxford University Press.

———. 2009. The risk management of nothing. *Accounting, Organizations and Society* 34(6): 849–855.

Preda, A. 2017. *Noise Traders*. Chicago: University of Chicago Press Economics Books.

Rona-Tas, A. and Hiss, S. 2010. The role of ratings in the subprime mortgage crisis: The art of corporate and the science of consumer credit rating. In *Markets on Trial: The Economic Sociology of the US Financial Crisis: Part A*, 115–155. Bingley: Emerald Group Publishing Limited.

Rose, N. and Miller, P. 1992. Political power beyond the state: problematics of government. *British Journal of Sociology* 43(2): 173–205.

Said, E. W. 1978. *Orientalism*. London: Routledge.

Salmon, F. 2009. Recipe for disaster: the formula that killed Wall Street. *Wired Magazine* 17(3): 16–20.

Salz, A. 2013. Salz Review: An independent review of Barclays' business practices. Retrieved March 15, 2014, from http://www. barclays.com/content/dam/barclayspublic/documents /news/875-269-salz-review-04-2013. pdf.

Sants, H. 2010a. Do regulators have a role to play in judging culture and ethics? Speech to Chartered Institute of Securities and Investments Conference, London, UK.

_____. 2010b. Can culture be regulated? Speech to Mansion House Conference on values and trust, London, UK.

Scharfstein, D. S. and Stein, J. C. 1990. Herd behavior and investment. *American Economic Review* 80(3): 465–479.

Schein, E. H. 1986. What you need to know about organizational culture. *Training & Development Journal* 80(1): 30–33.

Schneiberg, M. 2013. Organizational diversity and regulatory strategy in financial markets: possibilities for upgrading and reform. North Carolina Banking Institute, 18, p. 141.

Schumacher, E. F. 2011. *Small Is Beautiful: A Study of Economics As If People Mattered*. New York: Random House.

Seligman, J. 1982. *The Transformation of Wall Street: A History of the Securities and Exchange Commission and Modern Corporate Finance*. Boston: Houghton Mifflin.

Shleifer, A. and Vishny, R. W. 1997. The limits of arbitrage. *Journal of Finance* 52(1): 35–55.

Sidel, Robin. 2001. Takeover traders are battered by GE-Honeywell deal fallout. *Wall Street Journal*, June 15, p. C1.

Simmel, G. 1950. The stranger. In *The Sociology of Georg Simmel*, edited by K. H. Wolff, 402–408. New York: Free Press.

Smith, R. C. 2010. *Paper Fortunes: Modern Wall Street; Where It's Been and Where It's Going*. New York: St. Martin's Press.

Sobel, R. 1976. *NYSE: A History of the New York Stock Exchange*. New York: Weybright & Talley.

Spicer, A., Alvesson, M., and Kärreman, D. 2009. Critical performativity: The unfinished business of critical management studies. *Human Relations* 62(4): 537–560.

Spicer, A., Gond, J. P., Patel, K., Lindley, D., Fleming, P., Mosonyi, S., Benoit, C., and Parker, S. 2014. *A Report on the Culture of British Retail Banking*. London: New City Agenda & CASS Business School.

Spradley, J. P. 2016. *The Ethnographic Interview*. Long Grove, IL: Waveland Press.

Stark, D. 2011. *The Sense of Dissonance: Accounts of Worth in Economic Life*. Princeton, NJ: Princeton University Press.

Swidler, A. 1986. Culture in action: Symbols and strategies. *American Sociological Review* 51: 273–286.

Taleb, N. N. 2007. Black swans and the domains of statistics. *American Statistician* 61(3): 198–200.

Terzi, N. and Ulucay, K. 2011. The role of credit default swaps on financial market stability. *Procedia-Social and Behavioral Sciences* 24: 983–990.

Tett, G. 2009. *Fool's Gold: How the Bold Dream of a Small Tribe at JP Morgan Was Corrupted by Wall Street Greed and Unleashed a Catastrophe*. New York: Free Press.

———. 2015. *The Silo Effect: The Peril of Expertise and the Promise of Breaking Down Barriers*. New York: Simon & Schuster.

Ulmer, B. K. 2004. Ivan Boesky. In *Encyclopedia of White-collar and Corporate Crime*, edited by Lawrence Salinger, 96–97. Thousand Oaks, CA: Sage.

Weber, M. 2012. *The Theory of Social and Economic Organization*. Mansfield Centre, CT: Martino Fine Books.

Weick, K. E. and Roberts, K. H. 1993. Collective mind in organizations: heedful interrelating on flight decks. *Administrative Science Quarterly* 38(3): 357–381.

White, H. C. 2002. *Markets from Networks: Socioeconomic Models of Production*. Princeton, NJ: Princeton University Press.

Wolfers, J. and Zitzewitz, E. 2004. Prediction markets. *Journal of Economic Perspectives* 18(2):107–126.

Wrong, D. H. 1961. The oversocialized conception of man in modern sociology. *American Sociological Review* 26: 183–193.

Zaloom, C. 2006. *Out of the Pits: Traders and Technology from Chicago to London*. Chicago: University of Chicago Press.

———. 2009. How to read the future: the yield curve, affect, and financial prediction. *Public Culture* 21(2): 245–268.

———. 2012. Traders and market morality. In *The Oxford Handbook of the Sociology of Finance*, edited by Karin Knorr Cetina and Alex Preda. Oxford: Oxford University Press.

Zelizer, V. 1983. *Markets and Morals*. Princeton, NJ: Princeton University Press.

———. 2004. Circuits of commerce. In *Self, Social Structure, and Beliefs: Explorations in Sociology*, edited by J. C. Alexander, G. T. Marx, and C. Williams, 122–144. Berkeley: University of California Press.

———. 2005. *The Purchase of Intimacy*. Princeton, NJ: Princeton University Press.

———. 2017. *Morals and Markets: The Development of Life Insurance in the United States*. New York: Columbia University Press.

INDEX

A NOTE ON THE TYPE

This book has been composed in Adobe Text and Gotham. Adobe Text, designed by Robert Slimbach for Adobe, bridges the gap between fifteenth- and sixteenth-century calligraphic and eighteenth-century Modern styles. Gotham, inspired by New York street signs, was designed by Tobias Frere-Jones for Hoefler & Co.